Rebuilding Adam: The Tragedy

Adam Elnekaveh

Woodbridge Publishers
1280 Lexington Ave STE 2
New York, NY 10028

Copyright © 2024 Adam Elnekaveh
All rights reserved

First Edition

ISBN (Paperback): 978-1-916849-80-8

ISBN (Hardback): 978-1-916849-81-5

WOODBRIDGE
PUBLISHERS

Disclaimer

This story is entirely true. No events, thoughts, actions, or situations have been fictionalized, though some may be slightly altered due to memory loss.
Names and identifying details have been changed to protect the privacy of certain characters. Some conversations and events have been edited for clarity and brevity.

Kata Beach, Thailand. May 28, 2018, 3:47 PM.

"Adam! Wake up, man!" Rene's eyes were wide as he took in my mangled body lying in a lake of blood on the pavement. Cars and motorcycles honked as they passed us, unable to see where my body had fallen in the ditch.

Rene tried to check my pupil response, prying my eyes open with shaking, bloodied fingers. He couldn't even find my pupils: my eyes were rolled back in my head, showing only white.

It was around that time that he noticed my head wasn't all in one piece. Brain matter was visible on the sandy sidewalk, mingling with the oil leaking from my ruined motorbike.

Rene looked up and around, desperately searching for help. He didn't understand how emergency services worked in Thailand, 8,650 miles from home. It was a tropical paradise until today, when I decided to blend in with the locals and ride my motorbike without a helmet.

I was expected to die at a Thai hospital. When my heart kept beating long enough for my parents to arrive from the United States, they were told that I would likely be in a vegetative state for the rest of my life. And that was if I awoke from my coma.

The doctors thought wrong.

I was either the worst or the best person to suffer such a severe injury affecting the motor cortex of the brain. I may have been the worst because, before a TBI, my self-image depended on my physical prowess and ambition. I was a fiercely independent business owner, making good money as a fitness trainer, an increasingly famous bodybuilder, and the developer of the app FitFlow. So waking up and finding myself unable to speak

i

or use the left side of my body probably hit me harder than it would most people.

On the other hand, after my TBI, I was able to use my athletic discipline, in combination with my refusal to quit, to recover what doctors described as a "shocking" level of function. I applied the same principles I had once used to transform myself from the skinny guy on the basketball team into a successful bodybuilder to reclaim my life.

Now, I want to share my story. As a side effect of my irrepressible mischievous streak, I'm told it's fairly entertaining.

I had to relearn how to walk, talk, and perform every task of a typical adult life. My mother wept the first time I managed to say "Mom" and "Dad," and again the first time I managed to propel myself in a wheelchair. Even after I regained my ability to understand speech and make decisions, people saw my disabilities and spoke about me as though I were not in the room.

However, this isn't just a recovery story. By the end of this book, I'd managed to have sex with my physical therapist and start a hot affair with a married woman who lived up the street. Her husband turned out to be—well, no spoilers.

I am not the person I was before. This experience has changed me profoundly. While my former self took many things for granted, I never will again. Losing the ability to keep up my extraordinary physical ability forced me to re-evaluate how people with disabilities in our society are treated, and what true strength is.

In the process, I learned a lot about ableism and disability. I learned that I grew up judging myself harshly on things that no one should be judged on, and that I vastly overestimated how much people cared about my physical abilities and my ability to appear "normal."

What I've achieved with disabilities is more colorful than I ever thought possible. My editor read through my 762,000-word journals and recommended I write a book just about my love life. Plus, she thinks I could do a side hustle as a dating coach! But for now we'll focus on my previous life as a star bodybuilder, my injury, and my recovery.

A TBI can happen to anyone. Over 12.5 million people sustain injuries like mine per year, and countless more are born with or sustain disabilities that will forever set them apart. But being "set apart" doesn't have to be a bad thing. I have come to learn that "fitting in" is overrated.

I hope my story will entertain as well as inspire and educate.

Yours,
Adam

1

Being Adam Rose

I was born in New York in 1991. My father, originally from Persia, and my mother, of Lebanese descent, both shared a distinctive background. Raised in Israel, they served as medics in the esteemed Israeli Defense Force. I was a smiley baby with olive skin, two dimples, and a pair of expressive dark brown eyes that I got from my mom.

By kindergarten, I was an uncontainable bundle of energy. In home movies, I can be seen running around in circles at full speed over and over like a maniac. I was already showing signs of the ADHD behavior that would make school challenging.

I developed into a skinny kid with spiky hair and a love of basketball and football. My father, Aba (which means "Dad" in Hebrew) loved basketball, and it became my ambition in life to make him proud by becoming an NBA all-star player.

I'll never forget my first day of high school. My Ema and my achoti (sister) Orit dropped me off at my new school. There was a helicopter circling the campus overhead because of anticipated gang activity. I cracked open my window and stared up at it as we pulled into the fenced-in front parking lot outside the basketball gym.

"Please remain indoors!" a voice from a megaphone above blared. "There will be a 30-minute lockdown from

7:30 AM to 8:00 AM." I later discovered this was due to suspicions of planned knife and gun fights on school property that day.

My shivering sister's eyes widened in her car seat. She was wearing a cute pink sweater as she looked pleadingly at me, affectionately holding my arm. "Adam," she said in a small voice, "this place is scary. Please don't turn into a bad guy."

I smiled, giving her hand a light kiss. "Orit, don't worry. That's never going to happen. You'll always know me. Have a good first day of school!"

I was excited for my orientation despite the ominous announcement. I walked around to the driver's side window as my mom opened it for a last goodbye. HHHS was the biggest campus in the entire San Fernando Valley, with the largest student population out of the 15 local high schools. Scholastically, I did fine in my first term there. Basketball, however, was a different story.

In the gym, monster-sized senior and junior players dunked, the shortest point guard towering at 5'10". The players were rowdy, loud and trash-talking. I sat in the corner, too intimidated to make eye contact with them. Everyone was so much bigger than me, and I doubted I could ever fit in.

"Get your hands off! I'll throw your ass on the ground!" a guy much bigger than me yelled, grabbing another player.

I was lucky to make a friend in Andre, a classmate from my first period Biology class. He was also a 6' basketball player, and we would crack jokes in class. Andre became my best friend and beloved teammate on the freshman basketball team.

Andre introduced me to another friend, fellow basketball player Rene Reyes. At first I was suspicious of a potential rival for Andre's friendship, but I soon grew to admire Rene immensely.

Rene was short for a basketball player, but his skills were magnificent. He was a freshman, but did not play on the freshman squad with Andre and me, nor the sophomores, nor even with the juniors. Instead, he played with the Varsity team. He was their starting point guard!

I began looking up to Rene as a friend and basketball teammate, studying his swift ball-handling and passing skills. I spent more and more time with him, hoping his skill would rub off on me. We began to eagerly look forward to the classes we shared. To this day, I still call him by the nickname I gave him: 'Chico La Vito.'

Despite my best efforts, basketball became unsustainable for me. I wasn't growing into a 6'4" guy, nor had I mastered the defensive moves needed to compensate for my size. Disappointed in my progress, I began looking for new outlets to prove my physical prowess.

Around this time, my parents divorced. It didn't affect me much emotionally because my mind was obsessed with thrill-seeking and sports. I was becoming more of a daredevil, jumping off pool roofs and racing motorbikes with my new school friends who shared these risky hobbies.

One day, while waiting for basketball, a few teammates and I snuck into the gym to lift weights. I discovered I could only bench press 40 pounds, struggling with shaky wrists after just four reps. For my biceps, I could hardly lift a 15-pound dumbbell to my chest!

"Dang Adam, you weak man!" my teammate Brian teased me as we left.

"Yeah, yeah," I responded, "I'll get better, though."

3

I meant it. My height didn't matter in weight lifting. The more I read about strength training, the more convinced I became that, if I put in the work, nothing could stop me from becoming stronger.

I started exercising by running up the 12 stairs in my mom's Encino home while holding old stainless-steel dumbbells. Lacking internet how-tos, I remained clueless about using the weights until my Ema noticed and gifted me a 90-day in-home CD program.

P90X's trainer, Tony, guided me through exercises. Recording my progress sparked the beginning of my journaling habit. I completed the 90-day P90X program eight times in two years, progressively increasing the weights by combining my mom's home workout weights with my old dumbbells.

When my home weights became too easy, I joined a 24-hour gym at the nearby Galleria mall. My training journal expanded as I incorporated new fitness techniques. I also started meal prepping, using my mother's barbecue to cook 16 chicken breasts, beans, and veggie bags weekly for school lunches, aiming to boost muscle growth with ample lean protein.

By my junior year, I gave up basketball due to my height, which never surpassed 6'. Despite feeling like I disappointed my Aba by not excelling in his favorite sport, I noticed my growing muscles drawing attention and boosting my social confidence.

"Yeah, Adam, you pretty big! Look at the dude's arms!"

"Yo, Adam, can you teach me how you got so strong?"

My friends weren't happy when I quit basketball, but they couldn't ignore my transformation. As I became a business major in college, my true passion was the gym. I grew to 6' and 162 pounds.

***

In my first year of college I got my first real motorcycle, a black-and-yellow '01 Suzuki 600 cc. Concerned for my safety, my mother ('Ema' in Hebrew) secretly had my Suzuki impounded while I was in class.

I, of course, responded by buying a more powerful '19 Yamaha R6 which I hid from my parents until the DMV outed me by sending my registration renewal to my home.

Ema pushed me to wear full protection while riding, including a Department of Transportation-approved outfit of helmet, gloves, pants, spine protector, and more. It was uncomfortable and heavy, but I followed the law and my Ema's concern.

"Adam," she would tell me, "I trust you on your motorcycle, but I don't trust the other drivers in LA!"

I particularly enjoyed my stylish R6 motorcycle, as it made LA traffic seem to vanish with my ability to weave between lanes. It didn't hurt my ego that the bike roared like a sports car when I revved the motor.

Alex Eskanazi, my mother's Peruvian-raised Israeli boyfriend, was a kind man and a skilled home and auto mechanic. He was a dynamic blue-collar Middle Eastern man who had already raised two amazing girls. Alex had been riding and building motorcycles for over 20 years. We became closer as he helped me to install a carbon fiber motorcycle wing, mirrors, and sticky-black adhesive outer rim tape. He even helped me to install an exhaust system that escalated the bike's Ferrari-like sound!

While I was in college, my mother adopted a white Maltese dog named Nelly. Nelly would never grow beyond six pounds, and we sometimes called her Three

5

Buttons as her entire body was white with just her dark nose and two eyes standing out like black buttons. I would squeeze-kiss her snout, calling her Little Puppy Power. Her breed was so small that she had the "superpower" to remain an eternal puppy in my arms.

As I took business coursework, Aba urged me to intern at his company. In 2012 I accepted an internship at the Agora Building in Sherman Oaks, working under his CEO John Wilson. However, the role involved monotonous marketing analysis tasks using my laptop. I was responsible for recording customer data, which became increasingly tedious, making each workday a struggle.

On lunch breaks, I strategized and wrote out my upcoming workouts in my beloved training journal. I was always researching and testing unique ways to exercise, challenging myself to progress. Each month, I would record what worked and what didn't. If a certain technique or movement felt good or seemed to yield benefits, I would carry it forward into the following month, conducting further tests and taking more notes.

As my height and size continued to grow, I thoroughly enjoyed the respect I received wherever I went. I felt that with my muscular physique, I was achieving invincibility.

I soon told Aba I was resigning—to start my own business as a personal trainer. I knew I could help others achieve the same kinds of strength and growth I'd created for myself, and people from around the San Fernando Valley agreed. My best customers were middle-aged people, often parents, who knew they needed help to stay fit amid life's many demands.

"Michelle, remember to try eating lean at this weekend's BBQ," I would remind one client, holding both her 4-year-old twins as they scrimmaged down her stairs.

By 2015, I was earning a steady income, charging $45-55 per session and averaging seven clients daily. But Aba did not enjoy seeing the time I was putting into my new chosen career.

"Adam, you are in a service job," he remarked one morning in the kitchen as he prepared for his commute. "You can only make a certain income, limited by how much you are able to work."

I took Aba's advice seriously and aimed to boost my hourly pay. I discovered that offering group classes could multiply my earnings. To promote these classes, I hired a videographer to record my workouts at the gym. The classes quickly grew, with 12-15 regular attendees paying $35 each. I loved coaching my clients and earning around $350 per 50-minute group session.

I was determined to keep growing, both my business and my muscles.

My main challenge for muscle growth was meeting the substantial protein intake needed. Although not a big eater, I adjusted my diet to consume six meals daily, primarily consisting of chicken breast, beans, and brown rice. This dietary change led me to barbecue over 30 pieces of chicken each week to meet my nutritional goals.

I needed to eat every 2 hours to continue gaining muscle mass. My trick was to play games, watch a YouTube video, listen to a podcast, or read the news to steer my mind away as I chewed.

As my physique and my strength continued to progress, I began to be interviewed by bigger and bigger influencer channels where I displayed my strength and aesthetic looks.

By 2017, my arms were 18 ½ inches in circumference. My chest and back carried prominent muscles, my quads were aesthetically defined, and an 8-pack of abs formed naturally due to my lucky genetics. I dressed in simple solid colors with my preferred Wally Maddison gym pants.

I learned that there was a distinction between being a "top bodybuilder" and a "top natural bodybuilder." "Naturals" were assumed to have limited capabilities compared to their colleagues who used performance-enhancing steroids and other drugs. On many occasions, I had colleagues trying to pressure me into using as they sat injecting themselves.

"Not for me, thanks," I would say. "I started lifting weights to look and feel good, not to create a dependence on drugs that can mess with your natural hormone production."

I never drank morning coffee, either. For an energy boost, all I needed was a pre-workout supplement, and the only pills I consumed were those containing amino acids, the building blocks of protein, for rapid bloodstream release.

Influencers liked that I studied hard and worked hard. I spoke knowledgeably about my methods and got results without promoting fad diets or snake oils. I was gaining fame as "Adam Rose," the natural bodybuilder from LA.

My signature move became what I call "clap-ups." This was an art where I flung my body above the pull-up bar to soar 5-6 inches in the air. Doing this allowed me to clap my hands while airborne, sometimes up to 14 times, before my body began to plunge back toward the floor, and I needed to stop clapping to grab the bar and catch myself. I would grin at the interviewers and videographers while I explained the mechanics of this signature move.

I achieved my heaviest weight of 202 pounds at 6'2" in 2017. I enjoyed no longer being the short, skinny kid on the basketball team, and sometimes, I still played pickup games with Rene and his friends.

By now, I was known to millions of followers of various influencers who had interviewed me. On one occasion I was interviewed by Rich Piana, whom I'd met at Gold's Gym in LA. Rich's interview with me gained over 900,000 views and led to me being interviewed by another popular old-school weightlifter, Ric Drasin (RIP), alongside Arnold Schwarzenegger.

Later, I was filmed by another fitness influencer who had more than 3 million followers. We each displayed our capabilities as he pressed a 150-pound dumbbell and I managed to press 130 pounds. The influencer, who shall remain nameless, was stunned at my abilities. Especially knowing that, unlike him, I wasn't taking steroid injections.

"It's really unreal Adam-man, how strong you are with no 'roids," he told me after our workout.

My favorite video of myself was not one of the prestigious interviews. It was simply me performing "clap-ups" in slow motion, making me appear to hover in the air for a full 3 seconds before falling back to Earth.

The video played with a soundtrack of Will Smith speaking in the background:

"For me, it has always been about being that guy who does what people say that can't be done. I think it started with trying to please my mother, trying to please my father, because they always wanted something higher, something better for me. It made me get to the point that I wanted to be something, I wanted to be a somebody. I

9

wanted to be the first person there, and the last person to leave. I think the road to success is through commitment, and through the strength to drive through that commitment."

As my body continued to grow, my confidence and self-esteem did too. I reached a point where I felt like I could do anything.

Invincible.

In 2015, I noticed that trainers were using social media more and more. This inspired the idea for FitFlow, an app which would automatically share workout activities on social media, check users into gyms using GPS, and sync with fitness monitoring devices.

Excited about the pioneering concept, I hired programmers, invested savings, and involved friends and family in testing the app. However, a crucial test remained: pitching the idea to my father, who was skeptical about FitFlow's potential.

Stepping into the G-Defy corporate offices, I was both intimidated and inspired. Aba's atrium had 80-foot ceilings, rock formations, and a fully stocked koi pond.

My father really created something big, I realized. *Now it's my turn.*

I was called into a room by my dad's assistant Jennifer, and grabbed a seat alone at the large conference table. I had dressed for the occasion, combing my hair and wearing a white button-up shirt with black slacks. I sat with my left hand's knuckles pressed to my anxious mouth as I anticipated my father's rejection or approval. It was more nerve-wracking than any pitch to a random stranger could have been.

Aba soon walked in and sat across from me with Jennifer. I signaled for my PowerPoint to be projected onto the wall behind me and stood up.

I spoke as the slides flowed by in the richly appointed glass-fronted conference room. I presented the FitFlow concept, employing screenshots to translate it into my father's preferred language: a traditional business plan.

"Joining the app is free," I explained, "but this is a GPS-driven social app, which means that our return on investment will come from in-app ads. Gyms, restaurants, salons, sportswear outlets, and other businesses will buy timed ad space to advertise their services to users who check in to the app at nearby locations.

"Users will download the app for the social media benefits, and time spent on the app will create new targeted ad real estate for retailers."

I could feel my eyes sparkling at Aba, trying not to speak too fast in my excitement.

Aba began to nod, looking every inch the conservative businessman in a blue-gray dress shirt produced by one of his own companies, Topix Marketing, and slicked-back hair.

He looked down as my presentation wrapped up. "I have no idea about this social media stuff," he admitted. "But if what you're saying is true, it's a good idea. If it really creates new ad space for sale, I can see the potential."

I took a deep breath and sat back, my hand sweating. Discreetly, I checked my phone under the table to see if the FitFlow beta app had properly checked me in at the office building.

"You have checked in to 'Gdefy'," read the message on my screen. "Enjoy your workout!"

Driving home, I almost howled with excitement. "Yes! We got this!" I wailed over my music as my car approached 70 mph. I began envisioning the commercials I would shoot for FitFlow with the help of my friends.

I began recording daily workouts to create exclusive content. I wanted to entice FitFlow users to subscribe for premium memberships by offering access to my recorded videos and virtual group classes. This way I could transform my personal training skills into passive income.

I was living the dream as 2017 opened up. My days were filled with workouts, client visits, and time with friends, while my nights were dedicated to planning my future business empire and corresponding with my coding teams.

For all of my social confidence and for all that many might have assumed I was a "ladies man," in my mid-20s, I had not had many serious romances. That was all about to change with the introduction of two women who would influence the rest of my life.

***

2

First Loves

I'll never forget the first time I met Donna. I was at the student recreation center when I spotted a cute girl next to the rock climbing wall. She was with two other guys, but there was something about her that drove me to head in her direction boldly.

"Hey guys, I'm Adam," I introduced myself, trying my best not to stare solely at the girl.

"Uh, hey Adam. I'm Ryan," said a 5'8" guy in a red shirt and sunglasses, seeming surprised by my approach.

I learned that the girl's name was Donna and she was a Moroccan-American Jew. I tried to maintain conversation with her two male friends, but found myself making playful eye contact with Donna. I couldn't keep my eyes off her. She had this angelic smile with incredible brown eyes perfectly offset by her tan skin.

"This looks pretty steep," I said, quietly smiling at her as the guys turned away to strap themselves into their climbing harnesses. I grabbed a foothold with my left arm, attempting to lift my body off the ground with one arm in an effort to impress her.

"Careful!" she chuckled, placing her hand to her mouth.

Soon, I worked up the courage to politely ask for her phone number. Donna smiled and hesitated, but ultimately blushed and gave it to me.

At home that evening, I spent a while working up the courage to call her.

"...hello? Yes. Adam, right?"

We made small talk about the rock wall and school. I learned that she intended to become a nurse like my mother. Unfortunately, I also learned that she already had a love interest: Ryan from the rock wall.

As I was about to say goodbye, she asked if we could be friends. But my childish ego wouldn't accept being friend-zoned. I respectfully declined her offer, wishing her the best. I paced around Aba's kitchen, disgruntled, before distracting myself with FitFlow.

Months later, I found myself filming a fitness video with my friend Brad at a nearby gym when a girl approached. Despite his attempts to get her attention, she bypassed him and made a beeline toward me as I completed my workout routine.

"Hey, Adam?" She squinted, her long straight hair falling over her shoulder. "Remember me? Donna?"

I kept breathing with my pumped-up chest, staring at her gorgeous face.

"Hey, Donna. I remember you," I responded. "You chose that other guy Ryan over me, right?" I teased as I began to towel off.

She rolled her brown eyes, smiling. "Well, it didn't work out."

"Oh." I wasn't sure if condolences or congratulations were in order, so I changed the subject. "How are you and your studies?"

Donna and I began talking on the phone again and soon decided to meet up. It was then that we began dating.

Donna was interested in my family's history. She loved how my parents grew up in Israel and met as medics in the army. She was charmed at how well I spoke Hebrew, being American herself and hardly speaking a few words.

Donna stood just 5'3", but she was wise beyond her years. I felt responsible to her in a way I hadn't with previous girlfriends, which pushed me to improve myself as a person. I was no longer just a "gym guy"; I was a man with a woman to love and protect. She was so unique and down-to-earth. She didn't even have any social media accounts!

Donna was very supportive of FitFlow. She believed in my ideas and expertise and supported me in my late-night conversations with my coding teams.

Despite my deep admiration for her, I soon realized that Donna and I were very different people. After just a few months of dating, she 'joked' that we should get married because her parents approved of me. She made it clear that she was not willing to explore physical intimacy until after marriage, which she hoped would happen soon.

There was nothing wrong with Donna's beliefs. Her character was impeccable, but our desires didn't align. Still being in my 20s and not having dated much seriously up to this point, I wanted to explore and have fun. She was already seeking a husband to create a family with.

My friends suggested I discuss this with her, but I felt that I would be asking her to change herself as a person. I loved Donna exactly the way she was, and didn't feel it would be right to ask her to put her goals on hold for me.

So, I made up my mind. I drove to her house and told her that I couldn't continue our relationship because I wasn't mature enough. As I gazed into her beautiful eyes, I became filled with remorse at knowing I had wasted her time.

"Donna, I love you, and thank you for everything. You've helped me a lot." I gently held her small hands. Finally, after a bit of hesitation, I let go and stepped back.

She looked at me with disbelief but nodded in understanding.

"Donna," I told her, "you've taught me so much about love, respect, and belief. Enjoy being with your friends, family, and I'm excited for your upcoming nursing career. I know you'll be great."

As the months unfolded, I felt the void where Donna's supportive presence used to be. But I knew I'd done the right thing.

As FitFlow approached its launch date, I decided against completing my college degree. What did I need a degree for if I was already running a successful coaching business and was about to launch a successful app?

My parents being highly educated medics and engineers themselves, initially did not receive my leaving college well. But I told them:

"Aba, Ema I research and study whatever I want to accomplish. I train clients in person, in groups, and have an international online audience. Kids go to school to learn business; I've already started two businesses."

I now shared an apartment with a roommate, Kaitlyn. We shared a 2-bedroom place in Burbank near my clients and my Galleria Gym. She worked hard, assisting Los Angeles media personalities and aspiring to build her own brand in the industry.

Meanwhile, I studied the histories of tech startups and observed my Aba's approach to investing in tech stocks closely. I was determined that FitFlow would be the next big startup and listened to numerous business podcasts and shows in an effort to make that happen.

I was now shooting and organizing commercials ahead of FitFlow's launch and training about 13 clients each day. I was still recovering from breaking up with

Donna, but one day while working out, a woman caught my eye who I could not ignore.

She was a Latina girl with an aura of cute mischief about her, a fit lean stomach, and oversized natural breasts. She radiated a warm but wicked energy as she stood exercising. I learned from friends that her name was Kaylee, and that she was a well-known winner of prestigious local beauty pageants.

Kaylee would always come to the gym with her bearded father, who aggressively eyed everyone, clearly hoping to intimidate men to stay away from his daughter.

One day in April 2018, I was at the gym with my friend from middle school, Nick, when I noticed that Kaylee's father had left her alone and gone to the restroom.

"Ey, hold up Nick, this is my moment to take my shot," I told him. Still sweating from exertion, I half-jogged to her side and introduced myself, smiling.

"Hello, I'm Adam. How's your workout going? Your dad's the best workout partner, right?" I said with a smirk.

"Hi, uhh, he's about to come back!" she responded, smiling nervously back at me.

Sure enough, he returned, approaching us with his patented stare. I smiled at him confidently, making his daughter quietly blush and look away.

Nick watched from across the gym, muttering, "Look at this dude..."

I kept smiling joyfully at her father, killing his aggression with kindness.

Kaylee and I began casually dating soon after. She and I had amazing sexual chemistry, the kind I had dreamt of exploring with a more conservative Donna. Kaylee was much more open, fulfilling both her desires and mine.

Meanwhile, the FitFlow marketing launch was approaching.

A week before, my old friend Rene Reyes suggested we go on vacation and have fun. He had just graduated from business school, a ceremony I happily attended with his father, Jose Luis Reyes.

"Congratulations, Rene," I gushed. "I'm happy for you, Chico!" I stood applauding him by the entry gate with his father by my side. Rene was glad I came to accompany his single dad, and he asked again if I would consider traveling with him.

I was nervous about traveling, with FitFlow's launch approaching and my new relationship with Kaylee budding. To my surprise, Aba encouraged me to go, saying I hadn't been on a vacation in years and that I deserved it.

"Go on the trip with Rene, Aba," Dad said. "If you believe in your app, Adam, tavod al ze *(work on it)* when you return."

In Hebrew, "Aba" or "papa" can be used as a term of endearment, showing affection while also attributing leadership qualities to the person. Aba also calls my sister Orit "Aba" for this reason.

I nodded, making my decision. I knew the destination I wanted to suggest: Thailand, a tropical paradise Aba and I had explored as a detour on some of his business trips to China.

Rene had never left North America and had mentioned wishing to see the Thai destinations I told him about while we were in school. He cheered when I told him that I'd decided to make this happen for us.

In high school, everyone looked up to Rene. As an underclassman he was dominating Varsity basketball, winning awards, and traveling to tournaments consistently. I was excited to be able to give him an exotic experience, and to me, this was one more sign of my growing success as a businessman.

Aba agreed with our selected destination when I told him of my plans over dinner.

"Okay, let's set it up," he agreed.

I hesitated. "Aval (but), Aba, I don't have enough money for this Thailand trip," I told him. "Everything I have is invested in FitFlow's marketing and some stock investments. We think adapting FitFlow for Android devices will cost even more than designing the Apple interface did."

Aba looked at his plate, nodding. "Why don't I help you pay for it with my airline rewards?" he offered. "I have enough for the tickets."

I stared. "Really..? Thank you, Aba!"

I called my 'Chico,' Rene, with the amazing news that I would meet him on May 21, 2018, in Asia! I felt free and powerful, about to have an amazing, unforgettable time. I contacted my development teams and clients, setting them up for my upcoming trip that night.

"Okay, Michelle," I texted her cell, "I'll be back in 2 weeks. Please stick to your assigned cardio and eat your lean meals. Please don't let your kids get you on that midday pizza and brownie buffet! See you in June when I return!"

Rene and I talked all week about our upcoming Thailand trip. I made a list of all the things I needed to be sure I showed him—things Aba had first shown me.

Kaylee texted me, "I'll miss you, baby."

I replied, "Yeah, babe. I'll be back soon."

Traveling with Chico La Vito, I happily thought to myself as I lay in bed the night before departure. This really is a new chapter for both of us.

***

3

Thailand

Total-memory recall: 97%
Age: 27
Weight: 197
Sources: Rene, Div, and Myself
Monday Morning. May 21ˢᵗ, 2018, 8 AM

I woke up with an aching chest from an intense workout with Nick at the Galleria Gym the day before. Then I remembered what day it was and jumped out of bed.

I jogged to my bathroom sink to put in my contacts, then darted into the living room, where my bags were packed for Thailand. I'd packed while blasting Kaskade's "Room for Happiness" the night before.

Ema (Mom, in Hebrew) was already at the front door with her Maltese dogs, Nelly and Poof, in her arms. She was here to take me to the airport and to make sure I got a chance to say goodbye to Nelly first.

I grabbed my car keys from the 4-inch tall bronze-stucco gorilla that held them on a table by the door. I purchased that gorilla on my first trip to Thailand when I was 12 years old and kept it as a reminder of that treasured memory.

"Did you pack your contact solution?" Ema asked. She was forever afraid that I'd forget it and end up injuring my eyes.

"Yes, Ema," I replied. "Toda she ate biyeet lazor, Dubi." 'Thank you for coming to help, teddy bear.'

My roommate, Kaitlyn, was making coffee in the kitchen.

"Alright Kate, I'm outta here," I said, setting my carry-on bag down and walking toward her for a big hug.

"Oh, okay! Bye dude!" Kaitlyn said, throwing her arms around my wide shoulders.

I playfully picked her entire body up in a hug. "You'll have the entire place to yourself when you get home!"

"Have a great time," she said when I put her down. "I'll see you soon!"

I smiled at her and followed Ema out the door, rolling my luggage by my side. "Say hi to Jen (Kaitlyn's secret crush) for me," I shouted, winking over my shoulder, then checked my FitFlow account to make sure it showed my location accurately.

Since I had administrative access to FitFlow, I could tweak the location settings. I tested these every time I went anywhere, seeking perfection. Last night I'd set my airport gate for the Thailand flight as a new location, listing it as "Thai workout."

I climbed into Ema's station wagon, and Nelly climbed into my lap.

"It's going to be tough to relax with the app launch being so close," I admitted to Ema, petting Nelly's soft white head. "But it'll be good to test the GPS system on a different continent."

"Hakol heeye Beseder Adahm." *'All will be good.'* Ema said in her motherly way. "Have you checked in with Rene?"

Rene had taken a different flight, arriving in Bangkok before me. The plan was for us to meet in Bangkok and then take a small plane to our real destination: Phuket. Phuket was 32 islands of pure paradise.

"Not yet," I hadn't felt the need to disturb Rene's post-graduation vacation.

Orit called as we pulled up to the airport's drop-off zone.

"Hey!" Her voice crackled over the car's Bluetooth speakers. "How are you? All set for your trip?" Orit sounded ecstatic.

"Yeah, Orit, we just pulled in."

"I'm so excited for you!"

"Thank you, Oritoosh. I'll send you lots of videos!"

"Okay, love you!"

When we arrived at the airport, I got out of the car, kissing Ema goodbye.

"Call me every day no matter what, mami," she said protectively.

"I will, Dubi. Bye, Puppy Power!" I delicately kissed Nelly's head and knocked on the rear window behind which Poof sat, snorting and wagging her tail.

I looked down at my FitFlow app as I walked. The icon hadn't turned its active green color but remained the glowing orange of a "pending" workout. I sighed as we were called to board and the icon still remained orange.

As we boarded, a text from Kaylee pinged my phone. "Baby, bye bye! I'm going to miss your eyes, and your hands grabbing me." Her text brought back memories of her on top of me. Remembering her sounds, her glistening body, the feel of my two hands cupping her breasts all brought a grin to my face.

Before switching on airplane mode, I messaged her back, "Mamacita, I miss you too, heading out. See you the second I get back, babe. :)"

Once we were in the air, I headed to the restroom, took out my contacts, placed them in the fizzling solution bottle and closed my eyes to rest them. Back in my seat, I turned on some relaxing R&B melodies by Usher. Excited to show Rene what good times were all about, I promised myself this would be the first of many FitFlow-funded vacations for me and my friends.

FitFlow's official launch date was set for July 9, 2018.

***

I arrived in Bangkok to find that my FitFlow app still listed my check-in as "pending." I submitted a new check-in location for Rene's hotel and jumped in a taxi.

The taxi drove me past street vendors selling vibrant foods against the gray backdrop of the city. It was very different from Phuket, where pristine nature stretched away on all sides. I unloaded my luggage outside the hotel, then stepped into the hotel's blue and white marble lobby.

"Hello, I'm Adam," I said brightly to the half-asleep older woman who was staffing the front desk. "Is my guy Rene here?"

"Halo, Adam. Flight good?" she asked. She scanned her computer screen and told me Rene was getting a massage at the upstairs hotel spa.

"Thank you!"

I rode the elevator up to the spa level, and walked quietly to the candlelit massage station. Rene was lying naked under a beige spa towel while a Thai man massaged him.

Finally, a notification pinged my phone: "You have checked into 'Vela Glow Hotel,' enjoy your workout!" I smiled, relieved.

Then I tiptoed toward Rene's bed. I announced, when I was only steps away,: "Back off my man! I'll take care of my own baby Chico!" I sprang onto Rene as the massage therapist looked on, nervous and unaware of our high school antics.

"Ey, Adam, Adam... get off me, man, damn!"

I laughed, rolling off to his side in ecstatic amusement. "My check-in algorithm worked in Thailand, man!" I boasted. "You have no idea how much I've been looking forward to this!" I threw my arms around him in excitement. "I'm so happy, man," I said, getting off him after a long moment. "Almost done, Cheec? Show me the room, sexy man!"

Rene got up, looking at the masseuse, "Yeah, we're done."

I kept putting my arm around Rene as we walked down to the lobby, smiling in disbelief that we were in Asia together. I'd spent years telling him stories of Thailand over lunch and in nutrition class.

We tried exploring Bangkok more, but the combination of the overcast morning, the dirty city streets, and the tense atmosphere made me eager to get to Phuket. Bangkok was a bustling city of trams, moped drivers who sped past without helmets, dirt roads, and a combination of smog, cigarettes, and barbecue smoke. Black market bootlegged DVDs, fake jewelry, electronics, and ripe fruits and vegetables were for sale in bungalows along the road.

Rene and I walked for hours around the edge of a large green park near the Queen Sirikit National Lake Rafts.

"This city is unique," I told Rene, "but the real paradise is just two hours that way." I pointed in the direction I thought was south.

"It's nice here though, man," Rene responded. "Food's good." He had enjoyed sampling three different Thai street food dishes and drinks I'd recommended and was toting leftovers in a plastic bag. Local fried noodles, warm mango with sticky rice, stir-fried flat noodles, and papaya salads—I wanted to give Rene the best of everything.

That night, I called Aba to tell him we wanted to go to Phuket the next day. He helped us move some things around, and we booked a flight to the islands for the morning.

"Let's get out of this city," I told Rene, "and I'll introduce you to heaven."

As we waited for our taxi the next morning, I opened FitFlow to set a new check-in location for our new hotel.

"Another fake workout?" Rene smirked, looking over my shoulder at the FitFlow app. He'd called me out before for my constant fiddling with it.

"Yeah, man," I sighed and leaned back. "Just over a month to launch."

As we drove down the streets of Bangkok, some things were difficult to watch. Beggars lined the streets in some areas, including disabled people with missing limbs who did not look well cared for.

"Rene," I murmured, looking across the street, "Can you imagine not having a home and not having arms or legs? How would you survive?"

Rene kept his eyes ahead. "I know," he said. We felt powerless to do anything about it. Even if we gave them a lot of American money, I knew there was a good chance this would just make them targets for potential robbery.

"Okay, screw this city, man," Rene said after we passed more disabled people looking impoverished and unhappy. "I'm glad we're leaving it."

I agreed.

***

As we stepped off the small plane, Rene gasped. "Whoa, it's so humid out here!"

"Yeah, man. Now we're near the water." I pointed toward the beach with its white sand and blue topaz waters.

After all the stories I'd told Rene of accompanying my dad here in high school, I was proud to give him the gift of the trip he had long dreamt of. To me, this was true fulfillment: the ability to provide for my friends.

We checked into our new hotel and spent the rest of the day exploring the coast. At night I introduced Rene to some of the 120+ bars along the notorious Bangala Road. Just 20 feet from the beach, the road hosted raging parties, dancing, drinking, live music, nightclubs, and its famous go-go dancing bars.

Boom, boom, boom, boom! Music throbbed through our bodies and shook the night.

"'ey, let's see you move, Chico-La-Vito! Varsity man!" I hollered to Rene over the noise. He had already started to shimmy. It had been an amazing day of spicy Thai cuisine, outdoor shopping, and 87-degree ocean water.

In the coming days, we'd go snorkeling and island diving as we enjoy our hotel's pristine ocean view. Its free breakfast buffet included over 150 entrees to select from and 8 fresh fruit juices. This place really did have it all.

We danced on the white sand to Coldplay as waves rolled over our ankles. We hiked, laughed, took photos, and snorkeled. During our 5-hour cruise, we visited Monkey Beach, home to hundreds of monkeys. The guides warned us about their sharp teeth. I'd had a past encounter where Aba saved me from an angry primate I didn't want to reenact.

After the cruise, Rene and I walked back to Bangala Road, where we continued to party, mingle with locals, dance with the bar owners, and enjoy beach-barbecued chicken skewers and a couple of Corona beers. We discussed our thoughts on Phuket, finding it preferable to Bangkok. Eventually, we gave up on walking and took a tuk-tuk ride back.

The following morning, Rene wanted to sleep in, so I went to have breakfast by the ocean. I used the time to review FitFlow's basic functions and took notes on bandwidth and data limits.

As I rose to leave, I noticed a beautiful woman sitting by herself in the corner. Her silk-dark hair fell across her shoulders, and she wore a pair of beach shorts with an elegant white blouse.

I walked past, giving her a smile. "Good morning. I'm Adam." She seemed to brighten at my attention. "Are you enjoying the long walk from the hotel to Patong?"

"Hi, Adam. I'm Div." I learned that she was a South African woman living in Australia, and had come to Phuket with her boyfriend. But after a stressful, nearly relationship-ending argument, she was solemnly eating breakfast alone. When Rene arrived for his first coffee of the day, I introduced them to each other and we all exchanged phone numbers.

After breakfast, I told Rene I needed a weighted workout. We walked into the hotel gym to find that there were only two cardio machines, two cable machines, and a 16-dumbbell set which only went up to 80 pounds. I took a seat while Rene hopped on the elliptical.

"What are you gonna do?" He asked, starting to walk.

I flipped open the training journal I took with me everywhere. "I need some compound muscle group exercises. A little chest would be nice." I picked up a couple of dumbbells and tested them. "I need your help," I told Rene then.

"What do you need, you crazy ass?" Rene asked.

"These are too light. I want to stack some weights on top of each other," I told him. "I'll show you, it's easy."

Rene got off his elliptical and came over, curious. "So, Varsity, take these 25-pounders," I instructed him. "I'm going to grab the 80-pounders and chest press them while you hold the 25s on top of the 80s."

He stared at me, his blue-green eyes wide. "Uh, okay, papi, you for-real crazy." He laughed. Fortunately, I had mastered this technique back when my at-home dumbbell set first ceased to be enough for me.

"Yo," I smiled, "be a brother and help me out? These are nothing."

In the end, Rene carefully held the 25s' hovering over my 80s' with his skilled hands. I pumped out 21 reps until failure.

"Whoo, see? Easy, Varsity-man!"

After our workout, we grabbed a tuk-tuk back and went back to Patong Beach. We got facials and foot massages, explored local shopping, and dined at the local restaurants. We also saw captive tigers, fed bananas to elephants, and observed Thai black bears together in an enclosure. On our return to the hotel via tuk-tuk, I was amazed by the blue scenic view against the white beaches and a red parasail floating above.

"The universe created something beautiful here," I said.

Rene nodded in agreement.

"I love you, man," I turned to look romantically into his eyes.

He laughed. "Hahaha, you too!" He shoved me playfully. We ate fried rice and pan-fried whitefish on the beach.

Div then messaged me, wanting to join us and get away from her drama-fueled boyfriend.

She met us as we headed to the lively Patong street coast. There was a Holiday Inn Hotel on Thaweewong Road. Aba and I always stayed here, right on the edge of the Patong Beach walkways overlooking the ocean.

"Rene, we should stay at this hotel starting tomorrow," I proposed. "This is the best part of the island! Remember it from all my stories back in high school?" I led Rene and Div through the hotel's white lobby and out the rear exit facing the beachfront. "See, Rene, you just walk outside," I took a step, "and BAM! You're in the center strip."

After showing Rene and Div the hotel pool, the larger gym, a Starbucks next door, and a shopping center across the street, Rene agreed to make this our last night at the Diamond Cliff Hotel.

"'Ey Rene, what you doing? Nothing, chilling at the 'Holidae-Inn!'" I sang to him, quoting the Chingy song from our school days.

Rene, Div, and I continued walking. We stumbled on a store selling tickets for the "Paradise Beach Full Moon Festival," an event being thrown at a local lagoon.

"What do you think?" I asked both of them. Rene and Div looked at each other. Then, Div winked at me in approval.

"Man, you know I'm in!" Rene smiled.

Rene and I took a walk along the sand while Div went to grab a burger. It was another crisp, beautiful day; all sun and no clouds.

"What do you think about your future, man? Now that school is done," I asked Rene as the sand filtered between our toes.

"I'm not sure," he admitted. "I think I wanna start training people, like we did in the hotel gym just now. I liked watching you feeling good and getting your workout in." He looked up at me, his blue-green eyes matching the sea behind him. "You've gotta show me how to start finding and training clients."

"I got you," I assured him. "I can teach you training and everything about setting up a business. FitFlow is almost ready for launch, and I'm quitting everything else. When FitFlow is a success, there'll be Thailand trips every year!" I raised my arms in the air in anticipation of victory.

I threw my left arm around Rene and turned to see Div waiting for us in the doorway. She looked beautiful in a dark salmon bathing suit, her skin glistening with sweat in the heat.

I spoke softly so Div couldn't hear us, "Rene, you are a born leader. You were a Varsity point guard freshman year! You controlled the game with your skill. I know you can encourage those who need a trainer."

"Thanks, man, appreciate you," he said quietly. I could hear the doubt in his voice.

We walked back to Div then, and I squeezed her in a friendly hug. The three of us returned to the Diamond Cliff Hotel together via tuk-tuk .

Div and I explored while Rene rested. We flirted lightly, taking photos of each other around the hotel as I arranged our new hotel for tomorrow. Div posed playfully for more pictures.

"Do I look sublime, Adam?" She asked in her South African-Australian accent, laughing. I chuckled as she sought out impromptu props and ended up dangling lettuce from the buffet over her head seductively for my phone camera.

We headed to the rear guest pool with its artificial waterfall. I posed, squeezing my shoulders together under the falling water.

"Adam, you have quite a strong, sexy American body!" Div complimented me, grinning as she snapped photos of my ripped legs, eight-pack abs, and shoulder muscles. I shot her a sharp smirk as I flexed.

That night, we left for the Paradise Beach Full Moon Festival.

We boarded a yellow bus with no ceiling in front of the Diamond Hotel around 7 PM. The yellow bus rumbled under our feet for 30 minutes, a tourist's Reggae music blasting from a boombox amid the others' laughter. Rene, Div, and I were instantly captivated the moment we pulled up at our destination.

"Now that's what I'm talking about," Rene said.

The festival had its own private beach with lights, coconut tree swings, lit fire poles, and a 50-foot dance floor bawling out Thai pop mixed with Spanish music. The moment Div, Rene, and I walked in, we settled by the torches and tree swings and were given 90-ounce ice bucket-cups. These were filled with Thai basil vodka and chilled Red Bull, rimmed with rainbow sugar and garnished with pineapple. We spent the night laughing, dancing, and speaking with other world-traveling tourists.

"Div, quick! Take a photo of my boy Rene and me on the swings!"

Rene and I sat on the tree swing, then left for Bangala road at 11:00 PM. After bar hopping until 1:00 AM, we snuck into the closed Diamond Hotel pool, creating our own mini-festival.

We swam in our underwear to Kaskade's "Room for Happiness." We laughed, danced, and playfully teased each other in the pool under the starry sky and blue lights.

The next morning, I woke up before Rene and video-called my mom.

"Hiii Dubi, maneeshma ma kore!" *'How are you guys? What's going on?'* I almost whispered, trying not to disturb Rene. "I miss Nelly. Kiss that Puppy Power for me, Ema. I love and miss you guys!"

"We miss you too, Danduni!" Mom said on speaker, "I just spoke to your cousin Nancy in Israel. She's much closer to you than us!" Ema said. "She said to call her if you need anything!"

When Rene still had not woken up as the call ended, I went out onto the balcony and stared at the beautiful horizon. I messaged and video-called my dad and three clients, eager to keep up with life back home.

When Rene finally joined me on the balcony, we checked out of the Diamond Hotel. We dropped our bags off at the Holiday Inn, then headed up the hill to visit the island's famous cliffs. I wanted to show him the Bob Marley Cafe.

The cafe was perched on wooden planks that didn't look terribly stable. If you went downstairs to the restrooms, your jaw would open in nervous surprise. But that was part of the cafe's charm.

"Beautiful, isn't it, Chico?" I asked him as we sat on the viewing deck by the green cliffs. Along the 250-foot plank walkway, you could see a few missing boards.

After breakfast, I wanted to show Rene more excitement. I remembered that a street vendor near our new hotel rented mopeds.

I explained my plan to Rene as I led us through the unfamiliar streets. His eyes grew wide.

"Hold up, I can't ride a bike like you, papi," Rene said nervously as we approached the booth with ten Yamaha NMAX motorcycles lined up waiting.

"It's easy," I promised him. "There's no clutch or gears, and the brakes are simple. These little things have tiny 150cc engines, Varsity-man." I pointed to the small rear engines as the manager, an elderly lady wearing a blue shirt with flowers on it, greeted us with a selling smile.

"Ahlo! Rent for two?"

I nodded.

"You so strong!" She exclaimed, buttering us up, but also seeming genuinely surprised as she got a look at my arms.

"Listen, we'll teach you ," I turned to Rene. "What's the worst that could happen?"

Rene still looked doubtful, but he allowed the manager, who introduced herself as Kinna, to give him his first lesson. I went to get food and a drink, strolling past children playing in my sand on the way back to them.

"Almost ready, my darling Chic-a?" I asked as I approached.

Behind Rene, a Thai family of six drove past, all perched precariously on a single moped. Neither the father, the pregnant mother, the three children or the baby on the woman's hip wore helmets.

"You don't have to wear helmets around here?" I asked Kinna.

"Uh, yes, need helmets," she said. "Not many do here. But, 1994 law says, need to wear helmet now. Please give passport!"

I smiled and gave her my passport as collateral. I'd get it back when we returned the bikes.

"Be safe, be safe," Kinna said as I revved up my engine, grinning with delight.

VROOM, VROOM!

"Let's do this, Rene. You got this!"

We began our ride at a slow 15 mph, making a left toward the mountains. I wanted to take Rene to Beach Karon. Rene rode his bike cautiously, staying behind the other riders on the road.

I did not.

Missing the thrill of my more powerful bikes, I took corners fast. Once, I almost lost control but recovered myself in a spray of gravel. Feeling intoxicated by the speed, I hollered to Rene: "Whoa, Chico, that was a close one!"

"Adam, go easy, man," Rene looked worried. "You're going too fast!"

I drove a bit slower, reminding myself that I hadn't ridden in five years. And this bike was not as powerful as my bikes back home; it was not made for the same maneuvers.

By 1:00 PM, we were driving along a twisty hillside. Beach Karon was the opposite of Patong: it was quiet, calm, and tranquil. Heavenly. This coast had just a few scattered cafes and a few sets of wooden boards leading to the empty, warm-sandy waves. We began riding slower, gazing at the spectacular views.

"Yo, set the bikes over there!" I yelled to Rene.

I smiled as I parked, excited to show Rene paradise.

We parked our bikes across from a seafood cafe-bungalow, just across a 12-foot-wide street from the white Karon Beach sand. It was so beautiful, tropical, and exotic: the perfect trip moment with Rene. I smiled, smacking the backside of his bike like I did Div's bottom the night before.

"This is pure bliss," I said as we grabbed the nearest outdoor table, facing the serene ocean view.

"Yeah, man, this is perfect."

After eating, we decided to walk to the empty, serene blue ocean. We started to play-wrestle each other along the water's edge, laughing on the sand.

"Oh my God, Adam, get off me!" Rene shouted, laughing. "Adam! Ugh, watch out, I dropped the motorbike keys in the water!"

I eased off a little. Sometimes, I forgot my own strength when I felt like I was the skinny guy on the freshman basketball team again. But I wasn't about to let him off entirely.

I continued tackling and recording him, holding onto my phone with my left hand. Finally, I fell back into the sand, roaring in laughter, "I love you, man!" I managed to wheeze.

"But seriously, though," I sobered, fishing his keys out of the water. "You know we're riding back together if you lose your keys, right?"

"Only if you promise to let me hold you by your waist," he winked at me.

This is blissful, I thought. *The best moment so far in my life.*

Two hours after arriving, we got back on our bikes and prepared to head back.

I felt amazing. I was just weeks away from the launch of my application. After that, I'd be back here every year with Rene at my side.

"Chico, let's not wear helmets," I proposed. "We're Varsity," I told him, using the term as shorthand for a sense of power and freedom. "And I want to blend in with the locals."

I had always hated looking like a stranger who didn't fit in with the team. I stuffed my helmet in my tiny seat-trunk. Rene nodded, unbuckling his as well. We began our ride across the island, merging onto the sandy streets.

I felt like I was on top of the world. I revved my engine.

"Let's go, Varsity-man!" I hollered, speeding up.

Behind me, Rene honked to get my attention. I brought my ride to a stop on the sandy pavement, then turned and drove back to where Rene was parked by the side of the road.

"Yo, you good?" I jumped off in concern.

"Having brake issues, man," he pumped his brakes to demonstrate.

I rolled my eyes. "What do you mean? These rides are good."

He looked at me nervously, "I don't know, man..."

"Move over with those pretty little eyes and switch bikes with me," I suggested.

We switched bikes, him trusting my expertise with the vehicles. I tested the brake of my new bike at an intersection. It needed a stronger squeeze than my original bike to come to a full stop, but it didn't seem like anything major.

Gotta do everything for him in this country, I thought, shaking my head and accelerating. I sped up a few times, hoping to show Rene how to use his bike more adventurously.

We were near the first of the green hills connecting the two coasts when we were flagged down by police who seemed to appear out of nowhere.

"Ah ah! No helmet, ticket!" They announced, walking up to us and pulling out pads of paper.

I stared. "Are you serious, man?"

The officers gave each of us a 496 baht ($14 US) ticket for not wearing helmets, forcing us to put them on.

Rene and I walked to the police camper to pay our tickets. I was frustrated. This trip had gone perfectly until the police showed up. As Rene and I watched, the officers pulled over several locals, too.

"Are you kidding me?" I vented. "No one wears helmets here!" Rene and I found ourselves at the back of an eight-person line, all waiting to pay fines.

I got more and more impatient as we waited. Why have a law that most locals never followed? It obviously wasn't doing anything.

Finally, we walked back to our bikes. I settled into my seat and revved my motor.

"Adam, are you really not wearing a helmet again?" Rene asked me.

"No, screw that. There won't be any more police booths on our way. Let's get back to the hotel and hit the pool with Div and some drinks. I'm over this Karon Beach."

Rene followed my example, leaving his helmet in his seat-trunk.

We set off on the road back to Patong's Holiday Inn. This time I drove even faster around the curves, speeding off my anger at the interruption to our perfect day. I gripped the motorcycle steering, accelerating faster with a turn of my sweat-slicked wrist, pulling further ahead of Rene.

At last, I smiled, feeling the wind on my face. I approached 47 mph as I rounded a hill.

3:45 PM was my last memory.

**

4

The Tragedy

Total-memory recall: 0%
Mental Capabilities: N/A
Total-Left: Paralyzed
Skin-State: Broken Skull, Multiple Dislocations, Cuts,
Infections, Scratches, & Numerous Stitches
Assistive Items: Hospital Bed, Ventilator, Cardiac
Monitor, Oxygen, IVs, and a Head Wrap
Mental Age: N/A
Current Weight: 197 lbs
Sources: Rene, Dad, Mom's Journal, & Alex

Aba stood in my hospital room as I lay on bloodied sheets in the Phuket Hospital Intensive Care Unit. My eyes were closed, my nose threaded with breathing tubes, my right arm stuck with an IV, and my head visibly dented and covered by a 4-inch line of stitches. My oxygen and heart monitors hissed and beeped in a steady rhythm.

Ssss... Beep. Beep... Ssss.

He walked closer, terror hitting him as the shock passed.

Ssss... Beep. Beep... Ssss.

I was missing 15% of my skull, which the doctors had to remove to save my life, sewing the skin shut back over the wound to prevent infection. My face bore bloody gashes where it had scraped across the road.

"Ma-kara?" *'What happened?'* Aba whispered. "What did he break?"

Ssss... Beep. Beep... Ssss.

Aba covered his mouth as two Thai nurses descended on me, checking my vitals. He had jumped on a plane the night before, as soon as he got the call from Rene alerting him of my accident. He'd flown for 15 hours with his wife Monica and his 1-year-old son Jacob, unaware of how severe my condition was.

Behind Aba, Rene slowly crept back into the room. His hands shook, clutching his hospital single-use toothbrush. He stood behind Aba for a long time. Then he walked back to the bench where he had been sleeping for the past 18 hours and sat, bending forward with his face in his hands.

... Beep. Beep... Sss...

A doctor tapped Aba's arm lightly. Aba hadn't heard the man enter in his state of shock.

"Mr. Eynekaveh?" The neurosurgeon spoke slowly with his thick Thai accent.

Beep... beep.

Aba stared at the surgeon.

"Sir, we've operated on your son. I realize instructions were to wait until you arrive, but time was of the essence. When Adam arrived, his head wound was open and bleeding." The surgeon tapped the right side of his own head. "Without immediate surgery, he would have died from traumatic brain injury or blood loss."

Aba took a moment to absorb this.

"There is one thing you need to know." The smaller man laid his hand on Aba's arm apologetically.

"What?" Aba demanded. "What bones did he break?"

"Bones are not the problem, sir."

"Not the problem?" Aba almost growled, shrugging off the surgeon's hand.

"We found engine oil in his brain. We have to operate again, clean, and possibly remove more brain matter due to contamination."

Beep... beep... beep... Sss.

Aba stepped closer to me, unable to hear anymore. "Is he awake?" Aba asked hesitantly.

"He is in a coma due to his traumatic brain injury," the doctor explained.

Ssss, Beep, Beep...

"Ani lo-yachol..." *'I can't...'* Aba took a step back, not knowing what to do next.

At this moment, his phone rang. It was Ema.

"Ramona, ani po *(I'm here)*," Aba answered without looking away from my body. The nurses were drawing blood now.

On the other end of the line, Ema was hyperventilating. She was in Minnesota, trying to get a flight home to pick up her passport. She'd spoken to my cousin Nancy, a doctor who was a family friend, Nisso (another cousin who was a cardiothoracic surgeon), and her boyfriend Alex back home.

"What did we do? ...Adam," she sobbed.

"Monda, ani po." *'I'm here,'* Aba said into his phone, trying to gather his thoughts.

He told Ema that I was in a coma, but he was here and would look after me. Aba was stunned each time he glanced over and saw me lying in the hospital bed with a dent in my skull.

Aba was soon asked for his signature on a consent form so the hospital could perform additional surgery on me. During the accident, motor oil and rubble had entered my skull cavity, becoming embedded in my exposed brain

42

tissue. The hospital needed to perform surgery again to clean it out.

Hearing this, Aba's confidence in reality wavered. The doctors' mixed Thai and English words became distorted and blurred.

My cousin Nancy called, telling Aba that she'd found a synagogue in Phuket that could aid our family with food and moral support.

By that time, Aba was sitting by Rene in the waiting room. After he accepted what had happened, he began to feel relieved. I was alive. I was alive, so there was hope.

Rene sat in a crumpled pile by Aba's side. He handed Aba my phone. The screen was now covered in dirt, rock rubble, and smeared dried blood.

Aba took my phone and wiped the screen clean. It showed missed calls and texts from Ema, Aba, Orit, Kaylee, Kaitlyn, Div, and several clients.

Another neurologist approached Aba and tried to prepare him for the possibility that I would never wake up. Rene walked out of the room, hiding tears, while Aba crept back into my hospital room.

Aba's wife Monica entered the room cautiously behind Aba, carrying their 1-year-old son Jacob. She rubbed Aba's back as he looked at me in my hospital bed, cut, bruised, and swollen.

Ema continuously called Aba's cell phone, asking for more information. The following day, she arrived in Phuket.

***

Ema saw Rene first when she walked into my hospital room.

"Rene, Rene, tell me what happened!" Ema almost grabbed him by his shoulders, looking up at him with red-eyes.

43

Beep, Beep.

Ema later told me she had never seen a soldier in such a serious condition during her time in the IDF. After my second surgery, the inflamed stitches on my head now covered eight inches of skin stretched over the indentation in my skull.

Beep... Beep... Ssss...

Ema stayed at my side and spoke only to me. She sat with her hand on my chest, feeling my heartbeat and singing Hebrew songs from her childhood. She'd tell me stories, explaining why we were here in the most comforting way she could.

"Adami aya lecha mashoo katan she kara eem Rene, aval hakol heye tov Dan Dan." *'You had something small that happened to you with Rene, but all will be okay, Dan Dan.'*

Rene continued to sit alone in the corner, looking down. Orit arrived from the U.S. with her boyfriend Richie soon after my parents, and she tried her best to console him.

After one four-hour surgery, the surgeons told Ema and Aba that I'd likely remain in a vegetative state due to the severity of my brain injury.

"We cannot make you any promises," my surgeon said regretfully. "With this damage..."

My family and Rene sat in the waiting room every day. Aba got everyone separate rooms at our beloved Holiday Inn. Rene slept in the bed that had been mine for luck and ate dinner with my family every evening. Alex Eskenazi called every day asking how I was.

On the 4th day of my coma, Aba sent Rene home.

"He needs to get back to his worried parents," Aba told Ema, then took Rene aside and asked him to pack his things. Rene refused, feeling obligated to remain beside me until I woke up. Aba convinced him by asking him to take paychecks for Gdefy employees bearing Aba's signature with him back to LA.

Orit eventually called Alex Eshkenazi and pleaded for him to join Ema for emotional support, though Ema had initially asked him to stay home.

"Alex, can you please come be with my mother? Eet szercha *(she needs)* your shoulders to lean on. Please, you are family."

Orit looked at my mom as she sat silently by my bed with tears in her eyes.

Alex didn't need to be asked twice.

"Efo ha gever tsaeir sheli *(where is my young man)* Adam," he said the very next day, rushing down the Phuket Hospital hallway.

"Shama—'there'—room 132," Ema gloomily responded, sniffing to herself.

"Don't worry mami, your strong son will get through this," Alex said.

"Ata lo maveen…" *'You don't understand…'* Ema tried.

Alex fell silent as he opened the door to my hospital room.

Beep… Beep… Sss.

Alex walked to my bedside in disbelief. Then he turned back to Ema, giving her a forced, confident nod. "Ooh heye beseder." *'He will be fine.'*

Three hours later, a nurse named Gemma was cleaning my face and washing my body. Gemma gently pried my eyes open, one at a time, to deliver lubricating eye drops.

Then she screamed.

"Ch̀wy d̂wy ch̀wy d̂wy...!'" *'Help help help help...!'*
She sprinted out of my room, looking frantically for a doctor.

"Dwngtā k̄hxng k̄heā dwngtā s̄ì khxnthækh!" *'His eyes, his eyes! Still wearing contacts!'*

A contact lens had now been in my left eye, unlubricated and unchanged, for five days. No one had thought to check for contacts, distracted by my obviously life-threatening injuries. Fortunately, it seemed that the right contact had fallen out during the accident. But the left eye contact had remained under my eyelid for 112 hours.

The hospital's eye specialist arrived. He lifted my inflamed eyelid to inspect the bloodshot cornea and carefully removed the dried-out contact.

"Oh no..." Ema breathed, watching him work.

Sss. Beep... Beep...

"C̄hạn mị̀ khid ẁā k̄heā ca dî h̆ĕn..." he pronounced finally, shaking his head in grief. *'I do not think he will ever properly see out of this eye again.'*

He turned to the nurses and said: "Reā xāc t̂xng xeā dwngtā thī̀ tid cheụ̂x xxk t̄ĥā k̄heā rxd." *'We may have to remove his infected eye, if he survives.'*

Beep... Beep... Ssss.

Since arriving in Thailand, Aba had been working on getting us a flight back to the United States. This was a challenge, as no one wanted the liability of flying a patient in such a dire medical condition through the air for 13 hours.

Alex Eskanazi kept whispering words in my right ear. He hoped I would remember: "Puppy Power, FitFlow, basketball. Adam..."

On the tenth day of my hospitalization, my surgeons wanted to speak with my family.

46

"S-sorry, but this length of coma, we w we.. do not think his brain will recover now to the point of awakening. If he wakes, possibly vegetative or paralyzed…"

Aba's eyes bulged. "Lo… lo shekoo!" 'No, no, shut-up!"

My mother became very light-headed as they spoke, and almost fell to her knees. Alex held her up.

"It's okay Monda, it's…"

My sister began to sob, reaching for Richie's shoulders, as my Dad continued to glare at the doctors.

"I believe in my son," he shouted. "He will be fine, and you will care for him at any cost!" Spit flew from his mouth in his fury. Aba was so loud that doctors, nurses, and patients in other rooms turned to stare in concern.

At that very moment, nurse Gemma ran from room 132, shouting her own announcement.

"He's awake! He's awake!"

***

5

Troubled Transport

Total-memory recall: 0%
Mental Capabilities: N/A
Total-Left: Paralyzed
Skin-State: Broken Skull, Multiple Dislocations, Cuts,
Infections, Scratches, & Numerous Stitches
Assistive Items: Cardiac Monitor, Oxygen, IVs, a Head
Wrap, a Cessna, Eva Air, and an Airplane Beverage
Cart
Mental Age: N/A
Current Weight: 174 lbs
Sources: Rene, Dad, Mom's Journal, & Alex

I lay there, unmoving, under the bandages and tubes. But my eyes were open. Ema approached me. "Adahm sheli! Adam… hi." Ema could barely contain herself, stroking my stitched-up head and scraped face. She placed her hand over my heart, feeling my heartbeat.

Aba threw back his head, looking up to the sky in relief. Then he looked back to the surgeons. "Don't ever doubt my son."

Ema would never forget the way I looked blearily at her and Aba.

Ssss, Beep…Beep.

My brain didn't seem to be able to coordinate movement properly. I squirmed in the bed. What memories I have from this time are almost blank.

Alex patted Ema's back as Ema stared blissfully into my eyes. "He's okay," Alex said softly, "You see, he's okay."

Ema couldn't hold back, grabbing and hugging my Dad. Then she returned to talking to me and stroking my dimpled cheek. "Hakol heye tov Adami, hakol heye tov." *'All will be well Adam, all will be well.'*

Aba immediately whipped out his phone and dialed Vital, our health insurance back home which was responsible for paying for medical transportation. He stood impatiently, tapping his foot as the phone rang.

"Yes, hello? Adam Elnekaveh is awake. I demand a flight to America." A pause. "No! Listen to me! You told me he could fly if he woke up from his coma. Now send the flight!"

He argued with Vital for 25 minutes as I drifted in and out of consciousness, and Ema cried tears of happiness.

"Adami-sheli ani-po, Mami." *'My Adam, I am here.'*

That day, I was deemed healthy enough to move from the ICU to a standard room, where Ema could sleep beside me through the night in a reclining chair. My intervals of wakefulness were still short, coming every few hours now.

Vital finally caved into my father's insistence and scheduled a medical flight to bring us home. While he was winning that battle, the Thai doctors assessed my consciousness. The head doctor approached my parents outside my new room.

"K̄hxthos̄' thì thảh̄ı̂ s̄eīyh̄āy māk." *'I'm sorry, much much damage,'* he said, pointing to the MRI images of my brain. There was a clear asymmetry between the hemispheres and black spaces on the right where parts of my brain had been removed.

A younger Vietnamese doctor with a mustache spoke up, saying I would likely be paralyzed on my left side. My motor cortex, he explained as best he could, was too damaged to allow me to walk. My left shoulder dislocation was due to a total lack of signals from my brain to the muscles responsible for holding my shoulder in place. It was possible that the part of my brain responsible for my left-sided motor function was the part the doctors had removed to extract the oil.

"Friend Rene said Adam is right-handed," the Vietnamese doctor tried to finish on a hopeful note. "Good, he still has his right hand."

Later, the same doctor told my mother I would likely need 24/7 care moving forward. She kept this to herself, telling no one.

On June 8th, 2018, my parents and I finally left the hospital to get on the plane returning to America. Vital had informed Aba and Ema that only the three of us would fit onboard. Orit, her boyfriend, Alex, Monica, and little Jacob were sent home via commercial airline.

Getting me out of bed was a new challenge. The second I was off my mattress, my left leg locked, and my left arm and shoulder sagged. Even when I was placed in a wheelchair, my left leg remained locked straight with muscle spasms. Attempts to bend it into a sitting position did not succeed.

Now, it was time to load me onto a mobile stretcher. At this point, my parents realized I didn't have my passport. Over the phone, a shocked Rene reported that it must have still been at the moped rental booth back on Patong road.

In all the chaos, he'd forgotten about my collateral when he returned his bike on his way out of the country.

He had been too much in a state of shock even to explain to the bike owner, Kinna, what happened.

Aba immediately followed Rene's directions to find Kinna's stand. He grimly walked up to the booth manager.

"Passport!" He tried to communicate, almost shouting. Kinna looked up at him, confused.

"What!? Who you?"

"My son, Adam Elnekaveh, is hurt. Give me his passport. Need American hospital right now!" He glared to make it clear that he would not leave empty-handed.

Kinna matched his frustration.

"Sir. Where is moped?"

Aba almost snarled but held back. "You will get your moped. I pay you," he said, touching his back pocket. "My son almost died. Now give me his passport. Emergency. America!"

Kinna's frown became remorseful. But only for a moment. "Pay."

Aba shook his head at her greed, violently digging into his pockets. "You know what this is, take it!"

My father refuses to tell anyone in our family exactly what happened next, what he paid or did on that busy Patong road. But whatever my father and mother did for me, I will be forever in their debt.

He got my passport.

When my parents finally got me to the airport, they were horrified to discover that the "medical flight" was a cheap Cessna propeller plane that appeared to have been in service since the 1970s.

"Alex ze lo *(this is not)* a proper medical plane," Ema gasped to my father. But my parents dared not reject the flight, uncertain if any commercial airline would agree to carry me.

The aircraft was not much bigger on the inside than a large van. Vital had assigned two nurses and a Dr. Watt to travel with us.

Fitting my stretcher and my life support equipment onto the plane was a nightmare. I still required a stretcher, multiple IV tubes, and tube-fed nutrition. The fact that it was a humid 92 degrees on the runway did not make it any easier.

It took 90 minutes, five runway helpers in lime green, three nurses, two doctors, and both of my parents to lift me onto the craft while I remained medically sedated. Everyone used small battery fans to try to keep cool.

"Push up! Push up!" Aba yelled, guiding the runway staff.

Finally, they managed to fit me through the plane's door. My stretcher almost slid to the floor.

"Strap him in!" Aba instructed.

"Ahlex..." Ema pointed at my machine, "ooh heeye beceder shama?" *'Will he be okay there?'*

At this point, the doctor onboard explained that the small aircraft could not make a direct flight to Los Angeles. It was to stop and refuel in Russia, East London, New York, West Alaska, and finally, Los Angeles.

My parents exchanged worried glances. But they saw no other means of getting me home.

The Thai pilot appeared and introduced himself as Pilot Chakan. He had dark messy hair, a gold watch, a typical white pilot's uniform, and a dark, full-length beard.

"Hello! How are we? We have a long ride ahead!"

"Get us to America for our son," Ema answered. The local pilot bowed his head, entering his cockpit with no co-pilot to assist on the long flight.

The airplane's engines started, and everything began to shake. Everyone held on, white-knuckled, listening to the engine sputter. Aba moved to my side, holding the bed rails to make sure I did not roll out.

Beep...Beep...

The medical monitors almost couldn't be heard over the rattle of the shaking plane.

Just 20 minutes into the flight my heart rate began to climb, alerting the medical staff onboard. After two hours, my blood pressure spiked. Ema knew that it was probably because of the altitude, with little or no cabin pressurization in the ancient plane.

At some point, Dr. Watt announced, "We need to land!"

When the pilot did not immediately agree, Dr. Watt moved up the aisle to stand beside him. "His body can't handle this trip! He just came out of a coma; now you're sedating him without air pressure?" Dr. Watt explained that if we continued, I could suffer seizures and further brain damage.

We landed as close as we could to the nearest hospital, which turned out to be in Taiwan.

The plane landed bumpily on the Taiwanese airstrip. The medical team rolled me off the plane with all my machinery, loading me into a Taiwanese emergency services truck. Aba immediately called Vital, prepared to threaten legal action over their choice of air transportation.

Stepping off the plane, Ema went pale. The Cessna's left tire had exploded upon hitting the Taiwanese runway, throwing out shreds of rubber. Aba's eyes widened in disbelief as Ema pointed out the ruptured tire. He immediately began yelling at Vital on the phone while Ema made a video of the damaged aircraft.

"We are taking photos," Aba shouted, "and will be taking legal action when I return! My son could have died if the doctor had not told us to turn the plane around! He could have died in this landing!"

Hours later, we reached the hospital on Gongye Road in Yunlin County, Taiwan.

I was slowly waking from the sedative that was supposed to sustain me through a 9-hour flight to Russia. The hospital offered me a catheter to collect my urine until I was fully awake but preferred me to wear disposable absorbent briefs as these had a lower risk of complications.

My parents soon realized that many supplies, including the absorbent briefs, would not be offered to us by the hospital, which was funded by Taiwanese taxpayers to serve Taiwanese citizens. Ema stayed with me in my room while Aba visited a connected shopping mall of stores, food courts, and pharmacy supply shops.

My parents took turns watching me while sharing a cheap motel room and wondering what to do next. They sat by me for four days, keeping me company and communicating with me, using hand signals as if I were a newborn. I was an infant with a scarred adult body and bloodshot eyes.

Ema read stories to me in Hebrew and applied ointment to my mangled face, cuts, and bruises. She waited hopefully for me to say my first words.

Aba continued to call Vital every hour, demanding a proper plane to take me back to America. On June 16th, 2018, there came a light knock on the door of room 012.

Aba answered, hoping it was good news. Two young airlift medics in lime green jackets stood there. "Vital sent us," they reported.

"What kind of plane did they send?" Aba demanded.

They told him it was a similar Cessna model 150E. He told them to get out.

Aba decided to cut Vital out of the loop. Aba and cousin Nancy called every major Asian airline, pleading for help. Thirteen of the fourteen airlines said 'no,' afraid to take on liability for my fragile medical state. However, the Israeli airline Eva Air, promised to consider it.

Eva Air wanted to help the son of two former IDF medics, but wanted a video to confirm my medical status for them. They needed to confirm that I could sit upright as safety protocols dictated for takeoff and landing.

Aba and Ema thought about how to handle this. The decision was made to dress me up and prop me up in bed for the Eva Air 'audition' video.

Ema held me as I snored, and Aba left on an errand to the H&M Clothing store down the block. He bought a brown hat to cover my indented skull, black shoes, black socks, a dark denim shirt, and a black jacket to hide my scars.

As he shopped, he reminisced about visiting H&M with me in Los Angeles, helping me to dress for my first date. He vowed that he would someday shop with me again.

While Aba shopped, Ema sat with me by my bed. Around 3:45 PM, I looked into her right eye and mumbled:

"Em-m Ema...Ah Ah-Aba?" I spoke through cracked lips.

Ema broke down, sobbing at my first words. Then she called my father, shouting into her phone.

"Bo Bo, who air medaber who air medaber!" *'Come, come, he's awake and talking, he's awake and talking!"*

Aba, too, broke down and sobbed—right there in the H&M, clutching the bags of clothes he'd just purchased. He ran all the way back to the hospital.

"Hakol heeye beseder Adahmi," Ema kept whispering to me, stroking my reddened face.

Aba burst into the small white room as Ema continued talking to me like a child. Then, I showed that I could say more.

"I..I I I.. I'm s s s orry, I'm sorry, p p please, sorry," I winced in confusion at my parents among the tubes and 'beeps.'

"Ata air Aba, ata bachayeem. Ata chie," Aba said. *'You are awake, you are alive. You are alive.'* "Ech ata Adam?" *'How are you, Adam? I love you.'* Aba embraced Ema. "He's awake talking. My son!"

I drifted off to sleep again, but it was clear that I was not vegetative. I was regaining brain function. Unfortunately, this led to complications. The next time I woke up, I got upset about all the tubes coming out of me. I was still strong enough for this to be a problem. When I began trying to rip out my feeding and IV tubes, then kicking and swinging with my good arm when a nurse tried to stop me, the hospital staff decided there was nothing for it but to restrain me.

"Don't hurt him!" Ema hollered at the three nurses and two doctors needed to control my right good arm and leg. But she understood that a feeding tube slightly displaced by my struggling could end up in my lungs and prove fatal.

When I was finally secured to the bed, Aba looked at the clothing bags he'd been holding. "Rimona kaneetee lo mashoo lechbe et harosh shelo." *'I bought him something to hide his head.'*

He took out the clothes and began to dress me, slowly and carefully, with me still restrained. He slid clothes onto my arms and legs, asking nurses and doctors to assist.

Next, Aba tried removing all the connected machines, tubes, and IVs. With the nurse's tentative approval, his goal was to get me sitting upright in a chair. For the first time since my accident, Aba tried to get me to follow instructions. He wanted me to sit up and smile at the phone camera, convincing the airline that I could do the same on their flight.

"Adam, I need you to smile. I'm going to say 'hi' to you, and you'll respond with 'hello' so the airline can see that you are doing well. Okay?"

This was quite a task for me. I had regressed to talking, thinking, and behaving like a one-year-old. There was no way for me to sit up without falling due to the total lack of muscle control on my left side. It took three nurses, a doctor, and my mother to hold me steady on the chair (while staying out of the camera shot). The moment they let me go, I would begin to slide over.

After five attempts, Aba noticed a gray safety harness belt from the Cessna flight, still left on the floor by my bed.

"Let's tie him to the chair," Aba said. Not waiting for a response, he grabbed the torn harness-belt. Ema held my body still, fearful that the medical staff would hurt me if they helped. Aba began wrapping the harness around my shoulders and the back of the chair. Ema continued to hold me. My neck had no support, and I dropped my head to my chest.

"Takzeekee ha neck shelo!" *'Hold his neck,'* Aba urgently gestured to Ema, opening the camera on his phone to record for Eva Airline.

Ema supported my neck and adjusted my hat to cover a few stitches that were poking out. She licked her fingers, removing some dried blood from my right ear, then kissed her finger and placed it on my swollen red eyelid.

"Ok yalla Alehx ooo meechon." *'Let's go Alex, he's ready,'* Ema said.

Aba took a 70-second video of me staring at his camera, wearing a brand-new hat and an unevenly zipped jacket. Ema stood inches away, out of the camera frame, waiting to grab me the moment he hit, 'stop.'

"Okay," Aba said, giving Ema the all-clear.

"Sababa!" *'Great!'* Ema proclaimed, grabbing my shoulders. She untied me, and I fell back onto the bed, asleep. My loving mother curled up beside me and kissed me.

"Lyla tov Danduni," *'Goodnight.'* Ema said. Aba quickly sent the video to Nancy and Eva Airline HR.

It took the airline 26 hours to assess the footage. Meanwhile, my parents stayed with me in the Taiwanese Public Hospital, isolated from friends and family.

On June 18, 2018, Eva Air agreed to fly me from Taiwan to Los Angeles, with conditions. We would have to have to supply all my medical paperwork and MRIs, as well as licensed travel medics to assist with the plane transport. We would have to purchase seats for all desired equipment, personnel, and travelers. For the medics, Nancy and Aba knew the right service to contact: Hatzalah (הַצָלָה) Co..

Hatzalah was an Israeli, volunteer-based emergency medical services (EMS) organization. Aba had grown up near their headquarters in his home city of Ashdod, Jerusalem.

The organization, learning of my parents' past service in the IDF, assigned a doctor, a nurse, and a 4-foot oxygen travel tank weighing 31.6 pounds in case of emergency. My astonishing Aba purchased first-class Eva Air tickets for myself, my parents, the entire assigned medical team, and even the oxygen tank. The cost was $11,200. Our flight was scheduled for the following day.

My parents told me that our celebratory last day was chaotic, from immigration at the airport to the Taiwanese doctor being late to sign the hospital paperwork allowing our travel.

"They are scared we might return," Aba joked to Ema about the medical staff as he began collecting our luggage.

Knock knock.

Pascal, David, and Eliyahu Anavi greeted us in our room. They wore bright orange sleeveless jackets and light blue kippahs adorned with a Lagad Baosher Symbol and communication devices attached to their hips.

Pascal, a Moroccan with light-colored eyes, was the leader. "Tov, Shalom anachnoo poe," 'Hello, we are here.' "Mah' atem sacreem memenoo lasot beel shelchem." *'What do you need for us to do for you?'*

While my parents waited by my bed, the Israeli team and the Taiwanese medics strategized about how to keep me safely sedated throughout the flight. They finally loaded me onto their rented ambulance in the evening.

The Hatzalah ambulance dropped my parents off at check-in so they could go through security and immigration. I couldn't go through security while lying sedated on the ambulance stretcher. Two immigration officers came out to the ambulance, and the medics showed me my necessary paperwork. I was taken to the runway by ambulance.

The ambulance drove us down the airstrip to meet the plane. At this point, the medics realized there was no way to load my stretcher onboard. It wouldn't fit up the passenger stairs.

The crew suggested putting my stretcher into the elevator used to carry food to the plane's storage area. The food elevator was 3 feet wide and 5 feet long, and I was 6+ feet tall. After 25 minutes, they managed to shove me onto the elevator at an angle, with my parents and four runway workers pushing.

They then discovered my stretcher would not fit through the aisle to my first-class seat. While they continued to try to make it fit, Ema peered out the windows and saw that airline stewardesses were holding all passengers, including the first-class occupants who would be seated near my assigned section, until they could get me settled.

In the end, an Asian flight attendant came up with a good idea: "Bed and roller too big! Give me trays, here, strap him, easy." They could fit my stretcher on top of the rolling food trays and get me to my seat that way.

After 45 minutes, I was safely strapped in. The attendants reminded my parents that, per law, I had to be seated upright for takeoff. However, they all quickly realized that I was too heavily sedated and couldn't be moved with the heart monitor and IV equipment in the way. They left me lying down after a few attempts, and my parents prayed that the head pilot would not make us get off the plane.

Ema explained to my irritable father that the pilot always has the last word, and he could decide whether or not we would take off and begin our journey home.

"Ooh lo moreed otanoo." *'He's not dropping us down,'* Aba growled.

The pilot came out of the cockpit. Ema looked up at him, taking a deep emotional gulp.

"What's the problem? Why aren't the passengers seated?" The pilot raised his voice, questioning the flight attendants.

"Captain," said the Asian head stewardess, "we have a passenger here with his parents and medical team. Due to his sedation and his injury, we aren't able to get him into an upright position for takeoff."

Aba became worried, clutching my bed rails with white knuckles.

"Oh, is this the Israeli boy who was in a coma?" the pilot asked.

As my parents nodded defeatedly, the pilot said, "Okay, guys, let's get the boy home. He's been through enough."

When my parents heard that, they almost burst into tears. They grabbed thankfully at the stewardesses, and Ema wanted to hug the pilot as well. After all the fighting they'd been through to get me here, we were finally going home.

The Israeli medical team spoke to my parents in Hebrew. "Shè hakol tov ve teeshvoo, teeshtoo yíne, ve gam teeshnoo," which means, *'It's all good, grab a seat, drink some wine to relax and get some sleep.'*

It was the medics' job now to get us home safely.

Three weeks after my injury, we were finally going home.

***

6

Sunset, Los Angeles

Total-memory recall: 1.5%
Mental Capabilities: 1.5%
Total Left-Sided Capabilities: Paralyzed
Skin-State: Indented Skull, Multiple Dislocations, Cuts,
Scratches, and Numerous Stitches
Assistive items: Hospital Bed, Wheelchair
Mental Age: 4
Weight: 158
Sources: Rene, Dad, Mom's Journal, & Alex

My family & friends knew more about me than I knew about myself at 28 years of age.

On June 19th, 2018, our plane arrived in Los Angeles around 6 pm. A Vital ambulance was waiting for us on the runway, and medics loaded me onto a tram to move me.

"Anachnew mekayem she haben shelachem tavree." *'We hope your son will get better,'* Hatzalah head, Dr. Pascal, told my parents as the Vital staff took over.

Much to my parents' dismay, they weren't permitted to join me in the ambulance due to liability concerns. They took a rideshare to meet me at the Vital hospital, tipping the driver extra to follow the ambulance closely.

I lay half-sedated, wearing an O2 mask, a helmet to protect my brain, a pulse monitor, and an IV. In the lobby, twenty friends and family members awaited our arrival.

A longtime friend of my Mom's, Yfat, had known me since I was a toddler going to sleep-away camp and playing basketball with her son. She shrieked when she saw me being wheeled in on my gurney.

"Ma'am," the medic said to my mother again, "we need control in escorting him in." He lifted my mom's reluctant arms off my gurney. "The hospital will contact you shortly."

Ema took a breath and held it, not wanting to let go of her son.

Yfat chimed in, "Teet-nee lahem mami." *'Let them, sweetheart.'*

Ema reluctantly let her fingers slip off my gurney's guide rail, and the medic took me away. Yfat threw her arms around my mother, hugging her as they began sobbing together.

"Hakol," Yfat sniffed. "Heeye tov neshama, hakol!" *'Everything will be okay, my life, everything!'*

"Ma'am, stay with your friends. We'll contact you when Adam is roomed," a tall medic said as he watched the scene of grief.

"New' tavoe-etee." *'Come with me,'* Yfat said earnestly, grabbing my mother's hand and taking her to the nearest restroom. "Kree seeme et ze." *'Here, put these on.'* She handed Ema a set of new striped purple exercise pants and a shirt to change into. "Pagashti eem megale aidot." *'I met with a psychic,'* she said. "You must take off the clothes you wore while Adam was in the coma."

Ema obliged, changing.

"This is a fresh start for you," Yfat said seriously, "now that you're back home in California. Ani kol-hazman heye poe." *'I'll always be here,'* if you need anything."

Yfat was soon asked to leave the hospital, along with everyone except my immediate family.

"Toda, toda raba Yfat," *'Thank you, thank you very much Yfat,'* my mother said exhaustedly. My parents had not slept in 20 hours at that point.

Orit took over, hugging my mother as the support phalanx disappeared through the glass doors. "He'll be just fine now, Ema! I love you so much!"

After being in Asia for nearly a month post-accident, we were finally back in America. I was to stay in the neuro-intensive care unit (ICU) at Sunset Vital Hospital.

The hospital slowly started to wake me up from the controlled sedation. My mother, father, and sister watched me closely. They wanted to catch any outburst from me before the medical staff did.

Beep...beep...

My irritated eyes began to peek open under my helmet.

"Wake up, Adami, lea'te lea'te (easy, easy)," Ema said in a voice like a caress as the doctors and nurses carefully removed the helmet I'd worn for the last 18 hours.

I slowly rubbed my eyes with my good right hand, running my fingers down the nose tubes. Just when it seemed I might be calm, I started to move—becoming explosively violent again.

"Arghhh! Arghhh…. Ahhh!"

Beep, beep, beep, beep, beep!

I was confused and frustrated. Why were there tubes coming out of me? Why couldn't I move properly? Waking seemed like waking into a nightmare. Drool ran down my left chin as I continued my rampage, trying to free myself from these restrictions.

My left side wouldn't move at all. Realizing this made me more frantic. I felt myself melting onto the bed frame, covered in medical cylinders and tubes. The scariest part was having no sensation on the left side of my body. I was used to my body doing what I told it to, with strength to spare.

I continued to kick and slap with my right limbs in frustration like a wild toddler, so I was restrained again. This made me thrash more as Ema quietly wept, trying to convince herself that this was temporary.

"Adam..." Aba said quietly, raising his hand as a shield from my kicks.

Beep beep beep beep! My heart raced.

Aba bowed his head to stare at the floor. I angrily deflected everyone in the ICU, including nurses, doctors, and even my mother and father's caring hands.

Now tied to the bed and staring around with red eyes, I finally calmed as exhaustion set in. Vital moved us into a private room across from the Department of Neurosurgery's front desk, perhaps so I wouldn't disturb the other patients.

I received my private room but was put on 'critical safety watch' for my injury combined with my antics. I would wake up, have another anger spell, and then fall asleep every fifteen minutes or so while my family watched.

Ema tried sleeping on the room's pea-green, plastic-nylon couch that night, but I woke her up every few minutes with my struggling. I displayed seemingly different personalities when I woke, sometimes helpless and confused, other times agitated and violent. When I wasn't restrained, I threw pillows across the room with my right arm.

The following day, Aba arrived at the hospital at 8 AM sharp. Considering the 75-minute commute through Los Angeles traffic from his home to the hospital, this was quite a feat. I was asleep.

"Knock, knock," two doctors dressed in light blue surgeon gowns, both wearing glasses, announced themselves before walking in after him.

"Good morning, how's Adam doing?" The head doctor, Dr. Firestone, spoke first.

Ema sort of shrugged helplessly.

Doctor Firestone took a step closer to me. "We reviewed your son's MRI scans to try to get an idea of the damage to his brain."

I groaned again in the background, sounding pained. Ema stood close to me, massaging my left arm and watching for any sign of violence. An assistant nurse scurried in to add something to my IV.

"First, I'm glad he's awake," Dr. Firestone began. "The amount of damage to Adam's brain will make recovery difficult. Your son has a severe traumatic brain injury, primarily to his right brain hemisphere. This is the side that controls his left-sided motor function and sensory perception, as well as some emotional and cognitive functions."

This wasn't anything my parents hadn't heard before.

"And as you know," Dr. Firestone continued, "15% of his skull has been removed. He needs to wear a helmet to protect his brain for the next few months until he's stable enough for a cranioplasty surgery to replace the missing bone with an implant. The good news is we have a manufacturer of plastic skull implants in Frankfurt, Germany. A plastic implant will mean Adam won't have trouble with metal detectors and such." Doctor Firestone tried to focus on the positives.

"Let's talk about recovery," the younger Doctor Andrew broke in, glancing at Dr. Firestone.

"Yes…" Firestone lowered his voice. My parents stepped closer, hoping for more optimistic news from an American doctor. "I don't believe your son will walk again," Dr. Firestone said slowly. "Or have any use of his left side."

Aba and Ema frowned. Can one moment of carelessness lead to lifelong paralysis?

"Now," Dr. Firestone continued, "there is a good chance that he will be unable to care for himself. But the brain is a very complicated organ. For this reason, we can't say exactly how much he may recover."

"Yes." Dr. Andrew broke in again, "He may recover some mobility." Dr. Andrew stepped aside as another nurse walked in to check my various monitors. "Right now, Adam has to rest, sleep, and relax so that his brain may recover."

The doctors left almost apologetically, leaving my parents to stew in their thoughts as my nurse set up my feeding tube for breakfast.

I violently pulled out the feeding tube four times, resulting in minimal nutrition for two days after my flight from Taiwan. I struggled with discomfort and agitation, prompting a nurse to administer haloperidol. My parents, shocked by the antipsychotic label, protested.

"My son is not psychotic!" Ema fumed, knowing that haloperidol had side effects which could be dangerous for someone in my condition.

My parents eventually learned that nurses with 'hostile' patients were given a small red pouch of antipsychotic medication to give patients in a state of emergency or violence. Haloperidol injections, especially in large doses, can cause further agitation, drowsiness,

67

blurred vision, internal bleeding, and blood pressure issues. In my fragile state, my parents did not want me put at risk of these dangerous side effects.

"Do you nurses know what my son is going through?!" Ema demanded as the front desk staff looked on, listening. "Get out of this room! I want to be consulted before any drugs are administered!"

Later that day, I woke up again and began mumbling curse words—that, at least, was progress.

From this time, I only remember my parents. Nobody else mattered or seemed real in my battered state. The rest of the details come from my mother's journal entries, kept meticulously each day.

I would later learn that Ema's journal was given to her by a family member concerned that I may not survive and that she may need help to grieve. Ema used the journal to record what she saw, and her entries became a primary source for the writing of this book.

My parents did not allow anybody to contact or visit me besides my immediate family during these early days. Only my parents, Alex Eskenazi, dad's wife, my younger half-brother Jacob, Orit, and my aunt Orly were allowed visitation.

My room became like a prison. I had no knowledge of nights or days. I was constantly awake, groaning, mumbling, and restrained to prevent me from ripping out my IV, feeding tube, or monitors. Ema sometimes tried to brush my teeth in bed. My left arm and leg were losing muscle and shriveling. I was now at 151 pounds.

"Shh calm Adami, shhh," Ema begged me each time I woke up and moaned in the night.

Aba carried his usual command across the hospital, intimidating everyone for my benefit.

Ema would sit alone in the lobby cafe each morning, while the nurses cared for me. She'd look out the glass windows at Sunset Boulevard and think about my athletic past, my app, and my plans, and wonder what the future held for me.

Now, I was not even aware of anything happening on the left side of my body. If she whispered in my left ear, I would not respond.

"Let's have a look at his current MRI," Dr. Firestone said to my parents one day. He led them into a room where the recent MRI images were held on a backlit board.

"With the trauma to his right hemisphere," Dr. Firestone pointed to a dark shadow on my brain, "I unfortunately do not believe Adam will gain much function back. I hope his cognitive function will improve, but we must be prepared for the worst."

The worst.

"I do not care what you say," Aba broke in. "My son will be okay."

***

Finally, I began to show improvement. I was becoming less violent, could mumble two to three words at a time, and I began to recognize more people. Ema still limited my visitors strictly.

My mother's closest friends, Ronit and Dvorit, had known me since I was a teenager. They were the first non-family to visit me in my new room, followed by Ema's girlfriend, Yfat.

Having been raised in Jewish culture, I always hid my grandly built muscles and tattoos from my parents' friends out of respect. Now, I was not able to do so anymore, lying in bed shirtless with my helmet on and my stitches showing.

69

The hospital forbade my parents from feeding me, deeming the choking hazard unacceptable.

"His brain doesn't understand how to chew or swallow," a nurse explained to my parents. But I despised being fed through the nasogastric tubes, which I persistently tried to pull out.

"He needs to eat," Ema protested, arguing with the nurses.

The staff explained that, without the proper instructions from the brain, they feared that my throat wouldn't know how to swallow and I could choke or inhale food. Inhaled food could lead to potentially fatal pneumonia.

Aba, however, believed I could eat. He was frightened by all the weight I was losing. I now weighed 142 pounds, fifty pounds less than a month earlier.

On the seventh day of my hospitalization, Aba walked downstairs to the Bistro Hospital Cafe and picked up two slices of warm cheese pizza from the buffet. He hid the food under napkins as he walked it back up to my room. There, he unwrapped the pizza and sat down on the right side of my bed, where he knew I'd see him properly.

"Eat slowly, Aba, easy," he whispered, handing me a cheesy slice. I chewed and swallowed successfully, albeit while drooling.

"You see! He can eat! Stupid doctors," Aba muttered to the empty room.

Ema's boyfriend, Alex, also helped me to exercise. He came almost every day to see me. He'd help me to perform foot- and knee-bend exercises with my right leg.

"Tov tov, Adam," Alex always motivated me by speaking as you would to a toddler. It was he who first got me to crack my first crooked smile while applauding me for my exercise achievements.

My crooked smile inspired both fear and excitement in Alex and Ema. On one hand, the left side of my mouth barely lifted at all, and my left eye was still red and inflamed. On the other hand, I was smiling!

Vital now deemed me recovered enough to assign me a physical therapist named Alvin. Alvin was a young Pakistani man who worked with me for only 15 minutes at a time. I was always made to wear my helmet, although my first exercises took place strictly in my bed.

"He didn't wear a kasda *(helmet)* in Thailand," Aba said to Mom one day after they were asked to leave the room to make room for Alvin to work. "Achshav who sareech leevosh kol hazman." *'Now he has to wear one all the time.'*

"Okay, Adam, let's hold a water cup together," Alvin would say. I stared at his right eye—at this time, I perceived nothing in my left visual field—as he brought a cup filled with warm water to my right hand. "Hold this cup, and don't spill it. Spilling water is bad."

I spilled 20% of the water on my first attempt, staring at my shaking hand. On my second attempt, I spilled less, eventually spilling none at all.

"Great job!" Alvin said, clapping his knee and facing me. "Can you touch your ear, Adam?" I confidently touched my right ear with my right arm. "Great, now your left ear."

I looked at him, confused. The entire concept of 'left' had been erased by the accident, along with any perception of the left side of my body.

"This is your left ear," Alvin said, holding my hand against my left ear. "And this is warm," he said, placing a heating pad on me. "This is cold," he placed an ice cube on my arm, re-teaching me the concept of temperatures.

I stared, lost.

The hospital continued to offer muscle relaxants and anxiety medications, but my parents wanted to steer away from the constant medication. I still was not sleeping through the night, despite the Xanax, and my parents began to wonder if it might be *because* of the Xanax. They set up a meeting with the Neurology department to discuss ending the constant stream of drugs.

The hospital was hesitant to stop medicating me. They were also uneasy about how many visitors my parents were bringing to my room, fearing that the visits might prove overstimulating and stressful to my recovering brain.

In the end, a compromise was reached: the hospital would not stop the medication but would lower the doses of the sedating drugs. Melatonin was added to help me sleep properly at night without sedating me.

I helplessly lay in my hospital bed as my red left eye slowly healed. I was still not actively moving my body outside of physical therapy, but I recovered at least ten pounds now that I was eating.

Through physical therapy, I was slowly able to sit upright in bed. For a couple of seconds. A few days later, I could sit up in a chair (after cramming my locked knee inward).

My first time getting out of my bed since my accident was July 2, 2018. I was required to wear my helmet as I did it. I groaned and mumbled as I moved, toddler-like. Vital said that the helmet would have to be worn any time I moved at all, cushioning my fragile unprotected brain until my cranioplasty, which was tentatively scheduled for November.

FitFlow's planned launch date came and went. I had no awareness of the date, and no memory of FitFlow.

Vital began sending me a speech therapist. Pat had long brown hair and was middle-aged, and he was sent to help me with three tasks:

One: I needed to be re-taught how to chew and swallow. Or at least Vital thought I did. During these sessions, I remained tied down because I was still getting most of my nutrition through nasogastric tubes—which I still hated.

Two: I had to be re-taught how to drink water, a process that involved patting my throat and back like a baby. This was supposed to notify my brain that there was liquid in my throat and hopefully signal the swallowing process.

"Okay, Adam, small slurps. Stay upright, please," Pat soothed as I began to cough. I coughed more and grunted, unhappy. Ema helped by patting my back. "Leevreeyoot, Danduni," she smiled at every bit of progress I made.

Pat's third goal was to teach me to speak. This would involve both teaching me to understand and physically form words with my mouth and throat. "Water, Adam, that is wa wa water," Pat would slowly murmur, moving his lips to allow me to watch them form the sounds.

The one thing I enjoyed about Pat's visits was getting to remove my helmet. "Okay, Adam," he would say, "Let's take off that helmet. We're not going anywhere."

Around this time, Aba contacted Rene and asked him to come by the hospital for a visit. Rene was also asked to bring my old friend, Nick. A nurse reported to my parents that I had been mumbling Nick's name under my breath as she checked my vitals one day.

Rene later told me how his heart raced excitedly when he saw my name pop up on his phone. It turned out to be Aba calling from my phone, but I was awake!

That day, Rene parked by Nick's side entrance on Hazeltine Avenue. Nick got into Rene's white Infiniti coupe. At first, neither spoke as the radio filled the silence.

"I can't believe this, I can't believe this, man," Nick said finally. "I can't understand. This is Adam—the strongest of us all. I wanted to bring our boy Allan to help me see him."

Rene nodded. "But you can't. Adam's mind is too fragile, he can't see too many people at once. That's what they told me, anyway." Rene stared into the freeway traffic.

"Well, what the hell does that mean?" Nick muttered.

"Just chill," Rene said. "His mom said he's getting better, learning to talk and stuff."

"Whattt?" Nick whirled to stare at Rene. "What are you saying to me? How bad was his accident, for real?!"

"Pretty bad, man." Rene continued staring glumly ahead. "We'll figure it out. Hopefully, he'll be good, dude."

They arrived around lunchtime.

"Hey! Your friends are here, Danduni," Ema said energetically, lowering the applesauce she'd been spoon-feeding me. Nick and Rene walked into the room slowly. "Look how good they look!" Ema added, prompting me to speak or react. I couldn't stop staring at Rene and Nick, but no one was sure I recognized them. "But they need haircuts," Ema joked, breaking the tension as they approached. "And cologne!" She winked at Nick, then turned and left the room. She realized my friends couldn't fully be themselves with her watching.

I drooled.

"Adam! Remember this guy?" Rene said. He grabbed Nick by the shoulders, "Look who I brought! Gotta tell ya—he missed his FitFlow check-in at the gym today!"

I stared.

Nick nervously stepped closer. "Adam, man, how you doing?" That was when I turned my head. I wasn't wearing my helmet, so the dent and the stitches were visible. Nick later told me that he nearly fainted at the sight.

Rene stepped between me and Nick, reading Nick's pale face. "He's just great," Rene enthused. "Getting better and stronger, right?" He rested his hand lightly on my left shoulder, not realizing I had no sensation.

I continued staring at Nick.

Nick took a deep breath. "I need my trainer back. Miss our workouts at the gym, dude." My eyes widened and lit up as I smiled a crooked smile.

"Yea, good," Rene said awkwardly. "He remembers going to the gym, winning 'best body.' He'll be back to his old self, leading the way in no time." Ema heard him as she walked back into the room, smiling in agreement.

Ema asked Nick and Rene to leave after just 20 minutes, hoping not to overstimulate me.

Around this time, I began to speak like a one-year-old again—in both English and Hebrew, which was a good sign. "Mei, Mie," I would try. "Mye, Myeem!" *'Water?'*

Four days later, I was a 7-year-old: "Fo, Foo, Food. Food with e e-eggs?"

Soon, a 12-year-old: "Yes, TV is on. Radio is playing."

My apparent ability to understand the world around me continued to grow. I was re-learning how to sit upright, turn, and move my hips while lying down. My left arm was still effectively dead, lying mounted on a pillow. It had lost five inches of muscle circumference in six weeks. My left leg was not much better.

I started getting bored, so my parents gave me my old phone. "Here, Adam, remember this?" Aba gently handed it to me. I held it in my right hand, looking confused about how to turn it on. "Slide your fingers to unlock."

I stared at my phone's lit-up screen, seeing my lock screen photo of a young man and a young woman exercising in the gym. The photo bore a title: "FitFlow."

Ema spent 15 minutes walking me through how to use my phone. I'd had a smartphone since 9th grade, but she explained it again while feeding me applesauce.

I soon relearned—and began to send disturbing messages to my contacts.

"Hadar hie hower youe doingi, itse me Ardam" I lay there squinting at my own poor writing. Some contacts began responding. Some were aware of my situation. Some weren't.

"Take away his phone," Aba said, after seeing some of my broken sentences. "Let's not overwork his brain."

I had indeed started to develop headaches from staring intently at the glowing screen, but I had told no one because I didn't want the phone taken away.

Nick decided to visit again, messaging Aba for permission. He walked into my room while my parents, Orit, and aunt Orly were visiting.

"Hello everyone! 'Sup, Adam, what's going on?"

"Hey Nick, good to see you!" Ema smiled. I drooled as I smiled too, staring into Nick's right eye. Dr. Andrew walked in shortly after and asked my dad for a private discussion to update him on my progress.

"Good, good," Dr. Andrew said as my father updated him on my accomplishments. He was holding a few paper brochures titled "Residential Care Homes." This was how we realized that Dr. Andrew had not come expecting to hear about progress but rather to present nursing home care as an option for the rest of my life.

"Yes," Nick overheard Dr. Andrew say to my father. "But I don't believe Adam will be able to walk on his own. His short-term memory may not recover…"

Aba put a stop to that, lashing out loudly. "How dare you! I don't want to hear that garbage! We are going to leave this facility and report you to the Better Business Bureau!"

Ema and Nick raised their eyebrows, now distracted from Ema's task of feeding me strawberry Jello. "I'm going to fly Adam to Israel for a second opinion," Aba declared.

Soon, Ema, my disgruntled Aba, and Dr. Andrew left the room to talk more in the outside hallway to avoid upsetting Nick and me. Nick stayed with me, alone together for the first time since my injury. We'd known each other for fifteen years. I stared at him with a blank look on my stitched face and slowly started to fall asleep in the bed.

"You'll be good, man," Nick stood, looking at my face under the helmet Ema had replaced before leaving.

Four months before my injury, Nick had picked me up from the Burbank and played me songs from an underground rap musician named Trouble.

"Listen to this, dude!" he'd enthused, turning up his car speakers. We'd both bopped our heads, listening to Trouble and Travis Scott on blast. We played Scott's album 'Rodeo' at the gym when we worked out sometimes and on the phone together each day.

"Listen for memories, bruh," he told me now, playing me the Travis Scott song 'Impossible' at low volume on his phone.

Nick was an aspiring musician determined to re-awaken our friendship's musical memories even as I slept in my hospital bed.

"You 'Impossible, Adam.' All you, man," Nick said quietly before he left.

My memory was still playing tricks on me. Some days, I would call my parents "Ema" and "Aba," as was normal. Other days, I would greet them disconcertingly as "Alex" and "Rimona," which I had never called them before my accident. They wanted to see if I would remember Nelly, another beloved family member whom I hadn't seen since leaving for Thailand.

On July 11th, 2018, Ema brought Nelly to my room. Ema had gotten her certified as a service dog so she could come see me. When I saw Nelly, I smiled my crooked smile.

"Cute dog," I said, as though I'd never met Nelly before. Nelly scoured me with her little dark eyes, licking my bed but steering away from me. She must have sensed that something was off.

Ema stood by my dad, trying her best not to cry. "It's okay, Nelly," Ema said at last when it became clear that I wasn't going to recognize her. "Adam is sleepy." Nelly licked my lifeless left arm, sniffing my bed.

I dozed off to sleep as Nelly sniffed me and then looked away with her tail hesitantly curled in. Ema scooped her tiny white body off my bed and walked her out of the room, back to where Alex Eskenazi was waiting.

"Ahh, it's okay," Alex hugged my crestfallen mother. "His mind is still recovering."

As my recovery progressed, I demanded to be freed from the adult diapers and go to the bathroom normally. The hospital staff refused, however, because I was a huge liability if I should fall with my bad leg and hit my defenseless brain on something hard. They wanted to keep me in bed all the time for safety reasons.

My family also wanted to participate in my recovery by helping me with my physical therapy, but that always ended with fights between my parents and the staff. The staff said that this was another liability, that I could be injured if my family tried to have me do an exercise I wasn't ready for.

I became increasingly bored with the hospital room, getting the same bland injections for pain and stress and having the doctors and nurses come in to check on me. My parents could tell this was not good for me and wanted to take me, at least, to the enclosed garden downstairs.

One day, Aba had had enough. He decided to put me in a wheelchair himself and take me outside for fresh air.

"I'm through with this prison," he muttered. "Here, Monda, takzeekee et harsh shelo. (*Hold his head*). I'll put him in this chair I found in the hallway."

As my parents loaded me into my first wheelchair, my left shoulder went 'pop!', abruptly coming out of its socket. I felt nothing but looked around to see what had made that strange popping sound.

"Wait, Ahlex', ha yad shelo *(his arm)*!" Ema raised her voice, stopping him. Aba looked at me in confusion.

"I don't understand..." he muttered under his breath.

Dr. Firestone ran into my room, having glimpsed at the scene from the hallway.

"What are you doing? He can't be moved! He has no muscle tone on his left side at all—none!" He and a nurse placed me softly back in my bed, and he popped my arm back into its shoulder socket.

"Your brain is constantly working to keep all your limbs, ligaments, rotator cuffs, and everything else in place and operating," he explained, calming down. "Without those signals, even the slightest movement can lead to injury."

My parents were not fans of the U.S. hospital system at this point. The hospital never allowed anything to be done without a meeting or a doctor, neuro-nurse, surgeon, or even a psychologist to explain the risks of what might happen if I tried anything new.

While Thailand and Taiwan's medical systems had been frustrating with the language barrier, the second my parents had demanded anything for my care, the staff agreed. Here at Vital, it was a constant litany of rules, protocols, and regulations that needed to be followed to prevent the hospital from getting in trouble if something my family did injure me while I was in their custody.

Ema remained by my side during my stay, sleeping on the green couch beside my bed each night to make sure I was being treated to her standards. Ema developed back pain from sleeping on the couch, but she didn't let on that it was uncomfortable.

At one point, my father had to travel to China for work to visit new shoe manufacturers. He was gone for about a week and a half, and when he came back to see me, I began crying like a toddler upon seeing him from my bed.

"A a aba, ani-lo… rotsay, leote.. p p po, yoter, Aba." *'Dad, I don't… want to stay… here anymore, Papa.'* I pleaded, crying and grabbing his shoulder with my good arm. I drooled as my paralyzed left arm almost fell from its protective pillow.

"Te Te Te kach… o o o tee, me me me me-poe!" *'Get me… out, of-here!'*

Aba began to sob, hearing the truth of my experience. He immediately demanded a meeting with hospital personnel.

"Hey!" He yelled to a nurse in the hallway. "Your facility is emotionally hurting my son ! Get me a meeting! I want options for moving him!"

The meeting was granted—I suspect mostly out of fear of upsetting Aba. The meeting included four doctors, two case managers, and a few assistants seated alongside my parents at a long conference room table.

My parents first requested that I be transferred to a neuro-rehabilitation center called Renewal Ranch. They'd learned about Renewal Ranch from other brain-injured patients at the hospital, and it sounded ideal for my needs. Renewal Ranch was a medically sealed campus. A stay there included daily meetings with a full suite of physical and speech therapists, but the accommodations were hotel-like, and patients had mobility around the campus. Dr. Firestone insisted that due to my current disabilities, it wouldn't yet be safe for me to move to Renewal Ranch.

"Fine," Aba spat. "We are taking him home, out of this medical cave, back to the real world. And we want physical therapists to come keep my son physically challenged each day, so he's not just lying there."

The managing doctors and surgeon looked at each other, concerned. "Sir, what about his care like showering, bathroom use, and all the rest of his daily needs?" Dr. Firestone asked. While Aba spoke, Ema was texting Alex Eskenazi and my sister under the table, already recruiting support for the move.

"That's what the home therapist will teach him and his mom," Aba stated.

"One moment, sir," the medical staff began to speak quietly with Dr. Firestone. After a few minutes, they turned back to Aba. "We've conferred, sir, and Adam can depart. But let's have one last look at his brain."

Aba, Ema, Dr. Firestone, and a nurse trooped into the imaging room, where my MRIs were pulled out and displayed on the lightboxes.

Dr. Firestone took a deep breath. "First, I want to tell you that I understand as a parent myself. You want to free your son from hospital care. He's been in one hospital or another for nearly two months. But," he continued, "you need to be aware of your son's future." Dr. Firestone looked to Ema. "As I told Adam's dad, Adam will likely never have the brain functionality to walk, or move his left arm or leg. Right now he is not even feeding himself. He will need help."

Aba sort of growled.

"Damage to the brain's right hemisphere means that a patient will suffer from attention, perception, and short-term memory deficits," Doctor Firestone continued. "This can be even more problematic for self-care than mobility issues."

The nurse nodded along anxiously as Dr. Firestone looked directly at Aba.

"Sir," he said, "Adam being able to care for himself in the future is simply not likely."

For the first time, Aba allowed himself to consider this possibility. He looked brokenly at Ema.

"Thank you," he said finally, steeling his resolve. "I still believe in my son. He will be going home," Aba said. "We expect the therapists to arrive tomorrow."

He and Ema were sick of hearing the acronyms: TBI (traumatic brain injury), RHBD (right hemisphere brain damage), DAI (diffuse axonal injury). They woke me up from sleep and loaded me into a wheelchair. I was loaded into Ema's car by three nurses and a valet-assistant. Aba

82

loaded my first-ever Vital-provided wheelchair into his larger car. I was given a helmet for home and a new shoulder sling that was intended to secure my left rotator cuff so that my shoulder would remain attached to my body. My still-red eye looked around as they placed a sling-pillow under the wrap for the trip home. Mom looked at me, leaning uncomfortably to my right in her passenger seat.

As we drove home, my memory started to play games with me again. I forgot about having a two-bedroom apartment in the Valley with Kaitlin and thought we were driving to my mom's home where I grew up. I felt like a child as my left arm felt so heavy in my seat, dragging my upper body down.

As we pulled into the garage of my Burbank apartment, where I'd loaded my luggage into Ema's car to depart for Thailand, everything felt like a dream. I was confused, cradled in my extra-long hospital shirt and protective helmet, with my arm wrapped in a shoulder sling. We parked in my underground spot and waited for Aba to arrive with my wheelchair. The parking garage looked alien and unearthly to me, a dark and empty underground place. My body felt molded, shrunken into my seat. Sitting in a car was now a new experience.

Looking around the dimly-lit parking lot of my building, filled with about 15 parked cars, I didn't notice that my old Cadillac sport-coupe was missing. Once Aba finally pulled in and unloaded my wheelchair, he carefully aligned it with the passenger seat's door.

"Okay, Aba," Ema said, gently unbuckling my seat belt. I took an exhausted breath, managing my newly hurt body and mind. I had no energy to think. I just tried to stay awake and did what I was told, squinting my delicate eyes.

"Okay Adahm, nice and easy with your good side," Ema guided me through the process of moving me into the wheelchair. "Alex, ata-seem (don't put) any pressure o (or) pull on his left arm again."

Ema winced as Aba began lifting me. I was soon moved successfully and rolled into my apartment elevator. The next stop was the door to my third-floor apartment, guarded by a fake camera that I had installed myself.

Everything looked foreign. Nothing was familiar as I was rolled in. The entrance hallway with my red flower pot, clothes hangers, and the kitchen, dining table, and living room I had assembled seemed like they belonged to a stranger. I felt like a guest or tourist, remaining quiet as Ema pushed me through the apartment.

I felt no belonging here. I just breathed, not thinking, blankly looking at my parents.

Aba and Ema pushed me around my two-bedroom apartment, asking if I remembered anything. The only thing that looked even vaguely familiar was the color-changing LED light strip I had affixed to my cream-colored couch. I was left staring at my blank living room TV screen as my mom and dad discussed whether I would be able to get around with my wheelchair in the carpeted bedroom. Ema soon came out of the kitchen with a smile on her face.

We discovered that my wheelchair wouldn't fit through the glass doors onto the balcony. I soon fell asleep in the apartment's living room chair instead.

"Adam, bo eetea rega." 'Adam, come with me, please,' dad said, pushing my chair to my bedroom. He rolled me into my white bedroom, and I noticed a beige recliner chair to the left of my cream-colored bed.

"This is from my Gadget Universe Company," Aba told me. "You can recline it 100% to take naps on it whenever you need to." Ema came in holding the remote for the chair.

"Teare-elo later (show him) how to use it," she said, placing the remote on the right arm of the chair so that I could use it with my right hand.

A moment later, we were interrupted as the front door opened and Kaitlyn's hurried footsteps entered.

Ema and Aba brought me back out into the hall in my wheelchair. Kaitlyn wore a dark blue shirt and lighter gray tights and avoided eye contact with me.

"Hi...he's back?" She almost whispered, staring at the floor. I don't know what she had been told about the extent of my injuries, but she was broken-hearted to see me in person for the first time since the accident. I looked at her in happy wonderment, but she quickly walked across the living room and closed herself in her bedroom.

Later, I would learn the story of her being notified. Mom had called Kaitlyn from the airport in Taiwan shortly after we landed.

"Hello, hi Monda!" Kaitlyn answered brightly. "How are you doing? I've been *so* busy at work. Have you heard from Adam, by the way? I haven't gotten a message from him in a few days."

"Kaitlyn, listen..."

She did not, continuing to talk away while driving down the street. "I'll bet Adam is having so much fun with Rene in Thailand! I'm jealous, but he deserves some fun."

When Ema spoke again, the shaken tone of my mom's words finally registered. She heard the terms "accident, coma, head injury."

Kaitlyn almost drove off the road near my old elementary school, Emek-Hebrew Academy. She cried and sobbed for hours and days, in complete shock upon hearing the news. Unlike the others, she didn't downplay the injury in her mind.

"…Wait, not Adam. Can't be Adam. He has to be okay," she'd murmur to herself upon waking up in our apartment and remembering.

**

7

Burbank and Renewal Ranch

Total Memory Recall: 2%
Mental Capabilities: 5%
Left Leg: 2%
Left Arm: Paralyzed
Skin State: Indented Skull, Dislocation, Cuts, Scratches,
and Numerous Stitches
Assistive Items: Wheelchair, Cane, Arm Sling, & Ankle
Brace
Age: 10
Weight: 151
Sources: Rene, Dad, Mom's Journal, & Alex

The first night, Kaitlyn left to sleep at a friend's house. She saw me again when Ema knocked on Kaitlyn's door at 8 PM.

Knock, knock.

"...Hello, Katy. Adam wants to say 'hi' to you," Ema said cheerfully, holding my chair's handles. She was taking me on a stroll through the apartment complex.

"Wait!" Kaitlyn yelled from her bed.

She opened her door, and I stared, "....H h h h hi Keht...len," I mumbled to her under my helmet after a few seconds.

"Argh. So sorry, Adam," Kaitlyn apologized, carefully walking around my wheelchair.

I would not remember Kaitlyn leaving. I didn't understand at the time that she could not handle the change in me.

Ema also called Alex Eskanazi to stay with us for the first few evenings. She was going to stay by my side just as she had in the hospital, and she wanted helping hands nearby in case she had an emergency or trouble lifting me between my wheelchair and my bed.

I did wake up once at night, calling for my mom. Alex joined us to help me urinate. They gave me a bottle in bed, too frightened to get me out of bed at 3 AM. My mother converted back to her nurse-medic ways, always leaving me an extra water bottle, putting drops in my inflamed eye, and checking my temperature and my pulse with her hand.

It felt strange to be in a bed not belonging to a hospital. My mind and body were very tired. I slept hard, a full 8-9 hours, as my body worked to rebuild itself.

The next morning, Ema woke me up in her usual loving way, lightly removing my helmet and stroking my moist hair.

"Danduni, Boker-tov hegeeya, banoo yeled chamude…!" *'Good morning has come, here comes a cute boy!'* She sang, laying me on my back.

She stretched my arms as my left arm and leg quivered at being moved. Alex made himself coffee in the kitchen while Ema had me lay down on my back in bed. She slowly slid fresh socks and underwear onto my body, hesitant to add anything else. The tremor continued to shake my left arm for a full minute as we waited for it to subside.

To put on deodorant, Ema had me lie on my back as she lifted my arms, scraping my armpits with the deodorant stick. I followed directions like a robot. She attempted to brush my teeth while I sat in my gray wheelchair. My jaw was still very weak, and after a few strokes of the toothbrush, toothpaste foam would fall out of the left side of my mouth.

"It's okay baby, just try to keep hape-shelcha sagoor (your mouth closed)," she'd say, wiping my mouth. I looked helplessly in the mirror as Ema kissed me on the cheek.

I expected a hospital nurse to come and check my vitals at any moment. Instead, the first Vital occupational therapist rang the doorbell at 9 AM sharp as I sat desolate in my wheelchair.

"Hi, how are you!?" Ema excitedly greeted the therapist.

"Hello there! I'm Sahara." Sahara had gold curly hair. My short-term memory forgot why she was here, but I certainly didn't mind her presence.

"Adam, right?" She asked, walking up to me. "I'm Sahara. I'm here to show you and your mother how to complete your everyday tasks."

Still smiling, Sahara bent toward me.

I nodded as best I could. "'Kkkay," I managed.

"Great," Sahara enthused. "Let's begin. I think this is a perfect time to give you your first apartment shower." A moment later, she pulled from somewhere a one-armed, pale blue plastic seat with a suction cup at the end of each leg.

"This chair is water-resistant," she informed me cheerfully. "So you can sit safely in it while you shower."

I looked at the chair. *This is my life?* I wondered. My memory had recovered enough at this point to know that this wasn't right.

"Okay," Sahara continued. "Let's have your mom dress you in a bathing suit as you lay back on the couch."

Knowing Sahara was on a clock, Ema briskly changed me on the couch with her help. I lay helplessly naked in front of my mom and the therapist as my left arm trembled.

Sahara then wheeled me back into my bathroom and set up the chair with its suction cups stuck firmly to the shower floor. "Okay mom," she said cheerfully. "Let's get him into the seat as soon as the water heats up."

I fought the urge to apologize for the fact that they had to treat me like this, that I could no longer shower myself.

It took Sahara and my mom 25 minutes to bend my straight-locked left leg just one inch to clear the shower door. "Okay, Monda," Sahara instructed. "You stand behind Adam, by his hips. I'll stand in the shower and lift him so we can swing his leg around." Sahara strategically got into position as I winced, groaning. Mom held my hips as Sahara bent down, assisting my locked-razor knee over the door-entry.

"Okay, easy, easy," Sahara said as my mom tried her best to get her son onto the shower stool safely.

I looked gloomily into the glass-doored shower. As far as I was concerned, this was the first time I'd ever seen one.

"Okay, Adam, grab that wall handle, to lift yourself in," Sahara said as I stared in confusion. I vaguely remembered Aba saying he had added a 12-inch bar to my shower wall to help me lift myself in while I was in the hospital.

Thanks Aba, I thought to myself as Sahara and my nervous mother lifted me slowly up from my seat. My left arm and leg began to tremble and I was surprised when the water hit them.

Aba walked in then. Ema must have texted him about the exciting development that was my first shower.

"Okay, Adam, let's take off that helmet," Sahara said, unbuckling and lifting it off my hot-sweaty scalp as the warm falling water made the air humid. I sat on the shower seat, nervously hunched over and staring at the water running by my feet. I leaned to my dominant right side as Ema held my good arm, keeping me upright.

This was one of the first times I did not wear a helmet when I was out of bed, as far as I could remember, which made me quiver with hesitation. I knew that bad things could happen if I didn't wear my helmet. Aba stood by the faucet, ready to adjust the water temperature at a moment's notice, while Ema held me and the therapist prepared to wash me.

This was my first shower since May 27, 2018, at the Diamond Hotel in Thailand. I felt like a dog being groomed for the first time as warm water spilled around my body with all these people standing around me. I looked up at the shaving mirror suction-cupped to the shower wall but sat too low to see my reflection.

Sahara's gold curls dangled as she bent over me. The warm water started to splash over my chest and shoulders, and I smiled, remembering how I loved the sensation. A ghost of a memory of previous showers teased my mind.

In the shower, I morphed into a different being. I saw the water droplets fall on my skin and the mist rising from it. But I felt nothing. I was not connected to my body. I was someone else entirely.

I'll never forget Sahara's next words: "Okay, sweetheart, let's get that left side cleaned too!" She grabbed the mini-nozzle and aimed water to splash the left side of my body.

91

I saw the water hit my skin, but I felt nothing. No pressure. No temperature. No sensation. Nothing.

I sat in the shower, forgetting what task to do next in my haunted shock. Sahara began helping me rub shampoo slowly onto my messy, uncut hair, being very careful. She made sure my soapy right hand avoided the indented soft spot in my skull.

Ema watched, taking notes in her journal as Sahara washed the right side of my body.

"Don't worry mama, I have about 11 years of experience with patients," Sahara confidently said as Aba kneeled closer.

Soon, my left side was steered to face Sahara. "Okay hun, remember to turn your left side toward me please; it needs love too!" Sahara exclaimed, pointing the shower nozzle diligently at it. I felt my injured leg slightly for the first time as the water hit it directly, and that gave me some hope.

After a few minutes, she began scrubbing my entire body with my yellow loofah, telling me to stay upright in my seat so she could dry me off. With each scrub of my left side, my left arm quaked.

"Okay, great! That's all for today." Sahara finished drying me, ignoring the shaking left arm. "You passed," she announced. "Let's help you get dressed." Once I got completely dry and on my bed, Sahara showed me how to get re-dressed.

Ema asked Sahara about my left arm tremor. She explained that my brain was likely sending unsteady signals to my arm. But it could also mean that no signals were being sent or received since the part of my brain that got damaged controlled the left side of my body. And when environmental change or stress agitated my brain, random signals could be sent, causing uncontrollable muscle spasms in the left side of my body.

Ema listened, looking concerned.

Sahara dressed me in an oversized blue t-shirt, showing me how to pick up my shaking left arm with my right hand and swoop it into the left sleeve before putting on the right sleeve. I tried to mimic her actions but found I had no control. I tried a few times, flopping and sliding the t-shirt across the bed. Soon, I was too tired to keep using my right arm to lift my 20-pound left arm. It felt like a dead animal.

I gave up, lying down and closing my eyes. Sahara noticed my depression. "Don't worry, sweetheart," she encouraged me. "You'll get better."

In the weeks to come, Sahara and a physical therapist named Karen visited me three times per week for one-hour sessions. Karen, a pale girl with black hair, dared to encourage me to put some weight on my legs and attempt to stand.

I tried standing as Karen and mom tied a bungee rope around my waist to help support me. Both my legs heavily jittered while I stood, managing to support just 30% of my 155-pound body weight, and that mostly with my right leg.

In the end, I couldn't stand all the way up.

Karen also tried having me roll myself around on my bed. I'd use my one good arm and leg to grab the edge of my mattress and try to hold myself stable with a locked, unrelenting knee. I felt like a disabled seal. Karen wanted me to mentally reconnect to the ability to move my body. She placed me in the center of the bed and applauded me when I managed to move to another spot on the mattress, three feet away.

"Come on, Adam, come on! You got this!"

"Arrrgh," I groaned, trying to change position while dragging my left arm. I tried to crawl with just my right arm and leg. I couldn't bend my left leg because of the locked hyperextension from my brain's errant signals. My left arm was paralyzed and skinny in its sling, having absolutely no control. Each time my head turned to the right, a pool of warm drool fell from my paralyzed left cheek. I was re-learning how to move all over again.

This was especially painful when photos and videos from my past showed a dynamic athlete pushing, lifting, and squatting over 300 pounds for viewers and clients. My parents had made me a photo album from before to remind me of past memories, but it just discouraged me. Even scooting myself into a lying position was now a difficult and depressing task. I felt like I was floating in space with nothing to hang onto. I started to glisten with sweat, just trying to move six inches in bed.

Then, it was time to be re-taught how to brush my teeth. I sat in my wheelchair in front of my bathroom mirror, staring at a toothbrush. A new therapist, Patricia, applied toothpaste on my toothbrush and asked me to begin brushing.

"Okay, Adam," she said. "Just hold that brush against your upper teeth to start."

I brushed my teeth with my right hand, noticing my head leaning to the left side. My left arm lay in my wheelchair armrest, sling wrapped up. Somehow, I couldn't remember how to hold a toothbrush, and all these other body parts were distracting me.

"Try to focus on brushing slowly, so as not to throw off your balance," Patricia referred to the fact that it took conscious effort for me to avoid sliding out of my chair to the left.

I got confused, dropping my blue toothbrush to the floor a few times. Ema would pick it up and clean it each time. "It's okay, baby. Just brush slower." My eyes glistened as I stared at them in the mirror.

Over the days to come, Ema began taking me for more wheelchair walks around my apartment building. My room was on the third floor, three doors from the hallway elevator, leading to the underground garage or the roof. The roof had a few old tanning lounge chairs scattered around. As we strolled each day, relieving me from the monotony of my bedroom, I began having flashes of memories of my previous life.

"Ema, w-w-where Kah-k-Kaitlyn... right?" I asked one day.

"She moved away," Ema quickly responded. "Ee-lo-chola *(she was unable)* to pay her side of the rent."

The truth was that Kaitlyn was so shocked at my injury and disability, so horrified to see the roommate who had been like a brother to her with my indented skull, stitches, and half-paralyzed body, that she had moved out early with my parents' permission. She was so disturbed by what had happened to me that she began drinking and getting arrested, and was charged with DUI shortly after.

One night around 6 PM., Alex Eskanazi came over and surprised us with a bag of steak and chicken skewers.

"Adam," he told me, "I think you will like this meat. It's been soaked and marinated with many spicy herbs for three days!" He patted my back cautiously. I tried giving him a crooked smile under my helmet, still not speaking much but staring up into his right eye.

But I was confused. I stared at the kitchen stove and didn't understand how it was going to cook so much meat. Then Alex walked to my balcony barbecue grill, which had sat unused since the accident.

As an athletic bodybuilder, I had purchased that grill the moment I moved into that Burbank apartment with my first-ever balcony. I spent so much time BBQing on that $250 grill, standing on my 9-foot terrace, and talking to my friends on my phone speaker while I worked. I even purchased a three-foot-tall water fountain to have a nice serene background noise as I roasted my 20+ pieces of kosher chicken breasts for the week.

Alex was now lighting up my grill to cook. I suddenly felt my first stab of anger, glaring at him from the wheelchair.

That's my grill, I thought. *I know the perfect temperature, the perfectly-timed flip. That's my balcony, and this is my life. Back off!*

I missed the sense of ownership and control I had once had. I needed a break from my constant family visits, hospitals, rehabs, etc. I wanted my old life back.

But that wasn't possible. I soon shut my thoughts off, condemned by the wheelchair to stay inside. It wouldn't even fit through the sliding glass doors onto the balcony. I felt broken and weak with one arm gone, my legs unwilling to carry me, and part of my skull missing.

I ate inside, secretly grateful to be by myself. I realized I was not angry at Alex, the helpful and giving gentleman. I was simply feeling my first anger at my situation since pleading with my dad, "Get me out of here," at the hospital on Sunset. My left leg started to tremble in my chair from the emotional firestorm.

Alex was always by my side, assisting me and Ema each day. He'd even do small cycling and rowing rehab movements with me in bed when Ema thought the physical therapists from Vital were not available for long enough. Alex tried speaking to me and playing his favorite comedy show, New Girl, starring Zooey

Deschanel, for me. He'd sit by my side in front of the TV and laugh.

Alex had raised two girls as a single father. He'd begun dating Ema over ten years ago. I was the son he never had. Alex Eskanazi, I love and appreciate you.

Aba was always trying to do good things for me too, such as taking me to places like the beach, restaurants, or movies. One night, Aba took me to see the new Mission Impossible movie featuring Tom Cruise. I sat slumped to the left in my seat during the movie, helmet on my head, not remembering previous films and struggling to pay attention to this one. But I remember that the motion picture had a bank robbery scene, and dad suddenly hollered in the theater, turning to me:

"YES, Adam! YES!"

I looked up at him, almost frightened of his reaction.

"Yes!" He said to me firmly. "We got it! We got it, Aba!" Dad continued his rant, putting his hand up for a high-five. I tried my best to turn my body but couldn't make the turn to meet his hand with mine. Aba was seated with popcorn on my left side.

For a long time, I had no idea why my dad was so excited during that bank robbery scene. Much later, I would learn the truth: he was celebrating a big victory that would not be explained to me for some time.

One day, Ema and Aba, Orit, her boyfriend Richie, Dad's wife Monica, and my adorable half-brother Jacob came to my apartment for a family dinner.

"Adam, how was your day?" Orit asked me, trying to help me practice my speech.

I stared at her, trying to comprehend.

"You'll never guess what audition I had with my best girlfriend Skyler at Universal Lot," she continued, trying to get a reaction from me. I tried to listen, but the dead weight of my left arm beside my plate was so distracting.

Around 7:30 PM., I was staring at the chocolate-coated marshmallow treat on my plate, a Krembo, when a surprise guest walked in. It was Manny, of Manny's Barbershop on Magnolia Boulevard!

I had been going to him for almost a year before the accident, stopping in for a trim after my gym workouts or client classes. Often, Manny himself or his younger brother Nelson would give me my usual line cut. Manny was a big man, wearing a dark lime-green flowered shirt tonight. He walked up to me as we all sat finishing dessert.

"Oh man, Adam! How are you, man? Missed you hermano *(brother)*!" Manny smiled as I looked at him carrying his gray salon bag of haircutting implements.

"Adam, look who it is," Mom encouraged me. "It's Manny!"

I remembered him, but was confused to see him standing in my kitchen.

"Hey…Mnhny," I mumbled as Ema held my paralyzed left arm and wiped my mouth. Aba and Ema then rolled me to my bathroom as Manny set up his trimmers on my counter.

My hair had grown a lot over my left hemisphere, but my right side was sparser, especially around my indented scar. I sat in my chair wearing my blue shirt, some pants Ema had dressed me in, and my red helmet. After just a moment of sitting there in my wheelchair, I forgot what Manny and I were doing there. I was in a dream state.

Manny stood behind me, turning on his trimmer, "Okay, old friend. I remember last time you came in, a couple of days before your trip to Thailand with your high school boy?"

My stomach numbed at the mention of Rene and Thailand.

"Let's take off that helmet, my guy." I started to move my right arm to take off the helmet but stopped, embarrassed at the thought of Manny realizing how useless my left arm was. Manny sensed my embarrassment and removed my helmet himself.

"Love the apartment," Manny chatted, trying to stay upbeat. "I never knew how close you lived to my shop! And yet you were always late to our cuts," he teased. Then his jaw slightly opened as he got a better view of my face scars, neck stitches, and skull indentation.

"Okay, great," he said, almost stumbling over his own feet and walking toward the door, "just hold on for a second, man."

Manny nervously went back to my dining room. I heard his anxious tone as he spoke to Ema and Aba, "Is, is he okay…is he okay for a haircut?"

I heard Eskanazi speak up from across the 8-person seated table, "He's okay; just give him a light cut."

Ema agreed. "Just a trim, Manny. Aligning his sides."

He walked back to me. "Okay, sir, let's do this," Manny said, starting his clippers again. I shuddered in my seat, nervous as the loud clippers approached my head. Since Thailand, everything had seemed like a dream. I thought of the blue oceans of Patong and the Holiday Inn hotel on the corner, recalling them from past trips with Aba.

Buzzzzzzz. Manny began trimming the back of my head.

"So all is well, Adam?" he asked, attempting conversation. I felt him straighten my left-leaning head and felt the trimmer buzzing my rear scalp.

I half-nodded, trying my best to look natural and normal to him. After our failed attempt to talk, we both remained quiet in the bathroom.

I remember staring into the mirror as Manny cut my uneven hair. Every minute or so, I'd forget what was going on. What was Manny doing in my bathroom? Where was Nelson? I felt like I hadn't seen either of them in years. Cutting my hair took about 20 minutes, but it felt like three hours. It was the longest I had looked at myself in the mirror since the accident, and I didn't like what I saw.

"Looking good, Adam, like always!" Manny said as he finished up.

After we finished my haircut, Ema came into the bathroom and showered me with compliments. "There's my baby! Great work, Manny, love his sides!"

Manny eloquently bowed his head, grateful. My eyes soon crept to stare at my newly-cut head,

Cutting my hair short gave me my first good look at my indented skull. I stared at it shakily.

"Don't worry, baby, ze eekgdol-alze mami." *'It will grow over it.'* Ema warmly brushed my scalp with her hands. "Nobody will notice."

Ema paid Manny and handed back my cell phone so I could keep myself occupied again. I attempted some text conversations, too fearful to make phone calls.

After staring blankly at my phone for 20 minutes, I decided to text Rene, the one person I could really trust, who may understand my injury. It took me a few minutes to locate his contact information among my text messages.

Adam: Ey Renhe -8:03pm

Read

*Rene: Adam! Whats good man, how you doing? -
8:05pm*

Adam: Giod hhowes yyou?./ -8:10pm
Read

*Rene: I'm good, just visiting my mom's friends, you
had dinner? -8:12pm*

Adam: Ye diner writ family chikein -8:22pm
Read

Adam: Takr cari byeer! -8:23pm
Read

My conversation had improved (at least in my eyes),
which motivated me to try texting more of my friends:
Nick, Allan, Yaniv, my client Francisco, and some other
cousins. I continued to stare at my phone, now feeling
more comfortable but forgetting what I was doing roughly
every two minutes. I swiped around my home screen,
looking for something of interest. I saw my photos tab and
tapped it.

The first photo I saw was of a scene brightly lit with
purple lights. It grabbed my immediate attention.

It was a video of Rene and Div dancing at a Thai bar,
on Patong Beach, after we left the Paradise Festival early.
May 27th, 2008, at 8:46 AM Los Angeles time.

I quickly set my phone down, unable to comprehend
us smiling, being tourists. I looked out at my recently
rediscovered BBQ grill, across the balcony and over the
bank parking lot beyond. I slowly picked my phone back
up and opened my Internet tab. My Favorites section had
a few news sites bookmarked about tech, investments,
stock news, and the S&P 500 futures outlooks.

I stared, reading each tab headline but not clicking on any of them. My mind was already tired just from reading the titles of the first five favorite's tabs. I took another breath, my head aching as I attempted to read, looking around the room to call for Ema's help. I put away my phone for the rest of the day.

Meanwhile, Alex, Aba, and Orit took turns visiting and staying with me, giving my mom a break. I didn't invite my friends over during this time, not wanting them to see me in my half-paralyzed, helmeted state. One night, I watched a Saturday night movie with my sister and Richie. I sat on the couch with my phone, pretending to my sister that I didn't care very much about the movie.

I felt I needed to keep up the appearance of being cool and indifferent, being the 'big brother.' In truth, I was also a bit overwhelmed at being a third wheel in my own apartment while my sister and Richie talked.

"Want some chips?" Orit asked, walking to the kitchen to grab some. I remember staring at her from my beige couch as she looked through the kitchen cabinets around my snack bar.

I had never once been in my kitchen in my wheelchair. It wouldn't fit between the counters. My kitchen floor was like a ring of fire to me now. My eye twitched. I had hand-built those wooden Ikea cabinets, nailing them to the wall.

"No, Orit, g g good," I managed to respond to her.

Ema and Aba saw me beginning to want more in life, driving them to contact Vital every day to check on my acceptance to the Renewal Ranch.

I eventually learned that Aba used the near-disasters with Vital's medical transportation as a bargaining chip. Aba and Ema had learned just how dangerous it was to try to transport a patient in my condition in such a small plane—let alone one that was falling apart—and had learned about all the potentially fatal complications that could have occurred flying me in an unpressurized Cessna so soon after surgery.

Somebody on Vital's legal team knew it too, giving Aba tremendous bargaining power. If he decided to sue over the unsafe circumstance Vital had put me in with their medical transport services, Vital could lose millions.

Knowing that, Aba used the threat of a lawsuit to press Vital to cover rehab services for me well beyond what they would normally have approved for a patient who had no leverage.

In time, I would learn how common such behavior was in the American medical system. Health insurance companies would try to cover the cheapest or least care possible, even arguing with doctors about what care was medically necessary. But they knew they tended to lose millions in a single lawsuit, so they would do a great deal to please a customer like Aba, who they knew had a lawyer and a valid case for endangerment. Aba chose to take advantage of this: he was more interested in getting me well ASAP than in starting what could turn into a years-long legal battle over Vital's early treatment of me.

At some point in July, I had improved enough to pass the mental and physical evaluation required to finally attend the Renewal Ranch sleep-away in Downey, California. Vital's healthcare associates called me one day asking how I felt.

How was it, seeing more family and being surrounded by people? What was today's month and date?

"Mmmmondaey, Juuuly," I answered slowly.

We were accepted into Renewal Ranch on July 26, 2018. My mother excitedly packed our suitcases that night with Aba on the phone. Ema celebrated our Renewal Ranch acceptance like a Harvard acceptance.

The next morning, an ambulance parked outside my apartment building and drove us to the rehab center. I remember nothing of the ride over, but I remember pulling into the facility while lying in the ambulance bed as a safety precaution. The facility reminded me of a big campus surrounded by grassy fields.

"Welcome to Renewal Ranch National Rehabilitation Center," the ambulance driver announced to me and Ema, coming around to unbuckle me from the stretcher-bed. The multistory building had white-and-black patterned floors and huge glass windows allowing sun in. Renewal Ranch was a comprehensive center built to help with the recovery of seriously injured patients.

The front desk nurses checked us in briskly. "Hello, Adam, our very own bodybuilder!" the front desk nurse exclaimed, leading us to the hospital wing. The facility looked like a private high school on the inside, with its lockers and gyms populated by patients and therapists. I felt embarrassed at being helplessly pushed in a wheelchair with a helmet. The Renewal Ranch campus was the first time since the hospital I had been close to strangers, and it was overwhelming.

"You might not get a roommate," the guiding nurse said as we strolled. Ema nodded cheerfully, thinking we would have a room to ourselves. I slouched in my chair, blankly looking around the facility. I didn't know where I was, or why.

When we walked into my assigned room, we saw a plain white bedroom with a bathroom, a wall television, and two medical beds with curtains separating them. I looked over the room from my chair as the front desk associate asked us to pick a bed, and that was when I realized another patient might join me.

I chose the mattress by the window, overlooking a faculty parking lot. I hoped this would give Ema enough room to sleep on the nearby couch.

"Thank you, Adami," Ema said, holding our bags. I sat staring in guilt, unable to help Ema as she unpacked and inspected the bed with its instruments. The control dial had buttons labeled "bed up," "bed down," "nursing," and "front desk." There was also a big, red button ominously labeled 'EMERGENCY.'

"Ok, bo neere ech ha Renewal Ranch neera," *'Okay, come, let's see what Renewal Ranch looks like.'* Ema pushed my chair around the facility on that sunny day.

I remember passing a cafeteria with outside benches and tables next to an inner walkway with grills for chefs to cook for the patients. The grassy fields outside were neatly mowed.

Our initial tour of the outside was not very long, but once we headed back inside, I remember passing by a high-ceilinged gym to my left. I stared with great interest. Ema noticed my rare left turn in the chair, with my paralyzed left arm at risk of sliding off the supportive pillow pads. She quickly took my shoulder sling out of her purse and tied it around my arm for support.

"Watch it, baby," she said as we turned towards the gym.

Ema pushed my chair around the glass-enclosed fitness building, bringing us right up to the window. I remember peeking inside from my chair and noticing a rock wall similar to the one I met Donna on. A few touchscreen PCs stood, possibly used for patient check-in, and there were 20 treadmills, all standing in a line. I ogled at the grand gym, knowing that I admired it but not quite able to remember *why*.

We next visited hallways A and B. It was strange to see wooden handlebars lining every hallway to help patients walk.

"Okay, baby, according to this daily activity map, we will be assigned to come to this area each day," Ema said, half in Hebrew, as she pushed me down a long hallway lined with lockers. Everything seemed to be closed, possibly because we arrived on a Sunday. I remember peeking through the PT-hallway room 12-A and seeing a long room with two sets of 12'x12' blue athletic mats on each end and a tiny leg press machine on the right side.

"Ok, ze-ha *(this is)* physical therapy, Danduni," Ema paused by the door and tried to open it, only to find it locked.

As the day went on, we were visited by Renewal Ranch's speech and physical therapists. They wanted to ask me questions and get to know me on a more personal level. I was one of their few patients who were currently in a wheelchair, let alone who needed a helmet.

"Hello Adam, I'm Verona," said a speech instructor dressed in red.

"Hh hi hi I a ah Ahdahm," I tried looking up to make eye contact.

Ema had realized by now that my speech was impaired because my brain couldn't process the next needed word fast enough to pronounce it at a conversational speed.

I didn't comprehend or absorb much of what was said. I just continued to nod my head, seeing Ema smile-nodding as Verona described my new daily schedule.

The first night, I was getting ready to sleep as Ema fixed her couch-bed when a large security guard and a police officer with blaring radios at their hips stepped in. They were wheeling in a scary-looking young man with a bloody bandaged leg. He wore a red gang bandana and was handcuffed both to the arms of his wheelchair and at the ankles. At the sight of me and Ema, he started cursing.

"10-4. We have entered the facility," said the cop into his blaring radio.

The new patient stared at us aggressively, smirking with confidence. He didn't say a word. The guards slowly brought him into the room, ignoring us as they began securing him in bed.

Ema immediately got up and stormed to the front desk near my room, feeling the ominous threat. "Excuse me, police officers just brought in someone who, judging by the handcuffs and hostile attitude, has obviously been placed under arrest."

The night associate continued typing away, busy.

"Can we be moved to a private room," Ema pressed, "or at least into a place with someone who isn't in handcuffs?"

"I'm sorry ma'am," the associate replied, still not making eye contact, "but we are completely booked. There are no other available rooms."

Ema tried a few more times before giving up, returning to the room, and whispering in my ear: "Bo neeshev lo-ledabear." *'Let's sit quietly, not talking.'* The guards continued to care for the gangster boy, who we overheard them call 'Tony.'

"Ani po eetcha Adahmi, ani estakel acharecha," *'I'm here with you Adam. I will look after you,'* Ema said, an edge of hysteria in her voice.

"Get *off* me!" Tony screamed on the other side of the curtain. I heard him as I lay in my bed, powerless to move.

Ema sat next to me, holding my shoulder like a wounded soldier.

Two nurses entered, presumably to give Tony calming drugs. I stared helplessly at the possible inmate causing danger near Ema. Tony continued to become more aggravated and violent, with the security guards and the on-duty officer further tightening his restraints.

Tony began shouting obscenities now, thrashing and shaking the bed's rails. Spanish curses were interrupted by, "Get away weeyy," and, "Get off me credos *(pigs)*!" I heard the sound of spitting.

Ema later told me that as soon as I saw her become nervous and fearful, my mind transported itself back to a time before my body was half-paralyzed. In my mind, I was a strong, athletic man who would defend his mom's honor against this hostile patient. Unfortunately, my anger had the effect of impairing my motor control even further, making it challenging for me even to raise my right fist. Still, I did raise my right fist and pretended to punch the patient who was frightening my mother. Ema quickly telephoned my father for help.

While I continued to lie in bed shaking, she told Aba of the situation we were in. "Alex!? lachnoo, stachreem ezra!" *'Alex!? We need help!'*

As she spoke to Aba, Tony became increasingly violent. My parents began calling the facility managers and demanding that we be given a different room. Tony became so violent that the officer drew the curtain around the bed so that I wouldn't see further.

In my mind, sirens rang. "Wheeer! Wheeer!" I couldn't tell if they were coming from one of the room's EMERGENCY buttons or my own stressed mind.

The last thing I saw was Tony grabbing and pushing at the officers, continuing to scream. I quickly turned around on my good arm, hugging Ema in bed near my pillow. I tried once more to raise my arms into a fighting position, but only one side of my body responded.

"Johnathan, cover us!" A police officer shouted to the unarmed security guard as Tony refused to stop fighting. The antics continued until I was wheeled away from room 103.

Ema and the Renewal Ranch security officers discussed the situation amongst themselves quietly in the hallway. "Is this professionalism? My son has a damaged brain; he is recovering and cannot be exposed to this lunacy!" I heard Ema preach.

I lay there on my back with my numb arm and leg, confused at what I had just witnessed and felt. Eventually, I fell asleep in a dark 6-patient room.

That was my first night at Renewal Ranch.

***

8

Tremors

Total memory recall: 15%
Mental Capabilities: 10%
Left Leg: 2.5%
Left Arm: Paralyzed
Skin State: Indented Skull, Dislocation Sling, Cuts, and
Scratches
Assistive Items: Wheelchair, Cane, Ankle Brace
Age: 11
Weight: 150 lbs
Sources: Mom's Journal, Dad, Alex

Through the violent night, my parents weren't the only family members on the phone arguing with Renewal Ranch management. To mitigate the drama, the staff relented and gave us a private room the following day. Room 213 came with a single bed, a couch for Ema, and a television.

Ema woke me the next morning in my new bed.

"Boker tov hegeeya Danduni, banoo yeled chamude!" *'Good morning has arrived Adam, here comes a cute boy!'* she said, shaking my shoulder lightly.

I squinted half-open eyes.

"Lay and stretch ha *(your)* arms and legs, baby," Ema said. She slowly raised my paralyzed left arm as I lay stretching, half-pointing my good right foot.

"Tov, tase *(good, do)* the left toes, baby," she pushed and pressed my left foot down to help. The foot responded by trembling and spasming on the white sheets.

My eyes were bleary, and I felt as if my body didn't belong to me. According to Ema's journal, I didn't seem to know why I was there.

"I'll dress ve put deodorant on you," Ema said, holding up my arms to apply my favorite Old Spice. I lay helpless, not realizing that my position was cutting off circulation to my left arm.

"Raise your right leg," Ema said cheerfully as she slipped on my sweatpants. "I'll help you raise your left arm into the shirt." She left my red helmet off since I was still in bed.

"My baby looks perfect," she said at last, satisfied with her work.

Ema next gave me a bottle to pee in, having no assistance to get me into my chair and to the bathroom. I yawned, and in response, my left leg trembled.

Soon nurses came to run tests and check my vitals. They checked my blood pressure, blood oxygen, temperature, and examined my nostrils.

I lay back in bed, staring at the white ceiling. I was half asleep when Aba arrived to check up on me and Ema.

"Adah'm, aba ech ata?" *'Adam, papa, how are you?'* he asked softly.

"Okay…y. Ani tov, Aba," *'I'm good, dad.'* My head bent to the left as I looked out the room window, avoiding Aba's eyes. I think I remembered enough at that moment to know that this was all somehow my fault.

"Nothing to worry about, Aba; you are safe," he consoled me.

Aba left after he was satisfied that we were safe and comfortable. Shortly after, a cart delivered a monumental breakfast. They placed a tray bearing three plates on my lap and perched a glass of orange juice on my nightstand.

I stared down at the scrambled eggs, croissants, oatmeal, toast, and donuts while drooling from the left side of my mouth. My eyes widened in surprise.

Later, Renewal Ranch staff explained that the amount of breakfast food was calculated based on my daily intake needs. I had lost fifty pounds in two months, dropping to a skeletal 145 pounds on a 6'2" frame. Renewal Ranch wanted me to consume as many calories as I could to avoid fainting and other complications.

I was still sleepy from the long drive in, the new bed, and the hostile night. Ema noticed and ordered me my first-ever cup of coffee. Though 28 years old, I had always avoided the stimulants so many people used to stay awake. Ema strategically added cream and sugar to the drink before giving it to me.

I lifted the cup in my right hand and found the warm, sweet, creamy coffee to my liking. I nibbled a croissant and some scrambled eggs but ended up only eating about 20% of my breakfast buffet.

"Ahrbe," *'Much,'* I softly said to Ema, putting down my fork. Even as a healthy bodybuilder, I'd had to develop a strategy to force myself to eat enough to continue growing my muscles. Since my TBI, I'd had no appetite at all, and it didn't help that I could only feel sensation on the right side of my mouth.

"Tochal ma-ata yachol." *'Eat what you can,'* Ema told me as I sipped my coffee blearily. Food dangled from the left side of my mouth, and my heart began to pound from the caffeine.

The caffeine contributed to the nervousness I felt staring out the open door of my room. There were nurses, families, and patients hollering to each other as they started their daily routines. It was the most human activity I'd seen since my accident, and it felt overwhelming. I stared down at the floor.

"Knock, knock!"

My eyes slowly rose, my mind still sluggish.

"Hello there!" A tall man exclaimed. "You must be Adam, right? I'm Rene Ricard, your physical therapist! How are you doing? I hear you had a wild night."

He looked at Ema. "This your mother, Monda? Hello!"

"Hello," Ema responded politely. As Rene turned, she noticed that he had a scar on his scalp similar to my own.

"I'd like to give Adam an evaluation today so we can tell where to start his rehabilitation," Rene explained. "Adam, can you get into your wheelchair so we can go to the physical therapy room?"

I stared into Rene's right eye as he approached me, slumped in my bed. Rene was surprisingly strong, lifting my entire body into my wheelchair with practiced ease.

"There you go, Adam," he said cheerfully. "Remember, always engage your core! It will help you control your body when you move. Let's go for a ride!"

Rene pushed me into the hall. To Ema's and my surprise, he did not put on my helmet first.

"That scar is beautiful, Adam!" Rene enthused, admiring my bare head as I looked around, intimidated.

Fear pulsed through me as we rolled quickly with no support to prop up my left side. I slumped, feeling my left shoulder begin to come out of its socket despite the rotator cuff wrap. The arm would turn blue when the blood was cut off in this way, which Ema would notice before I did.

Rene paused to adjust my shoulder strap. "We must wrap this tightly now that you're moving around," he said.

I was confused about what was real: was this alien place a fever dream? Yet I also felt nervous and excited at seeing patients like myself moving around, talking, and laughing. The lockers reminded me of high school.

I looked around for Ema, wanting to call her for help like a little boy on my first day of school. She was hurrying after us, holding my helmet.

Growing dizzy in my seat, I heard Ema call out:

"Wait, Rene, too fast!"

She was right. My head and neck suddenly began to feel heavy and numb, lolling to the left. Rene slowed to a stop by the entrance labeled Hallway A.

"You know, Adam," Rene said, "you have one very good arm. You can learn to wheel yourself around without my help. What do you say, strong man?"

I sat in doubt but decided I would try my best. I nodded hesitantly. Rene smiled. He retrieved another wheelchair, sat down in it, and demonstrated how to wheel around using only his right arm and leg.

I stared, feeling useless as drool dribbled from the left side of my mouth.

"Lean forward," he demonstrated, "and lean to your right side. You can roll your chair's wheels with your right arm and use your right foot on the floor to help you turn."

To my surprise, watching Rene helped. I could see now how I needed to distribute my weight to control the movements of my chair. I gave it a try.

"You see!?" Rene asked cheerfully. "Just lean away from your dominant right arm as you roll."

Learning to wheel myself around was like being freed from a prison. I was always excited to 'drive' my wheelchair myself. It felt like going for a joyride in my car, not having to answer to anyone or ask for help or permission. I felt like a healed man, moving alone in a crowd.

Seeing my desire to learn, Rene put me on a full-day schedule of rehab. There was occupational therapy, eyesight training, speech therapy, and various physical therapists.

Rene next led Ema and me into room 12-A, the physical therapy center. I looked around the huge room at the other patients exercising on blue mats, doing yoga ball calisthenics, or riding stationary bicycles. One patient had their legs hooked up to some vibrating machine.

Overwhelmed, I stared around the room and forgot why I was there.

"Okay, Adam. You, me, center mat!" Rene tapped my left arm as he passed. I felt nothing where he tapped me.

In time, Ema would learn Rene's story. Now Renewal Ranch's head physical therapist, Rene had had his own head injury years ago. Like me, he was told of many things he would never do again. He proved every doctor wrong, and it was his intention to help me walk again.

After exercises on the blue mat, Rene rolled my chair back into the hallway and positioned me by the wooden handlebars running along its length. We were followed by Ema, a nurse, and an additional physical therapist.

"Adam, sit upright in the chair, please." The other physical therapist handed Rene elastic bands. He wrapped my hip, stomach, and chest with three of them. I nervously tried to sit upright, my left shoulder weighing heavily on me.

Rene connected the elastic bands to himself and the other physical therapist. He then bent to one knee by my chair. "Okay, my friend," he said, "I'm going to help you stand. I want you to grasp that handlebar by your side, tall man."

I stared at him, very nervous. Then, I looked to Ema for reassurance.

"You can walk, Adam," Rene encouraged. "I promise you."

The thought was daunting. And exciting. I leaned forward until my right shoe touched the floor.

"Great," Rene approved. "And now the left..."

I had no idea how to move my left leg, and I kept forgetting that it existed. I dragged my locked leg with my right hand until my left foot touched the floor.

"Good, Danduni," Ema almost whispered, watching with bated breath.

Rene smirked. "Great! Now grab that pole, and I'll help you stand."

I slowly grabbed the cold pole, squeezing my right trapezius muscle. Rene moved his supporting hands to my lower back. I sweated.

"Great! One, two, three!" The assistant physical therapist leaned back, pulling on the elastic bands around my chest and belly. Rene pushed, and Ema lifted my hip.

I stood up!

I stood on my right foot, my left knee still locked straight. Looking down at my feet, the vinyl floor seemed a long way away.

It was July 27th, 2018, at 11:35 AM. It had been almost three months since I last stood on the sandy Kata beach in Thailand.

I began to shake. Partly from emotion and partially from my locked left ankle and the strain on the right arm, which clutched the shiny wooden pole for dear life. My left foot shook as it hovered, not making contact with the floor. Fear washed over me at the thought of falling.

As my teeth began to chatter, Rene chimed in. "Great! Sit, Adam."

I managed to collapse into my wheelchair.

"How did you feel, being up at that height again?" Rene knelt beside me and lightly jabbed my right shoulder. "You will come back, I promise you!"

Ema's eyes filled as she stood behind me, massaging the circulation into my blue-gray left arm.

I smiled my crooked smile. "G-geood, t-t-tek, Re," I managed to stutter.

"Relax a bit longer," Rene suggested. "Then we'll try trekking down that hallway." He bent to manually re-bend my left knee and force my left foot down into its holster. "I want to see how far we can get."

I was already exhausted. I barely walked eight steps with Rene's help. My left arm, shoulder, and chest sagged lower with each step.

"Okay," Rene conceded. "Let's have you and mom roll with me to the floor mats to do some work with your legs."

I felt like a dead fish as I lay on the blue mat. I reverted back into my dreamlike state, letting other people move me. At one point, I had about ten hands holding me.

"Okay, easy, easy," Rene guided everyone in helping me.

Limping down Hallway A, clinging to the rail, was the most awkward of my physical therapy tasks. After five shaky steps, I would be applauded by Rene and my emotional Ema. By that time, my left side would have wilted inward to the point that I was facing the lockers.

With each step, I used the hallway railing to heave my left foot forward while my left arm dangled at my side. As I took my hunched steps, my left knee wouldn't bend, so I would have to swing it in a half-circle arc to move ahead.

"Agh! Ooh! Eeh!" I'd groan.

I will never forget hearing Ema applaud and cry quietly as she watched. She had been told that I would never wake up, never move, never speak again. Now, I was walking!

"Baby-sheli Danduni?" she would say to me as I struggled to walk. "Ata-roe mami, Hakol heeye beseder neshama-sheli! Ani-ve-ata." *'You see, baby? Everything will be okay, my life! You and me.'*

Rene did not understand Hebrew. "Walk easy, Adam," he would murmur at my side. "Take it smooth, no rush."

I would drool in concentration.

Around 12:30 PM, a lunch trolley would come through laden with sandwiches and chips. Sometimes, my eyes would begin softly closing in sleep. When this happened, Ema would hustle to grab me another coffee with cream and sugar.

"Bo Adami, moochan?" 'Come, Adam, ready?' Ema would ask as lunch ended. I would shudder away from the yelling patients and staff as Ema wheeled me to speech therapy.

Being at Renewal Ranch sometimes felt like being up on a stage: so many people around to watch me, judge me, and stare at my helmet. That most of them were recovering from their own injuries didn't matter. I was used to presenting myself to the world as a confident athlete. Now, I didn't want anyone to look at me at all.

Fortunately, Professor B-Jay's speech therapy room was directly across the hall.

"Hello, there he is!" B-Jay said as I arrived on my first day. "We were excited, expecting our first-ever bodybuilder! How's it been going, soldier man?"

I might have been flattered, except I couldn't remember what a 'bodybuilder' was. Memories of my old life flickered in and out of consciousness, and right now, I was confused by why people kept calling me that.

B-Jay was a big middle-aged man with a bald head. Ema smiled, answering for me as I was unable to think of the words to use. At that time, I seemed to speak Hebrew better than English—perhaps because Ema and Aba so frequently spoke it to me.

My wheelchair was rolled up close to the blackboard in a classroom, which was empty except for me, Ema, and B-Jay.

"Okay, Adam," B-Jay said, sitting by the blackboard. "Go ahead and remove that helmet. It's hot, and I'm sure you want a break from it." I nodded excitedly, looking at Ema for permission.

"Yalla ze-beseder, Adam." *'Go on, it's all okay.'*

I gladly removed my helmet, which was now suctioned to my head with sweat. The process of unclipping it and pulling it off with one hand was a slow one, and doing so showed off my indented head.

"Ouch!" B-Jay exclaimed. "Dear almighty, that was a pretty tough accident, eh?" B-Jay maintained his smile as Ema fixed my left hand, straightening it on the desk in front of me.

B-Jay and I first worked on my pronunciation using short-term memory stories and basic questions. Our lessons went something like this:

"Now, Adam, where can a little boy crossing the road go?" B-Jay would hold up photos to help me envision the scene.

"Uhh… hhh… Sss… sss s stawwore," I would manage, squinting at the photos in concentration.

"Great! Say it with me: sss sss *store*. Say, 'store,' Adam!" He would helpfully show me a photograph of a store. Then:

"Adam that's a gahrage... Gah-rage!" "It's hot! We need a fan. Say faaannn, Adam." B-Jay would show me photographs for each word.

After simple word exercises, B-Jay would challenge me to hold a conversation.

"Do you like movies, Adam?"

"Do yeae... do." I'd look to mom, seeking her help to communicate for me.

"Great!" B-Jay kept his eyes fixed on me, pretending Ema was not in the room. "What kind? Happy, sad, or, 'drah'-matic?"

If I couldn't answer in a few seconds, I would forget what B-Jay had said.

Near the end of our first session, B-Jay said, "Adam, understand: your life has changed. But keep doing what you can, and you will grow."

At this point in my recovery, I didn't understand what B-Jay meant. He saw something in me that made him believe in my recovery. Something I couldn't fathom.

In B-Jay's class, we saw how my brain ignored everything on my left side. There were two big markerboards in B-Jay's room. I would respond to words written on the right board but couldn't perceive anything written on the left.

The problem wasn't my left eye. It was the part of my brain's right side that handled information from both eyes about the left half of my world.

"Adam, look here!" B-Jay would yell to get me to turn my head to read the left-hand board. "Turn, Adam, just a few degrees!"

I didn't. I couldn't. I was so damaged, B-Jay had to stand behind me and hold my head, twisting it to read the left side of the board.

"Sorry, Adam," B-Jay would apologize. "We've gotta fight your brain!"

As B-Jay would gently twist my neck to read that side, my left leg would begin to tremble in my wheelchair. I would be overwhelmed by a headache. Tremors in my left arm and leg began happening more, like a sign of rejection from my brain. Every time I did something challenging with my left side, my left leg or arm would shake for at least twenty seconds.

"Okay, done for today, guys," B-Jay announced after an eternity. "Adam, go rest, please." I looked down to see my left elbow drooping off the desk. I was even more exhausted now and I wanted to sleep.

"Good job today, Dan Dan," Ema said quietly, massaging my left arm, which was turning blue again. I yawned, and was asleep by the time we rolled past Hallway A.

I woke up to find Alex Eskanazi bringing me barbecue for my first Shabbat dinner at Renewal Ranch.

***

The gigantic breakfasts became routine, as did the morning coffee, which I began to request. I did not realize it at the time, but I was developing my first caffeine addiction. I was also beginning to develop frustration with my wheelchair: a good sign, as it meant I wanted to take initiative and move around.

They made me try out this new therapy where I had to sit with an eye specialist. The eye doctor was a young British man named Dr. Polaroid. He first tested my far and near sight, followed by looking at my eyes through a special scope and watching how my eyes followed his finger through the air.

There was also physical therapy with Maria, who taught me techniques to augment Rene's. Maria was an older woman with black hair, and she was trying to help me re-learn to walk properly. "Nice, Adam! Try to look straight ahead as you walk!"

My hips pushed outward with each step, looking "like I was walking on shards of glass," in Maria's words. My left ankle and foot swiveled uncontrollably with each step.

"Sss h h h-hurtz," I moaned. My left shoulder felt empty and loose, and my body felt like a heavy weight I had to drag along. I imagined that if I closed my eyes, I would hit the ground with my left shoulder in the lead. But I was now up to walking twenty-two steps at a time.

Maria assessed my shoulder as I walked. She pulled up my sleeve, finding my left arm cold and turning gray again. "Monda, he now has about a 3-inch gap between his shoulder and the joint," she told Ema, tightening my sling further.

At Maria's advice, I got my first kinesiology tape. I fell back onto the physical therapy bed as Maria taped my upper left arm and rotator cuff tightly against my shoulder. "That should hold it in place for ten days," she said, applying the heavy blue tape to my skin. "The good news is that you don't need to wear the sling anymore!"

I nodded slowly and sat up, pushing with my right arm. "One, two, three!" Ema chanted, assisting Maria in pulling me up to stand. I stood lightly, swaying, but feeling free as a bird without my shoulder sling!

"The tape should help facilitate contractions of your shoulder muscles," Maria explained. "It can be worn during athletic activity, and can get wet while bathing. If you have any shoulder pain, you may benefit from improving the strength of your rotator cuff muscles."

I stared at her blankly: I'd understood about half of those words.

Later, Maria and I practiced 'sit-to-stands,' with two associates assisting me in standing from my chair. I was only able to stand—shaking with the effort—four times. I almost fell backward many times and developed headaches from the 'sit-to-stands.'

That was the scene: three or four therapists plus Ema, straining to pull me up to stand. Ema noticed that I never stopped to think: I just obeyed any commands instantly, without thought.

Around this time, B-Jay introduced some more complex thought exercises. "Okay, Adam!" B-Jay said, standing by his door as I was rolled in. "Today, we'll be playing the 'Do Something Else Challenge!'"

Ema pushed me, half-exhausted herself, into his room. "Sit facing me, please," B-Jay asked. "In this game, I do something, and you follow by doing something different, or bigger! For example, if I point at my nose, you touch your ears. If I point at a chair, you indicate the bench."

This might not sound challenging to you, but it was exactly what I needed. The one thing I couldn't do was unthinkingly follow B-Jay's orders or example. I would have to stop and think for myself about my options before acting.

"Let's begin," he said, bringing a small globe down from a shelf. "I'm pointing to this state, Delaware. What's different or bigger than Delaware?"

I stared, my head lolling to the left. Finally, I pointed, stuttering: "T t t t Te x x xas."

"Dan Dan!" Ema exclaimed, smiling.

"Good!"

At the end of our class that day, B-Jay had taken my helmet off for my comfort again. I pointed at my left arm in response to B-Jay pointing at his own wrist. Then, to beat his pointing at his eyes, I touched the top of my head.

It was the first time I'd felt my indented skull with my own hand. It gave me a new awareness of my TBI, and I immediately got a headache.

Ema noticed me wince. "It's okay, baby, drink water, neshama *(life)*," she rushed to my side with the water bottle.

"Ahh, all good for today, guys!" B-Jay said, understanding the reason for my sudden anxiety.

I sat, dismayed, as Ema rolled me back to my room.

"Good job today, Danduni," Ema said, trying to cheer me up. My eyes became gloomy with my new emotions at feeling my dented skull. I squinted under my helmet, jealous of the other patients walking the campus hallways freely.

I want to get out of here, I thought, finding relief by falling asleep in my chair.

Later, a therapist named Justine came to the room to train Ema and me on how to shower using Renewal Ranch's facilities. I was again placed on a light blue suction chair. At the age of 27, I was again being re-taught how to wash myself. As the water in the shower drenched my body, I couldn't feel it on my head, my left leg, or my left arm.

"Okay, Adam, place the body scrubber on your knees and then squeeze a little of the soap over it," Justine advised, pointing at the blue scrubber and the bottle of body soap. I followed instructions, feeling 'extra naked' as I showered with my taped-up left arm and two women standing nearby.

I practiced flossing and brushing my teeth with one arm, too.

"Nice and slow, Adam, or else your gums will bleed again," Justine advised. "And remember the left side of your mouth."

I couldn't make eye contact with myself in the mirror that day.

Even my body's automatic processes seemed to neglect my left side. We soon noticed that both my hair and beard grew more slowly on my left side.

My body felt strange to me. I was a tourist to being this injured, having previously inhabited another way of life.

In time, Ema's friend Ronit began visiting Ema and me. Ronit was a fellow Israeli, having been Ema's friend since her very first years living in Los Angeles. I had grown up playing basketball with her son, Edon, who lived just a few streets away.

Ronit started bringing us food as I grew tired of Renewal Ranch's bland offerings, and Ema never left my side to go to any restaurants. She brought my favorites: El Pollo Loco, Chipotle, and Subway sandwiches.

I remember walking outside with Ema and Ronit. It was then that I took my only cell phone video of Renewal Ranch, capturing the green courtyard.

Ronit always showed Ema and I pictures of our Nelly and Poof, whom she and her husband were taking care of. She and Ema smiled together, talking over Poof's and Nelly's behavior. I stared blankly from my wheelchair, leaning to the left.

The more I could do with the help of Renewal Ranch's therapists, the more I noticed what I couldn't do. The more I moved the right side of my body, the more frustrating it was that my left side was dead weight.

One morning, we were greeted by the nursing assistants who routinely came to take my vitals and perform various tests.

"Hello," the tiny nurse said, walking in with a male nurse at her side. "Unfortunately, our tests show that Adam has contracted a hospital-acquired MRSA staph infection."

Fortunately, I was not aware of any symptoms—they had apparently discovered the bacteria through a routine swab test. But Ema and I were required to quarantine for 48 hours and wear surgical masks to prevent us from breathing germs onto staff or other patients. We could only take our masks off when we walked outside. Mine would routinely fall off my left ear, and Ema would have to fix it for me since I could not feel that part of my body.

Rolling around the campus 'getting fresh air' during our quarantine was bittersweet for me. I would stare at the patients who could walk outside on their own with drool leaking from the left side of my mouth.

"Don't worry, Danduni," Ema assured me. "You will walk again."

One day, I must have looked particularly dejected because Ema stopped at a beautiful spot in the gardens and knelt beside me. "Okay, baby," she said, "keep your mask on and go for your own ride around Renewal Ranch." She looked out across the open grounds. "Go to the cafeteria walkway to the left. See the grassy fields, mashe ata rotse lasot, mami *(whatever you want to do, sweetie)*. I'll be across the street."

Since Ema was the only mother staying on her son's room couch each night, Renewal Ranch had given her a hotel room across the street for privacy. She rarely used it, but at this moment, she realized I needed my independence.

I remember rolling my chair in my mask, with my taped-up arm and helmet. I rolled first to the cafeteria we rarely visited. I looked around, trying my best to 'look normal' and fit in.

There were lines leading to a couple of chefs by a grill. I sat there, feeling bliss at moving by myself and seeing something new, mixed with nervousness at not having a wallet to buy food nor a cell phone to call Ema for help. A line formed behind me, assuming I was in line to order.

As my turn came up, I could not figure out what my next action should be. The chef stared at me, expectant. "E-e-e-elo..." I tried. It was my first independent conversation with anyone other than my parents or a therapist in months. "S-s-s steak, please?"

The chef looked up and chuckled. It was then that I noticed they were cooking scrambled eggs in a frantic process that gave me a headache to watch.

Despite my mistake, I soon returned to the room alone, feeling empowered by my independence.

I soon tested negative for staph infection and was approved to rejoin Renewal Ranch activities. The first morning I was rolled to the physical therapy center, where Maria waited by the door.

"Okay, sweetheart," Maria said. "Before you can practice walking with a cane, your foot needs support!" She pointed to my limp left ankle.

She walked to the box on the bed, opened it, and presented me with a black slip-on Velcro ankle brace. I stared at it, unsure what it was, but Ema nodded in understanding.

"I want to teach you how to attach this yourself, Adam," Maria explained, kneeling down by my feet.

Maria first took off my white shoe. "First, you place the heel cup on the bottom of your heel," she did this as she explained it. "Then, strap the Velcro around the top of your foot to secure it. Now you can slip your foot back into your shoe."

I stared blankly at the brace as Ema kept nodding, listening, and learning.

"Now," Maria continued, "I'm going to clip this attachment to your shoelace, and then it connects here." The moment she locked the final clip, the brace made the shoe intensely tight on my foot.

Maria helped me stand up. My left foot was usually floppy and loose, but now it felt very tight. My shoe was so tight; it felt like it couldn't breathe!

"How do you feel, Adam?" Maria smiled up at me. "No more loosey-goosey, huh?"

"Ata beseder Adami?" *'Are you okay, Adami?'* Ema asked, seeing my face.

I just breathed, staring around and looking lost.

"One step at a time, sweetheart," Maria said.

"But Maria, Adam will have trouble attaching this brace," Ema pointed out. She was right. I couldn't imagine voluntarily binding my foot so painfully.

"It will take time," Maria assured us, "but as Adam progresses, he'll get smaller and smaller ankle braces."

Ema and I said nothing.

"I'll be right back," Maria got up, smiling.

She soon came back holding my first cane and three long elastic bands. This wasn't a normal one-stick cane. It was a rod that stood up on a slip-resistant blue tripod. Maria held it out to me.

At that point, an entourage of four other physical therapists, including Rene, walked in from the neighboring physical therapy center. I sat nervously, forgetting the tight, itchy brace under the force of their attention. Gradually, my foot became completely numb.

"Big day! Let's do it, Adam!" Rene was almost shouting in excitement. It was my fourth day at Renewal Ranch. I'd gone from controlling my own wheelchair for the first time to attempting to walk with a cane in less than a week!

"Adam, please sit upright on the edge of your seat," Maria said as another therapist handed her the elastic bands. She wrapped the bands around my stomach, chest, and waist. I started taking deep breaths, nervous.

"This is just like what we already did, Adam," Rene told me, "but now, my man, you don't need to be cemented against those lockers!"

"Okay, Adam," Maria announced cheerfully. "Let's walk!"

I breathed again as Rene slid his arm around me with Ema, Maria, and another therapist helping to pull on the elastic bands. I rose slowly from the wheelchair.

"Remember what I told you on your first day, Adam: engage your core!" Rene encouraged me as I groaned, putting weight on my numb left foot.

Once I was standing, Maria handed me the desolate cane. "Hold this tightly, sweetheart."

To me, the cane felt like a 10-pound, 15-foot long metal pole stretching from the floor to the ceiling. There were about eight hands on my body in different places, holding me up.

"Looking good and tall!" Maria exclaimed, standing by my left shoulder. "I want you to take a few steps into the room, then we might hit the hallway. Now Adam, small steps forward please."

I looked across the room and momentarily forgot how to walk by placing one foot in front of the other.

"Easy baby, we are here," Ema encouraged me, but I could hear the nerves in her voice.

I was terrified. It's hard to say if that was because I hadn't walked without the aid of a bar to hold onto in two months, or because there were now five people staring at me expectantly.

I stepped forward with my right foot, my left leg with its locked knee pointing out behind me. I hesitantly swung it in around my left hip, almost falling in the process. Rene braced my body tightly with his own.

"Nice and easy, man," he advised calmly in my ear. "Take your first step with your left, like this," he demonstrated, moving his own left shoe forward.

"H h h h head..." I winced.

Ema jumped in. "Headaches! He has headaches. Let him sit and drink water." She let go of me for the fifteen seconds that were required to run and grab my water bottle.

The next time I listened to Rene and tried to lead with my left foot. My left arm, shoulder, and even the left side of my chest started to droop toward the floor. I took very small, two-inch steps with my cane while feeling the elastic bands, hands, and ankle brace squeeze my body.

Ema tried her best to hold onto her son for dear life, while also trying to record for Aba who was rushing down the freeway to see my first steps in person. Ema was quietly sobbing with joy.

I soon began shaking from my teeth to my feet.

"Okay, let's sit, Adam. That was great!" chimed Maria.

I walked seven steps with my cane that day, covering about five feet. My hips and butt shot back with each step, like I was stepping on broken glass. Setting my left foot down on the floor would cause me to sway to my right, almost tipping over. Still, I was eagerly taking steps.

My left foot was somehow both numb and itchy under the ankle brace by the time I sat down, exhausted. I felt like I was wearing a weighted vest on my left side.

"Sit, baby, drink," Ema told me, handing me water. I was sweating as I sat in the offered chair, drooping to the right. My taped arm felt much better now that I was sitting. Its weight still pressed down my body, but now the chair I was resting on could absorb most of it.

I leaned over and all five people in the room reacted, thinking I was falling forward. In fact, I was attempting to scratch my itching left foot under its brace. My left arm flopped uselessly as I leaned down.

"Easy, Adam," Rene cautioned me. "Don't move so quickly, stay slow with that arm."

Aba soon burst in and asked, "Adam can walk? Seriously, can walk?!" He smiled wickedly for his once-vegetative son.

"Aba ani beser toda." *'Papa, I'm so thankful.'* Aba found me and came in for a hug. "They said you'd never walk again!" Aba held me with all the love he could give. He was in absolute paradise.

I returned his smile with my own crooked grin, still breathing hard from the effort of dragging my body five feet.

Ema soon pulled Aba aside for a conference on Renewal Ranch's 'frantic' approach. To her, it seemed like they were pushing me hard. I squinted over at Aba, Ema, Rene, Maria, and the other therapists who were talking nervously about me.

"Are you sure it's safe for him to try walking like this so suddenly?" Ema asked.

"Renewal Ranch does know about his diffuse axonal injury, right?" Aba asked. "They said he'd never walk again."

That was the first time I remember hearing Aba say how severe my TBI was, or suggest that I couldn't do something. It angered me as I sat in my wheelchair, listening to my parents say it was too much to ask me to even take a few steps. I could not accept those words. All at once, I was frustrated with all the 'safety' equipment strapped to my body. I began to unclip my helmet...

Ema and Rene walked over as Aba and Maria continued to talk tensely in the corner. "Adam, it's okay to take off the helmet. But make sure an adult is present when you do it, soldier," Rene said, smiling. I didn't say a word, but groaned slightly as I tried to listen in on Aba's conversation with Maria.

Maria soon joined us and began showing me how I needed to try to always keep my left arm pulled tight against my body. I felt no sensation as I watched her fingers press on my arm, trying to show me the way.

"Okay, round two, Adam," Maria said as Aba gave in, smiling at the thought of seeing me walk.

The hands of the four therapists all seemed glued to my body as Ema and Aba stood apart, watching.

"Who yachol, ata teere!" 'He can, you will see!' Ema whispered excitedly to Aba as I painstakingly stood up again. I started with my left foot first, focusing on putting one foot in front of the other.

"He's walking!" Aba exclaimed. "He's walking!"

I dared not glance up to see Aba and Ema hugging one another, for fear of losing my balance. But in a lucid moment, I wondered if Aba was seeing a future of possibilities for me unfurling in his mind.

"Alright, great work, Adam," Maria said again, guiding me to sit back down. I was dripping with sweat— but satisfied, like after a good workout at the gym.

The whole time I walked, my left toes scraped against the floor. My right hip, knee, and quad were totally spent.

But I had done it. I could walk.

***

9

Electrical Shocks

Total memory recall: 18%
Mental Capabilities: 15%
Left Leg: 4%
Left Arm: Paralyzed
Skin State: Indented Skull, Dislocated Sling, Cuts,
Scratches, and Numerous Stitches
Assistive items: Wheelchair, Cane
Age: 13
Weight: 150
Sources: Mom's Journal, Dad, & Alex

T he next thing I remember is being rolled across the hall and being introduced to a tiny therapist named Jane.

"Hello, Adam and Monda," Jane smiled. "Adam, first I want to say congratulations on your first trek with the cane!"

I would later learn that Jane had over 12 years of experience treating patients with traumatic brain injuries, but what she did was a puzzle to me at this moment.

"Now, Adam," Jane sat down by me and untangled a couple of wires connected to a black box with a dial on it. "This is called an e-stim. It stands for 'electrical stimulation device.' This will be your new enemy."

"My enemy?" I will never forget her strange, dark choice of words.

"There are two cords here," Jane held them up, "and I will be hooking them up to your left arm, chest, and shoulder." She placed one red and one black pad on my left forearm, each of them trailing a wire to the black box.

"The e-stim sends small amounts of electricity through your muscles to 'wake up' nerves that are not receiving signals from your brain. In time, this may help your brain to recognize these muscles and nerves again."

I stared at her, feeling safe with Ema sitting right beside me.

"I'm going to start you off with a light electrical pulse to stimulate your nerves. You ready?" She smiled, setting the e-stim box in her lap.

I nodded, though I still felt apprehensive with the new tight brace squeezing my ankle.

"Okay. Let's begin. Just breathe easy…"

Zzzzzzzzzz!

I watched in amazement as the fingers of my left hand began to move! For a moment, I thought Jane had cured me! Then I realized I had no control over the movements. They were coming purely from the electrodes on my arm and the machine in her lap.

I felt a light tingling and a sensation of warmth building up in my left forearm. That was still progress, as I had felt nothing in that limb since my accident. As I watched, Jane smiled a little wickedly and continued to turn the dial on the machine up higher.

Then, the pain started.

"Ahhhh!" I shouted. Ema patted my back anxiously.

"Okay, so that's your tolerance limit," Jane said, lowering the dial.

I could still feel the e-stim vibrating through my entire body. Through my taped-up arm, my helmet, and my foot brace. What was odd was that I felt the sensation even more intensely in the right side of my body. The e-stim must have done something to my brain. Ema watched as I winced, my eyes watering.

"Adam, I would like you to focus on moving your left arm as I continue to administer these pulses," Jane explained. "We'll start with low intensity. I believe you can regain the use of your arm with this technique."

I nodded, unthinking, and soon felt painful electrical pulses running through my body again. I groaned.

"Good," Jane murmured. "Let's focus on moving the arm, Adam. Try to visualize your left arm moving. Your mom told me you used to do bicep curls with 50-pound dumbbells. Visualize that movement. Imagine it happening again."

"Arrrgh…" I kept groaning.

"Good," Jane approved. "Okay, stay with it!"

"Arrrg!"

Jane stared at the dial in her lap. "Okay—again!"

That was how my first session with 'e-stim Jane' went. For 45 minutes, electrical pulses were sent into my left arm over and over again.

"Argh, argh!"

"Yes. Visualize! Move! Move it!" Jane called confidently as she sat beside me. Ema looked on with hope.

"Okay, Adam," Jane said finally. "Drink some water. It's lunch time."

Relieved, I reached for the water bottle Ema offered.

"That's it for today," Jane declared. "From now on, I'll be seeing you for daily 40-minute sessions with the e-stim."

I looked at my mom, almost begging for help to get me out of the e-stim assault.

"Adam, I know it's not fun," Jane said, softening. "But the e-stim is made to help people in your situation. It can help the brain to notice your arm and leg in ways that other treatments can't."

Fortunately, with my short attention span, I soon forgot about my least favorite part of my new daily routine. I heard the lunch trolley soon coming for us and the other patients in the main physical therapy room.

I didn't want to move. My helmet sat on my indented skull while my legs felt weak and numb. My left arm still tingled, and my left ankle brace still itched.

"Bo eetee neshama sheli, bo noochal chsat." *'Come with me my life (or soul), let's eat a little,'* Ema said, rubbing my hand and leg.

Rene knocked on the window that separated us from the main physical therapy room. "Come join us, bodybuilder man!" His voice came, muted, through the glass.

I watched Rene take his cell phone from his pocket, and remembered that I had a cell phone too. I was consciously trying to imitate a 'normal person' as I reached for my right pocket, noticed it was empty, then touched my left pocket with hope. That was when I realized I hadn't touched my phone or even seen it since moving here, what seemed like weeks ago.

That night, I was laid flat on my back; my usual sleeping position since my accident. Ema slept curled up on her couch-bed just three feet away from me.

"Okay, baby sheli," Ema murmured, "teeshan tov. Eze yafe aseeta ayom!" *'Okay, my baby, sleep well. How great you did today!'*

I glanced at my feet under the white covers, wondering if I would ever be able to use them normally again. It was now August 2018.

In the morning, I was awoken by Ema's usual love singing: "Boker-tov hegeeya!"

"Where am I?" I wondered, blinking and expending great effort to turn my head and look around.

After my breakfast, coffee, and my ride to the physical therapy center, it was back to practicing with my new cane. My right side always turned outward as my left side drooped in. But I was getting better at balancing on the cane, my third leg. My hips continued to shoot back with each step.

"You must move every day," Rene told me, "to strengthen your brain's connections with your arms and legs."

After just 10 unbalanced cane steps, I would almost fall over as a headache began to overtake me. I wanted to progress faster, but my body just wouldn't do it.

"Okay...not feiling eso gret." I could only speak if I stood still, unable to multitask walking and talking at the same time.

Ema was always inches away, adjusting my brace, my helmet, and massaging my left limbs when I failed to notice their circulation being cut off.

"Good job, Danduni," she would murmur.

I always did what I was told, with no thought beyond brief moments of wonderment and confusion. I would sometimes apologize to Ema or Maria if I failed to meet their goals for me or was forced to ask for a break.

As the days of August passed, Ema saw me become more eager to get out of my wheelchair. Slowly but surely, my sense of independence was beginning to return.

"Ema (or Rene, or Maria)," I would ask. "Practice, walk?"

I started to pay more attention to other Renewal Ranch patients, most of whom were hurt but could still walk and use both hands. I would raise my 'good' arm when I saw them performing normal activities, even rising from my wheelchair when I could. But then I would see my increasingly skinny left arm dangling at my side and feel that my attempt to blend in was futile.

My arm remained wrapped, with the blue tape being reapplied by Maria, Rene, or Jane once a week. The daily 'Jane-Stim' sessions also continued without pause. Here's how one of those sessions went:

Jane stuck the ominous red and black pads on my forearm. "Close your eyes and breathe, Adam. Focus on visualizing your fingers moving."

I squinted, aware of Ema watching hopefully in the corner. I tried hard to move my fingers as the electricity began to tingle up my arm, but still received no response from my muscles. After a few attempts, Jane would begin to raise her voice, trying to elicit an adrenaline rush in me.

"MOVE IT, ADAM. MOVE!"

I got nervous but excited as I stared down at my dead arm.

Jane moved closer to my ear, almost spitting on my helmet. "Come on, Adam. DO IT!"

I squirmed in my seat. All this focusing was giving me a headache. I flinched in surprise, but my arm remained motionless.

Jane looked up at Ema. "It's okay, Monda. Soon, hopefully, it will move. Let's be happy that he's awake and walking, with no seizures so far."

I didn't look at Ema, afraid she would be disappointed by my failure. My paralyzed arm lay exhausted and numb. I was uncomfortably drooping to my left side, so I swung my body and arms around to try to adjust.

"Whoa, whoa, whoa, watch it, Adam!" Jane called out, grabbing my taped shoulder. I looked down to see blood oozing down my forearm. Someone had left a pair of scissors on the bed, and I had just driven my left arm directly into them.

It was a light cut that only needed a band-aid, but it unnerved all of us. I had felt nothing when the scissors cut my skin. What else might I not feel?

"I'll have a hand stretcher delivered to your room, Adam," Jane said, looking down to see that my left hand's fingers were curling into a frozen claw. "It's called a Golden Glove brace. Your mother will help place your hand on top of it and train your fingers to relax. Call it a form of hand training, like your old strength training!"

As the days passed, I became anxious to go home and get back to my life. My parents started petitioning Renewal Ranch to allow this, but Renewal Ranch felt it would be a liability to let me leave before my craniotomy, which would at least replace the missing part of my skull with a protective covering. After some time, Renewal Ranch agreed to allow them to take me home for a day trip. I had to be back by the evening.

Ema and I were thrilled. The next day, we left for Aba's house to barbecue and have some family time.

"Okay, Adam, seem et hakasda shelcha-please." *'Put your helmet on.'* Ema said, helping me get into her car along with two rehab associates.

On that sunny day, I watched cars whiz along beside us as Ema drove. She was nervous about driving me in a car, not an ambulance, and she was driving slower than the other cars as a result.

As I was leaving Renewal Ranch for the first time, I felt free – almost as if from prison.

Seeing my Aba's tan Jerusalem stone house was a shock. It felt like years had passed since I'd visited the place where I lived during college. I wheeled myself around his backyard, trying to demonstrate how recovered I was. I tried to hold a conversation with Aba as the sun rays poured over us, but I was still stuttering badly.

"How's work, Aba?" I asked him as his wife joined us on his deck.

From this hilltop, I could also see my old 24-hour gym building, and Aba caught me staring at it.

"You miss the gym, Aba?" Dad asked cheerfully as I continued to gaze. My thoughts were not clear, but I knew the sight of it made me sad.

I tried my best to not stutter, taking ten or fifteen seconds to think of the appropriate words before speaking. But still:

"H h h hows s s sh sh shoes g go sales... going?" I caught Aba's beautiful blonde wife chuckling at my attempt. I sat back in my chair wearing my helmet, as exhausted from speaking as if I'd just finished one of B-Jay's classes.

"Ken Adahm, hakol tov eem hanaliem," Aba answered. 'Yes Adam, everything is good with the shoes.'

Aba, Ema, and I ate together as a family. We had invited my sister, Orit, but she was caught in an exciting video shoot on Sunset Boulevard. She promised to drive to Renewal Ranch to see me the following week.

Ema and I soon said our goodbyes, and Aba helped us back into the car to start our journey back.

"Okay, Danduni, we are back," Ema murmured as I wheeled through the glass doors. We made an effort to abide by all their rules in hopes that I would be discharged soon.

Once I could ride in a car and use my wheelchair better, I became eager to spend more time in the real world. Recognizing this, my parents would tell Renewal Ranch they were taking me for walks, but instead snuck me off-campus to nearby restaurants.

It was a challenge to rise out of my wheelchair and get into the car using one arm and leg, especially with my left knee's habit of locking with my leg sticking straight out. Aba or Ema would have to bend it manually so that my left leg could fit into the car.

Slowly but surely, I improved in my performance in my 'classes.' I could take a few more steps with my cane each week. It began to bother me that I wasn't allowed to take my cane with me outside of my physical therapy sessions; the staff was too worried that I would try and walk with it unsupervised and fall, and injure myself.

"Adam, I have good news for you," Maria said one day, clapping. "I'm only going to put two elastic bands around your waist now!"

That's what 'good news' was like at Renewal Ranch.

Alex Eskanazi came a few times to applaud my cane walks in the hallways. Rene and Maria both worked with me, incorporating sit-to-stands, manual leg extensions, and assisted bicycling where they would wrestle my disabled foot into the exercise bike's pedal-holsters. B-Jay and I began to work on simple math calculations and continued to work on my pronunciation.

"Okay, Adam, what does that add up to?"

"F-f-f-f fourteen."

We also began working on reading comprehension, color-matching, and shape identification. My attention span was beginning to get longer as my brain recovered, and I could do more without getting a headache. Around this time, Ema walked me around the Renewal Ranch campus to meet Aba, who was going to take me to lunch at a nearby Italian restaurant.

"Ata-seem et ha kasda haze, Aba," *'Don't put that helmet on papa,'* Aba said as we got in the car. I removed it, nervous but happy, glancing at Ema's retreating back to see if she noticed.

Aba parked about nine feet from the restaurant's doors, so I could be easily rolled through in my wheelchair, which was crammed, folded, into Aba's back seat. It took Aba about 20 minutes to wrestle the chair out of his car, unfold it, and roll me those nine feet into the restaurant.

Fortunately, the restaurant was mostly empty and not too overwhelming. I felt good not wearing my helmet, feeling more normal than I had in weeks.

Soon, Ema and Eskanazi took me out to Benihana to see how my mind would handle being close to a chef who was slinging knives around while loud birthday celebrations happened at nearby tables.

That was my first time holding chopsticks since the accident. I separated the conjoined chopsticks by biting them instead of using two hands to pull them apart. I hoped no one would notice my improvisation and was grateful that actually using the chopsticks only required one hand.

"Ema, it's loud," I complained quietly as we watched the chef cook our fried rice.

I was taken for another evaluation a few days later, which led to Renewal Ranch recommending that I stay another week. Ema begged me to follow this advice, reminding me of how far I'd come at Renewal Ranch. I could now walk and speak a little, and even perform simple writing and math tasks.

I eventually agreed—which meant we had to get Vital to pay for another week. I learned that Vital had paid out $85,000 for my medical care and rehabilitation so far! I did not learn, yet, that this was probably in part because they were terrified of being sued over the Cessna incident in Taiwan.

Vital agreed to the extra week at Renewal Ranch. My parents asked Renewal Ranch staff to let me stay at my apartment for one night before my final week began. Vital said 'no' initially, citing liability concerns. We were able to convince them by signing paperwork to release them from liability if anything happened to me while I was outside the facility.

"Okay, Adam, sign this waiver. If you have any injuries, Vital and Renewal Ranch won't be responsible for the costs of your treatment, so let's be safe," Ema said, handing me a pen.

I signed quickly, eager to get home.

On the final night before we were going to be officially allowed to travel to my apartment, Ema was helping me out of the wheelchair and onto my bed after a long day of rehab tasks. She took my helmet off and assisted me in using my good right arm to push myself out of my chair.

I lost my balance. She tried to catch me, and we both fell. I hit the floor with no helmet to protect my indented head.

"Ugh!" I groaned as Ema crawled frantically to her knees to check me.

"I'm sorry, Danduni! I'm sorry!" Ema was in tears as she looked around for the emergency button. She pressed it, fearing the worst: a direct hit to my exposed, already-damaged right brain.

"Ema, okay…" I said, lifting my head off the floor. I'd managed to catch myself with my good arm. I was fine, just waiting for her to help me up. "I'm okay, all fine," I said.

"Adam," Ema whispered, helping me up, "if the facility realized ata nafalta *(you'd fallen)*, there'd be no way they'd let you spend the night babayeet machar! *(at home tomorrow)*!"

When the supervising nurse hurried in in response to the emergency call button, Ema put on a calm face.

"Sorry. I pressed the button by accident," she said with an apologetic smile. The nurse nodded and left, and Ema put her hand on my arm. She took a deep, shaky breath. "We have to be careful," she said softly.

It was a reminder of how careful we needed to be at all times, at least until my cranioplasty.

The next day, we woke early so Maria could retape my arm before heading home. My memories still escaped me, so I thought we were going to Ema's house in Encino where I grew up, not my apartment building. I looked up in confusion in front of my apartment.

Ema asked, "Ech ata margeesh, baby?" 'How are you doing?'

I replied, "Okay," not wanting to upset her.

That night, she rolled me out onto the apartment balcony, carefully navigating the narrow doorway, to look across the parking lot and the valley below. I felt lost but slowly began to feel that I belonged here, in the 'real world,' more than at the rehab facility. Ema also gave me my phone back.

Now, as though for the first time, I looked at the videos and pictures of my past social life. Sitting in the beige recliner in my bedroom with my feet up, I scrolled past the Thailand album and on to the rest of my life.

In one video taken on May 5, 2018, I was spending time with my friends Nick and Allan while buying a cheap piece of art for my kitchen. Later, Allan recorded while Nick and I held the canvas out of my car's moonroof since it wouldn't fit into my Cadillac.

Looking at the photos, I struggled. I had trouble connecting the images with my current life.

My friends and I had fun, laughter, and silliness. We cracked jokes and bobbed our heads to the song "Krew/Time Afta Time" by Trouble. In another video, Kaitlyn was drinking tequila in our kitchen. She was with her girlfriends, and her crush Jen was tipsy, licking salt off her fingers. On May 16th, I had recorded myself playfully kissing Kaylee while she was on the phone outside her house.

How fluidly I moved both my athletic arms in the videos. How effortlessly I talked with my companions. Sadness at my current state began to gnaw at me.

The video that pained me most was taken on May 12, just a few months earlier. I lay naked with Kaylee in my bed. Holding my phone to record us both, I declared: "I can't keep up with her...crazy." She kissed my chest, pressing her body against mine and looking self-satisfied. I suddenly remembered lying with her and feeling accomplished, having the most beautiful girl in the gym all to myself.

Watching the video, I began to tear up.

"Look at you," I thought. "Look at what you were like. Look at the fun you were having. Now look at yourself..."

The past began coming back to me. The past in which I was the smallest, weakest guy, built like a 12-year-old in high school. How I trained for ten years to become a confident, accomplished teaching athlete, having fun

146

throwing around hundreds of pounds and performing 'clap-ups.' Six months ago, I'd been consuming six meals a day in an attempt to break natural bodybuilder records, leading fitness classes, and giving interviews that were watched by millions of people.

Now, I couldn't even be alone without a babysitter.

While I wasn't yet ready to see anyone, I did try messaging some of my old friends. Unfortunately, every one of them responded in confusion. They couldn't understand what I was trying to say, or why I sounded so different from before.

Tommy Moreimi (cousin)

Adam: Hi Tommiu. -4:08pm

> *Read*

Tommy: Hey, whats good Adam! -4:10pm
Adam: You ar ok?. -4:10pm

> *Read*

Tommy: Haven't caught up with you in a minute monster man, hows FitFlow coming along? The app not working no more at my gym BTW! -4:12pm

Adam: FitFlow cool thank wer carrr? -4:12pm

> *Read*

Tommy: Don't understand, you drunk or what lol!- 4:14pm

> *Read*

Tommy: Ima call you later at dinner... -4:14pm

I shut off my phone, feeling overwhelmed. I felt I'd exposed my weakness to the world.

I couldn't hold their confusion against them. I was not the person I used to be. How do you tell all your friends that you may never be the person you used to be again?

As Ema and Eskenazi helped me into bed that night, I wondered how I was ever going to have a normal life.

Mercifully, I slept amazingly well in my old bed. I was beginning to feel connected to my place again.

***

During that last week at Renewal Ranch, I just went through the motions, completing each exercise or activity presented to me. I ate as much food as I could, starting to gain back a bit of my healthy weight. On what I hoped would be my last day in the Renewal Ranch facility, Rene gave me my final test.

"Adam, you have been doing much better," Rene told me. "You can now take almost 50 steps without stopping. But I have one last challenge for you."

He took my chair to the emergency stair entrance, helping me stand and walk into the stairwell, opening the heavy white door to welcome me in. I walked in with my cane as the door closed, hitting my left foot.

"Oops, that door swings fast," Rene commented, trying to divert attention from how slowly I was moving.

I took a nervous breath, as I always did when starting to walk with the cane. Rene stood by me, placing his hand on my shoulder in the warmth of the unairconditioned stairwell.

I looked up at the intimidating flight of red-painted stairs.

"Alrighty, Adam," Rene said. "Let's see you walk up these steps. I want you to be prepared for how much work you still have ahead of you, my friend."

148

I looked at Rene, confused. I was just gaining confidence in my ability to walk on a flat floor with a cane. I hadn't imagined he would think me capable of walking up stairs. But I nodded in agreement to the test, accepting the challenge.

I trusted Rene, Maria, Jane, B-Jay, Dr. Polaroid's vision therapy, and all the other workers at Renewal Ranch. They had set the stage for me to excel each day I stayed there.

"Okay," Rene began. "Stand right in front here. I'm going to be on your good side in case you need to align yourself. The banister will be at your left," Rene said, stepping up beside me.

I stood, staring blankly up. The stairwell was too tall for me to crane my neck and see all the way to the top from underneath my helmet. I looked around for Ema, seeking her assurance or permission, but she was not there. I was on my own.

"Before you step, Adam, a precaution," Rene took out a single elastic band and tied it around my waist, looping the other end around his own hands. "You know the drill," he said.

I tried to take my first step with my good right foot, only for my left knee to lock, knocking me off balance. I flailed!

Rene caught me by my hips. "Hold on there, partner! I know you don't trust that foot, but that side can't be left behind. It's part of your foundation." He straightened his own left knee, mimicking my locked leg. "You gotta step forward on your left, put weight on it to force it to bend! Put weight on your bad side, teach it to bear weight!"

I looked at Rene, unsure what kind of 'bear' he was referring to. But soon I took a quick, uncertain step with my left foot. He caught me again.

149

"Little fast there, Adam. Breathe. There's no rush," Rene advised.

I looked at his arms and hands, feeling jealous that I may never be able to use my left hand as gracefully as he used his. But I said, "G g got it," and swung my left leg up the first step.

"Okay, lean forward. LEAN!" Rene hollered, slightly scaring me with the reminder that I could fall backward and hit my head on the cement.

I took a deep breath, staring at the steps above me. I placed my right foot on the step in front of me, the biggest step I'd taken since my TBI.

Rene stood closer as I made it two steps up from the cement floor. "Very good! Make sure to lean on your left side. I know your body wants to lean on your right, but fight it."

I kept nodding, squinting with concentration as though I were solving a math equation. Figuring out how to distribute my weight to make it up the stairs was complicated. It felt like a puzzle. We kept going for 35 minutes. As Rene helped me lift myself up, holding my waist at every step, my left arm swung wildly forward and back. My left leg remained locked straight when I took my weight off it, and my left shoulder and chest drooped toward the pavement.

Astonishingly, we approached the fifth floor of the staircase.

"I am so proud of you," Rene said ardently. "Stay focused."

Proud of my own achievement, I felt my chest swell with confidence as I glanced back at all the stairs I had conquered. But then I felt fear: there was no doctor or team of nurses waiting to catch me. No reliable mother.

But that just proved, I thought, that Rene's belief in me was all I needed.

As we turned around and headed back down the steps, I no longer needed the cane. The banister was enough.

Ema soon came through the heavy emergency door to greet us. She stepped through while I was still a flight of stairs up and stared, her eyes wide with surprise and anxiety.

"God, Rene," she called, "are you sure Adam can do this?"

"I have full confidence in him, Monda!" Rene said firmly.

Reaching the top of the 90-step stairway took a heavy toll on my limbs. After Rene carefully guided me back to my chair, my left knee locked and would not bend. It took Rene and Ema both massaging my knee to create blood flow for fifteen minutes to slowly bend my foot back down into the chair's foot holster.

"I am very proud of you, Adam," Rene said as he massaged my knee. "The doctors, surgeons, and medical staff all said you would never be able to do this!"

I sat, smiling crookedly.

Later, Ema and I headed to the physical therapy center to visit Jane and Maria one last time.

"Alright, Adam, are you ready to go home?" Jane asked. She gave Ema a finger stretcher, a roll of blue Kinesio-Tape for my shoulder, and an intimidating e-stim box for me to take home.

"Make sure he uses it twice a day!" Jane said to Ema, loud enough that I knew she wanted me to hear too. "I know it's tough, Adam," she said to me then. "But it will pay off."

Ema smiled, congratulating me all the way back to the room. She started packing our things.

"I am so proud of you, Danduni. Chekeenoo *(we waited)* so long to be let into Renewal Ranch, and when you got accepted aseeta *(you completed)* everything!"

Soon, we took what I hoped would be our final stroll through the halls of Renewal Ranch. I sat in my chair and looked around, feeling happy.

But as we drove home on the highway, I wondered: What do I have to do next to leave this tragedy behind?

***

10

Old Friends

Total memory recall: 22%
Mental Capabilities: 18%
Left Leg: 7.5%
Left Arm: 2.5%
Skin State: Indented Skull, Dislocation Sling, Scratches,
and Numerous Stitches
Assistive items: Wheelchair, Cane, & Ankle brace
Age: 14
Current weight: 150
Sources: Mom's Journal, Dad, Alex, Myself, Allan, Nick,
& Delilah

Being home from Renewal Ranch meant being surrounded by reminders of my old life. This led to a nearly constant state of confusion. Waking up in my old bed, on my first day—but wearing my helmet—felt strange. I was in the apartment I had started renting with my income as a bodybuilder-entrepreneur, but the next thing I noticed was the paralysis in my left arm and leg.

"Boker hegeeya Danduni," Ema said, smiling as she woke her son who had returned from the dead. '*Good morning, Adam.*'

Ema handed me the usual water bottle to pee in, since getting me into my wheelchair and to the bathroom first thing in the morning would be too difficult. She had me lay on my back, holding my arms over my head and wiping deodorant on my armpits. In a few minutes, Alex Eskanazi would come in from his temporary quarters in the room that had been Kaitlyn's to help Ema heave my body into my wheelchair. She'd wheel me to the restroom, brush my teeth, and wash my face as I sat half-asleep.

Ema would make breakfast in my kitchen as I sat in my wheelchair next to the couch, staring at the TV. She continued to nurse me, bringing me water and fruits, checking my taped arm, and making sure the sun was not sparkling in my eyes.

I had no awareness of goals, or basic needs. These things lived in my brain like distant echoes—I could feel faint emotions and urges from time to time, but could rarely make enough sense of them to act on them.

When I wasn't trying to walk, my foot brace lived on my nightstand beside the brass monkey who held my car keys. I didn't remember the significance of either object.

Aba and Orit came to visit, sharing the duties of watching me. I barely moved under my helmet and only spoke when asked questions. I watched the show New Girl on TV, with Alex Eskanazi sometimes joining me to talk about it. I wasn't a very good fellow fan, because I didn't process or remember much of what happened on the screen.

One day, Ema set up a trip for me to visit the local mall with my friends, Nick and Allan. She'd traded in her silver Mercedes C-300 for an SUV to make transporting me easier.

"Excited lee-rot *(to see)* Nick ve Allan?" Ema asked brightly, driving us to the parking level near the mall's top floor food court to meet them. "Nick is always asking about you."

I scratched my itchy ankle brace.

"It's gonna be fun baby, seeing them."

I'd already forgotten who we were meeting.

Ema grabbed her purse. "Let's sit and wait for Nick and Allan to help," she suggested, sitting in the car. The alternative was for her to flag down a stranger to help her move me into my wheelchair, which she did frequently when she took me out on her own.

"Have to pee?" she asked tentatively, taking out an empty water bottle holding it out for me to use. I did need to pee, and she knew this would be easier in the car than in a mall restroom.

Soon, Nick and Allan pulled up a few cars from us.

"There he is!" Nick said proudly, tapping on my car window. Nick wrapped his athletic arms around me as the shorter Allan got my chair out the trunk. Nick wore his usual all-black attire, while Allan wore a maroon hat with jeans.

"I got you brother, no sweat," Nick said, raising me into my seat.

Today was the first time I'd been away from Ema and Aba's watchful eyes in public since my hospitalization. According to Ema, I had asked for such a trip several times. I had (and have) no memory of these requests, but she carefully documented them in her journal and set about planning to make it happen.

"Looking good, Adam," Allan said, walking around to push my wheelchair.

Seeing Nick and Allan, I became childishly excited. We'd been friends since middle school, when we'd bonded over rap and fashion.

Ema handed my rarely-used phone to my friends. Allan closed the car door behind me as Nick prepared to push me into the mall.

"What's up man, remember me?" Allan asked. "What's shaking?"

"Have fun, guys," Ema smiled, seeing my friends prepared to look after me. "Be careful with him, Nick!" Ema discreetly threw my pee-bottle into one of the parking garage's trash cans as she got back into the car.

Nick turned to me, "Yo, Adam, where you wanna go dude? Let's walk around the clothing stores first?"

I felt free, like I'd been released from months of house arrest. I sat joyfully with my helmet perched crookedly on my head. Surrounded by the sights and smells of the mall, I barely noticed how my left arm and shoulder drooped inward as I looked around.

Seeing so many people walking and laughing, I began to feel insecure. I was once the strongest man in any room, the trainer who people looked to for inspiration. As an entrepreneur, I was the go-to guy for my friends, often the one leading us into adventures. I decided to unclip my helmet's lock as we rolled past the pretzel stand.

"Yo, you sure brother? Allan looked unsure how to react, wanting to protect me but deeply feeling my desire to fit in with the crowd.

"Let's just take it easy with him, Al," Nick proposed, looking at me with understanding.

We continued to walk, scouting clothing stores and people watching. We joked as Nick and Allan chuckled at my slower cognitive ability combined with the remnants of my old sense of humor. It was clear that I was in there—but I was a bit slow.

"S s s sale, with a s s shirt," I would try to join the conversation like in the old days. But my head and body slumped, and I had trouble following Allan and Nick's conversation.

Then I noticed someone familiar.

A lean girl was walking toward us, wearing gray fitted pants that showed off her shapely legs and a white top that revealed a strip of tanned stomach. I soon realized she hadn't noticed me—because when she did, she gasped.

"Adam?! Is that you?"

She whirled and jogged over, leaning down to give me a tight hug in my seat.

Then I remembered. Delilah: a girl I'd met at my gym and dated for a few weeks, months before I left for Thailand.

"H h h h hi, D d d de de Delilah you hi, great?" I tried to act my normal self, but my nervousness at meeting her in this condition didn't help my brain to put words together.

Slowly, she realized something was wrong. "We should stay in touch," she smiled brightly, but her smile was a little frozen.

She hurried away to join her girlfriend as I stared after her, feeling that I should have said something more but not knowing what.

Nick smiled, tapping my shoulder, "Hey hey, yeee, look at my boy!" He quietly boasted.

"Look at Adam—still getting girls' attention!" Allan agreed, watching Delilah go. "Dude, she looks amazing, man. How do you know her, lucky?"

"Yo, Allan," Nick chuckled, "this dude got some stories. We ever tell you about beauty queen Kaylee?"

I later found the confidence to message Delilah, and she offered to come by my apartment. I was so excited that I skipped my usual afternoon nap.

I needed a nap each day around 3:30 or 4 PM. By 4 PM, I would feel groggy and unfocused, and if I didn't sleep, I would be unable to stay awake past 7 pm. Usually, Aba or Ema would place me in one of Aba's Gadget Universe recliners for a few hours of shut-eye in the middle of the afternoon. But today, I was too excited for

Delilah's visit. Since I couldn't pace, I wheeled myself around the apartment in anticipation.

When Delilah knocked on my door around 6 PM, I barely managed to open it by reaching up from my wheelchair with my good arm. Delilah had to open it the rest of the way, letting herself in. Ema had discreetly disappeared to give us privacy.

Delilah was born to an Uzbekistan military family, so we had some common experiences with my parents having met through the IDF. Today, she stood in my doorway in a tight blue outfit that displayed her curves, before bending to hug me enthusiastically.

"I'm so happy to see you again, Adam!" she exclaimed, biting her full lips as she pulled back and looked at me. "I miss seeing you at the gym."

I stared into her right eye, nervously smiling at her from under my helmet. I couldn't remember how to host a guest and was unsure what to do or say.

"G g g good...see you, how things, been while," I managed. She nodded and began to delicately push the door open, cuing me to move aside so she could enter. She walked gracefully to one of the high-top white kitchen stools and lowered the seat to get closer to my eye level before sitting. I watched her; grateful for the time her movements gave me to search for something to say.

"Wow," Delilah beat me to speaking, looking around. "Haven't been here in a while. How are things with your life and family?"

My insecurity heightened. What could I tell her that wouldn't sound tragic?

"You t t tell, how are things f f for you, D d d Delilah?" I strained to pronounce her name correctly.

She sat back, catching onto the rhythm of my speech. She spoke slowly as she updated me, saying things I soon forgot.

"Adam," she murmured then, "one day, I was training and I noticed you'd been missing from the gym for a while. And as I was leaving that day—this might sound crazy—I was approached by two different women in the parking lot, a few minutes apart.

"Both of them had a very similar message to me about God, spirituality, faith, and all that stuff. Which normally doesn't happen to me, especially at the gym. I was on social media later that day, and there was a post by your sister, Orit, asking for you to 'wake up from your coma.'"

Delilah paused, lost in her own thoughts as I struggled to process her words.

"For a few minutes, I couldn't believe what I was reading. I started to cry."

She inhaled; leaning down to touch my left leg.I felt nothing.

"Even though we weren't in touch after we stopped dating, I still cared about you. I was afraid you would not wake up."

I gulped, wondering how much she understood about my brain injury.

"I felt so powerless about your situation; I just hoped you'd survive."

She sniffed. "I just kept praying that you were alive, and hoping everything was going well."

Delilah began tearing up, sniffing and moving nearer. I sat back, nervous about a 'stranger' moving so close. This was the first time since my injury I'd been so close to someone who wasn't family, a medical professional, or a decades-old friend.

"Then, as I was walking with a friend at the mall, I saw a guy in a wheelchair. After a moment, I realized it was you! I was beyond happy to see you alive, but I also realized how it must feel for an athlete of your caliber to be in a wheelchair." She looked at my helmet. "Do you remember apologizing, saying that you did this to yourself at the mall?"

I didn't. The frequency with which I was told I'd said things I had no memory of was one of the most unnerving parts of the injury. It was as though most of my own life, even what had happened minutes or hours ago, was inaccessible to me.

"I could barely keep myself from crying in front of you and your friends," Delilah's voice cracked. "I rushed out of the mall and started bawling again. My friend was choked up as well. She didn't know you, but she'd never seen me crying that way."

Delilah moved closer to me again, touching my shoulder as I leaned away. Her eyes glistened as she looked at me. "Then you texted me saying that you've always respected, cared for, and appreciated me." She looked down. "That you were sorry you didn't have your amazing body anymore."

"Adam, I wanted to slap you so hard for saying that!" She lightly nudged my chest. "You don't realize how much I care for you, and how happy I am that you're alive, do you? I don't give a crap if you have muscles or not, I don't even care that you're in a wheelchair. It pisses me off when you start talking about rebuilding your muscles, Adam!" Delilah looked up at me as I struggled to pay attention to her words.

I desperately wanted to be in this moment, but my brain was fogging over again.

She noticed my departed stare. "Adam," she said softly, "if you ever need someone to talk to, or need any help, I am always here for you."

"Th-th-thank you," I managed. It was now nearing 7 PM and sleep was threatening to take over me.

"Keep in touch," she asked, and leaned over to hug me again. "Please keep in touch, Adam." She gave me a light kiss on the cheek before departing.

As she left, I told myself that the kiss was an expression of friendship. There was no way she could be romantically interested in me in my current state, after all. I was sure of that.

I fell asleep in my chair almost as soon as she shut the door.

Later, Ema woke me up for a shower. It would be my first real shower since returning from Renewal Ranch.

"Ok Danduni, I set up ha shower chair shelcha (*your shower chair*)," Ema said as she undressed me. Aba had come by to help.

"Shamatee she haya lecha date eem-meesheeyeet!" *'Heard you had a date with someone.'* Aba smiled.

"Alex al-tevaishi oto (don't embarrass him)," Ema said, protecting me.

I just sat staring around, watching Ema gather my clothes. The bedroom door remained wide open as I was rolled by Aba, completely naked, to the bathroom. Passing the open door, I nervously wondered if Kaitlyn would see me. How would I explain the situation of being naked, wearing a helmet, being rolled by my parents into the bathroom in a wheelchair to her?

Then I remembered. Kaitlyn was gone. She hadn't lived here in months.

Together, my parents lifted me from my wheelchair onto the shower seat. It took them 15 minutes to bend my locked-straight leg and get it into the shower stall. I took an anxious breath as Ema turned on the water and droplets poured loudly at my feet.

"Yalla Alex, teekanes eeto *(come on Alex, go in with him),*" Ema said. I sat, 27 years old, 151 pounds, and helpless as warm water splashed against my feet. My feet were covered in red scars from the accident.

"Ani hoce etze me-bachoots, ani lo olech beefneem Rimona." *'I'm doing it from outside; I'm not going in Rimona.'* Aba said.

I was washed, scrubbed, and shaved by my parents.

Why is this happening to me?

After Ema scrubbed my body clean, they put me back in bed. I quickly fell asleep.

As weeks passed, Aba and Ema kept calling Vital to inquire about more rehab for me. My Aba's wife and their adorable smiling son Jacob, Orit, and her boyfriend came to visit a few times. Nick met Ema and I for breakfast on the boulevard, and Rene came by often.

I barely spoke. I was often in a dreamlike state, and when I was more lucid, I was embarrassed by my injuries. Ema spoke hopefully to me.

"Hakol-Heye Beseder Adahm." 'All will be good,' she said any time I asked questions about my future.

Most days, I lacked the motivation to roll myself around my Burbank apartment, so Ema or Aba did it for me. There was nothing to see here, and I didn't have any sense of independence. I was brought water, smoothies, fruits, snacks, chicken, and barbecue from my balcony. From morning to night, I watched TV in the living room, having no perception of the passage of time. Getting virtually no exercise, I remained weak and skinny.

Ema was very supportive, always massaging my arm and speaking to me in Hebrew.

"Ech ata margeesh ayom?" '*How do you feel today?*'

"Do you remember this pizza? Was that good?"

She did the same thing she had when I was a baby, giving me so much love and affection. But I could barely respond. She did not let that discourage her.

"Those popsicles used to be your favorite, don't you remember?"

As she spoke, I vaguely remembered visiting Israel as a child, always eating popsicles at gas stations and markets.

Every day, I wore my helmet and sat in my wheelchair. I was never given my cane, and had no incentive to walk around the apartment. Ema would sometimes set up the e-stim and finger stretching, which was easy because it could be done while I was watching TV.

Aba took me for daily lunches, picking me up from the apartment to give me a change of scenery. Out from under Ema's watchful eye, he would tell me to take off my helmet for the drive. He knew I hated being seen with it in public.

My left arm still weighed about fifteen pounds despite all the muscle loss, and it was a dead weight on my left shoulder and chest. Even my teeth were affected as I began to grind them from the effort of holding it up. Ema propped it up on a pillow when I sat stationary by the TV, but any time I was mobile, it became a problem.

Ema was perpetually there, in my apartment kitchen. Cooking, cleaning, organizing, supervising.

One day, Aba picked me up for one of our lunches. As we drove home, I asked, "What was the hardest thing you ever had to do in your life Aba?"

In reality, I said this half in Hebrew, stuttering—the original words are lost to memory. His response is not.

He said, "Your injury, Aba."

What he meant was that it was difficult for him to watch me suffer and to fear for my life. What I heard was that I was the greatest burden he had experienced.

Alex Eskanazi continued staying over, assisting Ema as often as he could. I continued to neglect the left side of my mouth if left to brush my teeth unsupervised. Ema often had me pee in water bottles when we were alone as she could not lift me onto the toilet by herself.

My parents continued calling Vital every day to demand more rehabilitation for me. Finally, Vital proposed that I be evaluated for eligibility again. Vital assessed me, and to my parents' relief, offered to provide me with rehab at one of their facilities the following week.

At this point, the medical care and rehab I had received would have cost us over $100,000 if we had been paying out-of-pocket in the American medical system. Fortunately, we had good Vital insurance. More fortunately, in a twisted way, the near-disaster with my air transport had given my family an unusual kind of leverage. If Vital had not feared a lawsuit, who knows what could have happened.

On October 13, 2018, Ema, Aba, and I attended our first day at Vital's rehab unit. It was a white space surrounded by empty blue mats. The other patients had suffered heart attacks, strokes, and ligament injuries, mainly due to age. I sat in my wheelchair with Ema and Aba behind me as five older patients arrived with their loved ones and caregivers.

It was a completely depressing scene.

We sat in a circle, me the only patient under 65, and the entire experience felt more like a funeral home than anything else. I missed the Valley at Renewal Ranch, a wide, sunny campus full of trees and grass. I missed Rene winking at me and believing in me, and B-Jay's jokes that made me laugh.

"Monda, take his stuff," Aba barked, stepping into the marbled hallway. "My son is 27, not 75. What encouragement can you give him?" Aba demanded of the therapist as Ema rolled me quietly away down the hall.

"Hakol heeye beseder neshama." *'Everything will be okay, my life, my love.'*

At home, my parents called Vital again and dove into another argument. Ema and Aba informed Vital we were going to search for a more 'uplifting' rehab environment, and that Vital should pay for the facility we found, since the elderly rehab group was obviously not appropriate for a 20-something recovering from a severe brain injury. Over the next few days, Ema, Aba, and I drove up and down the boulevard searching for a rehab clinic that could meet my needs.

First, we went to a small facility next to the Encino Hospital. It was run by an Israeli man, Lagad Baosher.

"Shalom koolchem!" 'Hello, all of you!' He said, greeting us.

Lagad introduced us to his facility, making promises to us for my progression. I simply stared around as Aba and Lagad kept discussing costs. I was uncomfortable with the facility, finding its atmosphere oppressive. Ema noticed, and we left.

Later that night, Ema and Aba sat at my kitchen counter and talked.

"Traumatic Brain Services is supposed to be really good," Ema said. "Shamatee al-ze eem od Ema she aya shama be Renewal Ranch," *'I heard about it from another mother there at Renewal Ranch.'*

Aba was on his phone, using the Internet to search for options. "Oolie," *'Maybe,'* he murmured to Ema.

In the end, nothing he found looked more promising than TBS that Ema had heard about. And so, that was where we went for our next rehab "interview."

***

11

Traumatic Brain Services

Total memory recall: 23%
Mental capabilities: 19%
Left leg: 8%
Left arm: 2.5%
Skin state: Indented skull, dislocation sling, and scratches
Assistive items: Wheelchair, cane, & ankle brace
Age: 14
Current weight: 150 lbs
Sources: Mom's journal, Dad, Alex, Myself, Lina, Becca,
Dr. Torando, & Dave

I'll never forget my first drive to TBS. I dozed off and woke to Ema shaking my paralyzed left arm and chirping, "Tareree chamuda!" *'Wake up, cutie!'*

TBS was in a multistory blue-gray building on the boulevard, across from the Office Depot where I'd bought my school supplies from kindergarten through college. Beside the building was a strip mall with medical, vision, and therapy offices, a sandwich shop, a vegan grill, and a sushi bar. The TBS building's automatic doors opened onto a black-and-maroon marbled lobby where the elevators were located.

"5th floor, Danduni," Ema said, stooping to kiss my cheek after pressing the button. Aba stood disgruntled, not optimistic about TBS after our recent experiences. I sat in my chair, leaning to my right in my dreamlike state. The elevator opened to reveal carpeted floors, a glass-fronted check-in desk, and a hallway with rehab patients walking back and forth. The number of people made me nervous, just like my first day at Renewal Ranch.

My parents and I were given a tour. I couldn't focus very well, but was glad to see younger patients like myself talking in the treatment rooms. "You like, Danduni?" Ema asked, leaning down to speak into my ear. We were led by a receptionist, peering into tutoring rooms with learning tools and blackboards. Down the hall was a lunchroom, like a smaller version of Renewal Ranch's cafeteria.

When we came to the exercise and physical therapy room overlooking the boulevard's Office Depot, I perked up. The room was huge, twice the size of Renewal Ranch's physical therapy center. Three trainers were training a slew of patients on the treadmills, some using harnesses suspended from the ceiling to help them stay upright. There was also a wide exercise bed and treadmills, ellipticals, and bicycle machines, all fitted with medical assistive gear. I could even see my favorite childhood restaurant, Tony Roma's, through the windows. I felt at home.

"Wow," I said quietly, taking in all the equipment and the mostly-young patients. This was exactly the kind of gym I needed right now. The only downside was that when I looked around for my beloved dumbbells, there were none.

The operations manager, Ms. Lina, greeted us outside her office. "Hello everyone, welcome to TBS." She smiled at us from behind red-rimmed glasses. "Let's discuss Adam's progress so far and what we can offer him here." Ema and Aba wheeled me into her office. "TBS has occupational therapy offerings for motor skills, as well as physical therapy and cognitive classes," Lina explained.

"We have speech therapy sessions and group activities as well."

I think I was visibly excited at this point. Ema, too, was smiling at Aba, even as he frowned at the prospect of getting Vital to cover the cost.

Lina soon took us through the building again on her own tour. I paid more attention to the patients this time, noting an even mix of teens, 20-somethings, and older patients.

"Adam, what do you enjoy in life?" Lina asked me as we walked. "Uh…gym," I said instantly.

At the end of the day, my parents were given an unbelievable price tag: $975 per day to attend. "Vital will cover this," Aba muttered darkly.

One evening, Aba sat down next to me in a chair at my apartment's dining room table. "Keebalnoo et ha-kesef, Aba." *'We received the money. Papa.'* "Now you can get the real rehab that you need. I'll make sure of it!" he said vehemently.

I nodded, tentatively excited.

Early the next day, Ema took me back to Vital to get my first physical since my accident from my doctor, Dr. Herb Tornado.

Dr. Tornado was a middle-aged man with light brown wavy hair. He had been my doctor since I was 11-years-old and had seen me grow from a 5'4" skinny boy in 9th grade into a 6'2 athlete-bodybuilder-fitness coach. But he hadn't seen me since the accident.

Seeing me in my wheelchair and helmet, he looked away from me and to my mother, visibly shaken. "Hello. Uh, well, good news, Monda. I, uh, have ordered a handicap sticker for your car."

169

I stared at Dr. Tornado from my chair by the corner of the exam bed. I couldn't remember why we were at the doctor's, since I didn't feel more hurt or sick than usual.

"Thank you, doctor," Ema said. "Adamee, tageed-toda." *'Adam, say thank you.'* Ema looked at me.

I turned my head to the right, clutching a cherry lollipop someone had given me in my right hand. "T t t thanku," I stuttered.

October 17, 2018, marked my first day of rehab at TBS. Ema used our newly issued handicapped hanger to park right by the door. Lina greeted us again, wearing a red and blue dress suit. Beside her stood a small woman in green scrubs.

"Hello all, I'm Becca!" The head physical therapist was animated as she introduced herself. Becca was 5'2" with shoulder-length red hair complimenting her green scrubs.

"Hello, Becca!" Ema responded to her enthusiasm. "This is Adam."

"Hello, Adam!" Becca exclaimed, looking at me before Aba could introduce himself. "You ready, captain?"

I didn't enjoy how fake Becca sounded with her wild enthusiasm about the smallest things. But I did enjoy the idea of having a young woman for a therapist.

As Becca rolled me through the facility I became self-conscious, noticing that most patients could walk on their own. Some used canes, but all moved independently, talking and laughing. I looked up, trying and failing to be part of Becca's rapid-fire conversation with my parents.

Soon, we were in the physical therapy room, and Becca was helping me to stand up for the first time since Renewal Ranch. Nearby, two patients were using the ellipticals while another ran on a treadmill with bungee-harness support. A fourth was doing intense core exercises on an exercise mat. I squinted as I looked around from underneath my helmet. My left knee was completely locked, and I looked at the ground as my limbs began to shake. For a moment, I forgot why I was standing up, feeling like the center of attention. Drool dripped from my left lip as I imagined that everyone in the room was watching me.

I then tipped over, almost falling as Becca grabbed me around my waist. "Hold on there, cowboy!" she exclaimed as I breathed heavily, as though I'd been jogging. My body felt so heavy, so unpredictable. I'd forgotten every tip Rene, Maria, Jane had taught me about how to move.

"Hold him, please!" Ema exclaimed, running to help Becca. At that moment, I felt the worst of myself; hurt and helpless. I had been half-dead in Asia and at Renewal Ranch. But not in Encino. Not in my home San Fernando Valley. I don't want to be like this here, where I grew up.

Becca held out her hand to stop Ema from approaching. "I've got him, Momma!"

I was given water and a rest. Then, Becca tied my waist to the ceiling with a harness and a blue-and-black snakelike bungee cord. The harness supported some of my weight, so my legs did not have to hold it all. I stood up crookedly, standing without the help of a handrail or cane for the first time since my accident. I thought of all the times the doctors had told my parents that I would never walk again.

Ema kept her composure this time, watching me closely. My legs started to tremble, and Becca handed me a new single cane without a tripod base. Under their watchful eyes, I began to walk. I felt myself wanting to impress Becca, showing her, my mom, dad, Lina, and

171

even the other patients in the room my capabilities. "O o ok o ok k got i i it," I said quietly, taking a momentous 12-foot walk with Becca's guidance. The process took 18 minutes. "That's it," Becca soothed. "Nice and easy Adam, just stay upright." Her head didn't quite reach my shoulder as she walked beside me.

My knee brace itched as I began to joyfully sweat. I almost fell numerous times, but soon, Becca was asking me to walk faster.

"Don't worry, hun," she assured me. "The harness will catch you if you fall. Let's see what you can do!" More confident now, I made my way through a mini-obstacle course Becca and the other staff had set up for me. Becca stayed beside me. There were small, padded stairs to step up and obstacles to step over. I stared down intensely at my untrusted left foot as I worked through the course.

After watching me perform, Becca recommended an 8-inch mechanical brace for my left leg. It helped, but this was yet another weird-looking contraption hanging off of me, covering 40% of my left leg. And I couldn't put it on by myself. My head started to ache, and I winced. Aba and Ema noticed, stopping my first physical therapy session then and there. Drool spread across my cheek as Becca and Ema both massaged my left knee to re-bend it into my wheelchair.

In my chair again, my confidence faded. I spent the rest of the day being wheeled to classes for behavior, speech, cognitive function, and occupational therapy for my left arm. Once I forgot about "not fitting in" in my wheelchair, I enjoyed being rolled around by Ema in the bright-clean atmosphere of TBS.

As Ema rolled me around, she'd sometimes have to stop to put my left foot back into its ankle-holder, or to

172

perch my left arm back up on the arm rest after it slipped off. Sometimes other patients would pass by, glancing at me curiously. Seeing patients around my age made me feel at ease about recovering. It was like I was back in high school or college again, with even the promise of a normal social life.

Sometimes I dozed off in my chair. "Lee-torer Adami, anachnoo poe." 'Wake-up Adam, we are here,' Ema would say, stroking my cheek.

Group sessions showed that each patient had their own problems. Some moved perfectly, but were suffering mentally. I began to think that those conditions were tougher than my own physical injuries. I witnessed patients screaming, running into walls, and scratching themselves. A nurse, June, handled medications and sometimes had to give emergency doses.

The group classes at TBS were the first time since my injury that I had the opportunity to interact with new people who weren't professional caregivers. This both excited me and made me nervous.

"Okay," the therapist of the day would tell us, "everyone turn to the person to your left and ask them their favorite meals to eat!"

Ema helped me turn my head and my seat. In this way, the group sessions would get us to practice having conversations.

"Hi, I, Adam," I said nervously to a young male patient one day as I was rolled past him in the hall.

Ema noticed and smiled, trying to help the conversation continue. "Adam, ask his name," she urged, like I was an elementary schooler making friends.

But soon, my attention span or my short-term memory gave out, and Ema continued rolling me along when it became clear that the conversation had ended.

The last stop before lunch was the occupational therapy room for left arm and finger movement. Trying to use my left arm continued to be exhausting, as did tolerating the pain from the e-stim. My arm felt so heavy and dead by my side, slowly falling out of the Kinesio-Tape.

My occupational therapy instructor was Dave Isaac, a middle-aged man. "Okay," Dave would say at the beginning of sessions. "Let's begin with some weight-bearing movements."

The first time he said this, I looked at him, not understanding the phrase. "A-bear..?" I asked slowly, thinking of the big, furry, ferocious animal. "Wha...wha... weight... bearing," he smiled as he pronounced the words slowly, allowing me to process every syllable.

"Weight bearing," Dave said as he sat upright in his seat and demonstrated, "is when you stand up, place your left arm and fingers on the table beside you, and press your palm against your surface so that your hand supports your weight." He demonstrated the movements. "This is a reminder to your brain that there's an object in front of you, and your left arm can be used to press against it."

I glanced at my left arm where it hung, dead-looking in its Kinestape.

"Okay, Adam, let's stand up." Dave pulled me out of my wheelchair with Ema's assistance, moving us to the blue mat in the back of the room. He helped me spread my paralyzed fingers on the mat beside me, stretching them.

"See, that wasn't so bad. Now stay upright, bud," Dave said as I looked up at him, nervous to attempt anything with my left arm. "Now, Adam, push your body's weight onto your hand to remind your brain of the limb," Dave guided me as Ema watched, touching my back for reassurance. I continued leaning my body on my left hand. My hand slid off the mat, with no feeling from the shoulder down on that side. I couldn't focus on what Dave wanted done, and had no control over the limb anyway.

"Oops," Dave noticed my hand slide off the mat. "Okay, stay up. I'll push your hand down against the mat to keep it there." I felt nothing as he pressed his hand down on top of mine. "Now, push your body weight into your left hand," he instructed again. I firmly pressed down, Ema grinning at my efforts.

"Good!" Dave exclaimed. "Now hold that for 15 seconds." He looked at the watch on his own left wrist and began counting.

I felt jealous, seeing his left arm move fluidly. I held my breath and sweated with the effort of keeping my weight pressed on my left arm. My ankle brace itched, but I couldn't scratch it.

"We have to do these weight-bearing tasks every day," Dave said, looking down at my shriveled arm. "Try to practice at home over the weekend, okay?"

I stared back at Dave blankly.

"What do you like to do these days, Adam?" Dave asked. "What makes you happy?"

I tried to think of what made me 'happy' in my current state and came up empty. I thought about Kaitlyn. *Where is she?*

"What did you do last weekend, Adam?" Dave prodded, and I realized he was holding a roll of purple Kinesio-Tape. I stared at the tape, forgetting the question.

"I've got to re-tape you," Dave explained, reaching behind me. "But Adam, let me give you an idea. Why don't you create a notebook to write down what you do each day? You can record memories that your brain may not hold, and also work with your writing skills. Call it a journal. It'll help you to collect memories from the present and the past."

That conversation led to the creation of the journal that would become this book. You have my undying gratitude, Dave.

After occupational therapy was lunch. Ema rolled my overwhelmed self to the lunchroom where patients were grabbing food.

"First Danduni, let's wash your hands," Ema rolled me to the corner restroom. She and a handrail on the wall helped me to stand by the sink and let me wash my own hands for the first time since my accident. My left hand flapped, limp, as my right hand washed it.

Ema brought sandwiches for us to eat as we sat on a bench together. She asked how I was feeling. I was silent, letting my mind heal from the exertion. I tried not to stare jealously at the other patients who talked and laughed fluidly, effortlessly.

After lunch, it was time for my cognitive development class. Associate Professor Paul Allan was a middle-aged man with a harsh expression who was relatively new to TBS. To Ema and me he seemed insecure, looking to prove himself to his colleagues. This made him very demanding compared to the other staff.

Although he gave me some interesting topics and assignments, he could be harsh if I did not give the "right" response. "No, that's incorrect Adam. Do it again." He would repeat himself with noticeable frustration. "Again, Adam, if the lady went to the mall with $35, what could she purchase based on the prices we have discussed?"

His intensity gave me headaches that I tried not to reveal.

Mr. Allan was by far the toughest professor I'd had since my accident. He would ask me about my thoughts, relationships, decisions, and my progressing recovery—which might have been nice, but I was afraid to answer in case a "wrong" answer displeased him.

After Dave suggested I start a journal, I made a habit of opening the Notes application on my phone. I labeled a tab "Thoughts." My first sentence, the only one I could come up with the first day I tried to journal, was this:

"I miss me."

As my physical therapy progressed, Becca had me walk with the single cane regularly. Sometimes I would even walk on the treadmill, staring out at the Office Depot of my childhood. Becca's strategy was to have me stand on my legs every day, to continuously remind my body to use both legs when I walked. Each day spent at TBS challenged my core, legs, hip, and brain.

Soon, I started a new kind of therapy. There was a room at the far end of the physical therapy hub, which I could now walk through on my own with the help of a cane. The room was a comfy, enclosed space with a dark blue reclining chair similar to my bedroom's Gadget Universe recliner.

Laura was a young woman with a brown ponytail. She stood up from her own chair to greet Ema and me for my first session.

"Wow, hello there!" she said. "Welcome, Adam."

Laura helped Ema walk me to the recliner beside a wall which, I realized, was covered in white fake fur.

"Okay, Adam, you comfy?" she asked.

"...Uh, yeah," I responded.

"Danduni, ata rotse mayeem?" *'You want water?'* Ema asked, watching me settle in. I shook my head as the lights dimmed, drawing my attention to the three candles that burned on the table in front of Laura's brown chair.

"Okay, Mama, he's fine," Laura said, lighting another candle. "May we please have some privacy?"

Ema was visibly hesitant to leave us alone. She'd trusted the other people she left me with like Nick and Allan, but she didn't know Laura at all.

"Ani heye poe bachootz Adami," *'I'll be outside,'* she said finally, walking out and closing the door behind her.

"Okay, Adam, you athletic-looking man, tell me about yourself!"

Laura settled into her chair. I stared at her, not knowing what to say.

"First things first," she prompted me after a long moment of silence. "Remove that helmet, get comfy, and trust you are secure in that chair!"

I carefully took off the helmet, secure in that action only because Ema had left the room. I wiggled, realizing that the recliner felt secure and happy that Laura was a 'girl.'

I now realize that this was psychotherapy I was receiving, but I have no memory of what Laura and I talked about at that time. Ema was not there to observe and remind me later, and no explicit notes made it into my digital journal.

As time went on, TBS reminded me more and more of Renewal Ranch. This was never more true than when an occupational therapist named Gina shouted at me to move my left hand, trying to motivate me with adrenaline just like 'e-stim Jane.'

"Look at your arm. Think of moving it. Again. Again. Again!" My left arm lay dead and still.

"Careful with his hand!" Ema pleaded.

I continued to try to move the arm, but was defeated each time. Despite my arm, I was experiencing major improvements with walking, talking, and cognitive reasoning. TBS doubled my daily fish oil dosage to encourage my brain to heal. I increased my food intake to three meals a day plus fruit and snacks.

I had now graduated from my wheelchair, able to use my cane to walk short distances around TBS or my Burbank apartment. But the wheelchair still went everywhere with us in Ema's SUV since I couldn't walk much more than 25 steps without needing it. My left knee always locked, forcing me to swing my leg in wide circles, and my arm dangled freely, dragging my shoulder down.

At this point, the surgeons felt I had healed enough to perform my cranioplasty surgery. Manufacturers had been hired to create a skull prosthesis matching the shape of my head and brain based on MRI data, and after the surgery, I would finally be able to discard the hated helmet.

It had been six months since my TBI, and I was still wearing clothes Ema picked out for me and mostly awaiting orders to tell me what to do. I began attending appointments, meeting doctors, surgeons, and scanning technicians for my upcoming surgery. Once the plastic skull implant was inserted under my skin, only the scars from the stitches would show evidence of my head injury.

"No more!" Ema said, trying to get my enthusiasm up. "No more helmet after this!"

As my days at TBS became more routine, I began to immensely miss my independence. I missed the freedom of something as simple as showering alone.

One day while I was in the shower, Ema stepped out to fetch a forgotten towel. I decided this was my chance to stand up amid the warm water splashing on my head and body.

I was 6'2 and missing 15% of my skull when I chose to rise up, helmet-less, in the steamy shower. I used my functional arm to turn the hot water faucet toward my face, taking a deep breath and closing my eyes. I pretended things were normal, that I'd escaped this nightmare. I grabbed the wall handlebar for balance as the warm water poured over my face.

I'm sorry, sorry, please let me come back, I repeated this now-frequent mantra in my head. *I am down. Please, I am trying.*

As I stood, my paralyzed arm began to tremor with the effort. I didn't care. At that moment, I was begging for any kind of refuge from my injury. It felt powerful to stand on my own, controlling the shower head by myself. For a moment, I felt alive and free, like I was living alone with Kaitlyn again.

I breathed in, feeling peace. My knees were beginning to shake, but I stretched my hips and my left leg under the warm water. I felt good. This moment felt good. Free. A needed escape.

Then I heard the door open. I refused to look in that direction, away from the warm running water.

"Adahm!" Ema yelled. "You crazy? Sit down! You have no idea the risk you are taking, with nothing but skin between your brain and floor!" She rushed to the shower and began gently but firmly tugging me back down toward the shower seat.

"Ema hakol beseder y y y y yesh lee et ah...ugh, ah handle la chzeek." *'Mom it's okay I—ugh—have the handle to hold.'*

She continued to lecture me, in tears now, about being responsible and safe with my recovering body.

"Please sit down! Wait until your surgery," Ema pleaded. I understood and sat down, obedient. She fixated herself on reminding me that I couldn't take these kinds of risks with a severe TBI.

That night after the shower, Ema night fiercely dried me, overly attentive and hasty.

"Dubi! ow you a a a are hurting m m me!"

Recognizing my need for freedom, Ema began to leave me to be supervised by my TBS caregivers without her added scrutiny. It was bittersweet to be attending TBS alone. Sweet because I could function independently enough not to need parental help. Bitter because this meant I now needed a TBS associate to help me use the restroom.

TBS had male associates like Dave, Jim, or even Mr. Allan follow me in. Not just to stand outside by the restroom door, but to stand in the restroom with me as I peed! This made me not want to drink water to avoid having to use the restroom, which probably was not good for my health or recovery.

Dave or Jim or Mr. Allan would stand facing the door as I unzipped my pants. My attempts to sneak off to attend the restroom alone were unsuccessful, especially since I would often almost immediately trip over my own feet.

"Adam, don't forget you need someone with you!" my therapists would innocently call, mistaking my sneaking for forgetfulness. This drove my desire to escape from TBS.

Then, it happened.

One night, Ema, Alex Eskanazi, and I were sitting outside a Mexican restaurant, eating grilled chicken tacos under sparkling lights and palm trees. Ema and Alex were speaking quietly to each other in Hebrew in the serene warmth of the night. I was gazing out over the restaurant crowd, my mind quietly humming as it often did while people conversed around me. Nearby, a waiter was holding a tray of margaritas using his left arm. Suddenly, I had the urge to move my left arm and mimic him.

And I did.

For the first time since the accident, I felt my lateral shoulder muscle connect to my elbow. I felt it contract. I raised my left arm to chest height.

Ema dropped her napkin, almost screaming. "AHH! Oh my God, oh my God Adami! It's MOVING! Your arm!" she pointed dramatically, as though I might have failed to notice. I stared at my arm, transfixed.

The urge to move it had arisen from deep within me, spontaneous, yet for some reason, certain. It was as though my brain knew that it was time, that at that exact moment, it had completed healing enough for a trial run.

I moved my skinny arm for about 20 seconds before it fell flat onto the table, exhausted. I then began moving my arm from side to side on the table. I finally looked up to see Alex Eskanazi's eyes wide in disbelief, and Ema crying quietly in her seat.

After the first exhausting feat of movement, I could only raise my arm about three inches for a few seconds at a time. But it had been completely useless for six months before tonight. I felt nervous, like my newly moving arm was on a battery that would soon run out.

Ema was so excited that she whipped out her phone to take a video for Aba, who was traveling in China for work. But by the time her camera was out, my arm was completely drained. I couldn't even get it to twitch.

"I can't believe you moved your hand!" Ema enthused as she dialed Aba for a video call. "I'm so proud of you. I was so worried!" We would later wonder why this huge development occurred randomly during that dinner and not on the exercise bed while Gina hollered at me.

"Yes!" Ema cheered, Aba now on video call on her phone. "Keep moving it, Adami sheli!" *'My Adam.'*

Magically, after a short rest, I was able to do as she asked for 10 to 15 seconds. When my arm started getting tired and feeling over-used, it slowly became immovable from sheer exhaustion.

I felt my newfound mental connection to my arm gradually deplete until my arm became paralyzed again. My crooked smile began to fade, along with my temporary fulfillment and happiness, as I continued trying and failing to move my arm. I became so frustrated at the return of the paralysis that I flung my entire arm from the shoulder, knocking a glass of water off the table. It shattered as it hit my knee on its way down to the floor.

"Uh oh," Ema said, staring at the broken glass scattered around my good foot.

"It's okay, it's okay," she soothed me. "We'll get someone to help clean it up." She bent to pick up the largest bits of broken glass from the floor as Aba laughed from Ema's phone speaker on the video call.

"Ooh keemat shama!" *'He is almost there!'* He bellowed.

Ema continued to clean up the glass, whimpering as she found a sharp piece resting on my ankle. Exhausted, I bent over in my chair to munch on my spicy chicken tacos.

I will never forget being woken up the next day by Ema, extra excited. The first thing she asked me was to move my 'new' left arm as I blinked blearily, still half-asleep.

I tried, but my arm barely twitched half an inch.

"It's okay, baby," Ema soothed me. "Take a breath."

I tried again, and depressingly failed. We later learned that it was not unusual for a damaged nerve connection to be dysfunctional in the mornings right after waking up.

I did my best to appreciate my improvements as the date of my cranioplasty approached. I was becoming nervous at the thought of having surgery. I had never consented to surgery before: all of the surgeries after my accident were conducted while I was in a coma, completely unaware. Now, thinking about being rendered unconscious and having people cut into my head freaked me out.

One day, I asked Aba what I could expect from the surgery process.

He smiled. "Adam, when you are put to sleep, you'll wake up in what feels like the very next moment, not believing the surgery is already over."

***

12

Golf Balls

Total memory recall: 23%
Mental Capabilities: 20%
Left Leg: 10%
Left Arm: 3%
Assistive items: Wheelchair, Cane, TBS foot brace, and
Golf Balls
Age: 13-14
Weight: 151
Sources: Mom's Journal, Dad, Alex, Edwin, Myself

Lina, Becca, and Dave were elated to hear about my arm.

"Yes, yes! Hello, big man. You got it back!" Dave grinned as I limped in with Ema at my side. My parents had told everyone they knew of my progress.

"Hello Monda! Exciting day!" Dave congratulated Ema. "Have a seat. Let's start the day with some weight-bearing exercises."

Unfortunately, the partial recovery of my arm was not entirely positive. Now when I exerted myself, I could feel my left arm violently cramping. On the plus side, I now had some ability to relax the spasming arm at will. On the down side, it hurt.

Following Dave's advice, I had begun carrying a blue journal with me to scribble notes on physical paper, just as I had tracked my fitness progress during my bodybuilding years. Now I tracked everything.

It had become clear that Dave feared my memory might get worse rather than better, and that I may end up unable to remember anything without a written record of my life. My written reminders to myself to text friends or ask questions of my family and therapists had already been helpful.

Written Entry September 10, 2018 @ 1:30pm "I wentv Allan class"

Written Entry September 11, 2018 @ 11:30am "Becca nee raise"

Written Entry September 13, 2018 @ 3:40pm "Fun talkc Lora"

Written Entry September 14, 2018 @ 12:00pm "Nurse rumbring pells"

Sometimes, I would find myself staring at my open journal with no memory of what I had written just seconds before. The written words sat on the page like alien messages. I had no memory of the me that wrote them.

As time passed, my journal filled with notes, scribbles, and the occasional torn-out pages when I became unbearably frustrated with my limitations. On several occasions I misplaced my journal or my pens for days at a time or mislabeled dates, forgetting what month I was in. But through my journal, I ended up with a nearly-continuous, highly detailed record of my time at TBS. This has been one of the primary sources for writing this book.

At first, I needed to sit at a proper desk to write. With only one arm, I couldn't hold the book in my lap and write in it at the same time. Writing on paper felt oddly therapeutic, but when a writing desk was not available, my phone's notes app sufficed for taking digital notes.

On one occasion, Ema pointed out to me a difference between my right and left sides in how I'd been sitting in my wheelchair.

"Wow Adami, teere *(look)*!"

On the right side, the chair was deeply indented from the weight of my right arm and shoulder pressing into it each day. But the left side of the chair was perfectly smooth. My left arm and shoulder had been drooping inward, too weak to press into the chair.

Ema looked worried at this asymmetry.

The time came for my TBS 1-month review. Ema, Aba, Lina, and I filed into a room where group therapy sessions were sometimes held.

"Let's get situated," Lina took a seat around the grand oval table. "Today, we'll review Adam's progress here at TBS so far."

My instructors entered the room one by one, each giving an assessment of my progress and their thoughts about my future treatment. Becca endorsed my enthusiasm for recovery and my progress with the cane and physical exercises.

"I can tell Adam was a dynamic athlete," she proclaimed. "His persistence is unmatched! We just need to refine his motor skills and help him to develop more fluid motions." She winked at me.

Dave was next. He praised my newfound ability to move my left arm.

"It's amazing! After having part of his brain removed, we were unsure if Adam would ever move his arm again. But, Adam, show them how it moves, my man."

I started moving my arm in a humble, partial bicep curl, staring down the table at everyone watching me.

"You see?" Dave exclaimed. "Great work! We'll continue moving the arm, strengthening it with exercises, and seek to refine Adam's control over his fingers."

Lina smiled at Ema and Aba. "We're very proud of your son's progression," she told them. "We definitely need to keep this up."

I continued to move my arm for as long as I could, feeling it slowly 'run out of batteries' before going limp again.

A group therapist instructor named Dan had less glowing reviews of my performance. He reported that I "did well," but lacked attention span and did not put as much effort into my work with them that I did into my physical exercises. That was no surprise: I'd been the same way in school. Movement excited me, but when made to sit still and listen, my mind went blank.

"Now, Adam, how do you feel you are doing at TBS?" Lina asked. All eyes turned to me. Lina, Dan, Aba, and Ema all stared attentively, waiting for my answer. I sat slouching to my left, in my wheelchair at the end of the table.

I wanted to run away from their attention. I knew my speech was not up to scratch, and the anxiety made my left eye hurt and highlighted the itch of my ankle brace. I struggled through brain fog for something to say.

"Think I d d doing, okay," I responded, feeling my throat clog up.

After hearing from Laura, it was Mr. Allan's turn to speak to the group. He arrived late, leaving Lina sitting with us in annoyed silence for several minutes.

When he finally walked in in his usual button-up attire, he surveyed the room and smiled a superior smile. My eye twitched in anxiety.

Mr. Allan took a chair to my left side. "Hello, I am Paul Allan, Adam's speech therapist." He began to speak quickly, using technical terms I didn't understand to explain my speech disability. As he finished his assessment, he predicted that it would take me at least five years to begin to speak normally again—if I ever would.

"Honestly," Mr. Allan finished, "I do not think he will improve much more. He has made little progress in my class, and his brain damage seems severe."

This was the wrong thing to say. Aba already had an unfavorable view of Mr. Allan from hearing Ema and I's commentary on his classes.

Aba got to his feet, huffing majestically. Lina and Ema turned to him with wide eyes, sucking in their breaths.

"Who the fuck are you?" Aba demanded, staring down at Mr. Allan. "Who do you think you are? This is your diagnosis of my son? No wonder he makes no progress with you—you scare him. You have made your opinion of his abilities clear from the start."

Aba almost spat in Mr. Allan's face, leaning forward. "You think you can assume someone's future?" Aba demanded. "This is my son! He woke when doctors said he wouldn't, he is walking despite the surgeon's predictions, so shut your crummy little mouth! We looked you up—you have only been working in this facility for fifteen months. I never want you to speak to my family again!"

Aba looked sharply at Lina. "He is not associating with my son anymore. Adam needs someone else. I'll tear this man apart if he comes near Adam again!"

Mr. Allan sat back, gulping in fear. He walked out of the room without a word as Aba continued cursing him in Hebrew.

189

"Ya sea-nee tarnegol mefager ben-zona, chalela, ben orshdod yeled katan."

Lina sat steepling her fingers nervously as Aba grumpily drank his water. "This meeting is over," he declared then, wiping his mouth. "We got what we wanted. Adam will get his surgery and continue to get better. Tell that asshole speech professor that Adam will be a dynamic leader. It's in his blood."

All I heard was Aba's expectation of me, which I was sure I could not meet.

Dynamic...leader? Aba, I am nothing.

I, who had once justified my existence with massive muscles and social media interviews, now could not even walk across a room or form a coherent sentence.

Ema seemed apologetic as the meeting ended. But from that day on, Professor Allan never talked to me again. If I ever saw him in the hallway and asked how he was doing, he would hastily answer, "Yes, good, thank, you Adam," and hurry away. Years later, I would learn he had been let go by TBS.

For me, the most exciting thing now was to focus on walking. I learned to swing my locked knee more skillfully, transitioning more smoothly between that motion and the easeful movement of my right side. My left knee remained locked, requiring manual help to bend it. But I learned to work with it more efficiently so it inhibited me less.

In the mornings, I would rise out of bed with Ema's help, reaching for the cane that would allow me to walk to the bathroom. I learned my brain would not work as well first thing in the morning, which was normal for brain injury patients.

My recovery depended on neuroplasticity—my brain's ability to rewire its remaining cells to compensate for the tissue and connections that were destroyed. These delicate new circuits could be temperamental, especially when I was exhausted or newly awake.

Each morning the toes of my left foot cracked when they made contact with the floor, loosening up from a night of involuntary muscle contraction. I would groan as my brain attempted to drag me back to bed for more restorative sleep. Sometimes, I would tip over, falling back into bed.

"Oof, Adahm!" Ema would yell, pulling me upright. She prompted me to put weight on my left foot each morning to get me into the habit of using both sides equally.

"Ahh, ugh, tight," I mumbled.

If I exerted myself too hard in the morning, my left arm would spasm and shake. I'd have to stretch it before attempting to walk.

When I stood, I'd tower at 6'2" with my entire body balanced on my right leg. As Ema encouraged me to let my left leg share the burden, she'd have to help me by putting her arms around my waist and pulling my weight over to my left side. This was not a comfortable process, but if I had hopes of re-learning to walk without assistance, I had to continue strengthening my left side. Toward that end, Becca had now banned me from using the wheelchair. I walked with my cane, or I did not get around at all.

I'll never forget the first day Becca put me on the treadmill. She tied my dangling left arm to the heartbeat sensor readout at the front of the treadmill so it would not flop and get in my way.

"Lean forward," she reminded me. "And let's start slow. Your left shoulder is still delicate, and you could pull it out of its socket. Okay. Go!"

I felt a new wave of confidence in my recovery as I stood upright, without a cane or someone's arms around me.

Freedom.

Before she started the machine, I stood atop the platform like an athlete. I took a deep breath and closed my eyes, a wave of fulfillment washing over me.

When the treadmill started to move under me, my locked left leg swung wildly, out of control. I barely managed to rein it in. The process was not what I would call "graceful," but I continued.

Within a few minutes, I leaned to the right. I had already forgotten the existence of my left hand and Becca's warning.

But after a few more weeks of training, I was able to walk 55 feet without stopping. Double what my starting distance was at TBS.

Arm rehab with Dave was less fun. Despite my inability to move my wrist and fingers, I was able to lift my entire arm but then got sidetracked with a leg spasm. For months, I had no movement in my arm, so Dave was excited with my progress. Next, he placed a bucket of golf balls in front of me.

"Please pick up this ball, kind sir."

I tried humor, smirking crookedly as I swiped the golf ball up with my good hand. It may have been the first intentional joke I made since the accident, even if it was to cover for my disability.

"D d dohne."

Dave shook his head, smiling. "If only it was that easy, man. Now, let's work on your left hand."

Dave emphasized precision, guiding me through stretching exercises. Progress was slow, with 45 attempts resulting in three successful movements. If the accident didn't kill me, occupational therapy would!

"I know it's tough, Adam," Dave sympathized. "But it will get better. I have faith in you, young man."

I stared at Dave, hungry now as lunch time approached. I was also cold.

"D d dave, can help, cold," I pointed at the sweater I'd brought with me.

"Sure," He replied. "Let me show you how to put on your sweater yourself!"

Surprised, I followed his instructions. I first needed to raise my left arm and stick it into the sweater's sleeve while holding the sweater with my right arm. With that done, I could use my right arm to pull the sleeve tight over my left arm and finally reach behind me and slither the right arm into the remaining sleeve.

This operation took me about fifteen minutes and eight tries to complete successfully. Exhausted, hungry, and dazed, I asked Dave to put the sweater on for me. If I put my left arm into the left sleeve at the wrong angle, it would become snagged and it would be impossible for my right arm to pull the left sleeve all the way on.

"Please help, Dave... Argh t t t tough," I'd request, wrestling with the sweater. He would take the sweater back off my left arm and we'd start again.

I found that as long as I remembered to put my left arm into the sweater first—no easy task given my short-term memory issues and lack of awareness that my left side existed—I could gain enough control using my "good" side to wrestle my sweater onto both arms.

When I finally got the sweater on, Dave cheerfully zipped it up for me and sent me to lunch. By now, I couldn't move my left arm at all, having exhausted it to the point of uselessness. I used my right arm to maneuver as I ate a tuna sandwich, while my left arm lay limp and my left leg jutted out under the lunch table.

Days at TBS meant treadmills, picking up golf balls, and Kinesio-Tape.

I'd often recite a positive affirmation I'd been working on since my injury. *Yes, you are severely hurt, yes a broken skull, yes, a brain injury. But you woke up, you are walking, talking, and moving forward.*

There were days when I repeated this affirmation in my mind nearly constantly

The toughest "homework" I was given by any of my therapists was Dave's assignment to do weight-bearing exercises on my left hand while I brushed my teeth.

"Rega rega, mami," Ema would peel back my fingers, stretching them. "Okay, Adami, press your hand into the counter."

The problem was, I only had enough concentration to press my hand into the counter *or* brush my teeth. If I focused on doing one, I'd forget to do the other. But in time, I got the hang of it.

I fantasized about going back to my old gym, but knew I wasn't invincible. I now knew I never had been.

The gym was always my refuge. It was the place I felt most powerful and alive. Exercising at TBS without an escort gave me a small taste of freedom. Maybe, just maybe, I could go back to the gym soon.

I began to imagine what that might look like. The logistics involved in maneuvering my partially paralyzed body onto the familiar pieces of equipment alone were formidable.

When I asked, Ema contacted the gym to resume my membership. But she was terrified that I would hurt myself if left alone with all the heavy equipment, and she insisted on accompanying me for my first visit.

13

Return to the Gym

Total memory recall: 25%
Mental Capabilities: 20%
Left Leg: 10%
Left Arm: 3%
Assistive items: Wheelchair, Cane, & TBS foot brace
Age: 13-14
Weight: 152
Sources: Mom's Journal, Dad, Alex, Edwin, Myself

Ema parked in the very front handicapped space of the underground parking garage.

"Okay, mami, ata moo-chan leze?" *'Okay, dear, are you ready for this?'* She asked. glanced at my left arm as though speaking to it directly. She then reached out to touch it, now speaking in Hebrew. "You woke up—now let's see what you can do eem Adami!"

I tried to hurry out of the car, not wanting to be seen using the handicapped sticker at my old gym. I limped the 25 steps to the parking structure elevator, my left leg swinging out in wide circles. Still, I smiled a crooked smile as I thought of returning. I still weighed 40 pounds less than the last time I'd checked in here, but now I was at least walking again.

I attempted to outpace Ema with my cane, wanting to walk through the glass door by myself. My trapezius muscles clenched painfully behind my neck as I hurried, and my left shoulder began to sag inward in my haste.

I tried to open the glass doors on my own when I reached them, but I was already sweating from hurrying across the parking lot. I drastically underestimated the weight of the doors, and instead of opening them, I went sprawling on the pavement, with my cane and helmet clattering as they hit the concrete.

Ema ran to my side. "Adam! Adam! Ata beseder? *(Are you okay?)* How's your head?"

My cheeks burned with shame as I said, "I okay Ema, step, no p p problem." I brushed myself off, trying to act casual. It took Ema and me a solid 10 minutes to heave my body up from the floor.

Ema helped me dust myself off and straighten my carefully selected gym shirt. "You know," she said softly, "I know you want it all back. But remember, you had one heck of an injury, Adahm. And it has been less than a year. Like the hospitals said mami, patience please. Ata *(you are)* fragile."

Ema then opened the door so I could cane my way into the reception area.

Returning to the gym after a 6-month absence was unlike any feeling I'd known. The smell, the treadmills, the pop music filling the room felt like a dream. This place was at once profoundly familiar and totally alien.

In the past, I'd had friends, video editors, clients, and thousands of followers and fans to whom I broadcast my gym accomplishments daily. I had built an entire app around the premise of doing that. I had once squatted and benched 325 pounds, heaving my 195-pound body 10 inches above the pull-up bar for clap-ups.

Now, I could barely cane the eight steps from the lobby doors to the reception desk. Ema followed, watching me like a hawk, while the receptionist eyed my helmet and cane dubiously.

I tried to check in using the gym's fingerprint reader while Ema dived in front of me and explained the situation to the young man behind the front desk.

"I must watch over him for safety," she explained anxiously, trying to get us both in with just one gym membership. Meanwhile, I tried to punch my phone number into the membership keypad, but kept forgetting what it was.

"Uh Ema, uh, w w whats my number?"

"You see?" Ema glanced from me to the receptionist earnestly. "Please, my son is disabled. Can I please just follow him for safety?"

I cringed at her words as the front desk receptionist stared at me gloomily. I stood staring doubtfully at the automated check-in pad with my cane, helmet, taped-up arm, and drool dripping from the left side of my mouth. From the gym beyond, whoops of victory, sounds of clanking equipment, and upbeat pop music echoed, haunting and enticing me.

Unsurprisingly, the receptionist agreed to let Ema accompany me rather than sending me in alone.

Wow, I'm back here! I did it! I almost shouted in my head. Once, the doctors believed I would not live to see the United States again.

As I walked the gym floor, my old sense of dominance returned. I began to feel invincible again. Until I looked up and saw people walking with ease on the stairmaster, bending both their knees and ankles effortlessly. Jealousy burned within me.

"Do you need help with him?" a receptionist asked, following us through the gym entrance and peering at me anxiously. I stared, overwhelmed, at the sight of someone jogging on a treadmill with beautiful fluidity. I then hunched over and discreetly caned my way to a back corner of the gym, where the dumbbells were.

I remembered striding confidently, perhaps arrogantly, through this gym with my tight tank top hugging my bulging muscles. I remembered the looks of admiration and jealousy I had gotten.

Now I was on the other side of that equation, and I had no idea what to do. What exercises could I even perform with my current abilities? I imagined other gym members staring at me again, this time in a negative way as I hobbled toward the weight room, my left arm dangling limp at my side under my helmet. I wondered if anyone would even think I could be the same man as that star bodybuilder.

"Do you want to do cardio on bicycles, Adahmi?" Ema suggested, catching up to me. I could not imagine how that would work with my locked knee and limp ankle.

Around me, familiar pop music continued to play and the rhythmic sound of machinery filled the air. But the familiar sounds were dominated, in my mind, by the *clink, clink, clink* my cane made on the gym floor as I walked. My head began to pound.

Finally, I reached the dumbbell rack that held the small pink "grandma weights," as I had once thought of them. Frustration surged within me as I realized these were likely the only weights I could safely use.

"I'll get the weights, Ema," I said, determined to at least get the grandma weights for myself.

I limped over to the dumbbells, my knee brace concealed beneath my baggy gym pants. Dropping my cane an inch from the rack, I bent over and curled my right hand around a 25-pound dumbbell for my warmup. I was able to lift it just two inches off the rack, tottering on my right leg before realizing this had been a mistake. I needed something lighter. Praying no one had noticed my failure, I reached for the 15-pound weights next to the 25s instead.

My traps clenched behind my neck as I picked up the 15-pounders, realizing belatedly that I wasn't engaging my core properly to perform this minor lift. But after a moment, I was able to begin curling the single 15-pound dumbbell with my right arm, my first return to a gym exercise routine in nearly six months.

I ignored my negative thoughts and let a dreamlike bliss state overtake me, imagining I was back in my old life. But as I stood curling the 15-pound dumbbell with my right arm, my left arm began to cramp and spasm at my side. Then it shot out as my elbow locked just like my left knee, forcing the limb straight. I immediately stopped curling, feeling embarrassed in my hidden dumbbell corner.

"Y y you f f freaking kidding now," I quietly stuttered to myself, angry at my own body. I gently re-racked the desolate dumbbell and asked Ema, "Can you bring this shama *(there)*... small corner?" I picked up my cane and used it to limp to an even more hidden crevice in the back of the gym.

Ema did as I asked, bringing the small dumbbell to me in the secluded corner. I almost fell over as I took it in my arm again, briefly forgetting to exert force on my left leg to keep myself upright. Once I righted myself, I began my right bicep curls again, my left arm still sticking awkwardly straight out.

I counted 20 bicep curl repetitions while Ema cheerfully looked on. I felt a small but honorable rush of adrenaline through my invigorated bicep as I stared at myself in the gym mirror. Ema nodded in approval.

"Great work, Adami! Now what about 'ha sahd-yameena *(your left side)*?" My crooked smile disappeared as I stared at my impossibly locked left arm, realizing the hopelessness of performing bicep curls with it.

Still, I wondered if I'd be able to get the fingers to close around a dumbbell handle like one of Dave's golf balls. I felt the entire right side of my body pulse with warmth, coiling into a training stance in remembrance of my bodybuilding days. But my left side was numb and unresponsive.

I lifted a weight with my right arm and set it down near my left hand hopefully. Then I looked up and around, as though waiting for Ema or Becca to help me. But no, I shook myself out of it. I wanted to do this by myself.

I used my right hand to open the fingers of my left hand. They twitched weakly, curled tight. I spent five minutes trying to open the fingers without outside assistance. Nothing worked.

In frustration, I grabbed the dumbbell again with my right hand and used my right hand to shove the weight between the fingers of my left. Getting those fingers to clench tighter was at least something I could do. I tried to lift the 15-pound weight with my left arm. And tried. And tried. I couldn't do it.

Finally, I stared at Ema in complete awe at my lack of ability. "Know your limits, Adam," Ema said gently, having watched this whole struggle. I looked around now to see if anyone else was watching. Fortunately, they weren't.

In resignation, I let the dumbbell fall from my left hand and reached for my cane where it leaned against the dumbbell rack. I began to limp away from the weights, heading for some of the other machines.

"Try lighter weights, baby," Ema called after me, rising to follow. I ignored her and limped toward a chest press machine near the middle of the gym.

I now had an audience, having caned my way into the middle of 20 or so fellow gym-goers in my frustration. I was too frustrated to care what people thought at this point, so I approached the chest press machine, figuring I could do this with one good arm.

"Amigo? Adam...? Mohnsta man...?" I then heard a familiar voice and felt a tap on my right shoulder. Slowly turning on my right foot as my left leg quaked beneath me, I stared into the right eye of a bearded, 5'6" man who was staring at me in concerned confusion.

"Ahhdam, todas bien amigo?" 'All is good, friend?' My gym buddy Edwin asked. I stared back, having no idea what to do or say. I almost fainted from embarrassment.

Ema quickly intervened, shepherding Edwin to a more private area for a talk. "He is doing well, getting stronger every day," Ema said to Edwin in a low voice as they huddled together. But her voice was not too low for me to hear, and it struck me that they were speaking about me in third person as though I wasn't there.

"Okay," Edwin nodded in understanding. "Por favor keep me updated, This is crazy to see..." Edwin waved to me as he picked up his bag and left the gym. I wondered if he left because of me, or if he'd already been on his way out when he saw me.

I took a deep breath and resumed my attempt at using the chest press. I had once been able to lift the entire 200-pound weight stack that came loaded on a standard chest press machine. Now, I approached the empty machine and slid myself into the seat with Ema's help, still clutching my cane with my good arm.

"Put here?" I asked Ema, setting the cane beside the machine. Ema grabbed the cane for safekeeping instead, not trusting my decision-making capacity at this moment.

In retaliation for Ema ignoring my judgment, I decided to take my helmet off as long as I was firmly positioned on the chest press seat. I then leaned down and moved the weight pin, lowering the weight to 40 pounds (and praying that no one was watching me make this change).

To my delight, I was able to complete the chest press 40 times using my right arm. But when I switched to my left arm, I couldn't move the 40 pounds a single inch. My left leg with its locked knee flailed beneath me as I tried.

Before I could stop her, Ema noticed and moved the pin again, lowering the weight to just 10 pounds. I pretended I didn't see her action and continued to struggle with the machine as Ema tried to bend my left knee and tuck my leg in properly.

"This something, c c can't believe, this…with, g g grandma weights," I stuttered, unable to comprehend this new reality.

"Let's go," Ema suggested. "This is too much."

I smiled an unhinged, crooked grin of determination. "Guess cardio, if anything," I countered. Ema smiled at my determination and handed me my cane, but I tossed it back.

"No, if doing no weights and cardio, b better least try, walk, to machine, normal."

Hearing this, Ema picked up my helmet and began trying to place it back on my head. I first dodged, frustrated. But the look in Ema's eyes stopped me.

"Please be smart, Adam," she almost whispered. "It's not worth it. Not until after your surgery." Her eyes lingered on the indent in my head where my skull should have been.

Defeated, I let her strap the helmet on me, accepted the cane in my right hand, and headed for the cardio area.

As I walked, I passed the stairwell leading down to the gym's bottom floor, which had been the site of so many of my life milestones. Meeting the gym's most exquisitely beautiful girl, Kaylee. Nick taping me for my followers to see. The same soundtrack from those not-too-distant days still blared from the speakers by the stairs.

I wonder if I'll ever be able to go down there again.

"Try the bicycles," Ema called out, walking a few steps behind me.

"Nope, can't do that or the elliptical."

I thought with dread of how we would tuck my left knee and ankle into the stirrups of a bike, how I could even begin to bend those joints normally. But when I saw the lower-seated bicycles, I reconsidered. Perhaps the stirrups on these would be enough to hold my left foot in place, and perhaps the motion of my right leg on the fixed gear would force my left knee to bend.

I tried sliding into one of the seats, still holding my cane. I overestimated my motor control and fell the last four inches into the seat, hitting with a thud.

"You really need to take that risk?" Ema asked, shaking her head. "Have you not already been through enough?" She leaned down and grabbed my cane as I stared down at my hyperextended left foot and knew I would need her help to get it into the stirrup.

"Can't bend leg," I admitted finally. "Put it in shoe case-holder?"

Ema leaned over and did as I asked. "What will you do?" she asked. "Ask a stranger in the future if you come here by yourself?" This was how she'd gotten help getting

203

me in and out of my wheelchair in parking lots for months.

"Maybe," I said, trying to shove my left toes into the foot holsters. I then easily got my right foot inside the other brace, reminding myself of my old capabilities.

"Good. Let's do some cardio," I announced, and started to pedal. I kept a smooth rhythm going for about a minute as I looked around the gym, feeling almost normal. My left arm lay lifeless across my lap as I watched other gym members walk past, talking and laughing with friends, and using the dreaded ellipticals.

I closed my eyes and breathed in, trying to find acceptance. My right foot moved perfectly, but my left foot was all over the place. My right leg ended up doing all the work as my left foot swung around, along for the ride. I began discreetly massaging my stiff left arm with my good right arm.

After around 6 minutes, according to the bike's timer, I began to get tired.

"Let's go," I rasped to Ema, closing my eyes in embarrassment as I remembered that I'd brought my mom to the gym. "Done now."

"Okay," Ema agreed cheerfully. "Bo kneelech." *'Let's go.'*

We got up slowly, taking a full six minutes to disentangle me from the bicycle machine, gather my cane, and get me upright.

Walking out of the gym, I realized something. "I was on my right leg the whole time," I murmured to myself. "Becca would yell."

We retraced the 20 steps to the elevator and soon stepped into it together.

"You did good for your first trip back, Adahmi," Ema said approvingly. "Rotse mayeem?" *'Want water?'* She grabbed a bottle from her purse and offered it to me. I rejected it as my left arm twitched numbly at my side and my right arm pulsated with every tiny bump of the elevator.

Couldn't even wear my headphones, I thought to myself, plunging back into the negative feelings. I had always worn my DrumClub Airbuds to work out, but now who knew how badly music in my ear might distract me from the conscious effort required to avoid falling over?

As we left the shopping center, I gazed at the Cheesecake Factory where I'd worked in high school. My whole world was falling apart. My gym had once been my escape from life, but it could no longer be. My damaged eye twitched as I leaned on my right leg. Suddenly, I wanted to scream, yell, rip, bang, tear, run, and jump to get away from my current world.

But I couldn't.

After stuffing me into the car, Ema asked me to turn my left leg inward so she could place her purse next to my left foot. I did as she asked, still frustrated.

"You see," Ema pronounced as I moved my left leg on my own. "Look at your progress, Danduni! Ata ayeetah *(you were)* paralyzed in the hospital just a few months ago!"

"Still t-terrible," I quietly said to myself, remembering what I could do before.

As we rode the elevator back up to my Burbank apartment, I stared at the elevator buttons, resisting the urge to mash them all in frustration. I went straight to my recliner and slept for two hours.

To this day, I believe that was not because of a need to recover, but because of a need to escape. Part of me didn't want to ever wake up.

When I awoke, Ema brought me chamomile tea and began to cut my toenails. My mind was blank, loosely contemplating my failed reunion with my beloved gym. For the millionth time, I felt embarrassed about my injury—mostly because I knew it was my fault. The brain fog at least allowed me to forget about life. I forgot so thoroughly that I let the mug of hot tea slide from my hands, not noticing as the scalding water spilled across my numb left arm.

"ADAM!" Ema shrieked when she stood up from trimming my toenails. "Teere!" *'Look!'* She ran for the first aid supplies. "Ay, lo ergashta etze mami!?" *'You didn't feel it!?'*

I stared at my red skin as Ema arrived to clean up. "I'll bet if that was a protein shake you would not have let this happen!" she quipped.

"I'm sorry, metooka *(sweetheart),*" she said soothingly to my left arm, "Adam didn't mean to hurt you."

I asked Ema for my cell phone, which I had not looked at in days. I wanted to honor my first gym visit with a reward. I went to the Wally Maddison website.

Before the accident, I had worn Wally Maddison pants to the gym, to work, and even out to dinner. My favorite feature was the 4-inch zipper pocket on the right side, the perfect size for my car keys with an elegant metal-edged waist-tie. Wally Maddison pants were pricey, at nearly $80 each. Before my success in my training business, I had only bought a pair when I really needed a new one. Right now, I didn't know what I had in my bank account, or in my closet, and I had no real sense of how money or numbers worked. I swiped with my thumbs and ended up purchasing $400 worth of medium-sized Wally Maddison pants—a size down from my old large—using the credit card saved in my phone's browser.

"Thank you for your order, Adam!" A satisfying message on my phone screen read.

The next morning, after my usual morning stretches, Ema proposed that I try to put on one of my own socks. I optimistically took one of the sports socks she offered me in my right hand and began trying to pull it over my right foot.

This proved more complicated than I'd expected. Even with normal range of motion on my right side, it was almost impossible to get the sock to roll over the foot without using my left hand. My short attention span didn't help: I spent so long trying to get the sock on that I forgot what I was doing and looked at Ema, clueless about why I'd been bent over like that.

Ema smiled. "It's okay, baby. Ksat ve ksat." *'Little by little.'*

Ema helped me use my cane to the bathroom and complete my left hand exercises while brushing my teeth. She opened the toilet lid for me to pee, since bending over to do so was a challenging task with just one good leg. I sometimes thought that lifting toilet seat lids could be a rehab task, as it required so much focus on balancing on both feet while bending over. But I kept this thought to myself, not relishing the thought of it being added to my TBS routine.

When we arrived at TBS that morning, Ema accompanied me inside for the first time in weeks. I was surprised to see Becca and Dave waiting for us together. They normally taught separate classes, and this signaled a major change of routine for the day.

"Morning, Adam!" Dave said cheerfully. "Your mother told us you had your first gym workout yesterday! How did it go, monster man? Felt good?"

I stared at him and Becca, wobbling on my good right leg. "Big fun." I wondered if they could detect my sarcasm through my speech difficulties.

"Adam, I'm here today to work with you and Dave." Becca looked at me through her sparkly glasses as other patients filed past us. "I'd like you to lay across this bed while Dave assesses your wrist. I want you to bench press this bar."

The 'bar,' she held was a green, plastic baton weighing just 1.5 pounds. I didn't know what to think, say, or feel. I remembered once drawing gasps by bench-pressing significant fractions of a ton.

But recovery had to start somewhere. Ema helped me lay my helmeted head on the bed. "Danduni, let's see those chest muscles," she encouraged me.

Becca held the bar over my face. "Okay, Adam, grab it please."

I immediately snatched it fluidly with my right arm.

"Great! Now the left, please."

Damn.

It was 9 AM—still a bad time for my injured brain. The prospect that I might fail felt like adding injury to the insult of TBS trying to mimic my old beloved gym routine with a 1.5-pound plastic baton.

As I struggled, Becca grabbed my left arm and pulled it up to meet the bar, wrapping my frozen fingers around it. "Okay, set!" she declared. "Let's press, bodybuilder man."

My eye twitched at the use of the term "bodybuilder" as I tried to bench press the 1.5 lb green baton. My left arm began to tremble, first a little, then violently until I was afraid the baton would fly out of my left hand.

"Okay, Adam, breathe, and try again," Becca encouraged. I tried again. The same thing happened. I gave up.

"Keep that wrist locked straight," Dave suggested. "Focus on your left side and push through your elbow instead of your hand."

I tried again. My left arm began to shake violently again.

"Okay that's it, Adam. Get some water, please." Becca grabbed the baton from me like it was a crayon. My ego hit a new low as I stared, watching her gracefully dangle it from her left hand as I stood up. This frustration was killing me.

I remained quiet as Dave, Becca, and Ema congratulated me on my efforts. Sweat formed on my brow as I suppressed my rage. Later, Ema and Becca left me with Dave.

"Okay bud, let's work on your grip strength." He handed me a black metal "finger resistance machine" like the world's tiniest bench press, and wrapped the fingers of my left hand around it. "Sit up," he instructed me, "and squeeze as tight as you can."

I remember squeezing the metal ornament grudgingly, staring into Dave's right eye as he motivated me.

"Yes, yes! Squeeze, Adam, and your strength will return!"

That word, 'return,' pushed my efforts to their highest level. I squealed as I squeezed harder.

After about 20 minutes, Dave had us return to the dreaded golf ball pickups. My upper neck, strained from the past two days, refused to allow any muscle isolation or fine motor control for my arm, wrist, or fingers.

By the time I finished my first "class" of the day at TBS, I already wanted to sleep. Fortunately, I had psychotherapy next; Laura was amenable to the idea of me lying on her reclining couch and closing my eyes to rest.

At lunch, I felt chilly. My left arm had begun to spasm involuntarily when I got cold, so it was important that I fix this.

I wanted to zip up my sweater for warmth, but didn't want to ask for help with it after the disastrous morning workout attempt. Instead, I sneaked toward the restroom. I somehow managed to avoid being noticed, despite caning my way over with my left leg flailing out to the side. Once successfully locked in the restroom alone, I resolved to figure out how to zip up my hoodie myself.

I carefully put the sweater on, navigating my left hand into the left sleeve before pulling everything to my right. Once I triumphantly pushed each hand through its sleeve, I used my right hand to lift up my trembling left hand. I managed to make my left fingers pinch the two sides of the zipper tracks together while using my right hand for the more demanding task of pulling the zipper up the length of the sweater.

This was all staggeringly complicated. I began to breathe heavily, sweating again. I wanted, needed, to make this happen after the failures of the last two days.

Victory! I was able to pull the zipper up under my chin.

Outside the bathroom doors, I could hear therapists urging patients to hurry up and finish their restroom breaks before lunch ended. I realized the sweater struggle had taken a full 30 minutes. Still, swollen with success, I closed my eyes while I peed, confident that I could aim for the toilet based on body awareness alone.

I missed. But no matter! I had just put an article of clothing on by myself and zipped it up for the first time in almost a year. I imagine I caned out of that bathroom with the biggest smirk on my face.

Ema greeted me in the emptying cafeteria. "Hi, Danduni! Surprise! Let's go out for lunch!" Then she realized the direction I'd come from and noticed the lack of TBS staff following close behind me. "Shh, Lo meshoo sareech lavo eetcha la betshemoosh?" '...Doesn't someone have to come with you to the bathroom?'

I didn't say a word; just waited hopefully to see if she would notice my zipped-up sweater.

Later, as I waited for Ema to come check me out of TBS for the evening, I stared down at my phone. For the first time since the accident, I checked my Instagram page.

I still had 74,600 followers. I sat, slouching with my cane beside me, and scrolled through posts chronicling my own past achievements.

I began to delete everything. Not archiving, but that unthinkable word: deleting, forever erasing 70% of my Instagram content. I deleted videos of myself bench pressing 325 pounds, slow-motion videos of my 'clap-ups', FitFlow marketing videos, and more. It felt like I was cleansing myself of a past I could never return to.

The next day, Aba had a new proposal for me. In the course of his research, he'd come across a treatment called HBOT: Hyperbaric Oxygen Therapy. I had no idea what HBOT was—I usually couldn't remember the time or day, let alone information about new therapies—but Aba was adamant that this would help me recover. Ema seemed less certain.

After TBS that day, my parents took me to visit a local "O2 facility." Ema held my numb left hand as we walked in. Limping into the lobby of the "oxygen store," I admired an interesting, expensive-looking statue, and we were greeted by a smiling receptionist.

"Hello everyone, welcome! I'm Chase. Adam, I heard about your story. You feeling alright?"

I stared at him, irritated at being dragged to a new facility after a full five-hour day at TBS. If I had to go somewhere for extra recovery work, I'd rather be at the gym. My parents and Chase talked about the package deals and the time commitment involved in HBOT therapy while I stood uncomfortably, my tight leg brace and left arm tape pinching me.

The "HBOT chambers" were tubes where a person would lie down while pressurized oxygen was added, which was supposed to give more oxygen to tissues that were struggling to heal from injury. For a brain injury patient, according to Chase, this should help the brain to recover faster.

"This place is like a Dragon-Ball Z sanctuary, Adam," Chase proclaimed. "You go into one of these," Chase pointed to the submarine-like metal tubes, "and just relax and breathe." He breathed in with his hand on his chest, demonstrating. "But we'll have to take away any devices that could cause a spark. That means no car keys, no nothing."

I gazed out the store window and at the park across the street, staring longingly at the green grass and basketball court. It was the same park where a 10-year-old "Dancing Adam" had once performed Ricky Martin at the summer camp talent show.

"While sitting in the tube," Chase continued, "your ears may feel plugged as the pressure is raised. It's like

212

being on an airplane as the pressure drops. Swallowing, chewing gum, or squeezing your nose while holding your breath will equalize the pressure and make your ears 'pop.' The pressure in the chamber will reach 2.5 times normal air pressure..."

I tuned him out, absorbed in the basketball players across the street.

"Hyperbaric oxygen chambers force more oxygen than normal into your blood vessels, which is known to promote healing in damaged tissues." Chase walked us around the empty blue tubes. "The air we're breathing right now contains only 21% oxygen. HBOT has been used by professional athletes for decades to treat concussion—"

Aba jumped in. "Adam's brain injury is very severe. Can your treatment help someone like that? Half his skull is missing, and—"

"Don't say that in front of him!" Ema hissed in a loud whisper.

Chase smiled and focused on me. "This type of oxygen being pumped through your lungs will be a good thing, Adam."

I was lost in memories of Camp Encino. Campers lined up on those basketball courts each morning, singing.

"Little Sally Walker, walkin' down the street. Didn't know what to do so she stopped in front of me..."

I remembered our joyfully confident little boy voices. I leaned on my cane and wondered if I would ever be able to use both my hands and both my legs on the basketball court again.

I breathed in, closing my eyes. I needed to sit down, having stood for far longer than usual listening to Chase's long-winded introduction.

"Ema, s seat?"

"Ken neshama-sheli, shama," *'Yes my soul, right-there,'* Ema said quickly, indicating a nearby maroon-colored couch.

I hurried over, my locked left knee swinging out as usual. The couch was lower to the floor than those I was used to at TBS or my apartment, and I fell the last several inches as my motor control gave out. I got comfortable and tried lifting my left arm onto the armrest with my right hand to look like I was lounging comfortably.

See, Ema? Sitting normally. No need for rehab anymore!

Chase kept talking. "When an HBOT session is complete, you may feel lightheaded. Mild side effects include claustrophobia, fatigue, and headaches."

Ema glanced around nervously. "He already has a lot of headaches, and gets fatigued easily…"

But Aba was determined. "He'll be just fine. This will help. We'll take your 30-session package, please."

"Great!" Chase said brightly. "We'll have Adam start tomorrow after his TBS sessions. We'll reserve tube 1 for him." Chase was clearly thrilled at the sale as Aba signed the contract paperwork.

I watched in increasing frustration. I was like a child, carried from place to place and told what to do. A few months ago, that had been fine—my brain had been too busy healing to take any initiative. Now I was walking, talking, and bored.

"I'm going to go in with him," Ema decided, examining the long metal tube as Aba turned and walked out. "He shouldn't be in there alone."

"Okay, no problem," Chase agreed. "But it will be a little tight for both of you to squeeze in there. There's only one oxygen mask, which Adam will need to use to get the benefits of the treatment."

Ema nodded. "That's okay. I need to make sure his head stays safe."

Chase turned to me, smiling brightly. "You hear that, partner? Your parents will do anything to help their son! It's an honor to witness your amazing folks."

I simply nodded, trying to follow Aba out without being overly rude to Chase. I wanted to be done with this place.

At the end of the day, I felt very glad to be back in my recliner. The Wally Maddison pants had arrived, and Ema brought me the light grey bag from the mail.

"Adam! Ma kaneeta?" 'What did you buy?'

I had no memory of ordering the pants. "What Maddison?"

Ema inspected the bag, grinning. She opened it with a pair of kitchen scissors. The sight of the pants jogged my memory of the order.

"For gym, Ema," I told her, smiling crookedly.

I was determined to go back.

***

14

Hyperbaric Oxygen, TMS, & Cranioplasty Surgery

Total memory recall: 25%
Mental capabilities: 22%
Left leg: 15%
Left arm: 7%
Skin state: Indented skull & scratches
Assistive items: Wheelchair, Cane, & TBS foot-brace
Age: 14
Weight: 154
Sources: Mom's journal, Dad, Alex, Myself

October 4, 2018 - first day of HBOT
Ema opened the heavy glass door for me, and I limped obediently into the hyperbaric oxygen facility, my locked left leg swinging outward with each step. We were greeted today by a new front desk assistant, a woman.

"Hello," she greeted us. "Adam, right? Come on in!"

As we walked into the chilly room, I saw that one of the oxygen chambers was already occupied. I wondered what problem that customer was trying to fix.

Sssss. The sound the tubes made was not comforting.

"There he is, big and strong," Chase was waiting for us. "You ready, brudda-man?"

So this is my life now. I thought longingly of last week's visit to the gym. I would so much rather be there.

Chase opened the door of the blue oxygen chamber. "Adam, you'll be inside for an hour, so use the restroom first." He pointed to the back of the store. "We won't be able to open the door during the treatment without disrupting the pressure."

I started toward the restroom, and Ema quickly rose to follow me. "I'm okay, Ema," I said quietly, irritated by her worry. She hesitated, then let me walk on without her.

Finding the restroom in a new place by myself was another milestone of independence. I even managed to lift the toilet seat on my own. During this process, I discovered I couldn't urinate while also attempting to move my left arm. This apparently was too much multitasking for my injured brain.

After finishing the complicated operation of washing my hands, I stared down at how my Wally Maddison pants fit my legs. They lay perfectly, making me feel good about my appearance. I wanted to show them off. I wanted to train those muscles. But the car key pocket of the pants was empty.

Will I ever have my own car keys again?

"You took a long time, bud," Chase said, peering at me when I emerged, secretly thrilled to have used the restroom on my own.

Ema was ready and waiting to climb inside the oxygen tube. "I am going inside," she said to me. "You give your cane to Chase, ve teeshev-ala, ye *(have a seat, and)* pull you beefneem *(inside)*. Get in with your helmet on."

Getting both of us into the tube proved to be a challenge. I ended up wedged half-in, half-out of the tube, my feet unable to fit.

"Okay, I have an idea," Chase said. He found a handle with suction cups on both ends.

217

"Attach this to the wall," he told me, "and use it to pull yourself up."

I nodded, swelling with pride as I managed to close the fingers of my left hand around the black bar. But I had to use my right hand to push it above my head and press it to the inside of the tube until I felt it suction on.

"Rega mami *(slow down dear)*, easy," Ema tried to scoot out of my way.

"Good, there you go..." Chase seemed relieved as I pulled on the handle, inching my feet further into the tube.

The suction bar came away from the wall with a sharp pop, dropping me abruptly. My helmeted head hit the tube's metal wall with a clink.

"Adam!" Ema screamed, her voice amplified deafeningly in the small metal space. "How's your head? Adam?!"

I winced, struggling to form a response.

"Sorry, Adam!" Chase hovered anxiously. "You alright?"

I was fine, thanks to the helmet—which I now wished I'd been wearing in Thailand.

"Oho...okay," I managed, "heh-met fine."

We finally managed to fit Ema and me inside the chamber and close the door.

Sssssss, the ominous sound began, close, and all around me. Chase started a movie on the tube's spark-proof screen. Ema had selected a comedy.

Ema kept reminding me to swallow to pop my ears as the pressure built around us. The feeling was bizarre, like sinking deep underground.

After some time, Chase tapped on the glass window above us. "Mask on, please," his voice sounded faraway.

Ema nodded and grabbed the oxygen mask hanging on the inside pipe-nozzle above our faces.

I couldn't imagine anything less comfortable than this, being trapped in a metal tube with my ears continuously popping. I wasn't sure if it would be better or worse without Ema crammed in beside me.

"Okay, Adami, al harosh shelchah *(on your head)*," I ducked forward to make it easier for Ema to pull the mask over my face. Cold, crisp air filled the mask and then my nose. I remembered vaguely that this was 100% oxygen.

"Teenshom *(breathe)* Adami, teenshom," Ema said. I closed my eyes and started to breathe deeply, trying to remember how this was supposed to help. Ema watched the movie on the screen, but I had no attention to spare for it.

I sat, waiting for something to happen. Waiting to feel better. Ema massaged my left arm as she watched the movie. This had become an unconscious habit for her.

"I remember massaging this hand," she whispered, "and thinking it would forever be paralyzed. I'm so happy it's not, Dan Dan."

I was already mostly asleep, my body taking the enforced stillness as permission to nap. Eventually, something beeped, and Chase knocked again.

"Take off his mask. You're almost done."

He soon released the pressure. "Sssss!"

"Alright," Chase proclaimed when the depressurization was complete. "You've resurfaced! Watch your toes!"

My body wasn't happy after being crammed into a metal tube for an hour. When we got out, my left arm and leg were more frozen than usual. Even Ema had to stretch to restore normal circulation to her limbs. I stared out the window again at the basketball courts across the street.

"Dan Dan, ata beseder?" *'Adam, are you okay? How do you feel?'* Ema asked as I limped out of the facility.

I simply shrugged, too exhausted to speak.

Three times a week, I completed HBOT sessions. Wanting to be part of my recovery, Nick joined me in the tube once instead of Ema.

"Bruh, this is harsh," he rasped as the pressure rose. "I can't inhale, dude." He squinted, his eyes watering as he tried to watch the movie on the screen.

After 27 sessions—90% of the way through Aba's package—I snapped. I reached a breaking point, telling my parents how frustrating it was to have every waking moment of my day filled with therapies. I didn't feel that HBOT was helping, and I pointed out that between TBS and HBOT, they had me booked solid from 9 AM to 7 pm most weekdays.

They let me end HBOT early, but Aba continued his search for new treatments.

After HBOT ended, Ema began regularly dropping me off and picking me up at the gym. My workouts were limited by my helmet, my knee brace, and my left arm. Anything that required two equally functional arms or legs was out of the question. I realized I would have to create two different workout routines: one for my right side, and one for my left.

I worked myself up to exercising for half an hour at a time. I hoped that if I kept going to the gym, I could rebuild my left side just as I had built myself up from a scrawny teenager into a leading steroid-free bodybuilder. Challenging my right side felt great. My right side moved so fluidly that I could imagine myself as a monstrous athlete again, being interviewed about my techniques.

As soon as I incorporated my left side, the illusion of normalcy vanished. I sometimes skipped my left side altogether because I didn't want to be reminded of how things had changed. In time, I switched to working out my left side first. I decided this was the "tax" I had to pay to be allowed to feel powerful when working out my dominant right side.

On one of my first visits to the gym, I went straight to the leg machines, reasoning that my left leg was stronger than my left arm. This was bittersweet: the leg machines were directly in front of the bench presses, including the one with extra weight that I had begged the gym to purchase for me the prior year.

One evening, Ema took me to visit Aba after a workout. He had something to tell me.

"Aseetee research ve matsati od rehab-method la injury shelcha." *I did research, and found another rehab method for your injury.* Aba told me. "T-M-S." he pronounced it slowly. "Transcranial magnetic stimulation."

He explained that TMS used magnetic fields to stimulate brain cells. It was non-invasive—the electromagnets were strong enough to work through the skull. I would simply sit in a chair as the operators pulsed magnetic fields at my brain.

The TMS coils would deliver short, powerful magnetic field bursts designed to stimulate my nerve cells, improving their function and the connections between them. In theory, this could relieve the pain and spasticity in my left arm and leg, and potentially restore some function.

"That oxygen was bullshit compared to this, Adahm!" Aba enthused. "We have an appointment for tomorrow at 7 AM."

I stared. I didn't normally have to be at TBS until 9 AM. Waking up two hours early to go through the painful routine of stretching, dressing, and limping out the door with my cane did not sound ideal. But I'd do as I was told.

I attended TMS sessions at a place called NeuroPulse twice a week after TBS. These sessions were shorter than HBOT sessions, which had been 70+ minutes. NeuroPulse was only 30 to 40 minutes; it was much more comfortable. The machine, a black couch with metal rods, aimed to boost serotonin and create new connections in my brain. Revka, the technician, would adjust the rods near my head while I watched Friends.

Despite initial hope, no miracle occurred. At this point, my parents accepted that the only cures for me were time and rehab. Nothing else was going to restore my abilities.

At last, the day came for my cranioplasty surgery. Ema, Aba, Orit, and I traveled again to Vital's hospital on Sunset. I limped into the lobby with my cane and helmet, refusing the wheelchair Ema offered. We walked down an enormous hallway, into an even grander lobby, and waited.

This would be my first voluntary surgery. Ema finished the paperwork as I tried to look like any other patient. My phone buzzed: it was Orit's boyfriend, Richie, texting me his well-wishes for the procedure. I was too nervous to reply. The thought of going under anesthesia terrified me. I couldn't fathom allowing someone to render me unconscious.

I was assigned a young nurse named Timothy who walked me through the steps of surgery. He began to do something with the IV station behind the wheeled bed I'd been told to sit on.

"Let's take off that helmet one last time," he said, and I brightened at the thought of never needing it again. I did my best not to flinch as he stuck needles in my arms, including an injection of muscle relaxants. He connected me to a heart monitor, and an ominous "*beep...beep...beep*" began. I looked away as Timothy grabbed my right arm and inserted a plastic IV tube into the vein, trying to be stoic.

"Ain't nothing to it, big man," Timothy reassured me. "You ready for the show?"

Ema looked annoyed at his casual tone, but I understood that he was trying to calm me.

My memory blinked in and out.

Why am I in the hospital again? Did I do something wrong?

My parents and sister watched me as I lay, connected to many tubes and monitors, in the foreboding pre-surgery prep ward. Timothy rolled me into the surgery room, and my parents gave me their well-wishes. Ema was in tears as she wished me strength, while Aba looked stern and determined.

We passed through automatic double doors. I looked around for familiar faces, hoping that would calm me. I recognized no one. The surgical room was big and loud, and surgeons and nurses bustled hurriedly around.

Clink. Timothy stepped on a lever, locking the bed's wheels and bringing it to a standstill.

Nearby, I saw something that looked unsettlingly like a piece of human skull sitting on a tray. I fidgeted, knowing that would be inside my head soon. My nervousness kept rising as the doctors chattered over me about the necessary drugs and pieces of equipment. The fact that I didn't understand the words they were using did not set me at ease.

I stared up at the halogen bulbs above my bed.

Finally, a familiar face appeared. Head surgeon Dr. Rudy had met my family and me in our pre-surgery talks. I gave him a crooked smile as Timothy started the countdown to sedate me.

I heard a ringing in my right ear as the doctors and nurses encircled me. Timothy patted my shoulder one last time.

I felt very loopy, lying there in the surgical bed. I remember making a joke right before I fell asleep.

"F f feeling great, all aboard tise train r r ride."

I was gratified to hear a doctor laugh somewhere in the hazy distance.

The world faded into blurry darkness.

**

Timothy stood between me and the white hospital ceiling, waving a finger in front of my face. The world was a groggy blur, but I managed to follow his finger with my eyes.

"He's fine!" Aba announced triumphantly, somewhere behind Timothy.

I listened to the familiar beeping of the heart monitor as my family talked excitedly in the distance. I felt glued to the bed, too exhausted to move. When I felt like I could move my right arm a little, I wiggled my fingers under the hospital sheets just to prove that I could.

Ema and Alex Eskanazi kept watch over me. Ema was preparing to stay the night. I struggled for something intelligent to say and asked Eskanazi how he was feeling after his mother's recent passing.

"Ken *(yes)* Adam, I will never forget my beautiful, dear mother haya-la betseem *(she had balls/courage)*. An amazing mother like yours. Hakol tov *(It's all good)*, Adam. She was a great woman and is in a better place. But I miss her very much..."

Then sleep overtook me like a freight train.

I didn't know where I was when I woke up. I peered around the room to see Ema curled up on the couch beside my bed. I felt the urge to apologize to her for all the uncomfortable couches she'd slept on since my accident.

"Ema...? I'm sorry, Ema, I'm sorry f f f for everything, I...I...sorry, Ema."

In a moment, she was at my side, examining the bandages wrapped around my head and feeling my heartbeat with her hand on my chest.

"Boker tov hegeeya Dan Dan. Hakol tov mami, ech yashanta?" *'Good morning. Morning has come. All is good, baby. How did you sleep?'* she asked lovingly.

We were in a small room with a hospital bed, an IV, a TV, a couch, and a glass window overlooking Sunset Boulevard. I lay in bed half-naked with no phone and no helmet.

Ema checked her phone. My cousin in Israel, Nisso Morami, was having his own surgery today. He had been born with medical problems that now required the amputation of his right leg.

Despite having health challenges from a young age, Nisso got a police internship as a teenager because the police were impressed with his bravery. At 12, he was featured on an Israeli talk show discussing his life as a disability patient and a 15-year-old police intern.

As I navigated my own disability journey, Nisso became my role model. However, in my post-surgery sleeplike state, I had little awareness of the outside world.

Nurses kept coming in, giving me food and asking me if I wanted pain medicine. Each time I declined, my headache no worse than what I'd become used to in recent months. I had no complaints, and no real thoughts of the future either. I was annoyed by the bandages around my head, and Ema brought me a mirror in hopes that if I could see the bandages, I would feel better about them.

I remained in bed for 14 hours post-surgery. Dr. Rudy came in to assess my condition, and to my surprise, he handed me my cane. "Feeling good, Adam?" he asked. "Why don't you walk around the hospital wing, get some exercise?"

I nodded eagerly. As Ema secured my ankle brace, I began looking around for my helmet.

Then I remembered. I would never need to wear a helmet just to take a walk again. I smirked to myself, suddenly feeling more "normal" than I had in months.

A nurse came to remove the many needles from my arms so I could stand and walk.

I reminded myself to use my left arm and leg as I limped down the hall. Doctors, nurses, patients, and visiting family members strolled past me. I turned to Ema, glancing at her for reassurance in this busy and unfamiliar place.

"You remember this place, baby?" Ema asked as I looked around.

I didn't. But after seeing that I was walking on my own without a problem, Ema went back to my room to begin packing.

That moment—knowing Ema trusted me to walk around a new place on my own—felt so good.

This is the new me. Not a victim in bed. A moving man!

I was on my way back to my old self.

But I was still limping. And caning around without my helmet—or pants, given that I was wearing a hospital gown—I began to feel vulnerable. Growing nervous, I soon bumped into a passing nurse with my numb left arm.

"Ooh, srry."

My locked knee swung in wide circles, my trapezius muscles pinched my neck, and my left arm swung uncontrollably as I made my way across the hospital.

After about 60 steps, I found an empty chair and sat, breathing heavily. It felt great to take a stroll, moving freely with the cool air from the hospital's ventilation system hitting my face. But my body was not as ready as my mind.

"Hello, Adam!"

I looked up, and to my shock saw my old speech advisor, Pat. He looked overjoyed to see me walking around.

My only memory from my first stay at Sunset returned to me: I'd hallucinated that I was at a sleep-away competitive basketball camp, which I thought was in Donna's old gymnasium. I'd thought that Pat and Alvin were "basketball therapists," coming to challenge me with exercises as part of the camp. Only now did I recall that memory and realize how my brain had tricked me.

I tried to speak fluently as I thanked Pat for all his help in my first days of recovery, standing on my cane and leaning on my right foot. It felt good to get to thank him while standing on my own two feet. I even took a risk by shaking his hand—trying to conceal the fact that I almost tipped over in the process.

I said my goodbyes to Pat, stuttering. Then I directed my focus back to my feet on the floor and continued my trek through the hospital. I explored, half-expecting Ema to appear and summon me back to the hospital room. I felt like I was breaking the rules by walking around alone without a helmet as I limped on and looked at the other patients in their hospital rooms.

Can't believe I ended up here, I thought, recalling the years I'd spent building my physical strength and leadership abilities. I'd hoped to be a successful son.

Look at me. One simple mistake brought me here.

Suddenly, I was aware of my limitations. I wanted to leave the hospital and never come back. I turned and limped back toward Ema as quickly as I could.

"Hi Adami!" Ema greeted me when I limped in, huffing and sweating. "Ech haya *(how was)* your walk?"

I eased myself back into the bed, exhausted. Ema slipped off my ankle brace and began to massage the reddened joint. "Hakol heeye beseder Dan-Dan."

I began to think affirmations to myself as I stared at the weather forecast on the hospital room TV. *I'm going to the gym again*, I reminded myself. *I bought myself new Wally Maddisons. I don't need oxygen therapy or TMS anymore. I don't need my helmet, and I don't need any more surgeries. Hopefully ever.*

I looked at Ema as she texted her brother David, Nisso's father, while massaging my left ankle. "Dubi, let's go home," I suggested hopefully.

Ema stopped massaging and stared up at me with wide eyes. "Dubi?!" Her eyes filled with tears. "You called me Dubi, Dan-Dan!" She launched herself at me with a hug. This was the first time I had called her by my old nickname for her since the accident.

Ema soon asked a nurse if we could speak to Dr. Rudy about leaving. The nurse looked doubtful, saying my surgery had been "significant," but promised to ask him to see us. After a long time, Dr. Rudy appeared at my hospital room door.

"Hello, Adam," he smiled. "How are you feeling? I was told by the nurse that you wanted to go home?" He put a finger on my pulse and looked at his watch, counting my heartbeats.

"Y-yes, please."

"Adam, after a cranioplasty surgery, we advise patients to stay for three days so we can monitor the brain. Especially after a brain injury of your magnitude."

I frowned, sick of living in this bubble of constant recovery and care.

"Are you really feeling good?" Ema asked hopefully.

I looked past the doctor and Ema, at the beautiful sunny day outside. "Yeah," I carefully thought out the next words, "I am good," I said confidently.

Dr. Rudy watched me.

"D d dealt with hospitals too much," I tried. "Need...out, please."

Dr. Rudy nodded and began to test my reflexes.

"You'll have to keep wearing the bandages on your head—even in the shower. But I think you're fine to go home."

I let out an explosive breath I hadn't realized I'd been holding and smiled triumphantly at Ema. She looked torn between anxiety and hope.

"You're sure he's okay, doctor?"

"I think so, Monda."

As soon as Dr. Rudy left, we made our way to Ema's SUV. I happily caned beside her and turned my unhelmeted head to look around. I almost galloped to the car, and had to wait for Ema to catch up so she could help me bend my knee to get into the passenger seat.

"How does it feel, not wearing ha kasda *(helmet)* Adami?" Ema asked.

I felt happy and fulfilled.

Ema kept glancing at me as she drove home. "Feeling good? No headaches?"

I nodded my helmetless head. "Ye…let's throw helmet -away y y," I proposed.

Ema chuckled softly. "Adam, I hope you now understand the importance of safety and protecting yourself."

I nodded, glancing down at my ankle brace and my numb left arm. "Yea. New leaf."

When we arrived back at my Burbank apartment, a stream of family and friends began to filter in and out, congratulating me.

"How does it feel?" Ema asked again that evening, staring at me anxiously.

The big fuss felt odd to me. I felt fine and didn't really understand the seriousness of a cranioplasty surgery.

Ema's friends kept asking the same questions.

"How do you feel, Adam?"

"Ata margeesh beseder *(do you feel good)*? You had a part added to your skull—that's frightening!"

I didn't know how to react. While replacing part of my skull with plastic sounded like science fiction, it also sounded much simpler than the other surgeries I'd had. It was what it was, and I didn't understand the need to harp on it. All I wanted was to be normal, walk around without a helmet, and maybe go to some restaurants with my parents!

That was how I felt until I took the bandages off my head, anyway.

When the time came, I stood in the bathroom, slowly unwrapping the white cloth with my good hand. My mind strayed to what I would wear for my next visit to the gym—and then I saw the scars.

I almost fainted. Enormous, inflamed stitches crisscrossed the left side of my shaved head. They started above my left ear, arched up to the top of my head, and down to the back of my skull. Dried blood was crusted between the thick rubber threads.

I stared at the stranger in the mirror, a chilling feeling of horror rising in my gut.

Can't run. Can't scream. Would scare Ema.

I touched the scars around the stitches, leaning on my cane in my right hand. I then washed my hand, as though it might have been contaminated from touching my own skin.

I killed myself in Thailand.

Tears welled up in my eyes. "I destroyed myself!" I finally screamed in frustration. "Ema, I'm disgusting!"

Ema hurried in from the kitchen. "Don't worry, Danduni. Your hair will grow in soon. Be zman ze-amar ha (in time they say the) scar will fade until you can barely see it anymore."

I didn't believe her, and I don't think she believed it either.

"Your head is fully round now, Dan Dan!" Ema tried. "No more dent!"

I looked to the floor, unwilling to face Ema or the world beyond. The sight of my own head was a constant reminder of my one mistake. This was one of the hardest moments of my recovery.

On Monday, I got ready for TBS. I felt the usual morning pain and stiffness in my left knee as I walked to the bathroom, my weight on my right leg.

"What do I do now?" I thought to my horror-mummy reflection.

Ema was cooking breakfast cheerfully as I caned into the kitchen half-dragging my left foot. I didn't say anything, not wanting her to look at me.

"Adami, how about a hat?" she proposed when she saw my face.

I got one out of the closet, a dark blue NY baseball cap. But I didn't feel "normal" when I looked at my reflection, bald under a baseball cap with a cane in my hand.

Disgusted, I took the hat off and went to TBS without it.

15

Stitches Removed, Asking to Work

Total memory recall: 30%
Mental capabilities: 28%
Left leg: 20%
Left arm: 10%
Skin state: Fresh skull scars & scratches
Assistive items: Cane & ankle brace
Age: 15
Weight: 159
Sources: Mom's Journal, Dad, Alex, Rene, Nick, and Myself

The week after my cranioplasty, I stumbled into TBS on my own, using only my cane, ankle brace, knee brace, and shoulder tape to support me.

"Hello, Adam!" Lina admired my newly bare skull as I caned past her. "Looking good and mighty strong!"

I frowned. *You don't know what 'strong' is.* I remembered lifting 105-pound dumbbells the day before my accident.

But I was making progress every day. I was speaking faster, stuttering and slurring my words less often. I was moving more smoothly, and I felt more free to get up and walk when I wanted to. My daily fatigue was beginning to fade.

I missed my old body so much, but I was starting to see the benefits of TBS. Becca's therapy and Dave's daily golf ball pickups were leading me towards independence.

There were things I didn't enjoy; mathematical assignments and cognitive reasoning exams. But even my old self had not enjoyed those activities.

My toughest moments at TBS were the exams. I would sit at a desk and answer questions about written stories, math calculations, and more. I became so fed up with these exams that I began to mark random answers on the multiple-choice sections to speed things up.

One day, my frustration reached its peak. I was given the usual, repetitive cognitive test by a therapist who proceeded to play on her phone as she supervised me and the other patients. One patient held a pen awkwardly, drawing circles aimlessly on his paper. Another stared at her test and drooled. I looked at my own questionnaire.

This is not me. What am I doing here?

I got up and caned decisively out of the room.

"Excuse me, Adam," the therapist called sharply after me. "Where are you going, young man?"

I turned to her and took a deep breath. I set down my cane, making a point of standing without it as I strained through my anger to find the right words. "I don't want to do this." I gestured around the classroom, restraining myself from wincing as the cane slipped from where I'd leaned it and clattered to the ground.

"What is this going to give me?" I demanded. "I want to make money like my Aba."

The therapist looked taken aback. "Uh, okay..."

I limped out of the room and sat in a chair near the physical therapy hub to watch Becca and two other therapists training patients on the treadmills and bikes.

Occupational therapy, on the other hand, challenged me in ways I enjoyed. As my motor control and cognitive skills advanced, Dave introduced domino puzzle walls, light-up touch-sensitive surfaces, and pads mounted on the walls that I could reach for. I did as I was told in the "classes" that stimulated me, but I had less and less patience for activities that did not.

My family set up a meeting with the TBS leadership to address something that made me deeply uncomfortable. Why did TBS still insist that someone accompany me into the restroom?

"If Adam falls and injures himself while he's here, we could be sued or worse," Lina explained, glancing at me with sympathy as we all sat around a TBS conference table. "A lawyer would say we had been negligent."

I frowned. It was already challenging to lean my cane on the wall, unzip my pants, and lift my shirt with just one functional arm and leg. But having to do that in front of one of my therapists?

I began drinking less water, so I wouldn't need to pee. My parents and therapists soon noticed this, and a more hostile meeting ensued, with Aba demanding that I be treated with privacy and respect. TBS reluctantly agreed to a compromise: I could pee by myself if I agreed to only do so while a therapist stood outside the closed restroom door, listening for any signs of trouble.

Every day felt like a fight for normalcy. I knew I had only won this battle because my parents argued for me— I would not have been able to argue so eloquently, or so forcefully, for myself.

I wanted to grab my Ema and Aba and hug them for being by my side. Not only in this meeting, but with everything. I didn't know how to express how much I appreciated them helping me after such a horrific injury, for which I had no one to blame but myself.

The next week, Ema and I visited my surgeon, Dr. Rudy, to remove my cranioplasty stitching.

At this point, my hair had begun to cover the surgical scars. The dried blood had washed away in the shower. I had never had stitches before, save for self-dissolving stitches that were once used for a cut on my face. So I was not expecting this appointment to be brutal.

We walked into the hospital and were taken to a room with a nurse preparing a scary-looking scalpel.

"Hello there, Adam, have a seat," the nurse named Angelica smiled at us.

"Okay hun, take a deep breath." Angelica began to lay out creams and salves. I sat still with my cane on my lap, not realizing what was coming.

Ema did realize it. She reached for the cane I had precariously balanced on my knees. I didn't let her take it, wanting to assert my independence.

"Okay, let's turn your head, Adam..." Angelica edged toward me, noticeably tense.

Angelica started assessing my head delicately with her gloved hands. I felt like I was back in school, being inspected for head lice. Then, she reached through my hair stubble and gently grasped a loose thread of stitching, pulling it slowly. It felt uncomfortable, like a thick hair being pulled out from the root. I thought I could feel the rubber stitch tickling my skull on its way out.

"No problem on that one, right?" Angelica asked brightly.

She began digging deeper into my scarred head with her fingers and the scalpel she'd discreetly picked up while I wasn't looking. It felt as though she were pulling my actual hair out, sharp pains shooting through my scalp.

I winced, but managed to remain silent in front of Ema. My eyes glazed over, staring at the floor.

Nurse Angelica continued removing stitches and wiping blood from my skin. Then I saw the length of stitching she'd pulled out of me: seven inches so far.

I sat there gripping the chair's armrest with white knuckles, starting to sweat. The removal of the stitches proved to be the worst pain I had felt.

Ema massaged my hand. "Ata yachol Adam, hakol heeye tov baby." *'You can do it Adam, everything will be fine.'*

After twenty minutes of removing stitches from under the skin of my scalp, I was transported into a numb, dreamlike state.

When Angelica finished, I sat back, shivering. Now Dr. Rudy walked in.

"Thank you, Angelica," he said as she walked out, smiling sheepishly at me.

"Adam, you've gone through it, left and right, guy! Those stitches and that cranioplasty implant weren't easy! I applaud you!"

Some warning would have been nice.

I'd written down questions for Dr. Rudy in my journal, but now they'd flown from my head.

"...Bookeh, Ema?" I almost whispered, and Ema handed me the notebook. I reached for it with trembling hands. Then I pulled the hood of my sweater over my head, self-conscious as Ema and Dr. Rudy stared at me like a newborn attempting to speak for the first time.

"Hello Doctor," I managed finally. "Thanks. So...few q q questions, for you, doctor."

"Yes, Adam." Rudy sat back, smiling. "Of course. Shoot."

"O o ok…first, do think I ever walk…or be normal?"
I restrained the urge to scratch my now-itching head as I
asked the question.

Dr. Rudy chose his words carefully. "I cannot answer
that, Adam. We are unsure how you, or any traumatic
brain injury patient, will progress. This is especially true
since you did have some brain cells removed in
Thailand."

I looked into his right eye, taking a deep breath at his
response. "Doc, will I die younger, or sooner?" I asked
him, a bit embarrassed by my erratic speech.

The surgeon took a breath, "Remember that every
injury is unique, Adam. But patients with traumatic brain
injuries usually live a long life."

I slowly nodded and gazed at the floor in deep
thought.

"Last thing," I glanced at Ema. "Will I ever be able to
move this arm smoothly? It feels like a dead thing,
annoying."

"Time, Adam," Dr. Rudy shook his head. "Honestly,
be glad you woke up from the coma. Many of us thought
you would remain in a permanent vegetative state. I can't
imagine the journey you've had."

"You see, baby?" Ema smiled. "Be glad and
appreciate life. The important things."

I nodded, unsure how to feel. I slowly got up,
grabbing my cane in my right hand, and thanked the
doctor for his time.

"Stay strong, Adam," Dr. Rudy told me. "You are
already through the toughest part."

As I limped out of the hospital room, I heard Dr. Rudy
talking to Ema. "Listen Monda, he has a tough road ahead
of him. He's so young…"

In the weeks to come—without the consent of TBS—I began walking without a cane. It was clumsy going, but I was motivated by the fact that I was the only person at my gym to use a cane. I had been strengthening my legs during my gym visits, and now that I could replace my helmet with a hoodie to cover my scars, I decided to take this step toward looking "normal."

The first time I tested this ability, I left my cane on a bench and limped to an exercise machine about eight feet away. I stared at my feet, concentrating hard.

I could not bend my locked left knee at all, but I could swing my entire left leg in a wide circle without leaning on a cane or falling over. My right leg and core muscles must have been getting used to the operation. My left arm still flailed, but that was not a problem as long as no one was close enough to bump into it.

To my delight, I made it to the machine I'd set my sights on! I then did several more "laps," walking between the bench and the exercise machine. Only after eight minutes of unassisted walking did I pick up the cane again.

I was ecstatically proud, smiling a crooked smile under my hoodie. That day was one of the greatest accomplishments of my life. I planned to show Ema and Becca my achievement the very next day at TBS.

I restrained myself from telling Ema about my feat that night, wanting to surprise her. The next morning, I asked her to accompany me to TBS for the first time in weeks. Smirking with self-satisfaction, I led Ema past Lina's head office. I don't need you anymore, I thought, anticipating my final graduation from TBS.

"Adam, good to see you and momma today!" Becca greeted us in the physical therapy hub. "You ready for the usual treadmill and lateral footwork?"

I could restrain myself no longer.

"Uh, Becca, I can walk now w w w without a cane," I announced.

I set my cane down, anticipating Ema's look of pride. I didn't intend for it to clatter loudly to the floor, but when it did, I pretended I'd done that on purpose. Making a statement. A mic drop.

I then proceeded to walk the floor of the physical therapy hub unassisted. I wore a huge grin as though I'd won an award when I walked about ten feet. I had planned to walk fifteen feet, but found my arm windmilling and grew anxious as I approached another exercising patient. People moved unpredictably, and I didn't want to get too close.

"Great job, Adam," Becca's smile was tight as I limped back to her. "I don't want you to keep walking without your cane quite yet, though."

My smile disappeared. "But I can w w walk!"

"Yes, Adam," Becca agreed. "But you can easily lose your balance. Look there!" She pointed behind me and I turned to see what she was pointing at.

While I was distracted, Becca sprang forward and shoved me lightly, trying to knock me off-balance. But she was unsuccessful, my 6'2" frame outweighing her small body.

"Okay," Becca admitted. "He's doing pretty well. But he should continue using his cane," Becca turned to Ema, expecting her to be the enforcer.

"You hear that, Danduni?" Ema asked. "Let's be safe."

I must have been visibly put out because Becca added: "Adam, you are not walking correctly. You are getting from point A to point B, but you are not controlling your movement well. That will get you into trouble."

Now it was Ema who could not restrain herself. "Rebecca, he is walking though! At least it is a start, right?"

"Yes! Don't get me wrong, Adam," Becca amended. "We'll continue to work on your walk. But you should use your cane while you're at home or out in public when you don't have the bungee harness for safety."

"Okay," I said, defeated.

Ema soon left, giving me a kiss goodbye.

Later that day, I was surprised to learn that I'd tested at one of the highest levels of patient cognitive abilities. My memory, speech, and even my last hated exams had shown that I was ready to graduate from my least favorite classes.

My hair was growing back, so I looked almost normal even with my hood down. I could walk without a cane—however awkwardly. And I had all but tested out of the basic cognitive skills classes.

I was on the way to reclaiming my dominant mindset.

I started to walk without my cane whenever Becca wasn't around. I couldn't see how leaning on a cane would help me walk more "correctly."

I wanted my old life back. The life I saw when I scrolled through old pictures and videos on my phone. And to get it, I would have to push myself.

As my brain recovered, my boredom with TBS grew.

Ema sometimes took me out for lunch breaks to nearby restaurants. This was her attempt to quell my restlessness, but it wasn't enough. I soon began to plot to get myself excused from TBS.

One day, Aba took me to his favorite sushi restaurant during my lunch break. I decided to ask if I could begin working for his G-Defy sneaker company.

This request surprised Aba for several reasons. For one, six months ago, he'd been told I'd likely be in a permanent vegetative state; now I was asking for a job. For another, I had quit the last job he gave me to start FitFlow.

Now, those two things canceled each other out. I couldn't expect to run a business in my current condition, so where else could I work but for Aba?

Aba smiled at my request and said words I will never forget. "Lo-achav Adam, bezman Aba, bezman." *'Not now, Adam. In time papa, in time.'*

He took me back to TBS, where I had a few things to say to Laura about that.

Dave was at least keeping me engaged by expanding the range of motions we were training my left arm on.

"Okay, Adam, try to focus on holding your wrist up. Try not to let it fall toward the floor."

It took all my strength and focus to keep my wrist up, but the challenge was rewarding. I was slowly reclaiming a tiny amount of control over my left hand.

Dave instructed me to use my left arm in increasingly complex motions, reaching for my right shoulder, touching my chin, touching my right arm, etc. But my body was still frail, needing frequent water breaks and naps.

I'd go with Alex Eskanazi for cane-walks around my apartment building when he visited. We'd walk as Alex asked me about my life, my thoughts, and my rehab. Then we'd march back to my apartment for a barbecue dinner with Ema.

"Rimona, at seecrah leerot ech Adam olech tov!" Alex would gush. *'Ramona, you have to see how well Adam is walking!'*

"Tov-aval ooh sareech et ha cane shelo beyad?" Ema would agree, "Nachone Adam cmo-Becca amra." *'Good, but he needs to have his cane in hand, right Adam? Like Becca said?'*

Alex agreed with my logic about the cane and did not make me use it when we took our walks together. But he was willing to back up Becca that it might be safer to use my cane in crowded places until my walking was a bit more refined.

One night in December—the night of Ema and Alex's ninth anniversary—Alex had more wine than usual. This led to him becoming bold.

"Adam, what you think we go lasot (do) the stairs?" he whispered to me on the couch as his favorite show, New Girl, played on TV. I nodded in excitement, eager to try stairs without my cane.

While Ema was taking a shower, we snuck out together.

"After you, my friend," Alex said, holding the door of the emergency stairwell open for me. I walked into the warm, unairconditioned stairwell and looked up the imposing flight.

"There's a rail for your right side," Alex pointed out. "So hold onto that pole as we walk up, just like with Rene at Renewal Ranch!"

I nodded, my heart beginning to race as I looked at the task before me. I walked with Alex up the first step, then dramatically dropped my cane to the floor.

Don't need you, I thought, hearing it clatter.

"Okay, yalla grab that rail and let's try to bend your knee," Alex urged, taking a step to stand above me. I grabbed the shiny black banister and tried taking a step up the first stair without my cane. My left leg swung almost 360 degrees around my body before I got it situated atop the first of fifteen steps on this flight. I then pulled myself up and stood proudly, looking at Alex for his judgment.

"Okay," he breathed. "I'm going to stand by your left to block your leg from swinging." Agreeing, I tucked my left hand into my sweater pocket so it wouldn't flail.

Alex stood beside me with his right leg brushing my left leg, prepared to push back if my left leg went awry. "Just focus on bending your knee and moving your left leg forward," Alex encouraged. "Don't let it swing!"

I tried bending my knee again but failed, my leg swinging out instead. Alex's locked leg blocked it. "Concentrate Adahm!" Alex hollered. "Forward, not around!"

My hand holding the rail grew slick with sweat as I concentrated. I imagined focusing on the knee the way I did on my wrist in Dave's occupational therapy class, willing it to bend with all my might.

No luck. My mind could not connect to my left hamstring, knee, hip, or quad. We were only a couple of steps up and I was getting tired.

"Keep pushing," Alex encouraged me. I soon began to grunt and groan.

Eventually, Alex relented, allowing my left leg some room to swing up onto the next stair.

"Fine I'll take it," Alex breathed. "You keep trying to bend your knee, and I'll let you rise up, Adahm!"

Alex and I reached the top of the stairs. At the very top, Alex asked me to try raising my left knee to my chest as he assisted, helping me curl forward into a crouch to bend the joint. Determined, we walked up and down the four flights of stairs in my apartment building three times.

Alex kept applauding my efforts as sweat blossomed across my chest and stained my sweater. I even felt sweat dripping behind my knees.

Exhausted but content, I will never forget what Alex Eskanazi said to me as we reached the top of the staircase. "Adam, I swear to you, if you keep doing this you will walk without a cane one day!"

We were both so inspired by this experience that nightly stair climbs after dinner became our new evening ritual.

Ema was initially nervous about this, since Alex wasn't a licensed physical therapist. But she soon believed that Alex's heartfelt care for his only son was all the protection I needed.

At TBS, my bungee-treadmill training continued. My eyes frequently wandered to the Office Depot and Tony Roma's parking lots as I fantasized about being out there.

I can practice walking without my cane down there, and use the parked cars for balance if I need to. Perfect.

The temptation was always before my eyes, the places where I'd built so many memories. One day, I decided it was time: but walking out there would require some trickery.

Lunch at TBS ran from 12pm to 1pm. On that day, Ema had packed me a tuna sandwich, which I gobbled down quickly, then caned hurriedly to the lobby. I sat near the lobby doors, considering how to sneak out. The receptionist on duty, Martha, knew that my parents often picked me up for lunch.

I caned up to her desk. "Hello Mar, mom downstairs h h holding water for me, can go?" My voice trembled a little from anxiety as I lied, but I hoped she would chalk that up to my usual stutter.

"Where's your mom, Adam?" Martha glanced up from her phone.

"Downstairs lobby w w waiting for me, please." I looked toward the door anxiously.

"Okay," Martha agreed. "But hurry back. You usually need a parent to sign you out."

I smiled crookedly in victory. "Thank you."

This was my jailbreak! I escaped TBS on my own. My left leg trembled with fear and excitement as I headed to the parking lot elevator.

When the doors to the outside opened, I took a deep breath of fresh oxygen. I walked 40 steps, up to the door of the sushi bar across from the Office Depot parking lot.

Then I realized: I'd have to cross a six-lane street to get to the parking lot I saw through the TBS window every day. To do that, I would need to walk fast enough to make the crosswalk light, and I'd have to be able to lift my left knee up to mount the raised curb on the other side.

I looked up and down the road, clutching my cane and considering my options. I could turn right and walk toward Gelson's grocery store, where I'd face less of a challenge. I could walk the other way, toward the hair salon. Or I could try to cross the street, which even I did not think was wise at that moment.

I ended up settling for sitting outside the nearby Veggie Grill, eating alone and free.

The days went by like a dream. My parents gave in to my requests and called Vital to reduce the number of hours I spent each week at TBS. I continued sneaking out for lunch, saying I was meeting Ema but actually walking the surrounding streets without a cane. I took to hiding my cane in a janitor's closet near the entrance to TBS on my way out. Being in public with no wheelchair, cane, or chaperone was exhilarating.

I'm one of the crowd.

One day, I decided to try walking the TBS rear parking lot, which was rarely busy since only approved staff and patients could enter. I caned, my hips jutting out with each step. Thankfully nobody saw me, and I soon stood behind a beige Jeep. There were 30 or 40 cars parked in the lot.

Perfect.

I set my cane on the ground by the Jeep and began to walk, touching each car with my right hand as I passed. I counted 35 cars on my first lap around the lot, then took another lap before returning to pick up my cane. Becca's words rang in my ears: *Adam should continue to use his cane.*

Becca was wrong.

My left leg felt heavy as my feet skidded on the gravel and my left leg flailed. But I walked. On my own.

After about 20 minutes of laps through the parking lot, I was breathing hard. I had started dropping my bottom toward the ground in an effort to force my left knee to bend. I grabbed my cane to head back inside, not noticing that my right hand was black with dust from the cars I'd touched.

I was 20 minutes late to speech class after my 'lunch thrill.' It was worth it.

Unfortunately, my lateness helped TBS figure out what was going on. They called Ema, expressing their concerns about me 'vacating the premises.'

When Ema confronted me, I promised I'd stayed close to TBS. I just wanted some 'me time.'

That night, I slept the best sleep I'd had since my exhausting days at Renewal Ranch.

One evening, Ema had arranged for me to meet Rene and Nick for dinner at the Cheesecake Factory.

I was not in the best mood after a tough day at TBS. Why would they even want to be my friends? I ranted at myself in my head. I'm so helpless.

My memory failed me, and I have few recollections of that dinner. But I did journal about our conversations.

Rene, Nick, and myself were seated at table 27. The restaurant host—a job I'd performed there as a teenager—had to help me sit in my chair, across from Nick and Rene in the booth. I was embarrassed to need assistance, but Nick's mind was elsewhere. He kept looking around the crowded restaurant.

"Lots of cute girls here, fellas," he said to Rene and me in a low voice. "Check 'em out!"

I kept my head bowed, not wanting to attract attention.

"Adam, you usually always looking," Nick pointed out, concerned. "What's the deal, boss man? You looking completely recovered. I know I'll spot you on that 300 bench-press soon!"

I looked down at my left arm in my lap. *No, you won't.* I started rubbing my left arm with my right to encourage blood flow in the chilly December air.

"Yo, you good man?" Nick asked.

"Adam, really no girls?" Rene chimed in. "Wassup?"

The truth was, my sex drive had been nonexistent since my injury. In fact, I'm not sure I remembered why my friends liked women so much. I knew I preferred the company of women, but what Rene and Nick were talking about was alien to me.

I didn't 'check out' women: I just felt warm and loved when they were around, even as I felt anxious about impressing them for reasons I could not name..

For some reason, I didn't want pretty women to see me vulnerable. Which was how I nearly always felt now.

Today, I was just glad to be alone with friends, and I didn't want to attract the attention of strangers.

"You for real not checking out women no more, Adam?" Nick pressed, sounding worried. The table went silent as Rene reached for bread.

"T-t they won't even like me back," I said finally. "I path-pathetic,"

Nick shook his head, frowning. "Forget all that Adam, you good man. Ey, you even nutting bro?"

"Adam, you cumming dude, right?" Rene joined in, buttering his bread.

I didn't know how to respond because I didn't know what "cumming" or "nutting" meant. I had no memory of any previous orgasm, nor any idea what an orgasm would entail. As far as I was concerned, they were speaking Greek. I continued to stare at the menu I had once had to memorize for my teenage job.

"Yo, Adam, you got some..." Nick pointed at my bottom left lip, alerting me that I had food stuck to it. I quickly rubbed my face with my right hand. By now I wanted to run away from my old friends. I couldn't fit in with whatever this "cumming" was, and here I was being visibly oblivious to my own body.

When Ema picked me up that night, she witnessed more of my body's reaction to cold weather. All the joints on my left side would freeze up when the temperature dropped, and my left leg would stick out as immovable as an icicle.

We had a hard time getting me into the shower that night. In bed afterward, I lay helplessly frozen as Ema tried to rub warmth back into my limbs with a towel. She dried me for a full five minutes, but my body continued to spasm and shake. This drove Ema to wrap me in a beanie, scarf, and sweater, and make me hot tea as she tucked me in under my Scarface blanket. I'll never forget what a challenge that simple cold weather created for us.

At TBS, I continued doing golf-ball pickups with Dave and bungee-treadmills with Becca. Ema picked me up every day, sometimes arriving early to press Lina for updates on my progress. She'd sometimes talk to other patients, and on one occasion, met an Israeli man in his early 30s named Daniel Jookay Jack. Daniel had suffered a traumatic brain injury as well, and Ema became determined that we should be friends.

One thing she learned was that Daniel had tried to get his license to drive! He'd failed because he had frequent seizures, which posed a risk of him losing consciousness while behind the wheel. But I had never had a seizure. And I had full use of my right arm and leg. Was it possible, then, that I could drive again?

Not just yet. But the seed of an idea had been planted.

Visiting the gym after TBS remained my favorite activity. One day, I decided to start my workout with cardio. This meant I had to flag down a passerby to help me get my left foot in the exercise bike stirrup.

"Excuse m m me, can you please help get injured f f foot in brace?" I asked an older woman who looked motherly.

Once she had kindly strapped my foot in, I began pedaling, then sat back and began to people-watch. I enjoyed blending in with the crowd, now that my hair was back and the constraints of the bike hid my physical disabilities.

My chest tightened and my heart raced as I saw a familiar girl with long brown hair enter the gym. She wore grey gym pants and a black crop top that revealed her toned stomach and pierced belly button.

Kaylee.

A storm of emotions roiled in me as I saw her. I was happy. Excited. Sad. Nervous. Mostly nervous. I could not possibly keep up with the Adam she had known six months ago.

But I was too excited to restrain myself. I waved to her excitedly from my bike like Forrest Gump.

Her eyes widened and she started toward me. I panicked a little and looked down, feeling myself begin to sweat.

What do I do? What do I say? I can't even talk right!

Kaylee was steps away from me by the time I decided to throw my hood over my face in an attempt to hide any remnants of scarring that might peek through my hair. My teeth began to chatter and I wanted to disappear.

Help. Remembering my cane leaned against the bike, I smacked it to the floor to hide it from Kaylee's view.

Kaylee swayed her curved body coyly as she approached me, not realizing anything was wrong.

"Hi, Adam," she said, placing her cream-colored, manicured fingernails on the handle of my bike. "It's been a long time…" The gym fans blew her silky hair back from her face as she looked at me.

I was overwhelmed, my brain unable to process such beauty and attention focused on me. I told myself to keep staring at her right eye. I have no memory of our conversation, or if I managed to speak to her at all or just stared dumbly.

I know Kaylee spoke to me. I know I kept pedaling, trying to look busy. She was still talking when my left leg reached exhaustion and I had to stop, hoping she would think I was merely taking a thoughtful pause.

I remember that she smiled, then went back to her friends, laughing. I discreetly wiped a stream of drool from the left side of my mouth.

After Kaylee disappeared, I decided to attempt an upper-body workout. Seeing her had at least motivated me to work on my 'glamour muscles.' I decided on the dip machine to work my triceps, knowing that the tricep made up most of the total muscle mass of the arm.

I caned my way to the dip machine near the center of the gym, bent over, and automatically adjusted the weight to what I used to lift before my accident: 195 pounds. I used my right hand to wrap the fingers of my left hand around the left-sided dip handle, then grasped the right-sided handle with my good hand.

I stood between the handles and pushed. Nothing happened.

Realizing my mistake, I bent back down and adjusted the pin to a mere 40 pounds. Still nothing. I lowered it again, to 20 pounds. This time, I was able to do a few repetitions, but my legs and back soon began to complain about the position the machine required me to maintain.

My workout ended, and I texted Ema asking her to pick me up.

The following week, Lina visited one of my physical therapy sessions. The end of the year was approaching, and she was evaluating the new patients on our progress.

"Adam, I'm very excited for you!" Lina told me. "Your mom tells me you're walking up the stairs in your apartment building. I'd like to see you take the stairs here, if you don't mind." Lina invited me to follow her down a corridor off the physical therapy hub.

"Can you show me your strategies for walking down the steps, Adam?" she invited me, opening the door to the emergency staircase. These stairs were metal, covered with a blue slip-resistant material.

Lina took a few steps down the flight of stairs, then turned to look up at me. "Your turn! Let's see you stay to your left side!"

I grabbed the stair rail and took quick steps, my left leg springing out and dangling to the side as I leaned on the banister and focused on speed.

Lina nodded, watching me thoughtfully. "Okay, your mechanics are very loose. Now I want you to stand here." She reached out and gently shifted my body across the stairs to face the banister with my left side instead of my right. This meant I couldn't flail my left leg too much without hitting the wall, and if I wanted to use the banister, I'd have to grab it with my useless left hand. Which was completely impossible.

"Got it, sweetheart?" Lina asked, stepping to stand directly in front of me.

My head started to ache. I looked nervously down at Lina.

"Believe that you can do it, Adam," Lina encouraged me. "You can use your mind to control both sides of your body."

I took my first step down. My left arm jackknifed forward as my balance teetered.

Lina continued her pep talk as I looked down at her helplessly, feeling no connection to the left side of my body. How could I explain to her how impossible it was for me to do what she was asking?

This was how my first "semester" at TBS ended.

***

16

An Unexpected Home

Attainments: Cody Home
Total memory recall: 34%
Mental Capabilities: 30%
Left Leg: 22%
Left Arm: 12%
Assistive items: Cane, Ankle Brace, & Vibration Gun
Age: 15
Weight: 161
Sources: Mom's Journal, Dad, Alex, & Myself

I tried to keep my spirits up as the months passed, making time each day to think positive thoughts. I'd reflect on how far I'd come since the coma, which I only knew through the videos Aba and Ema showed me. Almost a year after my skull was cracked open on a sandy road in Thailand, I could speak full sentences, walk, feed myself, and brush my own teeth.

I daydreamed of a future where I might high-five my friends, laugh with them, and hug them. I fantasized about jogging in the park, playing basketball, lifting weights with both sides of my body, and being able to do "clap-ups" again.

But I was beginning to doubt that these things were possible. Carrying myself across the gym or picking up anything was still a challenge that required careful effort. My left leg still locked, and my left arm still flailed, bumped, and shoved passersby when I lost track of my left visual field. I thought of myself as a broken child.

I rarely saw my old friends or clients. I never opened Skype, haunted by memories of using it to talk to my FitFlow developer teams. I attended TBS each day, and my only thrills came from escaping my routine. I'd sneak out a couple of times a week, lying to pretend I belonged out there.

Becca was on to me.

One day, she called Ema in to join us for a session. As I limped in, expecting my usual bungee-treadmill walk, I saw Ema standing by Becca and beaming at me.

"Surprise, Danduuuni!" Ema exclaimed.

"Adam," Becca explained, "Since I am told by your mom of your desire to walk more during lunch hours, I'm assigning her to take you out today. Enjoy!"

I stared as other patients filed in to start their days at PT. This should have been good, but somehow being *told* to walk with Ema looking over my shoulder robbed my "lunch thrill" of its independence.

Becca knew what to do. "Adam, I want you to walk to Gelson's down the block. See how your body handles the walk. Rest and relax there, and return to me by lunch!"

This didn't feel like a challenge, but I was not good with numbers at this point. I didn't realize the grocery store was three times further than the distance I usually walked on the treadmill with bungee harness support each day.

I smiled as Ema and I passed Martha at the front desk on our way out. Later, I would understand why Ema and Becca chose Gelson's: getting there required only a right turn and a journey down a wide and uncrowded sidewalk.

"Ok, mami," Ema said as we approached the corner. "Keep your left side up, eyes forward."

I wished I didn't need the reminder.

A stream of cars flew by, and I tried to imagine crossing the busy street on my own. Overwhelmed by the sights, sounds, and smells of winter in LA, I lost track of the strategy I needed to keep proper form while walking. My left shoulder drooped, and my left arm swung as I hurled my left leg forward. I gasped for breath as my ribs struggled to expand under the weight of my shoulder.

"Okay, Adahmi, rega, rega, rega." *'Wait, wait, wait.'* Ema stopped me. "Ata rack olech kadeema *(you are just moving forward)* and hoping for the best! There's no rush. Remember the methods Rene and Becca have taught you."

Ema was right. With my left side flailing everywhere, each step was taking a huge amount of energy. I would be exhausted before we reached the corner.

I started forward again, this time more carefully. As I focused on keeping my left shoulder high and my left arm by my side, things began to feel easier.

But it was a long walk. I tried not to groan as I dragged my paralyzed foot. Ema and I had to take breaks, during which I thanked her for thinking to bring water. I drained the bottle before we reached the traffic light across from Gelson's.

Now I just had to cross the street. For the first time. Since Thailand. I stared as Ema casually pressed the crosswalk button with her left hand.

"Okay, teechake' la mamzor *(wait for the light)*," she said sweetly.

My heart pounded as I stared at the speeding cars.

"Okay Dan Dan, get ready," Ema glanced at me as the light turned yellow.

Thump, thump, thump, thump, went my heart.

Ema squeezed my left hand and stepped forward as the crosswalk light turned green. "Yalla-bo." *'Come on.'*

Ahead of us, the beige-and-white Gelson's sign loomed.

Ema helped me step off the curb, then began rushing at what felt like lightspeed in front of the impatient cars. I forgot my walking strategy as I hurried, shoulder hunched and limbs flailing. Ema almost dragged me as we neared the end of the street—and the end of the crosswalk's timer. I bent double as my left side seized up from the panic and the rush.

"8, 7, 6, 5, 4," the crosswalk light flashed the ominous countdown.

"Almost there, Danduni," Ema said, her voice tight but optimistic. With seconds to go, she helped me step up the six-inch high curb and sighed with relief.

Entering Gelsons, I was exhausted and wanted to sleep. We had walked for 40 minutes and my left arm had locked tight in protest of the insane venture.

"Here, baby," Ema suggested, "Tuck it in for warmth." She carefully moved my left hand into my sweater pocket.

At first, having my left hand tucked into a pocket felt awkward, but I grew to love this method as it meant I didn't have to worry about my left arm flailing and banging into objects or people. And the pocket did keep my hand warm.

After a quick coffee, Ema and I headed back to TBS. I didn't want to use my cane, but was too tired to argue about it.

"Hello, guys!" Becca greeted us when we returned to TBS 35 minutes late. "How did it go? Give me details!"

Ema answered as I sat down, covered in sweat and red-faced from exertion.

I didn't want to answer. The walk had been hard, but I desperately wanted to be allowed to do it again. To show Becca and everyone that I didn't need physical therapy, TBS, or that damn cane any longer.

As they talked, I noticed a young patient in a wheelchair who I hadn't seen before. He had glasses and messy, curly hair. He looked younger than me, and more injured. His arms were contracted, with his hands up near his face. His head was thrown back, looking at the ceiling, and he was visibly drooling. He was accompanied by parents and a nurse. My curiosity was piqued, as was my sympathy.

I was intrigued enough to eavesdrop and learn that he was Andrew Sharp, an 18-year-old race car driver for Bentley Motors. His father was a tech CEO who had enrolled his privileged son in horseback riding, ATV, snowboarding—and motorway racing leagues. His life sounded like a teenager's dream.

But despite the elaborate safety measures, harnesses, and professional racing helmets, he'd been run off the track at 132 miles per hour. His racecar spun and flipped over 47 times, landing Andrew in a coma for a year.

I shook my head. He'd been wearing a helmet, and still he'd been hurt worse than me. Sometimes, life just wasn't fair.

There was no speech therapy or gym visit for me that day. I was so exhausted from the long walk that, when Ema and Becca finished talking, I immediately asked to be taken home to sleep.

***

One week before my birthday on January 24th, Aba walked into my apartment with a big smirk on his face. "Adam-teeshma! Habieet-shelcha moo-chan!" *'Listen! Your house is ready!'*

I was lying on the couch, my head on a rolled-up towel Ema had provided. I stared up at him blankly.

'My house?'

"Monda," Aba turned to Ema, his arms spread wide. "Pick a day for Adam to take off TBS. We need to move him in!"

'My house?!' I strained to remember, thinking I must have forgotten something.

"Take a day off? No," Ema proclaimed. "He needs his rehab."

"Monda, it's for his birthday! I have been working on it for months!"

I was certain I was misunderstanding. So many things had not made sense to me recently that this would hardly be a surprise.

"Oolie *(maybe)*," Ema agreed grudgingly at last. "Just one day."

Over the following week, Aba hired movers to assist Ema and me in packing. I was in a state of shock and anxiety, not knowing what was going on. At some level, I understood, but I assumed I was understanding wrong. It was simply not possible that I could have a house to move into.

I had no idea where we were taking my things. I didn't even feel that I could help Ema and the movers, between my limited range of motion and my total confusion. So I sat, watching, as Ema, Aba, Alex, and the movers dismantled my bedroom and bathroom and packed my things into boxes.

I later learned that an 83-year-old man named Gilbert, who lived across the street from Aba, had lost his wife a few months before. I had helped host Gilbert at Aba's home for a few dinners. When Gilbert announced his intention to move to a senior citizens' home in Florida,

Aba asked about purchasing his house for me. This had apparently been going on since I'd been in my coma in Thailand.

There was just one problem with Aba's idea: Aba didn't have enough money to buy the house at its asking price. He asked Gilbert if he could buy the house for me for less, since he had exhausted all his money on my medical bills and treatments. Gilbert wouldn't budge.

Aba resorted to setting up cameras to let him know when Gilbert showed the house to prospective buyers. He'd then stand outside his home, trying to convince the prospective buyers not to buy the house.

Gilbert finally let up. He had attended a few of our Shabbat dinners before the accident, and he sympathized with Aba wanting to keep his disabled son close.

This was what Aba had been celebrating in the middle of the Mission: Impossible movie. He'd gotten confirmation that his bid to buy the 2-bedroom house just across the street from his own, for me, had been accepted.

As a mover left the apartment with the last of my boxes, Aba came to stand in front of me. "Your mother and I," he said softly, "will never give up on you. We believe you will live independently again. Soon, you can start working for the family business. In time, you will not need our help to live in your own home."

On my birthday, Ema and I got into her SUV and left my Burbank apartment for the last time. We drove up steep mountain roads, the car sometimes climbing at a 45-degree angle as we ascended a twisting, turning one-lane street.

The highest street in the San Fernando Valley is called Mulholland Drive. The street with my house and Aba's, just below it, is called Cody Road. As we wound up the hill, each sharp turn left me feeling groggy and nauseated.

"Slow, Ema, please," I squeaked while staring out the window.

"I know baby, I'll go slower. Ze-arbe." *'This is a lot.'* She let another car pass before slowly making a hairpin turn that made me hold my breath and clutch the armrest with white knuckles.

Finally, the road became flat. We saw Aba, Monica, and young Jacob cheerfully waiting to greet us on the curb. Ema pulled into the driveway of a single-story 1980s house with a white garage.

Ema unloaded my wheelchair from the trunk and helped me into it. I hadn't been using the chair much, but Ema told me the new place didn't have any elevators to make it easier for me, so I should rest my legs when I could.

Ema pushed my wheelchair up to the home's side door. I gathered the strength to turn my head to the left and saw a sea of grass, giant trees, and a footpath stretching away 90 feet below the house's terrace. I took a deep breath at the sight, tracing the downward spiral of the mountain.

Feelings and images flooded through me. Walking with Nick and Allan at the mall like a healthy person, smiling. Having dinner with Nick and Rene, talking and laughing. Did this house mean I could live a normal life again?

"Ema, will go in without wheelchair," I proclaimed, standing with my cane in hand. Ema took my hand to help me over the threshold, and I took my first unbalanced step into the house.

I had forgotten to stretch my legs and back when getting up from my wheelchair, and I dropped my cane as my left leg spasmed. I grabbed the corner of a wall for balance as I almost tipped over. My parents instantly grabbed me as Monica looked on, holding Jacob.

"Rega rega *(wait, wait)*, slow Adahm!" Ema sounded nervous. "Don't get overwhelmed. There is no rush."

Aba watched as I slowly re-balanced myself. "Bo, let me show you around!" He could barely contain his excitement as Ema began to peer around the white kitchen and the connected dining room.

I mostly looked at the floor to keep track of my feet.

"This," Aba announced proudly, "is your kitchen!"

A feeling of guilt began to creep up on me. *I don't deserve all this.*

Aba led us through wood-paneled rooms, including a guest bedroom and bathroom. "Ze-ha *(this is the)* dining room." He pointed and I saw a long table, behind which stood a sliding glass door that opened onto a balcony overlooking the valley. My heart began to race.

"Ema, mayeem?" *'Mom, water?'* I asked.

In reality, I needed a pause to process all this. I was insecure about losing my balance earlier, afraid my parents would decide that I did need their constant supervision after all. And this...this house...mine...

"Thanks Aba," I responded as he handed me a water bottle.

I sank into one of the chairs at the dining table. When I was ready to move again, we continued into the next room.

"The fireplace doesn't work," Aba said, "but we will install your TV here." A white couch big enough to seat four people stretched beneath a peaked ceiling.

"Good floors for the wheelchair," Ema observed, examining the hardwood.

"Wait for the best part!" Aba walked to the glass door. "Adam, come with me. Seem-ha-yad *(place your hand)* on my shoulder." I did as he asked, and Aba walked me toward the glass doors.

"You ready?" he asked. Then he slid open not one, two, or three, but four connected glass doors, spanning 17 feet! Aba smiled as a stiff, cold wind poured in, along with gleaming sun and birdsong. Ema hurried to join us as we stepped out onto a balcony that overlooked the green hills below.

"Alex, ze safe?" Ema asked nervously, staring at the long drop.

I didn't know what to say or do, staring in amazement.

"Grab the gate, Adahm," Ema encouraged me, indicating a white bar that stretched across the balcony. I pressed my hips against the gate for balance against the buffeting wind. "Put your hands..." Ema said, signaling me to grasp the gate with my hands for safety.

My heart raced as I stared. Below me stretched a view of brightly colored homes, huge trees, and hiking trails. I looked away, overwhelmed.

When Ema asked me to grasp the balcony rail with my arms, I forgot about the left one. Ema now tried to wrap my paralyzed fingers around the rail herself, but found she couldn't get my fist open. My left hand was locked stiff with tension. I tried to ignore the reminder of my disability as she stubbornly worked to pry my hand open and I looked across the valley.

The wind, doves, crows, and even hummingbirds sang around me.

"Thank you, Aba," I managed. "This. Too mm much." I looked up to see a brown hawk soaring above our heads.

My weight began to shift onto my right leg and my fingers trembled, their grip weakening. I tried to keep looking over the heavenly view, refusing to let my disability steal the moment. But the trembling continued, and my left hand fell from the handrail. Ema massaged my numb left arm like a wounded soldier.

Aside from the two hawks I counted, the doves, and the cawing crows, the balcony was serenely quiet. I had never lived on a street with green trees below, or without the constant din of traffic. Standing there felt like a dream.

Aba next had us follow him into the guest room, which held a desk and a bed. "Ema can sleep here," he proposed, "or it can be your future office or gym." From here, we could see Aba's own home through the front windows of the house.

"Come, let's see ha-cheder shelcha *(your bedroom)*, Aba," Aba said then.

The room he had designated as mine had the same cozy wooden ceiling as the rest of the home. I stepped in, seeing my familiar cream-colored bed and recliner from the Burbank apartment. My room was almost as big as my apartment living room, with an attached bathroom and walk-in closet. Two windows overlooked the valley below.

"Bo-teere et habetshemoosh *(come see the bathroom)*," Aba enthused. I followed him, and Ema followed me.

In the bathroom, a bathtub faced a five-foot-high window, which overlooked the mountain view. There was a glass shower stall and a brand new toilet.

I glanced anxiously at the sharp corners on the bathroom stall and the counter. TBS had mentioned the possibility of falling and hitting my head on a sharp corner as a reason I shouldn't use the bathroom alone.

"Let's start with the toilet!" Aba announced. "Telech le-ze Adam." *'Go to it, Adam.'*

I thought that was an odd thing to say, but I glanced at Ema for permission and then did as I was told. I stepped up to the white toilet.

"Okay," Aba instructed, "lean to your left."

I did so, annoyed that I had needed reminding to stand up straight. As I straightened, the toilet mechanically sprang open on its own!

Zzzz, the toilet buzzed, presenting its open bowl with a tranquil blue light glowing inside. I stared.

"You see?! Ptatsa *(boom)*! No more problems for your balance," Aba celebrated, walking to a wall-mounted controller I hadn't noticed.

"There's a motion sensor ala *(on the)* toilet," Dad explained. "I had it placed on the right, so you must lean to your left to activate it. Good practice. The controller will then clean the bowl, warm the seat, and flush automatically when you stand up. I've placed this block so you can rest your left arm on it as you sit. It even has a built-in radio!"

Aba pressed the button for radio transmission, and commentary on a sports game began to blare from a speaker on the toilet's side.

I didn't know what to say. I hadn't asked for any of this, and while I appreciated it, it also reminded me of my own perceived emptiness.

I did nothing to deserve this.

"One last thing," Aba finished, "I had this metal bar placed to the right of the toilet, so you can use it to help you stand after using."

I looked at the bathroom's black-and-white checkered walls and floor, at the two white faucets that stood side-by-side.

"Wow, Aba."

Ema also seemed nervous in the new bathroom, but for different reasons. "Toda Alex, aval en leze *(thank you Alex, but there is no)* bar like that in the shower for him."

"I think he will be fine," Aba explained. "I ordered slip-resistant flooring." He pointed to the checkered floor and smiled confidently at me, as though looking to me for agreement or approval.

"I, oh, ok Ema," I said, taking a step closer to her. "I'll be okay."

The barrier between the floor and the inside of the shower stall here was lower than in the shower at my Burbank apartment, which would help me get into it on my own. I wondered if Aba had intentionally chosen not to include a shower handle as a show of trust in my abilities, or if he had forgotten to get one in the midst of everything. I decided to believe it was a matter of trust.

"Ramona tealche bevakasha, te-nee ani ve Adam leerot ech who mashteen eem ha toilet haze..." *'Rimona please leave, let Adam and I see how he will pee with this toilet.'*

Ema left and I pulled down my pants with my right hand. The toilet raised its lid as I stood in front of it and leaned to the left.

"Okay," Aba instructed. "Teal-chats *(press)* the, 'open,' button again lashteen *(to pee)*."

He pressed a button on the wall and the toilet seat lifted with a whirring noise. I started to pee—then stopped as the lid began closing, apparently deciding I'd had enough time.

"You see?" Aba asked as the toilet closed and flushed itself. Then he pressed the "open" button again and the lid and the seat started to rise in unison. I felt dizzy as I stood there with my pants down, watching and listening to the buzzing electric sounds the motors made. As my eyes strayed from the blue glow inside the toilet bowl, I saw red LEDs on the left of the toilet tank reading:

Power
Energy Saver
Water
Heat Seat
Dryer
Flush
Sensor

Aba looked at me. "This is good for la-rehab. You must lean toward your left, or the sensors will think you have gone away and will close."

Aba and I spent a while practicing using the thing. I learned that if I shook my hips periodically while I peed, the toilet would continue to register my presence and stay open. This was an adjustment because I was used to holding as still as possible to avoid losing my balance.

Aba then showed me the walk-in closet, which was cabinets and drawers. He promised I could use these for general storage if I didn't have enough clothes.

"You also have a private entrance to the deck, Aba," Aba pointed. He led me out onto the deck, where we passed two small, waterproof couches. I soon stood by him, my right hip grazing the balcony rail as we looked over the houses below.

"What are you thinking about? Ata-ohev et habayeet shelcha *(you like your house)*?" Aba asked.

I watched a crow fly past a hawk who was perched on a nearby tree branch. "N no words, Aba. Toilet expensive, house?" I tried my best to converse with him.

"The toilet was cheap in China," he waved a hand dismissively. "Eighty dollars. I brought it along with some of my shoe inventory. The house cost is fine. Anything to have my son living next to me."

At the time, I didn't even know if eighty dollars was a lot or a little. But after a pause, Aba's voice was thick as he said:

"…כמעט איבדתי אותך אבא." *'I almost lost you, papa. Never again…'* Then he shifted his weight. "How are you with your rehab?" he asked cautiously.

I didn't want to lie. I told him I knew it was necessary, but I was increasingly bored and craved more independence.

Aba turned to me as the birds sang around us. "I know rehab every day is tough, but I promise you. Anything you are willing lasot *(to do)* for your body to progress, I will make it happen. Let's prove those doctors even more wrong."

A hawk screeched over the valley, as though to emphasize Aba's words.

"I got you this house and built you a whole downstairs," Aba said, pointing down. "'Ze-lemata *(the downstairs)* will be for tenants to live, helping you with the mortgage expenses. Let me show you."

We walked to the kitchen side of the deck, my left leg swinging in circles as I grew exhausted. Aba slid open a glass door, helping me into the dining room.

"Ani ere lo et ha-lemata Ramona," *'I am going to show him the downstairs, Ramona,'* Aba called as he walked toward the stairs I'd been avoiding.

"Gam-ani yavo lo ra-etee, ve lazor," *'I will come and help also, I did not see, also help,'* Ema responded. I realized then that she had been unpacking my pots and pans and washing my dishes.

268

My cane clacked loudly on the hardwood floor as I approached the stairs. Aba went down the first six steps, then turned to see if I needed assistance.

"Boh." I gave a nervous smirk, realizing he didn't know I could walk down stairs on my own now. I darted down after him, but my cane collided with the edge of the stairs and my left knee locked, causing me to pitch forward.

"Adahm!" Ema yelled behind me as Aba grabbed me. My ankle brace hit him in the shin as my left leg swung forward. Thankfully, I stopped my fall by clutching the banister in my right hand.

"Nice and easy. No rush, Aba," Aba soothed, holding my shoulders. I nodded and took the rest of the steps more slowly. The second half of the staircase had no banister, so Aba stood closer to me so I could lean on his shoulder for balance. Needing so much help felt like a return to the Renewal Ranch days.

"Almost done, Manny tells me," Aba murmured. We had reached a hallway, where Aba showed Ema and me a series of bedrooms and bathrooms filled with dust, boxes, and furnishings like mirrors leaned against the walls. I would later learn that Aba had ordered these rooms built from scratch after discovering unused space between the main floor and the mountain beneath.

My head spun as I looked at the rooms. The paint was unfinished, and scraps of various materials littered the floors. My eyes began to water as my body begged to be allowed to lie down.

In the end, both my parents had to place both their arms around my shoulders, almost carrying me back up the stairs. I was taken to my recliner, where I almost instantly fell asleep for two solid hours after the 45-minute house tour.

Around 4 PM, I blearily opened my eyes to see an unfamiliar wooden ceiling.

Zzzzzz, the chair lifted me into a sitting position as I scratched the cranioplasty scars beneath my hair. I patted my pants pockets, looking for my cell phone. To my alarm, the pockets were empty.

"Ema!" I called from my recliner, hesitating to even stand up in this unfamiliar place when I did not know where my phone was to call for help.

Ema smiled at me as she came into the room. "Hi Danduni. How do you like waking up in your new home?" She handed me my cane. "You like the ceilings, yafe-nachon *(they're nice, right)*? Very cozy." She helped me up, pulling on my limbs to stretch them after my nap.

"Come to the kitchen. I want you to see it and the laundry room!"

We trooped back through the house to the kitchen with its white cabinets, drawers, four-foot-tall island, and the white bar stools taken from my apartment.

"Beautiful, right? All clean for you!" Ema said.

I looked around, wanting to sit. Ema showed me how to do the dishes with my one-functioning arm. I could look through the window at a beautiful green mountain view while I worked.

"You just wet, then put the plate down," Ema said, showing me the strategy she had devised. "Then scrub and rinse the soap off."

I stood beside her, mostly on my right leg, and practiced. My body kept wanting to turn away from my left side, and it was a strain to face the sink head-on. I went through the motions in a dreamlike state.

Still, it felt good to do something with Ema instead of her doing it for me. I hadn't set foot in the kitchen at Burbank since realizing my wheelchair wouldn't fit past the counters. Splashing as I cleaned plates alongside Ema made me feel a sense of camaraderie. The house had a dishwasher, but Ema didn't want me to use it. Doing so required me to bend over near one of the sliding glass doors, and she was afraid I could fall through the glass panels.

"It's good for you to walk and use your hands," Ema explained cheerfully, "but take breaks when you need to."

Aba had made the down payment on the house, but he planned for me to pay the mortgage, utilities, and taxes after I returned to work, which he was confident I would do soon. I'd had no sense of money or numbers since waking from my coma, but Aba believed this was within my capabilities.

That night, my 28th birthday, was spent in my new home. I sat on the couch as Ema bustled around, unpacking and organizing things.

I wanted to love my new home, to feel joyful and fulfilled. But my cane and foot brace were constant reminders that I was not truly independent, and honestly, I was not sure I could live alone.

"Dan-Dan, let's go to the deck," Ema walked into the living room, "your room is almost set, but let's go see the mountain!"

Outside, the Los Angeles night was cool. I caned back to the spot where I'd stood with Aba earlier, and Ema immediately began prying my left hand open to close it around the balcony rail. I'll never forget my first time staring across the valley at night, the stars above and the windows of the homes below glowing warmly in the cold darkness. Crickets chirped, and an owl hooted. A few minutes later, a coyote howled.

"Happy birthday, Adahmi," Ema said, putting her arm around me and squeezing.

271

"Thank you, D-Dubi."

I stared at the tree branch where the hawk had sat earlier. I was jealous of everyone and everything, even animals that moved fluidly through the air.

"You have no idea what your father did, Adahm," Ema breathed finally, looking out over the distant city lights. "The flights, hospital-eem, underwear, food, drugs, rehabs...to get a flight from Israel to Thailand, back le-po *(to here)*..." Ema silently wiped a tear and continued to massage my hands in the cold night air. "He gave everything for his son to לִשְׂרוֹד *(survive).*"

I stared out, nodding. I couldn't fully comprehend what my parents had been through. My memories from the early days of my injury were still missing.

I grabbed the white railing, slowly leaning my butt to my ankles to force my left knee to bend. I found myself anxious about being so far from everyone. There were no roommates, no neighbors sharing the building, no people driving by. Just me, Ema, and the San Fernando Valley at night. The darkness began to seem eerie as I looked around.

"Aba left you another surprise, Adahm," Ema said softly. "Bo-teere *(come see)*."

We walked back to my bedroom, where I saw a 9-inch-long silver device lying on my pillow. I was almost ready to sleep, my eyes blinking slowly as the left half of my face began to sag. But I leaned over and peered at the device, curious.

"Don't know if you remember, aval *(but)* Jane at Renewal Ranch told us to get a vibration stimulator to use on your left arm, like an e-stim. The vibration sends fast nerve impulses up your arm, hopefully reminding your brain that it exists. Aba used to also sell this at his Gadget-

Universe business with that chair." She pointed to the recliner.

Ema laid me on my back to sleep, placing the Vibration Gun X4-750 beside my hips with my left fingers wrapped around its base. "Tackzeek-poe *(hold here)* for 20 minutes, Adahmi."

The stimulator was marketed as a health device, and in my case, it really was prescribed to stimulate my left arm. I had no idea, as I held it, that vibrators could have any other use.

Ema turned the gun onto the 4/10 strength setting and it lightly pulsated, jiggling my numb left hand. I could feel the vibration through my hips where the device rested, but not in the arm it was meant to be awakening. I closed my eyes, frustrated by the lack of feeling in my fingers, and almost immediately fell asleep.

Suddenly, it was morning, sharp shafts of sunlight falling across my bedroom from the windows. I had fallen asleep with the vibration gun on, and Ema had tucked it into the corner of my nightstand when she came in and found me drifting.

I studied my room, noticing my phone charging on the nightstand beside my Thai monkey sculpture. Now the monkey stood empty-handed: I had no keys to give it.

Hearing me stir, Ema hurried in. "Boker-tov Danduni! Let's get ready for TBS!"

TBS.

The new house had increased my desire to be independent. I took the deodorant stick from Ema and tried to apply it on my own. I tried to use my right hand to apply it to my right armpit, curling my arm so the deodorant stick's tip grazed my skin.

My biceps must really have shrunk, I caught myself thinking, remembering when they were too bulky to allow me to curl my arm so tightly.

"Very good baby, ha-soldier sheli," Ema approved.

My attempt to put on my own socks failed, but I managed to stand up by myself even though my left leg was locked, sticking straight out.

After dressing and brushing my teeth, I caned into the kitchen. Ema had made me a bagel with cream cheese and coffee. I chewed my breakfast, looking around the kitchen in the morning light. Almost everything in the kitchen was white, and the center island held a fake purple flower in a vase.

That day at TBS, Becca decided to try having me walk barefoot. This was quite the experience.

"Okay, Adam," Becca gestured for me to sit so she could remove my shoes. "I'd like for you to practice walking without your shoes or your ankle brace!"

Even though I despised the ankle brace, I hesitated. Ema put my brace on every morning before I got out of bed: I tried to remember if I had walked without it since the accident.

Becca removed my shoes, socks, and ankle brace and put me in a bungee harness. Having Becca nearby gave me confidence: she hadn't failed me yet.

I rose off the table-bed on my right leg and took a few unbalanced steps. My left foot was limp, its toenails scraping the ground. I strained to bend and raise my left knee.

"Okay, Adam," Becca said approvingly, "nice, but stay balanced. If you raise your knee too high, you might tip over!"

I was too busy focusing on my left leg to pay attention.

Despite the difficulty, Becca and I felt my first attempt went well. Becca even mentioned that someday I might not need the brace at all! In the short term, Becca said she would order a smaller, lighter brace for me since I didn't seem to need quite as much support as I used to.

I smiled, wondering if that brace would hurt less.

But Becca was also quick to caution me. "You still need to wear a brace, and use your cane, for now. Remember, today, you had the bungee harness keeping you upright. You wouldn't have been able to stay standing without it."

At lunch, I gobbled my food up quickly and completed an extra-long parking lot walk, feeling good. After TBS, I asked Ema to take me to the gym.

For the entire drive to the 24 Galleria Gym, I raved to Ema about walking with 'naked feet' and the prospect that the hated ankle brace could be discarded.

At the gym, I never liked having people open the door for me. I would feel extra helpless in this place where I had once been dominant. To avoid this, I went so far as to wait by a bench until there was no one around before tackling the glass doors, yanking one open with my right arm, and throwing myself through before I lost my grip. I carried out this routine today, then caned to the back, where I grabbed a yoga mat from the rack beside the 'grandmother weights.'

I scanned the gym for Kaylee, hoping to see her but *not* wanting her to see me.

I decided to see if I could perform bodyweight exercises. I found an empty corner and unrolled the mat next to the mirrored wall, then used my cane to get down on my knees slowly. This ordinary-looking action forced my left knee to bend, a major achievement for me.

I practiced lifting my body off the yoga mat in different ways for the next 30 minutes. I was able to do something resembling push-ups by planting both knees and both fists on the mat, then pushing with all my might to straighten my arms and lift my body. I could perform this movement for six repetitions before my left elbow began to shake.

After a rest, I would spread the fingers of my left hand open against the mat and do tiny, three-inch "tricep push-ups" similar to Dave's weight-bearing exercises. This routine resulted in my first real sensation of being 'pumped,' the warm feeling of blood rushing into tissues combined with the temporary expansion of muscle size.

I felt so good after accomplishing these exercises! My weight was now back "up" to 160—still 35 pounds less than before my accident, but 15 pounds more than I'd weighed at the low point coming out of my coma six months ago.

I was feeling great about myself for the first time since my injury as I got up to start my next exercise. Then I saw something that made my heart sink: right in front of me, another gym member was performing my beloved pull-ups.

I watched in awe as the man lifted his body above the bar again and again, replaying my lost ability to launch myself into the sky. My heart broke as I watched him do the exercise I would probably never do again. When he did stop, he went to another machine that was now impossible for me: the treadmill.

I went to a small cable machine. If I could do tricep extensions, a movement not too different from some of my bodyweight exercises, maybe I could begin to use the machines again. I carefully pried the fingers of my left hand open with my right, then wrapped them around the handle.

This time, I remembered to lower the weight to 30 lbs—once I could do tricep extensions with 225 lbs—and pulled.

My left elbow shot out to the side, and my wrist and forearm shook while my weight shifted to my right side. "Argh..." I hissed, unwrapping my fingers. Disappointed, I texted Ema, "Ready, please come."

I caned back to the gym exit, surprised by how my feelings had changed from heated excitement to cold defeat in such a short time.

I sat in the underground parking structure on one of the benches in front of the elevator. The metal bench was cold beneath me as I watched many gym-goers, families, and friends joyfully walk across the parking lot. Everything they did as they walked and chatted seemed to mock my disabilities.

How can this be my life now? I thought, dismally waiting for Ema. At that moment, I couldn't think of any of my accomplishments, my luck, or my recovery. I just felt empty.

"How was your workout, neshama *(soul)*?" Ema asked me as I got into her car. I plopped myself in recklessly, losing my balance before I hit the seat.

Ema soon made a right turn onto Sepulveda Blvd towards the mountains. I had forgotten that I no longer lived in my Burbank apartment.

I sat staring down at my phone while my cane leaned against my left leg. I watched videos of Kaitlyn with friends in the kitchen of the Burbank apartment. Videos I took with Kaylee in my arms. I wanted to shore up my hazy memories.

Glancing up, I noticed Ema driving the car up a familiar one-lane street at a steep angle across a hill. "Ema... W where?" I asked, puzzled.

I continued to stare, slowly remembering the street. "Visit Aba?" I asked.

But Ema pulled into a white 1980s garage with walls of cracking cement brick. "Habi-yeet shelcha mami *(your house sweetie)*, you remember?"

I looked up at her blankly. "Very. Forgot all this."

The memory loss did not help my self-esteem, but it did give me the benefit of blissfully witnessing the back deck for the first time again.

The sun was high in the blue sky, and two exquisite black-brown hawks circled overhead while birds sang in the trees below. The mountain view gave me a badly needed sense of peace after my emotional day. I stood staring out over the valley until Ema brought us fruit and water and sat by my side in the sun.

"What are you looking at, Adahmi?" Ema asked.

I had no words for what I was feeling. Ema told me later that I looked deep in thought, but they weren't thoughts that came with words that made them easy to explain.

For my first weeks in the new house, I was on my feet almost continuously. Having my own home made me want to live up to the image of "the man of the house" who was in charge. I wanted to prove to Aba and Ema that I was able-bodied enough to live alone.

Ema was onto me. "Dan-Dan, take it easy," she called from the kitchen one day as I used the couch to practice knee bends. "You don't need to put on a show for us."

I would cane around the house tirelessly for hours, finding exercises to do or items to organize, then fall into an exhausted sleep in the reclining chair.

By February 2019, Aba was the one to pick me up from TBS since my home was across the street from his. He loved having his eldest live just steps from his door.

"Ze kmo ba-aretz she' koolam gareem echad lead ashani!" *'It's like Israel, everyone lives next to each other!'*

Ema continued coming out in the mornings to wake me up, help me dress, and issue her daily challenges.

Putting on socks with my right arm was now an everyday task, followed by slipping on a shirt. I continued to need Ema's help raising my left arm, which felt like it weighed 100 lbs in the morning, but I was able to do almost everything else in the morning preparation process. And now waking up involved not just dressing and brushing my teeth but walking the length of the house to get to the kitchen for breakfast.

In the evenings, showering in the Cody Home was easier than it had been in my apartment. The floors were very slip-resistant, and the lower barrier between the shower and the floor allowed me to swing my left leg into the stall. The shower stall here was also wider, easily hosting my shower chair with the suction cup feet.

I now began to get annoyed with my shower seat. Once necessary, it was now an inconvenience as it took up much of the shower floor. As my confidence grew, I began to complain to Ema and Aba about the chair getting in the way.

I scrubbed my own body as my balance and range of motion improved. I still waited for Ema's assistance to shave or clean my toes, but it was no longer necessary for her to scrub my entire body or prepare my toothbrush.

"How do you feel about owning a home, Adahmi? Ze *(is)* it weird to adjust?" Ema asked me one night as I got out of the shower. I thought about how to respond as I held my left arm up to help her finish drying me. In a strange way, the new home was less of an adjustment for me than it would have been for most people: my memory issues and the seeming loss of my automatic habits meant that every day felt like I was adjusting to life anew, no matter where I was.

One morning, Becca greeted me in the TBS lobby holding a white box. "Oooh, Adam," she said, swaying with anticipation like a schoolgirl with a secret. "Guess what I have for you?"

She guided me to the physical therapy hub, where she sat me down on a table-bed and opened the box. It was my new ankle brace!

"Okay," she said excitedly, "so this wraps around your ankle by clamping to your shoelaces." She held up its elegant velcro straps to demonstrate.

This brace came in two pieces: One would clip to my shoelaces, and all I needed to do to put it on was wrap the Velcro around my ankle and clip the two pieces together. This meant I could put on this brace by myself, without help!

We tested my new ankle brace on the bungee treadmill, in an obstacle course walk, and with bodyweight movements. It seemed to work, and I was that much closer to independence.

One day, Aba told me he wanted me to go on a trip with him into the desert toward Renewal Ranch Mirage, Palm Springs.

He didn't tell me why he wanted this, but since it meant getting out of TBS for a day, I immediately agreed. Aba later asked Ema for permission to take me on this overnight "business trip," whose purpose was still not explained to me.

A few days later, Aba and I made the two-and-a-half-hour drive to Palm Desert in his convertible. As Aba provided a stream of running commentary, I realized that he was opening up a new G-Defy office and wanted me to be there.

"Adahm, Manny heeye shama lazor lanoo *(Manny will be there helping)* to combine two stores into one," Aba explained as the sun-baked open road stretched before us. Manny was one of Aba's long-time contractors, a man with expertise in construction and renovation.

At last, we arrived at the strip mall complex, where a beige fountain stood in the plaza, looking incongruous in the dusty surroundings.

I suddenly got a rush of euphoria: being here on a "business trip" made me feel like I was starting a new life. When Aba brought the car to a stop, I almost jumped out, excited, but the excitement caused my left arm and leg to lock up.

Still, I was determined to walk in to meet the workers without my cane.

Aba saw me struggling to move my left leg and hurried to help. He now knew the motions to help me stretch my left arm, leg, and lower back.

"...Ah, thank you, Aba." I realized it was the long drive that did it: I'd had no muscle movement and impaired blood flow to my left side for far longer than usual. We stretched for 20 minutes before walking into the G-Defy store-to-be.

"It's okay, Aba," he reassured me. "Breathe." He pulled on my left arm, hyperextending it toward his chest as he spoke. "Teenshom." *'Breathe.'*

When we stepped into the store, I peered at the construction workers driving nails into new hardwood floors. Aba stopped me, grabbing my left arm. Only then

281

did I notice it was bleeding: I'd smacked it into the sharp, unfinished door frame on the way in, cutting the skin.

Aba tended to the cut without saying a word, but I saw construction workers glancing at us.

"Sorry, Aba," I murmured, trying to turn my back so they wouldn't see.

Aba found a shirt somewhere—I later learned that it was Manny's—and used it to dab up the blood. As he worked, I glanced around at the mirrored walls cloudy with dust from the construction, the couches waiting to take their final places, and the empty shelves that stood waiting for inventory.

The workers continued to hammer nails and lay plaster as Aba wrapped my arm in toilet paper and the shirt, and the bleeding stopped. Aba then led me to sit on a couch covered in a plastic tarp and took command of the construction work.

"You, go with Manny and Fidel. Rafael, help Edmundo with the measures."

Aba was always commanding, but seeing him here was a new level. He used words I didn't understand, teaming workers up on tasks as he evaluated what needed to be done before the opening. I just stared, drooling a little.

I shook my head when he stopped to bring me water and ask if I needed anything. I wanted to contribute value, not take his attention away from the work.

At one point, I tried to help by leaning down to assist Manny in lifting a mirror. This would have been an easy task a year ago, but this time, I nearly fell over to my left side, unprepared for the weight. Aba saw this and hurried over to hold me up.

Later, Aba and I drove to a hardware store to pick up some fixtures for the new G-Defy store. As he drove, I noticed that Aba had only one arm on the steering wheel for most of the drive. Wheels began to turn in my head.

"What do you think about driving soon?" I asked. Driving wouldn't require me to stand up, so my left arm and leg didn't need to be a problem.

Aba glanced at me and was silent for a long moment. "Do you think you are ready to control a vehicle?" he asked finally.

"...I want to," I said, squinting as the bright desert sunlight beamed off his snow-white dress shirt.

"Okay...yalla, get in."

To my shock, Aba pulled over on the side of the empty road. Then he got out of the driver's seat and opened the door, gesturing for me to take his place.

I got out of the car, leaving my cane behind. I stood on the roadside for a moment, hesitating, then finally walked to the driver's seat of the pearl-white car.

Is this a mistake? I wondered as Aba got into the passenger seat. *He really trusts me.*

Getting into the driver's seat proved harder than anticipated. It required me to get in with my left arm and leg first. I couldn't get in with my right side and then pull the injured limbs in after me. I ended up plopping myself into the seat and scooting until I was in something resembling a comfortable position.

Then there was a new problem: some of the controls, like the turn signals, were on my left side. That meant I had to consciously remember to search for them since my brain would forget that they existed if I didn't remind it.

But operating the pedals and turning the steering wheel only required my right arm and leg. The clutch was to my right, as were the road signs.

What would Becca say? I wondered. *Would she approve?*

283

We'd chosen a perfect place for the test: the desert road remained empty, stretching into a flat infinity. If another car showed up, I'd see it a mile away.

My heart began to pound as I looked around at the mirrors, speedometer, buttons, knobs, and the navigation screen. I felt like I was in a movie, surrounded by so many controls. I looked down at my legs, seeing my T-shirt-wrapped left arm laying in my lap and my left leg in its brace. But my right arm and leg felt perfect. Aba leaned back in the passenger seat, his expression unreadable.

"Adam regel ala-breaks *(foot on the brake)*," he reminded me when I seemed not to know what to do. I nervously followed the instructions, and he pressed the engine start button. This last action explained some of my confusion: his modern sports car used a button to start, not keys in the ignition like I was used to.

His 6.0L V12 sports-engine roared. I gulped as I squeezed the steering wheel, shaking a little. I glanced down at his speedometer, which topped out at 200 mph. I began to sweat.

He trusts me. Aba trusts me.

I pressed my foot down on the brake and shifted into drive. Relief flooded me as the actions felt familiar. Some of my old habits still survived. I inched the car forward at 15 miles per hour, turning right when Aba pointed out a side road. Turning the steering wheel felt unnatural, and my left arm slipped off my lap to be crushed between my left leg and the car door.

I stopped the car. "Okay, fix," I said, trying to comfort Aba by looking like I knew what I was doing. I lifted my left arm with my right, placing it on my lap like a bag. "Okay," I breathed again, pressing the engine button and staring in confusion when the car did not start.

"Adam, relax," Aba urged me. "Look around. No other cars, no rush. Just you and me."

I looked around the dirt road. This side street was lined with palm trees and residential houses further down the block. I gave Aba a crooked smile, feeling better from his words of wisdom.

"Okay, Aba," he tapped my shoulder with motivation, "Ata-yachol Aba!" *'You can do it, Papa!'*

I began driving more fluidly then. I was still nervous, but I'd taken us this far and had no impatient traffic to worry about.

My head drifted to the left as I concentrated more on driving than on my posture. Drool rolled down the left side of my chin as I concentrated on navigating at 23 miles per hour. My clothes became saturated with sweat from the intensity of my concentration, leaving stains on my armpits and thighs.

If Aba noticed, he said nothing to break my concentration. My right arm gripped the steering wheel as though touching something forbidden. My left arm lay heavy on my thigh, smacking me when we bounced over bumps. My head drifted to the left as I focused on driving, forgetting my posture.

"Yofi, let's do some work on turns—WHOA ADAM! LOOK OUT!"

***

17

More Driving & Seizure

Total memory recall: 35%
Mental Capabilities: 36%
Left Leg: 30%
Left Arm: 13%
Assistive items: Ankle brace
Age: 16
Weight: 162
Sources: Mom's journal, Dad, Alex, Rene, and Myself

I almost hit the cars by the time I saw them. They were parked on the right side of the street, which I had been drifting closer to as my brain failed to process the existence of the left side of the road. I swerved, missing one car by millimeters.

For a few minutes there, I'd felt very pleased with myself. I was driving! Here was proof that I could go where I wanted to and look normal while doing it. I imagined that no one would stare at me or stop to ask if I needed help while I was behind the wheel. Plenty of people drove with just one arm most of the time.

"Adahm, easy, keep attention," Aba said, breathing deeply.

I got us back to the G-Defy store parking lot, and Aba half-jokingly asked me to try steering with my left arm. I peeled the fingers of my left hand back with my right and wrapped them around the wheel. My grip instantly slipped as my hand was slick with sweat, my armpits and pants soaked through with it. Later, Aba let me practice again near the hotel where we were staying.

"Good, Aba, slow. It's getting dark." I was developing a habit of forcing my eyes to scan the left half of the road. I sweated with the intensity of concentration. Around 6:30 PM, I yawned while we sat at a red light. Aba noticed that my left arm was shaking on my thigh and suggested we return to the hotel. I'll never forget Aba's impossible challenge to me over dinner that evening.

"Adam, you need to buy the Podiatry Book and learn about every foot condition there is. Then you can come work with me at G-Defy."

I nodded, feeling helpless. Learning from books was never my strong suit. It was why I'd had so much trouble in school. But I had to try.

I eagerly told Ema about my drive when we arrived home the next day. "Ema I, d d drove car with Aba!" She smiled and nodded, but I saw the uncertainty in her eyes.

"Ahlex, yesh lo-yad echad *(he has one arm),*" I heard her say reproachfully to Aba.

"Ramona who haya-beseder *(he was fine),*" Aba defended me.

The next day at TBS, I realized that my business trip with Aba had had a huge positive effect on me. I walked with more confidence and looked further into the distance. I wanted to walk further off of the TBS campus on my lunch break.

I skipped eating the sandwich Ema had packed and caned straight to the parking lot again for some practice walking without my cane in public. I left my cane by the usual Jeep and set off. As I walked, I found myself wanting something more.

I wanted to drive again.

287

Of course, that was not an option at the moment. I had no car of my own. But I could give myself a different challenge. I returned to the Jeep, got my cane, and walked to the nearest crosswalk. I took a deep breath and pressed the button.

My heart pounded as I waited. Could I really do this? This intersection was closer to TBS, but much busier than the one Ema and I had crossed. I stared at the 6-inch curb, planning how I would swing my left foot down onto the street.

"26," the crosswalk timer began to count down. "25, 24, 23, 22...." I rushed forward, swinging my legs, torso, and shoulders around wildly. I didn't make it across the street in time, but one of the cars stopped at the light was a big truck from which a Southern gentleman waved and shouted encouragement. He made it clear that he wouldn't let his lane move until I had safely crossed.

"Take your time, brother! All these folks can wait!" I smiled crookedly and waved back as I caned my way up to the ramp designed to let bicycles cross the street.

I was overjoyed to be out on my own. I felt like I was at an amusement park as I stared around, with no one to tell me what I couldn't do. There were so many places to visit. Stores, benches where I could leave my cane, people walking in and out of restaurants. I stood staring at Tony Roma's and reminiscing about my childhood birthdays there as I decided where I should walk first. I soon realized this parking lot was different from the TBS lot: this lot was busy. Cars constantly moved through the crowds, creating chaos.

My heart raced again as I considered what it would mean to step in front of one of those cars. My hand went to my phone, thinking I should call Ema to pick me up. I looked for a quieter area, and I found it: a corner near the nail salons. I caned there, already beginning to tire.

Okay, let's do this, I thought as I surveyed the relatively quiet part of the lot.

I carefully dropped my cane between two bushes, already panting from the exertion of getting myself here. I chose a blue SUV near the entrance as my starting point and began to take unsteady, unassisted steps along the edge of the lot. I swung my left leg forward with great effort, hunching over under the burden of my left arm. I made it to the next car, huffing with excitement. As I made my way around, I leaned on cars, light poles, and store signs for support.

After 20 minutes, I looked back at the bushes that held my cane. They seemed very far away. I turned to head back. I caned back to the crosswalk and stood by the light. I felt winded but proud. I was running late to therapy with Laura. I stood by the elevator, joyful from my 'escape,' half-hoping Becca or somebody had seen me out there.

I was still smiling a big, crooked smile when I knocked my cane against Laura's open door to let her know I had arrived. My experience of driving had given me a new perspective. After eight months of needing full-time caretakers, I finally felt like a man again.

When Ema picked me up that day, I asked if I could drive her SUV. She looked at me like I was crazy. "Lo, lo ma kara lecha Adam?" *'No, no, what are you thinking?'*

Ema kept reminding me that I only had one functional arm when the topic came up. I kept asking, like a 16-year-old who doesn't yet have a car of his own. Finally, the day came when she had to make a stop in her quiet suburban neighborhood near TBS before driving me home. She hesitantly agreed to let me get behind the wheel if we stayed in her neighborhood.

"Okay, nice and easy," she said as I climbed into the driver's seat. It was, thankfully, much higher up than the seat of Aba's low-riding sports car. "Okay, Dan Dan," Ema took a deep breath as I began inching forward, my left arm lying limp in my lap.

Ema kept staring at me anxiously, clutching my cane with white knuckles in the passenger seat. "Please drive slow, baby."

That was easy. Twenty-three miles per hour was still my top speed.

"ADAM!" Ema yelled as I stopped at a stop sign to let another car go. "Adahm, please look at your left!" Ema clutched the handle of her car door. "How did you do this with Aba?! Ot-pam *(again)* look at your left mirror, Adahm…"

During that ride, I realized that I was different around Ema. With her always being so ready to take care of every aspect of my life, I felt I could let go of some responsibility. This made me, perhaps, a little bit sloppier. I focused on looking to my left, determined to drive Ema to her Encino home. Things went smoothly for a few minutes, and then she looked at me again.

"Adahm, yesh lecha et ha license shelcha?" '*Do you have your driver's license?*' I realized that I did not have my license, wallet, or even my headphones with me. I also had no idea if my license might have expired in the last eight months.

"Okay, okay," Ema breathed. "Go up the garage ve zeuoo *(and that's it)*."

I obliged, noticing that my hand was already moist with sweat.

My mind played tricks on me. One morning, I woke up and looked at the monkey on my nightstand. "Ema," I asked sleepily, "W-here's car-keys?"

"No more car, baby," Ema said, then tried to change the subject. "Ayom bo naseem 'garbayeem lemala, echad, shtayeem, shalosh!' *'Today, let's put on socks! One, two, three!'*

I rose to grab the socks she offered as Ema playfully announced to me, "Teastakel eem ha drool ha-reshon shelcha ba-biyett shelcha! *'Look! Your first real drool at your house!'*

She was correct: a string of glistening drool was dripping from my mouth. I put on the new ankle brace on my own, and it was off to TBS.

After a day of speech therapy, cognitive therapy, and a group discussion class, Martha stopped me at the front desk on my way out of TBS. She told me to look at my phone about a "special pick-up." This was when I discovered that Rene had texted me over lunch, telling me he would be the one picking me up today!

Ey dude im coming to grab you at 4
Helping your moms out
Daddy I'll calllll you

Bosh - 11:10 AM

I was ecstatic! It still surprised me when my friends wanted to spend time with me since I was now unable to take part in most of the activities we had in common. I sat by the lobby, excitedly waiting for Rene. He soon walked in wearing the white American Eagle pullover sweater I had given him in 10th grade.

"Yoo, there he is, big man," Rene exclaimed. "Let's go bro! Oh, hold on, I gotta sign something?" Martha primly handed him a clipboard. Rene stared at it with his intense blue eyes. "Man, crazy how I gotta sign you out. Remember ditching class for Jack In The Box, Adam?"

he smirked as he scribbled the name of my high school ex, Tristy Edner, instead of his own name.

"Sir, your ID for confirmation," Martha asked knowingly. Rene was caught and eventually scribbled the correct name to match his ID.

I carefully folded my left knee to get my left foot under me, then stood to walk out of the lobby with Rene. "Walking got a lot better, man," Rene observed. "You're moving!"

"Still not, n-good," I said softly, trying to distribute my weight equally between my feet.

Once we got into Rene's white coupe, I examined the interior. "Infiniti," a logo said. The center console was lower, but had many controls similar to Ema's. I wanted to drive his car. I wanted to show him my progress, but it was also a beautiful vehicle that would have tempted me under any circumstance.

"Let me drive, Rene," I asked casually as he drove us down the Boulevard with both hands perched confidently on the wheel.

He glanced at me. "Bro, sure you can drive with one arm?"

"Yea, good," I responded to him. Rene looked back down the road, "Okay. I know you're driving your dad's expensive whip, and your mom's trusting you with hers. We straight, Varsity man." He pulled over by the side of the road.

My heart fluttered as Rene called me "Varsity." That was an inside joke: I'd never made Varsity basketball, but I'd always wanted to. It reminded me of the good times we'd shared, including the journey I took him on across the world.

I left my cane in the passenger seat in my haste to get to the driver's seat. I had to grab the car door to keep my balance.

"Easy, easy, bro," Rene soothed. "No rush, man, we good."

"Sorry, Re'," I mumbled. I slid on the driver's side seatbelt, grazing my taped shoulder in the process, and pushed the "start" button with confidence. "Okay, drive chill, man," Rene said, watching me.

I nodded excitedly, scratching my cranioplasty scar as I got oriented.

"Ey, let me see your cranio-scar," Rene requested. "Your mom told Nick and I not to talk about it. But show me, man, I wanna see."

I shrugged my right shoulder, holding his steering wheel with my only arm. "Nah, let it heal," I responded.

He jokingly "knocked" on the hood covering my head. "Ey, so is this really all plastic Varsity?" He shook his head at the thought.

We had never spoken about the injury I sustained on the Thailand trip. But now I wanted to enjoy feeling "normal," driving a car with an old friend. I focused intensely on scanning the Boulevard ahead.

Rush hour traffic was setting in, but I navigated smoothly with my one arm.

"Cool," Rene said, sitting back in his seat. "You can be my driver. That'll be cool!" He laughed as I felt my entire body shift to the right in Rene's leather seat.

I absolutely loved that moment. No embarrassment from walking, caning, or fumbling with my left hand. Just driving, like I might have in another life.

"Let's go to In-N-Out," Rene proposed. "I had no lunch today, and I'm starving from working with my clients!"

The thought of entering a busy parking lot made me sweat. In my anxiety, turning the steering wheel made me dizzy. But I wanted to impress Rene.

Do I take my cane, do I leave it? I wondered as I inched into the parking lot.

Where should I park? A handicapped spot? I don't have my handicapped pass.

"Take the drive-through," Rene proposed. "Let's stay in the car. Gonna text your mom to tell her we stopping for food," he said, pulling his phone out. "But don't tell her you drove, man."

I breathed a sigh of relief at everything he said.

I slowly pulled into the line, and anxiety seized me. How close should I get to the other vehicles? How close did I need to be for the staff to hear me order?

"Be cool, Adam," Rene reassured me. "Just signal; they'll let you pass."

I will be eternally grateful for Rene acting normal. This was the first time I'd driven with someone, and they hadn't yelled for me to avoid something. Rene didn't even feel the need to keep his eyes on me, texting Ema as I drove.

Rene's car was a sporty coupe similar to Aba's but sturdier. It moved perfectly under my right hand, and the peace I felt driving with Chico made it easier to remember the left side of the road. Rene took a phone call on speaker with a friend. I felt even better at receiving so much trust from him.

I had wondered if he'd ever trust me again after what I did in Thailand.

Once we got his burger, we switched seats as Rene thought it would be risky for me to drive too far without a license. At Rene's first turn, my left arm fell out of my lap and hit his center console. I didn't care. I was joyriding with my friend.

Rene drove us up the hill to my Cody Home. I stared as his left hand glided beautifully along the car's steering wheel while he ate with his right hand.

"Tell your mom I said 'hi,' and it was easy picking you up. No sweat!" He smiled as I opened the door. "Text me later man, maybe we'll go for another ride."

I smiled back, pulling my knee out of the car and grabbing my cane as Ema came to help me safely into the Cody Home.

"Hi, Danduni!" She paused. "Why you have ha *(that)* sweat stain?"

Only now did I realize I'd soaked my armpits and Wally Maddison pants with sweat in my intense concentration. I only sweated like that while driving.

At dinner that night, I finished eating my baked salmon while Ema held her water glass, moving her fingers across it to the soft Israeli music she had been playing.

"Adahm," she said finally, "I do not want to hurt your feelings, but all this driving that you are doing ze-arbe *(is too much)*." She looked at me. "I cannot sleep at night. Your mind's cognition ze *(is)* on ksat *(slight)* delay, and the thought of you driving in traffic keeps me awake with worry.

"Your progress is amazing Adahm," she continued, "but this driving is too much strain. Ata lo yodea mah ha-doctors amroo-ala recovery shel ha-moach shelcha." *'You don't know what the doctor's said about your mind's recovery.'*

I stared down at the right half of my plate. I didn't want to hear about the alleged limits on my recovery. But I didn't know how to express this to Ema.

She was still talking. "...guessing you were maybe driving with Rene, it's too much achshav *(now)* Adam..."

I looked up at her finally. "Sorry, I-I'm sorry, Dubi, need to drive, I want to d-drive, Ema. Please, I like it." I stared into her right brown eye, almost begging.

In my sleep that night, I dreamt that Nick, Allan, Rene, and I were having fun on a road trip. We were driving on a desert freeway similar to the one Aba and I had taken to Palm Springs, but we were driving Ema's SUV. We were laughing, talking, rapping, and eating as I guided the car on its gliding course through the desert.

In the dream, I was using my left hand to steer us effortlessly.

***

My TBS rehab continued, but I now desired more than just parking lot walks. One day, I decided to call an Uber to take me somewhere new.

I stared at my phone, wondering where I should drive. I could think of no places in the world beyond the mall complex outside TBS, the nearby Gelson's, and the 24 Galleria Gym. I finally remembered The Woodland Village—the restaurant where I had first moved my arm in front of Ema and Alex Eskanazi.

I pressed the "confirm ride" button and started downstairs, grinning wildly.

"Adam, eating downstairs?" Martha inquired as I passed through the lobby.

"Yep!"

Unfortunately, it turned out it was not that easy. Four Uber drivers in a row refused to pick me up, seeing my obvious disability as I approached their cars.

I eventually found a driver who did not seem to care about my condition. My heart pounded as I thought about how to get into his old Lexus without help.

I nervously knocked on the window, trying to remember the correct procedure. Did I need to ask his permission to unlock the door?

"Yes, Adam?" The driver asked me, rolling his window down.

I nodded.

"Yes, welcome. Get in, unlocked!"

I excitedly opened the rear door, trying to gracefully slide into the back seat. To my dismay, I couldn't bend my left knee. I tried frantically to pull the knee in after me with my right arm but kept getting stuck half-in the car.

Watching me struggle, the driver called: "It's okay sir, come sit by me."

The driver held my cane as I struggled into his passenger seat. As we drove away from TBS, I felt very accomplished.

So much for golf ball pickups, I thought, watching the world roll past us.

I stared out the window on a winter day in Los Angeles feeling sheer bliss. I fought the urge to text Ema, wanting to relish the moments of independence.

Slowly, I realized I wouldn't return from my destination on time. And if neither Ema nor TBS knew where I was, they could call the police.

I ordered a chicken taco like I'd had that night my left arm first moved. I stared at my phone as I ate it, considering my dilemma.

I could try calling another Uber and hoping TBS wouldn't call Ema when I was late. But that sounded too risky. At last, I nervously called Ema and asked her to pick me up from The Woodlands if she could.

"Adahm!" I could hear the panic in her voice. "I can't believe you are leaving TBS! You have rehab! Ani ba-achav ata-zoos!" *'I am coming now, don't move.'*

I tucked my phone in my pocket and looked around. I still had energy and excitement from my Uber ride. I paid for my lunch and decided to do some of my own 'rehab,' leaving my cane by a bush and walking without it.

Walking in public without a cane was always a monumental feeling. It's difficult to describe to someone who has never been bedridden for weeks. The doctors' dire predictions early in my recovery added to my joy at walking around on my own, with no nurse. No therapist. Just me, hooded to hide my cranioplasty scar and dragging my foot, not letting my arm or leg slow me down!

I walked carefully, staying near walls and signs so I could catch myself if I lost my balance. I walked past a glass-fronted shop called Cupcakes Delight, swinging my left leg in circles like a drunk ballerina as I went. I smiled crookedly as my fingers drifted along the front windows of new shops I'd never visited before.

There was a flock of children running up and down the sidewalk. Their passion for life seemed to mirror my own.

You can do this, I told myself. *You can be one of them.*

I had walked the length of quite a few stores when Ema arrived with fearful and angry comments about my "playing hooky."

"This was no good, Adahm. You should have called me!" She continued her rant as I folded myself to get into her SUV.

I still felt good about the trip, even if Ema did not agree.

"Adam, are you crazy!" She asked. "How did you pay? No one knew where you were. What if you got hurt? Don't do this anymore, Adahm!"

I looked out through the windshield as Ema massaged my left arm. I contemplated leaving my cane in the back seat and walking around the Cody Home without it to see if Ema would even notice. I decided to do just that.

As far as I could tell, Ema didn't notice my cane's absence. Not during dinner, while I helped with the dishes, or even when I showered! This solidified my decision to stop using the hated cane since I obviously no longer needed it.

Only the next morning at breakfast did Ema notice its absence. "Adahm, efo ha-cane?" *'Where is the cane?'* she asked.

"Left in car," I told her, raising my bagel as though in a toast. "Don't need."

As the months passed, I drove in the passenger seat with various friends and family members. My parents finally, reluctantly, called Vital to reduce my weekly rehab hours. I began preferring Ubers to being driven by Ema, having a greater sense of independence that way. But I still sometimes asked Ema to join me for lunch. Now that felt like a special treat rather than a constant necessity.

To my astonishment, Ema agreed to help me contact the DMV about getting a driver's license. The DMV told us it wasn't out of the question if I could pass a safety evaluation for people with brain injuries.

"It's good you haven't had seizures, Adam," Ema said as she made the appointment. "Having seizures like Daniel can lead to driving restrictions."

On March 8, Ema and I attended my appointment for a "post-injury driving test" at a local business the DMV contracted to evaluate brain-injured prospective drivers. I had to be interviewed and pass a test to receive my certification. I remember hobbling into the evaluation office without my cane and banging my left arm on a door frame.

I sat, my left foot trembling from excitement, and was given a 50-question exam paper. It was similar to the one I'd taken at 16 but with more questions.

I had to take breaks as my nerves shorted out my already-short attention span. Ema gave me water as I concentrated, hunched over my desk. In the end, I completed the "20 to 30 minute" exam in 55 minutes. I had to strain to remember things like how to behave when an ambulance was driving toward your car.

By the end of the test, I was disheartened. I had so much trouble with some of the answers that I was sure I would be deemed too disabled to drive.

Next came the eye exam. I tried to pass it without glasses, but in the end, I had to wear them in order to pass the vision requirements. I was then assigned to an interview-room with a young woman, Ms. Ares.

She and I sat face-to-face at a table as I looked into her right brown eye intently. My foot trembled under the seat, and I squeezed it to try to get it to stop.

"Hello there, Adam," Ms. Ares greeted me. "I'd like to ask a few questions to check your mental state as a possible future driver."

I nodded, curious.

"Does traffic on the road disappoint you?" she began.

I shrugged. "Nobody likes traffic," I said as naturally as possible.

"Do you ever feel angry and want to hurt yourself?"

I looked around the room for a hidden camera. "N-no."

"Do you ever injure yourself," Ms. Ares asked, "as a form of coping?"

I stared at her. "N-no?"

"Good. Thank you." She seemed to sense my unease. "If someone were to cut you off in traffic, would you get angry?"

"Not angry," I said carefully. "Happens."

"You wouldn't want to run them over or hit them with your car?"

I looked at the table in front of me. "I I would never do that, a good person a d d driver al m m my life."

Perhaps because of the stuttering, Ms. Ares asked: "Adam, do you have much trouble remembering things?"

"Sometimes."

"How often?"

I shrugged, looking at her helplessly.

"What kinds of things are distracting to you?" She asked. "Do you avoid them? How? Might that continue as a driver on the road?"

I described my process for focusing on myself to her and making sure I scanned both sides of the road.

I was surprised that the interviewer passed me. I was told later that I had technically failed the written exam, but if I was able to pass the interview and the practice driving test, I could get my license anyway. What probably saved me was that I had never had a driving violation in my life up to that point. Perhaps the DMV figured that my old good habits were likely to have survived the accident.

Aba and Ema were stunned when I reported that I had an appointment to take my road test.

After that DMV appointment, I was on top of the world. I was now a homeowner, able to walk around and participate in society without a helmet or cane. And I was about to get my license to drive my very own car!

I almost began to feel invincible again.

A few days later, Thailand's Phuket Hospital emailed my parents to check up on my recovery and progress.

Greetings Elnekaveh trakūl (family),

How is □□□□ - *Adam? Recovering ok?*
Please email for any assistance needed. We have relationships for international nursing homes if needed!
Thank you!
Nurse Gemma

I smirked, thinking about what to write back.

***

I awoke the morning of my driving test, practically bouncing with excitement.

"Boker-tov hegeeya Dan Dan! ready for today?!" Ema asked. My eyes shot open. "Bo stretch for me, baby."

I immediately began stretching with a crooked grin on my face, raising my arms and putting on my deodorant. Ema went to the kitchen to cook breakfast.

This is it! I told myself. *Freedom at last!*

Everything felt possible as I used Aba's new toilet. There was nothing to fear and nothing slowing me down. I was determined to live life to the fullest.

Then it started.

The fingers of my right hand began to go numb. My *right* hand. I stared in horror as tremors took over *both* arms and legs. The ground rushed up at me.

I woke up, dizzy and confused, in an ambulance. Everything felt far away, like a dream of another life.

I glanced around to see cardiac monitors and IV equipment hooked up to me. I realized after a moment that there was an oxygen mask on my face. Paramedics were

302

reporting vitals and passing supplies back and forth over me.

Where am I? How?

One of the paramedics noticed that I was awake.

"Are you okay, young man?" Just keep breathing. "Relax."

I learned that Ema had been waiting for me in the kitchen. She came to check on me when I didn't come in for breakfast or answer her calls.

She found me sprawled on the bathroom floor, convulsing. My eyes were rolled back in my head, and saliva ran down my cheeks. My body shook violently.

I was now learning what a post-traumatic convulsion was.

A post-traumatic convulsion is a seizure resulting from a traumatic brain injury. When the brain is injured, neurons can get overexcited, similar to the activity that caused the spasms in my left arm and leg. These storms of overexcitement can become so intense that they take over the whole brain, disrupting consciousness and resulting in full-body spasms.

Soon, I was sitting in a hospital with my parents at my side. Ema kept glancing at my face as she massaged my left arm while Aba looked around the room with his arms crossed in frustration. In my hazy state, I thought I was in some sort of international battlefield hospital.

A neurologist, Dr. Atman, came and prescribed me a medication called Depekot. It was to be taken each morning with water before I ate.

"Hakol heeye beseder Adahmi," *'All will be good.'* Ema gave her most consistent motherly phrase, massaging my arm.

"It could have been worse," she looked at me. "You could have been driving, at the gym, or in an Uber!" Ema took a deep breath, raising her own blood pressure with speculation. "No more of that for now, Adahm."

The fact was, it could have been a *lot* worse. Aba later calculated, by measuring the bathroom, that my head had landed just seven inches from the sharp corner of the counter. If my head had hit that, it could have killed me.

Dr. Atman eventually returned, handing me a bottle of pills. He advised me to stop drinking caffeine, as it could worsen seizure activity. He also explained that I should not drive or use heavy machinery, including gym equipment.

I listened to the long list of forbidden activities and immediately decided to ignore the prohibitions.

Finally, Dr. Atman warned me that I may need a live-in caregiver if I continued to have seizures.

Aba gave him a fierce look. "Teashtok ya-mefager *(shut up, you idiot)*," he said. Then he smiled at me. "Thank you, doctor. Let's go, Ramona." He extended his hand to help me off the bed. My left arm and leg were unusually stiff.

Just like that, I lost months of progress. No one wanted to take me for my driving test after the seizure, and with the prospect that I could be getting sicker, my days became sad. My friends were instructed not to let me drive, and TBS was told not to let me leave the facility. Ema insisted on escorting me to the gym.

After this, I checked out almost completely during my TBS sessions, resenting them. The missed DMV appointment nagged at the back of my mind. I wondered if they'd count the fact that I hadn't shown up against me in the future.

Nick texted me:

I have belief in you man. Adam, you will get stronger from this situation.

Later, I was told that if anyone reported my seizure to the DMV, I wouldn't be allowed to drive or get my license for at least three months.

"I hope that doesn't happen Dan Dan," Ema said as she searched state policies on her laptop. "If it does, we will have to fight it."

It was during this time that I felt most isolated. I had recovered enough to crave company and excitement, but I wasn't getting it. I felt despair.

I didn't really *want* to go out if it meant everyone was watching me, nervous that I'd have a seizure. I couldn't imagine how I was going to rejoin normal life.

One day in March, Aba brought me a new Apple Watch Series 3 to wear.

"Adam, I want you to wear it always!" He instructed me. He presented it as a gift he'd brought me to brighten my mood, but I overheard him say to Ema in Hebrew: "It will be good if he has another seizure or accident. It tracks his vitals, and he can always call for help as long as he is wearing it."

It took me (with Ema's help) 25 minutes to put it on my wrist for the first time. I chose my left arm so that I could use the touchscreen with my right hand. Once I got it strapped onto my disabled left arm, I couldn't feel it at all.

This was unsettling. The gray watch looked so bulky and heavy on my wrist, but I couldn't feel it. The watch soon accumulated dents and scratches from where I accidentally slammed it into door frames or countertops.

Aba noticed that I seemed defeated, and he thought of a plan.

"Adahm," Aba said, "we should visit Thailand. To give you closure."

I wasn't excited to return, given the memories attached to the place. But I did agree: it sounded better than continuing the monotony of my TBS classes.

"Adahm," Aba said as we sat on my couch together, "I know you are feeling down, aval ze heye tov lachzor chazak le Thailand! Le efo keemat ayeeta keemat met." *'But it will be good to return with strength to Thailand! To a place you were once dead!'*

He wanted to remind me of how far I'd come. Last time I was in Thailand, I couldn't even speak. The doctors had not expected me to ever speak again.

Ema wasn't thrilled. She saw my seizure as a major medical setback. I overheard her ask how 'closure' would help me.

"He's getting better," Aba insisted. "He's stable and stronger, walking without a cane. He will be fine. Ani estakle-elav." *'I will look after him.'*

I took a breath as I sat in my own home, being spoken about like I was not there.

Hearing my father express his confidence in me boosted my own. I decided it was time to show my parents I was looking ahead. I scrolled with my right hand on my phone and ordered four business books, selecting from among the bestsellers with the highest star rating. I ended up with *Total Money Makeover*, *The Intelligent Investor*, *Leaders Eat Last*, and *Life and Work*.

I ordered these books in part because I wanted to help Aba prove to Ema that I was recovering. But I also hoped that they would help me recover further. Somewhere in my mind, merely purchasing books like these would automatically boost my memory. I must admit, I also thought about how cool I would look walking around TBS with these books in my bag.

The final week before "Thailand Trip Part 2" went by like a recurring dream. I woke up in the same position every morning, my sleeping position restricted by my dead limbs. Ema would wake me up, give me a morning challenge, help me dress, and I'd be off to TBS for a day of rehab.

On one of the last days before leaving for Thailand, I asked Ema if I could try walking in my shoes without the ankle brace.

"Careful, Dan-Dan," she responded, "but okay. Bo-nere *(Let's see)*. Aval tee-ye lead ha meetah *(Be next to your bed)*."

Ema pulled my shoes on, tying them tightly for support, but leaving the brace at the foot of my bed. "Okay," she said. "Stand slowly."

I pulled my left knee in and got up, pushing with my right foot. I tried to step forward, but my left toes dragged brutally against the floor. Without a brace, my foot felt like dragging a 10-pound bag of rocks with my left leg. I stopped as Ema grabbed the side of my shirt, steadying me.

I tried two more times but soon sat back on the bed, groaning. "...I will never do that again."

Ema patted my back. "Ksat ve ksat Adahmi." '*Little by little.*'

I put my velcro brace back on, and we went to TBS.

That day, Ema informed Lina and Becca of my upcoming trip. They emphasized the need for me to take extra care on my trip because of my disability. They both spoke to us about the importance of using my cane when I walked.

I nodded earnestly when they encouraged me to wear my brace, but I didn't plan to return to Thailand with a cane.

***

308

18

Closure

Total memory recall: 38%
Mental Capabilities: 40%
Left Leg: 37%
Left Arm: 15%
Assistive items: Ankle brace
Age: 16 1/2
Weight: 165
Sources: Dad, Holiday Inn Desk, Leenda, and Myself

I didn't journal much during "Thailand Part 2," so I don't have many details. I remember being ecstatic about getting a break from rehab, feeling powerful at the prospect of flying across the world. I didn't always remember *where* Aba and I were going or why, but the prospect of taking a real trip was huge in my mind.

When the day came, Aba gave me the aisle seat on the airplane so I could cane up and down the aisle during the 18-hour flight.

This flight felt different. I wasn't anticipating delicious Thai food or tours of the beautiful islands. I wasn't clutching my phone or testing FitFlow. I wasn't calling the shots. I felt frail as Aba carried my bags, concerned about me losing my balance. When we sat down in our seats, I was already beginning to feel tired.

Aba helped me get comfortable in my seat by taking off my ankle brace. He alerted the stewardesses that I would need snacks and water regularly, and even followed Ema's instructions to make sure I used the finger-stretcher during the overnight flight. I kept my hood up, insecure about my itching cranioplasty scar.

"No hood-wearing heye in Asia," Aba told me, trying to make light of the issue. "Ze heye *(it will be)* too humid!"

I did at least get the satisfaction of turning off the phone alarm, which was meant to remind me that I should be at TBS while the ocean stretched below us.

Eighteen hours later, we arrived in Bangkok.

I don't remember landing, nor departing for Phuket. I do remember arriving in Phuket and seeing the familiar tuk-tuks on the street, taking my first breath of sunny, humid air, and being helped by Aba into a taxi at the airport.

We got out of the taxi to the honking of tuk-tuks and walked into the familiar lobby of the Holiday Inn. I limped behind Aba as he carried our bags.

"Remember the pool?" he asked. "Ve-ha *(and the)* gym? Rene said you guys never got to use it, but you used the gym at the Diamond Hotel, nachone *(right)*?"

I peered at the stack of dumbbells visible through the gym's glass door as we passed. They were larger than the Diamond Hotel's dumbbells: here, I might not have needed Rene to stack the weights for me. Then my gaze traveled to the pool, remembering laughing as I roughhoused with Rene and flirted with Div.

"Let's go, Aba," I responded, cracking my knees. He thought I would benefit from seeing these places again, but I wanted to get away from them fast.

I can't explain what I felt being back at that Holiday Inn. I caned through the halls at Aba's side, acutely aware of the rattling of my Depekot pills in Aba's pocket. The humidity in the air made my hand slippery on the cane. I didn't recognize the elevators as Aba and I got on them.

"Ani samtee *(I put a)* request for the room you and Rene stayed in," Aba told me as the elevator doors dinged open. Aba clearly hoped that if he could reproduce the trip Rene and I had taken, this would somehow help my healing.

My left knee swung out as I caned after Aba to room 730. I stared around the room but found I didn't recognize a single item in it. That was almost a relief.

The staff had left a plate of fresh fruit by our beds to welcome us. Aba placed my pills beside them on the nightstand, and I resolved not to use my cane anymore while we were here. I didn't want the injury I had suffered to "win" and change my life forever. I was going to prove to Phuket that I could recover.

From then on, I walked close to Aba so I could grab onto him if necessary. I told him I thought I would recover faster without the cane, and he agreed.

The sandy and gravel-strewn walkways didn't make walking easy. My locked left foot skidded across the loose sand and rocks as my left leg swung out. Aba had to constantly straighten my shirt, because my drooping left shoulder kept causing it to rumple.

We visited many of the places Rene and I had explored. With him, I had been so joyful and carefree, but now I was struggling to keep up with Aba. I had to stop many times for water breaks or sit as my left arm and leg trembled. I soon reluctantly asked Aba to carry a water bottle for me like Ema did back home.

Aba kept pointing things out. "Look at the boxing truck, Adahm,"

Shrill announcements played from the passing truck's speakers: "Monday night! Tomorrow night! See the best

311

of Thailand!' On a screen atop the truck, two Muay Thai boxers smacked their gloves together aggressively.

I was more preoccupied with the fact that every step felt like a TBS obstacle course, but with no bungee cord for safety and no Becca to catch me if I fell.

Patong Beach stretched about two miles, lined with over 300 stores, bungalows, umbrellas, and huts. Aba and I kept walking all afternoon, eating, shopping, and getting foot massages. We passed a street I recognized: a party canopy booth with the same banner I once saw while walking with Rene and Div.

"Paradise Beach: Full Moon Winter Festival."

I stopped in my tracks. "Aba...rega want t-to see this..."

"Mah ze *(what's this)*, Adam?" Aba asked, coming to my side.

"Aba, remember, that night," I explained. "Lights, music. Girl, drinks, bus."

He smiled. "Tell me what happened."

I didn't want to talk about it. But I remembered working out with Rene. Remembered walking on the beach and assuring my friend he would be a great personal trainer.

"Kloom, Aba." *'Nothing, dad.* I continued walking.

We continued hiking, visiting shopping centers and the street booth where Rene and I had rented our motorcycles. Kinna was not on duty today.

"You have no idea what happened here, Adahm," Aba was barely able to look at the closed motorcycle booth. I heard this as a condemnation.

If Rene and I had not rented a motorcycle...

Aba and I rented a dark blue pickup truck, and he drove us to Kata Beach.

312

Aba drove us along the coast. We didn't speak much in the car with its loud engine as it bopped us across the island. Aba soon turned off the Thai radio and opened the windows, allowing in the fresh breeze. I kept glancing across the blue ocean as tuk-tuks passed us, along with many helmetless motorcycle riders. I began to get nervous as I watched them, imagining what could happen.

"Now you see the risk of being too carefree, Adahm," Aba said, pointing to a shirtless and helmet-less young man riding a motorcycle past us. "I know you were a strong man, but you must understand your limits." He continued to glance across the green island, whispering in Hebrew.

Aba parked on the side of the road and walked with me stiffly hobbling at his side. This was someone's best guess at the exact spot where my accident had occurred. I had no memory of it. Aba walked with me to the place he thought I had fallen. We stood watching parasails out at sea as moped riders whizzed past us.

He took a deep breath. "Now that you're here, is anything coming back?"

"No." I looked out to sea at the people having fun. "Don't r-remember."

"Okay, Tavo-etee *(come with me)*," Aba said, turning back toward the car. His next stop was the Phuket Hospital.

Aba was very cheerful as he greeted the nurses, doctors, and even janitors at the hospital. I stared into the unfamiliar white rooms.

"That's where we were sitting," Aba pointed. "Your sister was always in that corner, and your mom always watched as the nurses performed their duties," Aba explained in Hebrew as we walked.

313

I didn't recognize the hospital at all, but I did recognize the sounds.

Beep, beep, beep.

Sssss, sssss.

We walked by the operating room where I had undergone my first brain surgery. Aba became emotional as he showed me around the waiting area where he and Ema had huddled, hoping I would wake up.

"I want to tell you, Adam," Aba said, his voice thick, "when the doctors said you may not survive...it tore me..." Aba then pulled me close.

I looked down in wonder. I couldn't feel Aba's arm on my left side.

I needed to stretch and sit, having reached my limit of walking without my cane. The jet lag didn't help. I found a yellow couch and slowly lowered my backside toward the ground to crack my left knee and ankle. My arm and leg trembled from exhaustion. Aba massaged my arm, noticing it turn gray. He helped me do some exercises with my left hand as my eyes stayed glued to the floor.

After rest and water, Aba introduced me to the head nurse of the Neuro ICU. Nurse Gemma, who had emailed us recently, had been one of my caretakers.

She was astonished. She excitedly called her associates as Aba re-introduced me, this time standing and conscious. Gemma teared up as she looked at me.

"He's alive and well!" Aba celebrated with her,

"Xô phracêā k̄hxbkhuṇ bādp̄hœl kār yeů̄xng h̄āy pị!" Nurse Gemma sobbed. *'Oh my God, thank God. So many cuts gone! His skull is whole again!'*

"Oh wow, Alex, wow, so tall!" she said, wiping away tears.

I smiled, not knowing what to do or say next. I could barely speak English, let alone Thai, and I was positive she didn't speak Hebrew. I focused on standing correctly. I wanted to look as recovered as I could for her.

Even being in the hospital and meeting my nurses didn't jog any memories. The last thing I remembered was getting that ticket from the Thai police.

More and more nurses gathered around to inspect me, and I could feel the emotional intensity in the air even though I couldn't understand their words.

Mixed feelings swirled through me. I was more confident in my achievements now, remembering how close I had come to dying. I was embarrassed that these nurses considered me standing up to be an achievement. I was glad my hair covered my cranioplasty scar. I was anxious about being the center of attention, fearful that someone would find some flaw in me.

I continued to smile crookedly as the nurses poked and prodded me in awe. I pretended I could keep up with the multilingual conversations and medical terms that were being thrown around. But my heart rate was rising, and I was beginning to tilt toward the left as my injured muscles flagged. A wave of dizziness came over me.

Aba noticed and whisked me away. I challenged myself to keep up with him as we walked back to the parking lot.

This is where my parents were told I may never wake up again," I thought as Aba drove us back to the hotel. *I need to be better to pay for my mistakes.*

It wasn't the disability that bothered me. I had respect for people born with disabilities, or who were disabled in unavoidable illnesses or injuries. I should have given myself the same grace. But in my mind, my disability was *my fault.* I had been specifically warned to wear a helmet and had refused.

I was always harder on myself than I would ever be on anyone else.

Back in the hotel room, I fell asleep instantly when my head hit the pillow.

After a two-and-a-half-hour nap, I woke up with renewed resolve. I'd walk around the island with my father as much as I could without any complaints or needs. This was how I'd push myself to become stronger.

Using the hotel bathroom was an unexpected challenge. There were no disability accommodations and no motor sensors, which meant I had to bend over to open the toilet lid or flush the toilet. I almost lost my balance and awkwardly yanked my left leg to support me while I performed these complicated tasks.

Aba noticed my struggle. "Tov (good) I got you the China-toilet. Aba," he commented. "Rega rega, ani yazor, (*Wait, wait, I'll help.*)"

I only glanced at my cane where it lay under my bed as we left the room.

Aba and I walked toward the Patong Beach lagoon, planning to cross a busy street to see the sun set over the water. Crossing the street was nerve-wracking. Thai drivers seemed to rely on signaling each other directly more than on traffic lights, which meant that if you surprised them, you could have a problem.

Aba and I stood on the sandy pavement, waiting to cross the intersection.

"Okay, Adahm, tee-ye etee *(stay with me),*" Aba said, putting his hand on my right shoulder. The light changed, but cars and bikes continued to move and beep.

Aba started forward. I tried to walk normally, but my left arm and leg swung out from my body. The slippery sand on the pavement didn't help.

The crosswalk light changed back to red much faster than the ones in America, and four other pedestrians hurried past us, half-jogging. The drivers then began honking and yelling at Aba and me to hurry across the pebble-strewn road.

"Pị kạn īhexa! Kฎ̃āng xarị!" '*Let's go! What is the hold-up?*'

My face burned as I struggled, wanting to look capable in front of Aba.

Aba grabbed me, almost lifting me as he pushed and pulled me across the intersection, bikes and cars whizzing past as soon as I stepped forward.

That was my "returning to Phuket" scene: a father carrying his 6'2" son. I remembered Rene and I driving our motorcycles through this intersection.

When we reached the other side, Aba set my feet down on the sandy sidewalk. We started to walk, and I avoided eye contact out of embarrassment. After a few moments of walking quietly, Aba stopped.

"Adam," he said softly, "ata stcreech lada-ate *(you need to understand)*. I feel partially at fault for what happened to you. You wanted to stay home and work on FitFlow, and I encouraged you to come here instead." Aba looked out across the sea in the warm night air. "I thought I'd lost my son. You children are my life's meaning—everything to me." His voice grew thick as waves crashed on the beach.

I tried to understand his feelings. But I knew my injury was *my* doing and no one else's.

"Thanks Aba. I promise...puts everything, have into, recover. Can do good things." The sincerity of the conversation hurt.

Aba and I walked for 55 minutes along Patong Beach. Without my cane.

317

I bumped into tourists who probably thought I was staggering because I was outrageously drunk. I didn't care. We passed vendors selling mobile phones, sun hats, suits, beachwear, snacks, and drinks. There was so much to see and so much to dodge as my left arm and leg stuck out like pieces of wood.

"Yofi Aba," Dad said, reminding me to push my left knee forward. "Drive your knee up! Drive, drive, drive!"

My left arm hyper-extended, and my locked left leg swung wide. The walk was like playing with fire, waiting for something to go wrong. I found myself wishing for my cane or even for a wheelchair. But I said nothing.

We were finally nearing the end of the Patong Beach trail, walking past flashing neon signs in the night.

I did it! I swelled with pride as we approached the club district. *I arrived! And survived! I can pass for one of them.* Tears pricked my eyes as I looked to where tourists milled around, talking and laughing together.

It wasn't just the distance I'd covered that made me proud. Once, any nearby conversation would have distracted me from the intense focus needed to move my left leg without falling. Once, walking down a crowded hallway was impossible because of the risk of smacking into other people and losing my balance. Once, not long ago, Becca had cautioned me not to walk on sandy or gravelly surfaces without my cane.

I was dripping with sweat and starving from the effort, but I had done it! I had walked the same walkway where Rene and I had spent our fun-filled nights.

Boom, boom, boom, familiar music blasted out of bars, carrying with it the frantic energy of the club dancers.

"Massageeh! Helloo, drink?!" the vendors called.
Boom, boom, boom, boom.

"Hello! Food, tuk tuk, o beer-o?"

I remember asking Aba to stay in front of me, feeling nervous about him watching me as I limped along.

"Don't go overboard," he cautioned me with a concerned glance, "but you are doing great, Aba."

We dodged around potholes and discarded beer cans as we continued. I stopped many times, needing a break as I began to lose my balance. Once, I leaned on a parked moped for help with a glut-bend and almost knocked it over.

Within the party district, we saw go-go dancers as competing clubs blasted music onto the street. Bangala Road had over 275 bars with performers, DJs, alcohol, televisions, lights, and waitresses charming customers to continue ordering drinks. I sat with Aba at a bar as he ordered whiskey. To my surprise, I did not feel uncomfortable on the 5-foot tall stools amid the upbeat music, colorful lights, and crowds.

Just one person rang in my thoughts: *Rene Reyes*.

I wanted to send him a video of this place so he could remember our good times. And I wanted to show him I was still capable, despite what Ema and Aba told him about my fragile state. I wanted to show him that I could still have fun.

Behind Aba and I, eight women stood dancing and calling out to passersby, enticing them to come in. I slid off my stool and walked toward them.

Aba watched me, turning in his seat. The girls greeted me, and I moved closer to them, clutching my phone in hand. I stumbled and swayed beside a Thai woman wearing a black bikini and held my phone up to record a video for Rene. She awkwardly looked back at her friends, confused about what to do.

Another girl brought a laminated sheet listing the drinks available at the bar. "Ayo! Drink for you?" I didn't want a drink, nor was I vying for the attention of the girls: I just wanted my best friend's acknowledgment that I was still a man, vital and young, capable of enjoying the same things we used to.

Aba soon got nervous about overstimulating me, especially with my recent seizure. He brought us back to the hotel, where I had an unsupervised shower (with the bathroom door open, so Aba would hear if anything happened).

It was an awkward shower as I tried to soap, rinse, and dry my whole body using only my right arm. But I did not complain. The independence felt good.

**

Aba and I woke up late the following morning. While Aba showered, I tried to dress myself. I grabbed the nearest shirt and spun it on my lap to find the correct side to slip my left arm into. On my first attempt, I put it on backward. "Ugh, okay," I breathed, preparing to try again.

In the shower, Aba whistled one of his favorite songs: Pink Floyd's *Hey, Teacher.*

Once I got my shirt on right, I moved to pull on my black bathing shorts. Thankfully, Thailand's weather did not require sleeves or long pants. I raised my left thigh over my right and clasped the front tie of the bathing shorts, arranging the leg-holes carefully and shoving my feet into them. I then stood up, my toes cracking with their morning stretch, and shuffled the suit up to my waist. Then I joyfully lay back on my bed to stretch my left arm and swung my trembling left leg up onto the mattress.

I remembered my ankle brace. I stared at it where it lay on the nightstand between our beds, wishing I could just throw on a pair of sandals like Aba. But I sighed and began the long process of inching socks onto my feet, after which I stuck my feet into my shoes and fastened the ankle brace on top.

Slipping on a shoe was complicated, with my inability to move my left foot on command. Stomping around to try to get my left foot all the way into its shoe was a long struggle each morning.

Aba finished his shower, and we walked to the breakfast buffet. Aba stayed on his phone, answering work emails. He called Ema next, letting her know that everything was going well, and checked in with his wife and little Jacob.

I sat listening to the pool waterfall out back and clutching my coffee cup. I had spent so much of my energy dressing myself I was grateful for the quiet time.

My eyes roamed over the pool I'd once hoped to swim in with Rene. I realized I still wanted to swim.

"Aba, go in w-water?" I asked.

Aba nodded. "Okay, aval Adam ata yachol leeschot?" *'But can you swim, Adam?'*

"Kneeye *(we'll stay)* shallow?" I suggested. I began to dream about my vacation with Rene, the fun I had created for us. I remembered him calling me 'Varsity.'

"Okay, telech-la *(go to the)* room," Aba instructed. "I'll meet you, but I need to talk to Phil haze *(about this)*." Aba was dialing a number on his phone.

The walk to the pool was straightforward, but the last 80 feet of open hallway was more challenging. The walkway was littered with rubble as an unintended consequence of its "outdoorsy look." I managed to get a towel and returned to the poolside to find Aba sipping hot water by the bar.

"Okay, telech-le-shama *(go there)*." He pointed toward the shallow end of the pool, closest to the hotel walkway.

I had no phone, hotel keycard, or wallet as I lowered myself into one of the chairs. I was just a 6'2" boy with arm tattoos and scars running across his shoulders, chest, and even under his socks.

Aba assisted me in taking off my brace, shoes, and socks and walked with me to the shallow end. I stared at the pool water, using sheer willpower to keep myself upright without a brace or bungee harness. It took us ten minutes to make the barefoot 13-foot walk to the edge of the pool. The four steps into the water were treacherous, despite the handrail.

Aba helped me in. "Okay, Aba, teechsot *(swim)*," he urged me. He demonstrated a breast stroke, but that did not help as I was only able to move my right arm and leg. Aba watched as I spun in the water, viciously trying to get both sides of my body working.

"Use-ha left, Aba! Ha left!" Aba splashed and shouted to encourage me, in what I suspected was partially an effort to distract the attention of passersby from my struggle. I felt overwhelmed in the water, with my mind racing to successfully multitask. *Leg, chest, arm, breathe, up! Leg, chest, arm, breathe...*

This 'water dance' lasted for about two minutes. Then, I began to kick back toward the shallows. "G-g gamartee *(finished)* Aba. N-no, more."

I was out of breath and lay on the cement pool floor, gasping and soaking up sunbeams after my most intense cardio experience since my accident.

Aba tried to make me comfortable. He laid a white towel on me, then lay back in a chair of his own. I was completely embarrassed and spent. I wanted to hide my dilemma, my scars, my difficulty, and my failure.

I soon told Aba I wanted to go back to the room, declining help when he offered it. His phone rang, distracting him as he spoke to one of his vendors.

"Phil! What? No! Never at that margin!" His loud words attracted my attention and I hurried away, grabbing Aba's key card.

About 35 locked-knee steps later, I entered the rubble-strewn walkway. I realized I had left my shoes and ankle brace behind on the pool deck in my hurry to leave. I looked down, not caring enough to go back, and continued.

Thankfully, my feet had had time to dry, and so, they were not as slippery. I felt the rubble digging into my bare feet, but did not pause.

Already embarrassed enough, I thought. My right foot felt the discomfort of walking on sharp stones, but my left foot felt nothing.

I got back to the room and fell asleep. Aba woke me up, staring at me with wide eyes.

"Aba, did you not feel…?" He gestured wordlessly at my feet. This was when I noticed they were covered with blood and bits of gravel stuck into the skin.

That evening, we walked less due to my sore feet. We ate dinner at a restaurant near the hotel.

My feet felt good as new when I woke up in the morning. I did develop scars on the bottom of my feet, but those just matched the scars on the tops of my feet from my accident.

Aba came into the bathroom as I brushed my teeth. "Visiting Thailand ze *(is)* a tax for you to pay with blood and scars, Adahm?" He shook his head in grim amusement.

I decided to attempt a workout in the hotel gym. Aba did not join, needing to speak with his shoe designers back in LA. I didn't mind the independence.

I entered the gym after lunch with no idea what I could do. There were no easy machines: just cables, cardio, and dumbbells. I avoided looking at the pull-up bar in the corner.

I decided to test my shoulder capabilities with some lateral flies. I stared at the dumbbell rack, deciding which weight to try first. I picked up the 10 lb, already feeling embarrassed at the low weight, and sat down on the bench to wrap my fingers around it.

My heart pounded as I tried to stand upright. I clutched the dumbbells and attempted a fly motion with my left arm, but after raising my arm just five inches, the weight slipped out of my fingers.

Clang!

"...okay," I sat down and picked up the dumbbell. I did 20 repetitions with my right side, then turned my attention to my left arm again.

I found some strategies for working my left shoulder by using my right hand to help my left hand. But that limited my range of motion and proved frustrating.

My left traps trembled, severely taxed. I went back to the room to sleep this nightmare away.

***

Our visit to Aba's factories in Guangzhou is another story for another time. When we returned to Los Angeles, Ema greeted us at the airport.

"Hi, Adam!" she said. "I hear you walked a *lot* in Asia."

I nodded happily, proud but also ready to fall over with exhaustion from the jet lag. When I walked into my bedroom back at the Cody Home, I was surprised to see a

324

stack of books on my bed–the business books I had ordered before leaving for Thailand.

"Danduni, you want some fruits?" Ema called from the kitchen. I picked up the book on top of the stack and carried it into the living room, wanting to at least *look* like I was reading.

"Whaii...!" Ema exclaimed when she saw me. "Dan-Dan reading business books kmo-Aba shelo *(like his father)*!"

The truth was, my brain was learning as much as it could from my rehab and the experiences I was having. I never even skimmed any of those books and completely forgot my intention to carry them around TBS.

The first days back home, Ema wanted me to attend TBS, even though Aba and I had gotten Vital to lower my attendance to three days per week. Aba and I won that argument, convincing her that I needed time to rest.

I began to post on social media again, sharing photos and videos from Thailand and my Cody Home. I was forever in love with looking out from my deck during the day, hearing and seeing the songbirds, crows, and hawks. It was spectacular to stare at the gliding birds elegantly soaring across the blue sky.

And yet, jealousy burned me at the sight of such graceful and powerful movements. I felt sure I would spend the rest of my life trying to mimic them.

When I was fully recovered from the trip to Asia, I decided to take advantage of my reduced TBS schedule to go to the gym more frequently. Thailand and China had left me with a renewed sense of motivation and a renewed sense of my goals. I had become convinced, as I once had in high school a decade ago, that developing my muscles was the remedy for my cognitive and social difficulties. I felt that all my desires could be satisfied by an intense workout.

As for so many bodybuilders, my bicep was my favorite muscle to train. But just getting my left hand to close around a dumbbell was now a struggle.

My first day back at the gym after Thailand, I chose a tiny 7.5-pound dumbbell and trudged to a bench to begin the process of using my right hand to wrap the fingers of my left hand around the weight. Then, I'd clench my left hand as hard as I could and hope for the best.

I tried standing on my right foot but realized that there was no way I could turn my left arm at the correct angle while standing. I then discovered that I couldn't lift the weight with my left arm *at all* while standing up. I was going to have to sit down and use a neutral hammer grip, which was less than ideal form.

I curled the 7.5 pounds for about four repetitions before my left arm and left leg began to quake. I switched arms and easily curled the 7.5 for 28 repetitions. The weight felt featherlight in my right hand.

When I perfectly curled my right arm, this would sometimes cause my left arm to shoot straight out and freeze there. This was my biggest moment of embarrassment in the gym—a place where I used to be a conqueror. I would have to stop bicep curling after just two or three sets, as the muscles of my left side grew progressively more deranged.

I tried to just be glad I no longer needed a helmet, a cane, a giant obvious knee brace, or Ema watching over my shoulder. I would leave the gym with mixed feelings: a "pumped" sense of having completed an intense workout and a sense of sheer exhaustion. I'd walk out of the gym feeling like a ghost, holding my left hand in my right to keep my rotator cuff in place.

"Alo, how was your workout, Dan Dan?" Ema would greet me as she picked me up.

"It went," I would tell her, massaging my left arm.

Ema's nursing eyes would linger on my left arm, wondering if I was working it too hard. But after a session with the e-stim and the finger-stretcher, I would feel a little better.

One day, after I had pushed myself in such a gym workout, Ema announced that she had a surprise for me. "Someone is coming to stay with you!" Shortly after, her friend Ronit walked in, holding a 6-pound Maltese dog.

Nelly stared all around the unfamiliar new Cody Home, her tail wagging wildly as I gave her a huge crooked smile.

***

19

Going Back to Work

Attainments: Driver's License
Total memory recall: 43%
Mental Capabilities: 42%
Left Leg: 34%
Left Arm: 15%
Skin State: Calluses and foot scratches
Assistive items: Ankle brace
Age: 17
Weight: 163
Sources: Mom's Journal, Dad, Alex, and Myself

I felt nothing but joy as Ema lifted Nelly to touch her little black nose to mine.

"I'm so happy you remember her!" Ema smiled as I began kissing Nelly's head. It made me so happy to have a life that would not judge me for my disabilities but would accept me as I was. The familiar feeling of petting Nelly was as thrilling as being behind the wheel again or going back to the gym.

"Puppy Power," I murmured to Nelly.

Ema teared up. "You called her Puppy Power!"

"Okay, Adahmi," Ema asked after I'd frolicked with Nelly for about an hour. "Should I take her back home?"

"No, Ema," I shook my head, not taking my eyes off Three Buttons. "Nelly, stay please, forever."

Being with Nelly jogged more memories. I remembered that Nelly loved being at eye level with me on the floor, enjoyed her head being scratched, and loved getting treats. I tried laying myself on the couch to get at her eye level, creating a sense of belonging with her.

Nelly loved to stretch after eating, sleeping, snuggling, and playing.

Watching Nelly stretch on the ground, Ema joked, "Adahmi ata roe *(you see)*? Stretch kim-he *(like her)*!"

I did. Stretching next to playful Nelly was much more motivating than being given stretching instructions by a therapist.

Our first night together, I wanted to cuddle Nelly, but it felt like Nelly was cautious after my long absence. Instead, she ended up huddled by my feet.

That next morning, Ema woke me and Nelly up by kissing us both.

"Hi Neluchka, how you slept with Dan-Dan?" Ema asked Nelly playfully. "Achshav yesh-lee *(now I have)*, two cuties to kiss!"

I groaned and began my morning stretches. Nelly curled up her small white body and made clear her intention to go back to sleep. Once I got through the painstaking process of dressing myself with one hand, I stood up and cracked my toes on the floor.

Standing in the morning was always a reminder of my injury. It often took more than one try, with me falling back into bed at least once before standing successfully. My weight always shifted involuntarily to my right leg.

In the restroom, the Chinese toilet Aba had bought me was a godsend. But whenever I accidentally leaned to the right for a few seconds, it would close and flush prematurely, reminding me of my disability. I'd have to stop my urine mid-stream and make the appropriate motions to open it again.

Ema made me my usual bagel and coffee to eat as we sat on my kitchen stools. This morning, I asked Ema if I could drive us to TBS.

Ema was hesitant, knowing my brain dysfunction was worse in the morning. "Adam, you have not driven during rush hour before."

I kept asking, and Ema ended up deciding to let me try on the condition that I would let her take over if we hit heavy traffic. I kissed Nelly goodbye and went out to Ema's white SUV. I opened her driver's side door and slowly slid in, bending my left knee with my right hand.

I slowly backed out of the driveway and started down the mountain. The first mile of Cody Road went easily as the valley view rolled past us. Approaching the first stop sign, there was a hairpin turn, and the driving got more challenging.

"Adam, Adahm ta-et *(slow-down)*!" Ema clutched the car door handle. I slowed and tried my best to remind myself to check the left side of the road. I counted seven sharp turns as I wound down the mountain, dodging cars parked along the narrow streets.

I parked Ema's car in the TBS lot, staring at the Jeep where I used to hide my cane during parking lot walks.

"Tell Becca and Dave I said hi, Dan-Dan! Don't leave at lunch today…" Ema cautioned, hugging me goodbye.

Riding the elevator up, I was bored already. I wanted more out of life than this rehab. But I needed to get my arm re-taped. So I limped into the lobby, eying Martha at the front desk as I walked past.

"Look who's back!" I heard Lina call from her office as I limped toward the physical therapy hub. "Adam is back, guys!"

I continued down the hall, turning right into the sports room with the bungee harnesses hanging from the ceiling. Becca spotted me.

"Perfect timing!" She enthused. "I noticed when you made that right turn into the room, your left ankle and arm weren't moving very fluidly. Let's work on that."

Becca did a quick review of my ankle brace, then laid out a blue mat on the floor. "Okay," she said. "I want you to make lateral movements like a defending basketball player does." I tried my best, and Becca periodically stopped and gave me instructions.

"When you do this, Adam, visualize a road full of obstacles you must avoid!"

Each time Becca asked me to hover my left foot off the ground, it trembled. Becca would stop and massage my ankle and tighten my brace before trying again. I tripped around, stumbling over my left leg as I moved. I panted with exertion, but inside, I *loved* this feeling.

I had to hold my left arm in place with my right as I walked to the occupational therapy hub for fresh Kinesio tape.

"Hey Adam," Dave said as I sat down, "how was your trip?"

I gestured to my sagging left shoulder. The tape was torn up from over a week of Thailand humidity and near-constant walking.

Dave re-wrapped my shoulder and assigned me to golf ball pickups and wall reaches.

When Ema came to pick me up, I asked if I could drive us to the gym. I envisioned reaching out of the window and grabbing the parking validation card, like Ema did. Ema argued but eventually told me to drive at 'a very slow creep' and agreed to see if I could get the ticket from the machine.

I did as we agreed, crawling through rush hour traffic. In the gym's garage, I maneuvered the car until the side was almost touching the ticket machine.

"Okay, Adami, easy," Ema said as I rolled my window down and leaned out.

"Le-ate!" *'Slowly!'*

I twisted and squeezed my right arm through the window, managing to grasp the paper card with my fingertips. I turned back to find that Ema had put the car in park because I forgot to.

That day at the gym, I wanted to try a chest press again. I'd realized that using dumbbells was the only way I'd be able to do this with my left arm. I limped over to the dumbbells and nervously stared at the weights, trying to figure out how much I could take.

Would 5 pounds be enough? Would 10 be too much? …was Kaylee here? Would anyone I know see me?

I settled on the 10-pound weights.

Walking with a dumbbell in my right hand almost felt normal, but the one I managed to wrap the fingers of my left hand around felt ten times heavier. I tried not to think about the fact that I used to chest press over 110 pounds as I began setting up with my two 10-pound weights.

I set a dumbbell on my lap, adjusting the fingers of my left hand as though fitting tetris blocks together until I managed to wrap them around the handle. Then I laid back. My right arm bent as it should have for this position, but my left shot out straight and rigid. Between my rigid left leg and the dumbbell feeling ten times heavier on my left arm, I almost fell off the bench!

My heart pounded as I realized I would need to lie on the floor to do this successfully. I grabbed a black yoga mat and unrolled it. Only after lying down did I realize I would need help to get up. Fortunately, there were two friendly-looking older men working out together nearby. I kept my eye on them.

Then I realized I couldn't find the dumbbell I'd been holding. Had someone stolen it? No. It was just lying on my left side.

Now, it was time to wrap the fingers of my left hand around the dumbbell's handle. I pressed the weights upward with both hands, remembering the day I'd found myself unable to perform this exercise with a measly 1.5 pounds. Today, I managed three repetitions with 10 pounds, though my left arm shook violently throughout the process.

On the third repetition, the trembling spread up through my shoulders, and I knew I was done. I sat up, my left arm dropping the dumbbell on my diaphragm and leaving me wheezing. I switched arms and began chest pressing with my right side, praying no one had noticed the fumble. I could have done 100 reps with my right side.

I peered back at the men exercising nearby and decided I had time for another round. But this time I had to pry each finger of my left hand open, and then hold them as they tried to close back up. Finally, I managed to force the dumbbell into my left hand before the fingers clenched again.

My left arm began to shake violently.

Come on! Are you f*cking kidding me?!

After a few deep breaths, I asked the nearby gym-goers for help.

"You injured?" One of them asked as he pulled my extended right arm.

"Thanks…yeh, somning ike-that," I mumbled, avoiding eye contact.

Part of me wanted to call it quits for the day. But I still felt that the "me" who came back from Thailand was a new man. I remembered that I had driven myself here.

I looked around and saw an empty abdominal bench. It had cushions to hold one's feet down, making it perfect to stabilize me for more chest exercises. I made my way over to the bench and sat, planting my feet securely under the bars. Then I began doing crunches. I soon realized that I was lifting almost exclusively with my right side. I even felt like I was breathing only from my right lung.

Frustrated, I completed a couple of abdominal sets and then texted Ema.

"Ani-yavo odmeate." *'I will be on my way soon,'* Ema replied.

I decided I had time to wash my hands on my way out. The washroom was 109 steps from the abdominal bench. I walked cautiously on the slick tile floors.

When I turned on the water, my left hand was shaking so badly that I could barely get it under the water. I washed and dried it as best I could, fluctuating between feeling pride at what I had accomplished and sadness at what I couldn't do. These feelings warred inside me as I waited for Ema in the parking garage.

Ema pulled up in her SUV, and all my sadness vanished when I noticed the back window. Two tiny white paws were pressed to the window, and a tiny white face looked around and sniffed frantically.

"Neyeee efo *(Nelly where is)* Adam?!" Ema asked Nelly playfully. "Enea-who!" *'Here he is!'*

I normally disliked being picked up by Ema, but seeing Nelly's little bouncing head and the three black buttons of her face filled me with the greatest joy.

"Hi, Nelly!" I exclaimed as she jumped onto my lap and licked my arms like she hadn't seen me in years. The feeling was mutual.

Later that night, I reflected on how I only felt capable of doing such exercises lying on the ground. I had never been the guy who got hurt or sick or even broke any bones! I was Adam, which had always meant that I excelled at fitness.

"What can I do?" I murmured as I sat with Nelly on the couch. The e-stim was plastered on my arm, with the finger-stretcher and vibration machine next on my list.

That night in the shower, I decided to see how far I could raise my rose-tattooed left bicep over my head. I planted both feet on the non-slip floor and began to lift. My body tilted to my right side as tremors moved up my arm. I was able to raise it about five inches before the uncontrollable quaking started.

Now that I had Nelly, each night, I would lay down in my bed and roll and crawl to snuggle her. Nelly was never a very affectionate dog, preferring to sleep on her own like the magically beautiful princess that she was. But I would still kiss and play with her until she gave a little growl-snarl and a warning bite with her sharp little teeth. Sometimes, we would flop down on the bed facing each other, and she would mimic my posture, laying the left side of her muzzle on the bed.

That next morning, I woke up with my TBS alarm and got dressed alone.

I asked Ema if I could have eggs for breakfast, borrowing from my past bodybuilder habit of eating egg whites each morning. Ema made me two egg whites to have with my coffee and half a bagel on the side. I watched enviously as she used both hands to crack the egg and separate the yolks. My breakfast included a Depekot pill.

Before we left for TBS, I took a quick walk onto the deck to stare at and listen to the birds. Alex Eskanazi had said it was significant that my home faced east—the direction of the rising sun.

I felt joy when I saw the usual brown hawk sitting alone on her top tree branch. I was thrilled to glimpse a scruffy baby hawk flying in circles around the mature bird. The young hawk kept gliding in circles just above the older hawk's head until the large bird flew away in annoyance.

This is amazing. I reached for my phone to take a snapshot of the view, sending it with a 'thank you' text to Aba.

After TBS that day, Aba came to the Cody Home to talk with Ema and I about having me come work with him.

Ema didn't think I was ready. "Wrack-haya lo *(he just had a)* break le *(in)* Thailand!" Ema preached to us in the kitchen as Orit sat outside on the deck.

Aba had promised me in China that I would work for him, and I had absolute belief in his words. A former army engineer, he was precise with his language and never made promises he didn't keep.

***

It was decided that I would work at G-Defy two days per week and attend TBS three days per week. My parents wanted me to continue attending TBS for as long as Vital would pay for it. Even Nick and Rene had taken their side, urging me to continue attending the rehab that they felt had helped me so much.

But I wanted out. I wanted a change.

336

As Ema served me my egg-and-bagel breakfast the next morning, she said, "Aba is really happy you are going to work with him. He has always wanted it since you were 12. Ata neescar kol kach rachok? (Do you remember back that far?)"

I nodded. For some reason, perhaps because it was so important to me, I never forgot my days spent working for Aba in my first official job.

Aba soon honked his horn as Ema walked me to his convertible sports car. She helped me into the passenger seat and handed me a water bottle, just like my first day at Renewal Ranch.

"Okay yalla, goodbye Monda," Aba said. He accelerated, and the first turn knocked my elbow off the center console.

I made myself comfortable as Aba coasted down the 405 freeway. I enjoyed the wind in my hair as Aba merged. I had only one thought: how good it felt to be playing hookie from TBS. There would be no tedious golf ball pickups today.

After 25 minutes, Aba entered the city of Pacoima. It was a working-class neighborhood filled with 7-Elevens, auto-shops and fast food restaurants with graffiti spray painted on every wall.

"Remember last time you were here?" Aba asked me. "To pitch FitFlow shelcha *(your Fitflow)*?"

I vaguely remembered, but the details were gone.

I was already tired when we pulled up to the G-Defy 33,000 square-foot warehouse. My anxiety grew as I anticipated what I might be asked to do today.

We were greeted by the sound of the artificial waterfall that poured into the lobby's koi pond.

"You recognize?" Aba peered at me.

I looked up the 80-foot ceilings and towering glass front overlooking the golf course. I *barely* remembered this place, and I felt like a stranger to it.

I glanced inside the lobby store, dark and empty at this early hour. The rows of shoes were beautiful, but they made my head hurt as I thought about how much a person would have to know to memorize all of them.

"Careful, cach et-ha rail *(use the rail)*," Aba reminded me as we began to climb the stairs to his office.

We crossed a catwalk overlooking the lobby and entered Aba's office. There, I sank into the furthest chair from Aba's, hoping this would keep his employees' attention off me. Aba powered on his PC as employees began to walk the halls outside. Those who noticed me greeted me with bright smiles and waves. I avoided eye contact, not wanting to be an object of pity.

I was supposed to be observing Aba to learn his job, but to my alarm, I soon found I couldn't focus on a conversation for more than a few sentences at a time. I couldn't tell if this was due to anxiety or if it was normal for me, but I strained hard to pay attention.

"Tell her to take those designs off the excel sheet, Jennifer." Jennifer was Aba's head designer. "They look okay, but they won't give the arch support our customers need. The ankles are too narrow."

Jennifer and other employees I didn't recognize rotated in and out of Aba's office throughout the day. I avoided making eye contact, trying to make myself as small as possible. I tried to take notes in my journal but struggled to summarize the conversations I heard. My mind frequently betrayed me and wandered in other directions.

I'd been so preoccupied with my physical progress these past months that I hadn't realized how far my cognitive capacities still lagged. TBS didn't expect patients to follow complex conversations. We were only spoon-fed simple requests and conversational exercises, and I was now realizing that was nothing like navigating the business decisions Aba had to make.

I have no memory of anything that happened for several hours after Aba's meeting with Jennifer. It was as though my brain overloaded and shut down.

My memory fades back in with Aba giving me a tour of the facility at the end of that first day. The facility was so big that it reminded me of my epic treks to Gelson's, or down Bangala Road. We ended with a tour of his Pacoima outlet store, home of the overwhelming selection of shoes we'd passed on our way in.

"You see ha-shoe colors, floors kmo *(like)* at the store in Palm Desert?" Aba pointed as we walked.

I tried to pay attention, but my mind was preoccupied with a new thought: *How am I going to drive myself all the way here after I get my license?* The drive in with Aba had been long and disorienting.

Clunk. I smacked a sneaker off a display as I turned a corner, and my left arm flailed out.

"Careful," Aba scooped the shoe off the ground effortlessly. "This is a lightweight sports shoe…" he went into detail about its characteristics as I stared at the name on the label: this shoe model was called an IONS.

The last stop on our tour was the employee cafeteria. "Vegam bo-etee *(come with me)*," Aba murmured, walking to the end of the cafeteria. We entered a high-ceiling space, where a spiral staircase led up to the top floor. "Don't *ever* use those stairs, Adam," Aba warned, pointing. "They would be very dangerous for you."

339

"Okay, Aba," I breathed. I tried to imagine driving myself into work and then navigating this place on my own.

For days, I accompanied Aba to work silently. I tried to learn as much as I could, but was afraid to speak.

One day, on our way back to the Cody Home, Aba pulled over on a quiet stretch of road outside of Pacoima.

"Okay, Aba," he said. "Bo-knee re *(let's see you)* drive me ha *(home from the)* office."

I was terrified but excited. Smiling crookedly, I plopped myself into the driver's seat and reviewed the buttons and knobs on the console before me. I made the drive successfully with a little direction from Aba.

At home I immediately fell asleep in my recliner, exhausted. Every day after that, Aba had me drive us home after work.

My need for sleep was decreasing, and I'd largely stopped taking naps after my days at TBS. I could now spend my afternoons at the gym, watching TV as I used my e-stim and finger-stretcher, or happily looking over the valley on the deck of my Cody Home. But going to work with Aba was something else. It left me drained in new ways like TBS had in the first days when I was learning to walk.

It would be years before anybody told me that the brain solidifies memories during sleep, and that was probably why I needed more of it while I was re-learning to do everything.

My growing confidence in my driving fueled my desire for independence. My parents didn't want me to contact the DMV, afraid they would refuse to reinstate my driver's license due to my seizure. But I continued to drive as often as I could and performed other tasks like dishes, dressing, and showering on my own. For me, completing these simple household tasks without help was exciting, proof that I could live on my own without supervision.

Ema seemed a bit shocked that I was able to complete all these responsibilities. I think she expected me to become overwhelmed with Aba's work. But as I spent time at the office, my attention span grew, and my anxiety faded.

I was pushing myself hard. Everything I struggled with, I blamed myself for since I had caused my accident. Even before the accident, I had been hard on myself. That was what drove me to develop my athleticism so intensely, feeling inadequate unless I could find something to be better at than anyone else.

But it wasn't all self-criticism. I'd also had enough of being treated like a fragile dependent since my injury.

I wanted my life back. I wanted autonomy. And I had to master as many skills as I could, as fast as I could, to get it.

After a few weeks of shadowing Aba, he announced that he wanted me to train in his call center. This meant I would learn the details of the company's products and how to navigate its sales systems. I would sit at a computer and speak to customers on the phone. The system should allow me to read answers off of employee information sheets if I needed to.

I was nervous and surprised at Aba's faith in me. I wouldn't be supervised in this role, meaning he was trusting me to handle customer orders and answer questions on my own.

One day in mid-May, Aba led me through the call center doors. The call center consisted of about 20 cubicles, each with a telephone, desktop computer, tablet, and catalog. Aba introduced me to the head manager, a man named Jam.

"Heyyy, this is the man I've heard about. Adam?" Jam asked, standing up from his chair. He was covered with tattoos and sported a faux-hawk. I would soon learn he played drums in a rock band.

"Hi," I nodded to him, pulling my shoulders back to stand tall.

"Okay Alex," Jam addressed Aba, "you can leave Adam here, and I'll take care of him!"

Aba nodded. "Lamed-memeno Aba," *'Learn from him, Papa,'* he said, patting me on the arm and leaving.

Jam's choice of words grated on me. *Take care of him.*

Yet I *was* nervous without Aba around. I felt like a two-year-old who had been left alone in an amusement park.

This was what I wanted: independence. Wasn't it?

"Okay, Adam," Jam instructed me. "Grab any open desk, I have Marissa and Letty joining us soon, and then we can begin the training."

I actually fell into the chair at the desk I finally selected, losing my balance while lowering myself to sit. A woman at a neighboring desk glanced over with concern as I focused on pretending I knew what I was doing. A slow sense was creeping up on me that there was no way I belonged in this room.

Maybe I should *be at TBS.*

But as I familiarized myself with the computer, I was surprised by my own ability to type and even operate the customer service headset with one hand. All the one-handed typing I'd done on my phone since the accident was paying off.

Letty and Marissa were young women who were also new to the call center. When they arrived, Jam beckoned me to join them all in a conference room. The long conference room table reminded me of TBS.

"The patented Verso-Shock system," Jam explained, "absorbs shock from ground up, converting it into energy that puts a spring in the wearer's step."

After 40 minutes of sitting and listening, my left arm began to cramp. Letty and Marissa glanced at me in concern as my muscle spasms progressed, and I grew visibly uncomfortable.

Finally, I awkwardly stood up and asked to speak with Jam privately. As we stepped out into the call center, I was overwhelmed by the snatches of conversation I overheard from the cubicles.

"...Yes sir, yes. And what is her shoe size? Yes sir, the shoes have been proven to help with all of those issues."

"..Yes, they are appropriate for bunions and plantar fasciitis."

"P Please Jam," I tried, "explain slower? Please," I tried again, "bit slower, explain company technology. Mind not able...uh, tough time, please."

I realized I had nobody here with me: not Becca, Ema, Aba, or even a doctor. I was all alone and needed someone to understand and support me.

Jam listened, looking concerned. Suddenly, I was opening up to him. "...was dead. Head, you know." I tapped my cranioplasty scar. "Please."

It was the first time I'd explained my situation honestly to someone outside of TBS. I had been terrified to reveal the extent of my injury to strangers, but opening up under Jam's compassionate gaze felt liberating.

Jam nodded. "No problem Adam, I got you, bud," he patted my back, which I struggled not to see as a gesture of pity. I stared at my feet as we walked back into the room, convinced that I could feel stares of judgment aimed directly at me. My left arm was turning blue as I sat and tried to hide it under the conference table.

The training continued for what felt like forever, with Jam and a woman named Rain explaining the features of Aba's shoes. I took notes as best I could with my right arm while my left arm hung under the table. I even drew diagrams in attempts to remember what the trainers were saying.

As I wrote, my mind blanked out. You'd think a person would understand what they were writing down, but Jam's words flowed directly from my ears to my hand with no comprehension happening in between.

'Learn from him,' Aba said. I tried to concentrate. *Need to make him proud.*

About two-thirds of the way through my first training day, I texted Aba to ask him to come get me. He came to salvage me just as Jam and Rain were about to explain the use of a shoehorn. After that, my memory fades out.

What I do remember is being home, wanting to spend time alone on my back deck. The green mountains were my refuge, and I tried to rehearse the names of the shoe brands I had seen that day as I stared out at them.

Mighty Walks, XLR8s, Energias, slip-on Mateems. slip-resistant Ions. My head hurt within a matter of seconds. I closed my eyes and took deep breaths.

The mountains gave me a sense of peace. I remembered Alex Eskanazi saying that the Cody Home was perfectly placed to receive healing natural energies.

"It could be key to his recovery," he'd said.

As I continued to demonstrate responsible behavior, Ema agreed to look into getting me my own driver's license. She made a thrilling discovery: Vital had never reported my seizure, so there was no formal hold on my ability to take my driver's test!

We scheduled my next driving exam for April 15th, 2019.

I was still concerned about whether I'd be allowed to drive with just one functioning arm. The DMV website recommended an assistive device to let me operate both turn signals from the right side of the steering wheel, which meant it had to be possible for people with just one arm to drive. But that wasn't enough to convince me when so many people had shown doubt in my abilities.

I carried my journal as I walked beside Ema into the DMV on the day of my test appointment. I felt as though I was being analyzed by all-seeing eyes as I limped up to the DMV desk and wondered if I should have worn my hoodie to cover my cranioplasty scar. I carefully filled out the forms with my right arm as Ema held the clipboard steady.

"Remember your left side," Ema whispered as I worked.

I was so cautious on the test course that the instructor asked me to speed up several times. I sweated more than I ever had as she took notes on her clipboard. I counted under my breath at each stop sign.

In the end, I was astonished to hear that I had passed. I could now legally drive anywhere I wanted! I was almost too shocked to be excited at first, unable to believe this was real. Still, I smiled as I stepped up to the camera to get my photo taken for my new license.

"Okay, feet behind the line," the photographer instructed me. I bumped my legs on the table behind me as I backed up. Then I gave a crooked smile as the camera flashed.

My second shock of the day was yet to come. When Ema called Aba to tell him I'd gotten my license, he told us to meet him at the nearby car dealership.

The question of how I would afford a car had been looming in the back of my mind. The plan was to have tenants move into the downstairs bedrooms of the Cody Home to help me pay for the mortgage, but no one was going to help me pay for a car. The theory behind my working for Aba was that I would earn my own money, but I was still in training there, and I wasn't confident in my ability to work 20+ hours per week.

When we arrived at the dealership, I learned something horrifying. Somehow, my seizure had not been reported to the DMV in a way that prevented me from getting my license. But my TBI *had* been reported in a way that caused my car insurance costs to skyrocket. I'd be expected to pay $400 per month *just* for insurance due to the insurance company's judgment that I had an elevated chance of being involved in an accident.

How much could I afford to pay for a car itself on top of that?

I felt overwhelmed. Finding a car that was easy for me to get in and out of and comfortable to sit in was proving difficult. We decided to delay the decision about which car to buy, and over a week passed before we found a model in the local area that both met my accessibility needs and fit into a reasonable budget.

Aba and Ema almost insisted on an SUV, worried about accessibility issues with smaller cars. I had been picturing a sportier sedan, but I couldn't deny that the higher seats of Ema's SUV were easier for me to get in and out of.

When Aba finally found a car that seemed both affordable and accessible, I was expecting to be disappointed. But we arrived on the lot to find that I actually liked it, and I took a moment to be grateful for how very fortunate I had been so far in my recovery.

Here I was, leasing my own silver car and training to go back to work, just one year after nurses had proposed that my parents seriously consider putting me in a long-term care home. If anything had been even slightly different, if Vital had refused to pay for proper care, if Aba had been less resourceful and persistent about advocating for me, if my family had been unable to pay the out-of-pocket costs—the consequences would have been unimaginable.

I still beat myself up for sabotaging my own life as an entrepreneur and leading bodybuilder. For refusing to wear that helmet because I wanted so badly to fit in with the locals. Because I believed in being invincible. But I was *still here*, preparing to start a job, living in my own home, and preparing to sign a car lease.

I promised myself I'd do my best to make my parents proud. It didn't occur to me at the time that, just maybe, being a little kinder to myself could have been on that to-do list.

In the end, I was ecstatic to get *any* car. While we sat at the dealership waiting to sign the paperwork, Aba helped me access my online bank account. There was $7,653.66 left of the money I'd had before my accident. I paid the $5,000 down payment on the new car without hesitation while Aba aggressively talked the dealership down on the total by offering to lease their floor model.

I smiled in the seat of my new car, running my fingers over the steering wheel. Sitting in the driver's seat felt *familiar*.

"Congratulations on your car, Adahm!" Aba threw his arms around my shoulders in celebration. I smiled at

Ema as she handed me the car keys, unsure how to accept such a great step forward. I then managed to drive myself back up the hill and park, excruciatingly carefully, in the Cody Home's garage.

I was able to give my monkey statue a new set of keys to proudly hold on my nightstand. And I was finally able to use the key pockets in my Wally Maddison pants.

***

Learning to work for G-Defy felt like being back in school. I would have to pass an exam to demonstrate my knowledge of the company's products before I could work independently with customers. I'd never liked exams, even at my best, but I was determined to pass this one. At night, I'd go home and make myself flashcards to try to help cement my memories. Anything for my Aba.

In the end, I scored 72% on the G-Defy exam. That wouldn't have gotten me an A back in business school, but I had passed by a comfortable margin. Scoring less than 85% meant I would be evaluated regularly on my performance, but I was given my own cubicle next to my new friends Marissa and Letty.

I had another moment of surreal shock as I found myself sitting at my own desk, preparing to take customer calls. What was I doing here? Were these people really about to trust me with their business?

To my surprise, actually working with customers was, in some ways, easier than training. I knew how to deal with a person who had questions or who was confused, worried, or hesitant. I had felt those things myself often enough over the past year, and seeking out information to answer a specific question was easier than trying to memorize every possible answer to every possible question.

We used a sales input system called NetSweet. It took Letty, Marissa, and me a solid month to learn how to use it properly, but it reassured me that I was not the only one who was confused by it. We'd have to enter each customer's information, painstakingly collecting their personal demographics, contact information, payment information, and sales information. Even keeping customers on the line long enough to get all this could be challenging, but if there was one thing I was good at after the last few months, it was asking for patience.

Speaking fluently required almost as much concentration as driving, especially when it came to clinical terms like "proper range of motion." I put tremendous energy into speaking slowly and clearly, and my elderly customers who were calling because they weren't comfortable ordering online appreciated this.

My parents had done so much for me. I was determined to make them proud.

***

20

Getting Overstimulated

Total memory recall: 43%
Attainments: G-Defy Call Representative
Mental Capabilities: 44%
Left Leg: 36%
Left Arm: 17%
Skin State: Scratches on feet
Assistive items: Ankle brace
Age: 18
Weight: 164
Sources: Mom's Journal, Dad, Alex, and Myself

Spending all day talking to customers was more intensive speech therapy than TBS ever was. The longer I worked at G-Defy, the less anxiety clouded my mind when I faced new tasks.

Here I was, earning money. I had colleagues who didn't see me first and foremost, as a rehab patient. I was delighted to find that I was able to successfully join in the office's inside jokes and even in a little bit of flirtation.

My partner in flirtation was Letty from my training group. I still hadn't felt physical attraction, but I knew that I aesthetically appreciated Letty and enjoyed being around beautiful women.

Letty was a work of art. She carefully curated her outfits, her makeup, and her hair, and her legs were beautiful. And even though she'd seen me at my weakest during our orientation, she seemed to want to be friends.

"So Adam," she asked me one day when we were alone, "what happened to you? Tell me."

I always tried to hold back details, afraid she would deem me too disabled to be her peer. But she always drew them out of me.

"I got into a car accident myself," she told me. "So I understand how tough it can be."

You have no idea.

I couldn't imagine that anyone so self-possessed could have an injury like mine. I found myself telling her more details of my injury, just so she would understand how much I had overcome. So she would forgive any mistakes I made.

Here was a friend who hadn't known me before my accident, who I couldn't disappoint by being different from before. She accepted me as I was, not as a patient but as a colleague.

We texted so much that Jam made a "no phones" rule to keep us on task. Then we began messaging through the company's NetSweet system, joking that the bosses couldn't stop us from talking. We had no idea that Jam could read all the messages we sent on NetSweet.

NetSweet Messenger: (May 22nd, 2019)

Letty: Hey! What time are you off?

Adam: now!

Letty: Whoa lol...Will be here till 4:30. Jam keeps looking at me lol. See you tomorrow?

Adam: yes of course everydat' :)

Letty: Mmmkay

Adam: ill miss you :(

Letty: tomorrow im in at 9:30. Miss youuuuu.

Despite my comfort with Letty, I was still insecure about my disabilities. I chose moments when she wasn't looking to walk to the bathroom, and I walked behind her to the break room so she wouldn't see the way I moved.

I'm not sure it worked very well.

"Adam, you have some cracker crumbs on your mouth, hun," she would alert me on our breaks.

I avoided messaging Letty after hours because I was convinced she wouldn't want to be friends with someone like me outside of work.

I had no idea if Letty knew that I was the owner's son. I took care never to mention it, not wanting to stand out. Aba clearly paid special attention to me, but that might have been because I was a worker with disabilities who was subject to regular review because I hadn't aced the entrance exam.

Whatever the case was, I enjoyed my new life. I gained more independence with each passing month, and I was beginning to believe that my dreams of being a leader might be within reach someday.

When my training audit period was over, I was moved to a new desk far from Letty. I missed my work friend, but being unsupervised was exciting. I had memorized the call scripts and could deliver them confidently, and I'd created a system for flipping through the catalog and the sales computer system simultaneously with just one hand.

I had also developed a method for standing up periodically to stretch my hips, leg, and shoulder. At first, I worried that this routine drew attention to me. But I soon realized that if I did it confidently, I could pass it off as an athletic training routine rather than an accommodation for my disabilities.

"Hello, thank you for calling G-Defy, the ultimate shoe for pain relief," I'd say in my friendliest voice. "H-how may I help you?"

"Great, Tim, thank you for your interest. May I ask you what in your life you want to…improve?"

I sometimes had to ask customers to repeat information, but they didn't seem to mind too much. Some seemed to appreciate that I was taking pains to get it right.

I learned to strategically pause between calls and take a deep breath to clear my mind of stress. If I didn't do that, my speech would slur more and more as the day went on.

One day, while driving home from work, I needed to fill up my SUV's gas tank. I hadn't had to do this on my own since my accident. I had to adjust my car several times to get it closer to the gas pump, then remember how to remove my gas cap. I had to take my credit card out of my wallet and leave the wallet in the car because moving around with my whole wallet in my pants would be too hard. After what felt like an eternity of trial, error, and strategizing, I thought I'd figured out a system.

I swelled with pride as I stood beside my car, joyful at filling up like a normal driver. But to my horror, I soon found that I couldn't hold the nozzle's release lever with just my right hand. After spending some time twisting my body around in an attempt to tetris it into a configuration that would work, I gave up and asked a fellow driver to help.

I still had short-term memory problems. I sometimes forgot to lock my car doors or close my windows, and on a few occasions, I even forgot to turn off the engine until I noticed its purr continuing as I walked toward the house.

Still, feeling my own car keys tucked into the pocket of my Wally Maddison pants was sheer bliss. Knowing I could go anywhere I wanted, anytime I wanted. And no one could stop me.

Recovering my abilities was a nonstop process. Every activity of the day, from putting on my clothes to driving home from work, required concentration and patience.

I'll never forget my first time driving to the gym alone. I drove up to the entrance, pulling my car so close to the validation ticket dispenser that the side mirror almost brushed it. Then, I twisted my body and stretched my right arm over my body to take the ticket.

"Nice and easy," I whispered to myself, repeating Ema's words to me.

I stretched my right arm.

I couldn't reach.

"Come on..." I took my foot off the brake and put it on the floor, using it to lift myself off the car seat to gain a few more inches. The car began to roll forward.

"Whoa!" I slammed myself back into the driver's seat and hit the brake. I finally settled on putting the car in park and opening the driver's side door, stepping unsteadily out to get my ticket.

Behind me, cars waited. I stuffed my body back into the driver's seat as fast as I could. I circled the garage, avoiding handicapped spaces. I told myself other people might need them, but in reality, I didn't want to draw attention to myself by using one.

I found an open spot and walked 140 steps to the parking lot elevator, clutching my water bottle. My steps kept swerving to the right, taking me dangerously close to oncoming traffic. I earned many honks and flashes of high-beam headlights as I proceeded toward the elevators in the dark garage.

Finally, I got there.

I rode the elevators up and hobbled past the front desk to enter the Galleria. I chose to start with a leg press, hoping that would allow me to fit in with the crowd since my right leg still worked almost normally.

Your legs are your foundations, I remembered Becca saying.

Despite my best efforts, my left leg was too hurt to do the presses. I completed 30-pound leg presses with just my right leg, then moved to leg extensions to try to loosen up my left side. Hamstring curls still proved impossible for my locked-straight left leg.

When I stood after each exercise, my legs would feel weak and numb. After about 20 minutes of work, tremors would begin to run up my left leg. My workouts were still short, but they gave me tremendous confidence.

After my first night of driving myself to the gym and working out on my own, I decided I had earned another pair of Wally Maddisons. The following week, I began driving myself to TBS on the rare days I still attended.

"Dubi, can I live alone now?" I asked Ema one Saturday as I grabbed my car keys from the kitchen counter.

She looked up from the dishes she was doing. "Adam, what about laundry, folding your clothes, and all the house chores? Can you change garbage bags on your own, or cook and clean?

She had a point. Getting a garbage bag into the can with one hand and one and a half legs sounded unimaginably complicated. Let alone hefting a full 13-gallon bag out of the can and walking it to the curb.

But I wanted to try.

"I have a dishwasher," I pointed out, "And I can— hang my clothes up, instead of folding them! I promise

I'll clean up after myself, Ema. Maybe I can hire a housekeeper for an hour a week?

Ema frowned, watching me. She wanted my independence, but she was also more aware than me of how much work she took care of around the house while I was struggling to get into my clothes or passed out in my recliner after work.

We settled on a compromise: she would move back into her own home and begin sleeping there instead of in my guest room, but she could visit to check up on me whenever she wanted.

"Gam *(also)* leave Nelly, please Ema," I squatted to rub Nelly's adorable head with my right hand.

Ema agreed.

I was very grateful to Ema for all her help, staying at my side almost full-time for the year after my accident. But I was also thrilled by the thought of living alone again, at the thought of such independence.

Living alone, I began to appreciate all the work Ema had been doing: cooking, cleaning, organizing, and even helping me when I got stuck getting dressed or drying myself after a shower. I had to learn to close my bedroom shades each night so the rising sun wouldn't blind me in the morning and to fill my water bottle to take to work or TBS with one hand. I had to learn not to leave the stove burners on, which took a few painful reminders before I got it down.

At work, I learned that call center workers were paid commissions on sales we made in addition to our hourly rate. I dedicated my whole being to being as helpful, knowledgeable, and encouraging as I could be to each caller.

"Yes, Shira, I w-would recommend our Ion styles to a nurse. They are proven to provide more comfort for long hours spent on your feet."

One day, the department received a check in the mail with a note attached from an 85-year-old customer. The customer, who had struggled to navigate our online ordering system, had written to thank me for being so supportive and attentive to her and for helping her to feel comfortable and confident in placing her order with us.

"Adam, congratulations!" Jam said in an email in which he transcribed the contents of the note, CCing Aba to notify him of my success.

"I wanted to take a few moments to tell you about the outstanding customer service I received from Adam yesterday evening when I called to order my first pair of your shoes. He was absolutely wonderful! We talked about the type of shoe I was looking for (I've recently had major back surgery), your company policies regarding purchases and returns, and how to contact Medicare. When I was ready to place my order, he was extremely patient, helpful, and professional.

"I'd considered simply ordering my shoes online, but I'm so glad I called instead and talked with Adam. He really helped me pick out the right shoes and did a great job explaining exactly what to do in case I needed to return them for a different size or color. So please let his supervisor know it's because of Adam's great customer service your company has gained another loyal customer! - Janet Anderson"

This message solidified my dedication to my job and to putting everything I had into improving my skills. More and more, I was beginning to believe I could reclaim the life of leadership that had once seemed lost forever.

"Adam! I saw the email you got! Amazing work." Letty announced at our afternoon coffee break, wrapping both her arms around me from behind. I almost stumbled backward in surprise but then relaxed and basked in her affection.

Letty's embrace did something to me. I caught myself glancing at her more and more. Although I wasn't sure what I felt, I liked being near Letty, and I liked looking at her even more.

Letty's long legs stretched out under her chair. I found my eyes lingering on her full lips and her hair as it dangled beside her cheeks...

Then, I forced my attention back to work. "Hello. Thank you for calling G-Defy."

I can do this. More and more, I was beginning to believe it.

I realized I needed to develop a relationship with our CEO, John if I wanted to advance professionally. Aba had delegated more and more responsibility to John as his own time was taken up, first by his infant son Jacob and then by my injury.

I'd quit working for G-Defy to start my coaching business years ago, fed up with John asking me to do monotonous work on spreadsheets for hours on end. I wanted him to see me as I was now, successful in a customer service capacity that suited me much better than analyzing numbers.

I had a plan. But life wasn't quite done hitting me.

The same day I resolved to befriend John, I got an email in my inbox. It was from Apple informing me that FitFlow had been removed from the Apple store and its creator account suspended due to nonpayment of fees for the past year.

As I read the message sitting in my car after work, a wave of helplessness overwhelmed me. The right side of my chest—the side that I could feel — ached and I had to gasp for breath.

All my hard work was gone. And I had to admit that I hadn't even been able to *think* about FitFlow during my recovery. My new life revolved around my injury and although FitFlow had once been everything to me, it was obvious there was no room in my life for it now.

I'd been gaining confidence with these weeks at G-Defy, successfully completing a basic call center role. But now my doubts swarmed back: would I ever be able to run my own business again?

I wanted a friend. A supporter like Donna had been when I was developing the app. Hopeful but terrified, I decided to text her.

How would I explain what had happened to me? Would she reject my friendship now as I had once refused to be "friendzoned" by her?

"Hey Donna," I typed.

A pause. Then:

"Message Undeliverable"

I stared. That meant she had blocked me. Well, at least she had done it *before* I was injured. Maybe she didn't want to open old romantic wounds.

Still.

"Wow," I murmured, looking up at the only handicapped sign in the G-Defy parking lot. "Do I deserve all this?"

I decided to at least email her. I wanted to respect her boundaries, but consumed with insecurity, I needed to know if we could be friends.

Hey Donna',

How are yuo,
I recently went thruoug a brain injury tbi they call it, would want your talks to help through this time thanku
Adam

She responded 3 hours and 22 minutes later.

Hi Adam,
I'm so sorry to hear about your crash. I can't imagine how awful that must have been for you and how challenging recovery must be. I wish you all the best in getting better as quickly as possible.

Adam, I don't mean to be insensitive in any way, but I have moved on and do not wish to see you or speak with you. I have been with someone else for over two and a half years and am very happy.
Again, I do wish you all the best with everything and a speedy recovery.

Donna

The truth was, I wasn't thinking of romance as something I could even aspire to at this point in my life. But I did remember that I had been the one to break up with her, and that I had once declined to be friends with her if we couldn't be lovers. I replied almost instantly:

No problem, I fully understand Donna.
Thank you for your time.
Adam

That night I snuggled into bed, reaching for my vibration machine. I used my right hand to wrap my left hand around the machine and cranked up the intensity to 3. I felt a faint throbbing in my paralyzed hand as I waited for my 20-minute session to end.

My mind swirled with warm thoughts about Letty, and then drifted to Donna. I wondered if Donna's boyfriend was Israeli or American, and if he shared her views on marriage.

Lost in my thoughts, I didn't notice the vibration machine sliding towards my pelvis, causing waves of pleasure that I hadn't experienced in ages and didn't fully understand.

My mind shifted to Kaylee, her body – the curves, the round butt, and full breasts.

Bzzz. The vibration machine caused a primal pulsing as it vibrated its way down my thigh and towards my crotch. Electricity shot through my genitals, causing me to suddenly stiffen and convulse into a release.

My right toes curled. I trembled in disbelief.

It was all beginning to come back to me now: my sexual pleasures and aspirations, the reasons for me and Donna's breakup. The wild nights I'd had with Kaylee. The reason I appreciated Letty's lips and legs.

Relief flooded me as I understood what I had been missing, what Rene and Nick had been concerned that I had lost. This part of my life had survived the accident, after all. Even after more than a year, there were still parts of me resurfacing every day.

I felt alive again.

***

The next morning, I spent some time standing on my deck before leaving for TBS. I stared up at the mother hawk who circled overhead, then down at the sheer 90-foot drop under my house and the canopy of trees below it.

What would happen if I jumped? the thought hit me out of nowhere.

A morbid curiosity snuck up on me as I leaned over, taking in more of the view straight down. I was already so injured, and I'd been left on my own in this house. Trusted with my own well-being, on the edge of a sheer cliff.

What would happen if I jumped? Would my parents realize something was wrong quickly? What would the outcome be? Would I be cared for as thoroughly again?

Would I die? What would that be like?

I had the power here to change the course of my life entirely, if I wanted to. On purpose, this time. No one could stop me.

I shook my head, dragging myself away from that alternate universe and off to TBS for the day's rehab.

In the days to come, I began to develop a warmer, more visceral attraction to women. I began to entertain the thought that perhaps women like Letty or Delilah could be more than friends with me. This shocked me because, in my own mind, I was a totally inadequate partner. I couldn't even embrace a woman with two arms.

More to the point, I worked so hard to meet my own standards of social acceptability in casual conversations. The thought of intimacy with a woman whose opinion of me I valued was *terrifying.* '

One evening, I had a conversation with Ema that scared me.

Ema had been my biggest encouragement and supporter. "He will recover, he will recover," she would tell friends, family, doctors. "Oooh Ya say tov." '*He will do good.*'

At dinner that night, I told Ema that I couldn't wait to be my normal self again. I waited expectantly for her to encourage me, but instead, she looked up from her dinner plate and fixed me with an intense stare.

"You know," she said slowly, "you were very lucky so far recovering, but there's much more to go, mami. It is possible you may not get all the way back to the way you were. Maybe instead, 80%?"

"Oh, okay," I responded. It was a reflexive response, a habit I'd developed of replying instantly to *look* like I'd understood while my brain was still processing.

Internally, I was blown away. I struggled to grasp the prospect of never being fully recovered.

Ema moved closer to my side of the table. "You should be very happy with your progress, Dan-Dan," she said. "You have come so far."

I avoided her eyes and picked at my dinner.

I wanted more. I had always wanted more. I wanted to be able to break a sweat at the gym to bulk up. I wanted to be able to help other people with their fitness journeys again. I wanted to manage or run a business, not just work in a call center. I wanted to support a family someday.

*S*till, she had a point: having come from being paralyzed in a hospital bed, I was exceptionally recovered.

For a few more weeks, I went to work and just enjoyed my independence. I got to work out at the gym whenever I pleased, then go home to relax in my own house. I felt like I needed this time to myself after spending so much time under the strict supervision of rehab staff, hospital staff, and "extracurriculars" like TMS and HBOT, etc..

At one point, I decided to take a break from TBS entirely in an effort to recreate what it was like to live life as a "normal" and uninjured adult. But after two weeks, I had to admit it: I was losing function in my left arm and leg. As tedious as I now found rehab, I still needed it.

Ema cheerfully agreed to send me back to TBS the very next day. But when I arrived in the morning, I was surprised to be directed to counseling first, not to the desired physical therapy.

"Hello, Adam. How are things?" Laura asked, looking at me from her cream-colored chair.

I had once enjoyed our talking sessions because they were less tedious and exhausting than physical therapy. Now, this made me nervous.

"I'm good," I replied, lying back in her blue guest chair. My recent experiences had changed me. As I stretched fluidly, I imagined that Laura saw me as a man, not a patient.

"Any new thoughts, Adam?"

I stared at her yellow dress, the way it complimented her dark skin. "I realize now," I said slowly, "how I've changed. I u-used to want to look like a strong guy, to stand out." I gestured with my right hand. "But now I w-want to be like all the others. The m-most important thing to me is to fit in."

Laura said it was great to see me growing in self-awareness.

After that, it was off to physical therapy with Becca. To my disappointment, there was no occupational therapy with Dave. As much as I had once hated the tedious golf ball pickups, I had to admit that I couldn't do without my ability to hold objects in my left hand.

The next day, I still was not assigned to occupational therapy. I didn't feel I was gaining much in leg training with Becca that I couldn't get at work or at the gym, so when I realized I was not scheduled for occupational therapy that second day, I simply grabbed my car keys and left. I ignored the front desk associate's attempt to stop me and drove to work.

Ema was disturbed when she heard what had happened, but I explained my reasoning to her. They weren't giving me what I felt I needed most, and work was a better place than TBS to practice walking and talking anyway.

At work, I was studying upselling tactics. For example, I could suggest G-Defy's special socks to go with a pair of sandals a customer was considering buying. There were ways to systematically find companion items that would be optimally appealing to the customer you were talking to. There were also ways to talk up the added value of purchasing several items at once rather than just one.

After passing CEO John in the hallway and exchanging a friendly greeting one day, I began occasionally texting him.

> "Hey John., Howr you doing today?"
> (Messaged 2:02 PM)
> (Read 2:34 PM)

> "Hey Adam! How are things going down there my guy, staying with the sales!"
> (Messaged 2:57 PM)

I wanted to visit his office upstairs to show that I was making an effort to build our relationship, but I couldn't walk up the 23 stairs alone. I hoped that one day, Aba might ask me upstairs to his office, or I might find a reason to invite John out to lunch or dinner with me.

Some days were really good. I accomplished what still felt like an astonishing amount, talked and laughed with my coworkers, went to the gym, and went home.

Other days were not good. I might become overwhelmed by the cognitive demands of the job and of socializing, or my body might suddenly fail when my gym workout had barely begun.

Those days would destroy me. My physical prowess was still so important to me, and finding myself unable to reclaim it was a nightmare. Every waking moment felt like an obstacle course as I heaved around an arm and a leg that felt like logs.

I still could not walk and talk at the same time. Walking took too much concentration, and so did processing words. I would have to strategize about how to keep activities separate, so I could give each my full attention.

"Can't explain to you Ema, m-my day, challenging," I told Ema one evening after a bad day. "Much to think about, hard find time to move-smooth."

"Keep doing it," Ema responded. "Every day, things will get better, mami. Hakol-heye beseder," 'Everything will be okay.'

One day, I attended TBS and saw Andrew Sharp. The teenage race car driver who had gotten into a near-fatal accident had not improved much since my first sight of him. He still couldn't walk or talk. His only form of communication with his family was the ability to give a thumbs-up. He was being wheeled into the physical therapy room, his arms flapping in distress at some pain or frustration he couldn't communicate.

His parents and caregivers flocked around him. Every time I saw them, Andrew's father brought up the rear of his entourage, and he was on the phone talking business. I eventually learned that he had used his business profits to have a private HBOT chamber installed in Andrew's room.

He was also taking Andrew regularly to an institute in Colorado. He spent an astonishing $8,200 per week on their specialized rehab program, which used something called "stem cells."

I'd heard of stem cells before. I remembered something about them being a medical miracle, but I couldn't remember exactly what they were supposed to do. Andrew's family was willing to do anything to try to revive their son, and I began to take an interest in what they were doing.

I shared my interest with Ema, and through Internet research, we learned that the Colorado clinic used stem cells that had been taken from the umbilical cords of newborn babies. It had once been common practice to simply discard umbilical cords and the blood in them, but when it was discovered that cord blood was rich in stem cells, companies started offering to buy the blood for use in medical treatments or freeze it for the family in case the newborn child should need it later in life.

The stem cells could be injected into patients with injuries in hopes that they would grow into new tissues, like neurons, that patients' bodies might not be able to make on their own.

I hesitated to ask my parents for this treatment due to the hefty price tag. I knew I would never be able to pay for it myself, on top of costs of living on a call center worker's salary.

Still. This treatment nagged at the back of my mind.

When I mentioned that I'd seen Andrew to Ema, her face fell. She felt his parents' pain keenly, and she told me what she'd learned from speaking with them.

His family had spent a full year visiting him in the hospital before he was well enough to be released. His father kept spending money on more and more treatments, trying to get his son back. But after four years of rehab, it didn't seem that Andrew would ever be as he had been before the accident. And he had three younger siblings, all still children who needed their parents' love and care, too. It was a wonder they made it into TBS to join him at all.

I realized then how lucky I was. How lucky we were.

I had always had mixed feelings toward the Sharp family. They always wore expensive clothes, drove expensive cars, and seemed distracted when they accompanied Andrew to TBS. Overall, they'd seemed privileged and uncaring.

But now I understood: they had been doing this for four years. His father saw his business profits as the key to Andrew's salvation, and his mother must have felt exhausted and hopeless.

The next time I saw the Sharps at TBS, I walked up to Andrew's mother.

"Hi," I tapped on Mrs. Sharp's shoulder, just back from my weekly Kinesio tape replacement with Dave. "I'm Adam."

Mrs. Sharp turned around and stared at me. I smiled in what I hoped was a disarming way.

"Want apologize t-to you for my thoughts. Heard about what your son has been through. If needs a friend to walk between classes or have lunch together, I can gladly do that. Wish him the best. I was very disabled in my beginning. But after a while and work, I doing better. Driving now, even."

Mrs. Sharp smiled. To my astonishment, *she* seemed shy around *me*. But she cautiously responded, "Adam, no problem. You are doing so well; keep it going!"

She seemed to miss my point. She didn't understand that I'd been judging her family for their wealth and their seemingly distracted attitude. Maybe that was for the best.

Although I still wasn't satisfied with the way I walked as I limped away from that conversation, I felt profound gratitude settle over me. My parents had given me so much, and all without the Sharp family's wealth. Even my own home.

The Cody Home seemed a vast expanse to me. It was 30 steps from the living room to the kitchen and a challenging 63 steps from the kitchen to my bedroom shower. Walking more than about 50 feet at a time usually required me to reach for walls, windows, chairs, and counters to lean on while I did a glut-bend to crack my knees.

As I had predicted, replacing garbage bags turned out to be the worst part of living alone. I could just about pull a full bag out of the bin and walk it the 30 steps to the curb outside. But getting the edge of a garbage bag around the rim of the 4-foot-tall garbage can with one functional hand was something else.

I would first have to "open" the bag, shuffling and shaking it in the air with my right arm to get it to unfurl. I would then do my best to toss it into the bin, hoping that the open center would settle inside the bin and the edges vaguely around the rim. I'd bend over, balancing carefully on my right leg, to secure the bag's lip all the way around the rim of the garbage bin.

It took me weeks to master this art.

As I became more independent, I realized that I did want a woman to share my life with. I was still nervous about my ability to be a partner, but I remembered the faithful support Donna had given me, the fun company that Kaylee had been.

I was still afraid to go to bars or clubs. Afraid to stand out in the wrong ways.

"Who wants this b-broken person anyways?" I muttered to myself on one dark day as I drove home from work.

Then I saw it, passing by in my car window. In the parking lot of a grocery store, a beautiful woman was pushing a cart..

Of course!

At a grocery store, I could lean on a cart to camouflage my injury. As long as I could keep my left hand on the cart's handle, no one would see that it hung useless at my side. My limp might not even be noticeable if I was pushing something.

I wouldn't have to tolerate bright lights, loud music, or crushing crowds in the grocery store. And beautiful women went to the grocery store all the time. Everyone went to the grocery store.

Maybe a simple trip to pick up some milk was all I needed.

I pulled into the grocery store parking lot and glanced at my reflection in the car mirror. My hair now covered my cranioplasty scar completely. I lifted my left knee out of the car with my right hand and limped to the line of carts where they stood waiting for customers. I used my right hand to wrap the fingers of my left hand around the cart's handle like a dumbbell. Then, I pulled the cart out and pushed it into the store.

For long minutes I paced the aisles, looking around in wonder. Here, there were people of all shapes and sizes.

None of them knew me as a rehab patient, and I could talk to them if I wanted to.

As my legs tired, my limp became more obvious. I abandoned the cart in the children's cereal aisle and fled in defeat.

Pathetic, I berated myself as I limped back to the car.

The 12-minute attempt at a thrill had left me broken. My left arm was turning blue from hanging at the wrong angle, my hip cramped from pushing the cart, and my right-sided ribs held all my weight while I pushed it. I sat back in the driver's seat, and checked my phone to find a text from Ema.

"Where are you? Home with Nelly? She didn't eat today."

I went home to feed Nelly and to strategize.

Bending over Nelly's bowl to fill it was a balance challenge, and I'd sometimes drool in concentration while I did it. I wasn't able to walk her outside of the Cody Home yet, not trusting my ability to navigate the hilly neighborhood on foot.

Playing with Nelly on my bed reminded me of my early physical therapy with Sahara, where she'd had me drag myself around on my mattress. Except playing with Nelly was much more fun. I would lay on my disabled side, snuggling her with my right arm as she flopped down on her own left side and looked up at me.

The next day, I had to pick up some milk for my protein shakes from the grocery store. Two beautiful women were walking in, chatting and laughing as I pulled up.

Okay, I took a deep breath. *Let's try round two.*

I lifted my left knee out of the car and trudged through the underground parking structure. My mission was to conceal my disability in hopes of looking like a magnificent, un-injured citizen. But all my confidence came to a screeching halt as I glanced at the heavy, rusty-looking grocery carts.

"Let's do this right," I murmured to myself, starting toward them.

***

21

Finding Love at the Grocery Store

Attainments: Delilah
Total memory recall 50%
Mental Capabilities: 44%
Left Leg: 36%
Left Arm: 17%
Skin State: Foot and shoulder scratches
Assistive items: Ankle brace
Age: 18
Weight: 164
Sources: Delilah, Mom, and Myself

The bright lights of the grocery store blinded me as I glanced around the florist area. Around me, older shoppers were browsing. I wrapped my fingers tighter around my cart's handlebar and took a deep breath. All I really needed was milk, but I hoped to find something more while I was at it.

What to do first?

I plodded towards the milk section about 85 feet away. I felt suspicious with my empty cart, but then I saw one of the pretty girls from the parking lot browsing the yogurt aisle. I tried to look as casual as I could as I strolled over and skidded my cart to a stop inches behind her.

"Hi, I'm, A-Adam," I said, not giving her a chance to notice my approach. I was in such an anxious hurry that I didn't even see her face until she turned. I almost winced with nervousness.

"Hello..." she gave the same nervous but curious look Donna had given me at the rock wall all those years ago. Terrified that she'd discover my disability, I apologized and began hurrying away. I nearly tripped over my cart's wheel in my rush.

I now realized that I had no idea how to strike up a conversation with a woman. All I could think was that she was judging my walk and my stutter. The thought was so loud in my head, blasting at full volume.

In my mind, the differences between who I used to be and who I was now loomed enormous. I didn't even give the people I met a chance to give me their opinion on the matter: I had already passed judgment on myself.

My confidence shaken, I put a carton of milk in my cart and headed for the register. This was enough of an adventure for one day.

Maneuvering proved challenging in the narrow aisles, with delicately stacked display items on every shelf. I would have to push to the right with my right thumb and to the left with my right pinky to keep the cart moving straight. This was strenuous, and I had to stop every ten to fifteen steps to adjust my grip and reaffix my left hand to the bar. Once, I knocked over an entire coffee display and hurried away, ashamed that I couldn't bend over to pick them up.

Doing all this while thinking, let alone speaking, was too much of a challenge for today. I resigned myself to this fact as I got into line behind two other customers. Only then did I realize that I'd been so excited about my adventure that I'd left my wallet in the car.

This filled me with terror: running out to the car and then back into the store with my wallet would not be easy for me. And it would surely draw attention to my disability.

"Hi, sorry," I stuttered when it was my turn to step up. "Left wallet in car. Can leave milk here?" The cashier nodded suspiciously. I undertook the long trek back out to my SUV, then back up to the register line. Behind me, other customers waited, visibly impatient.

So much for feeling normal.

I pushed my cart to the escalator that would take me back down to the parking garage. Customers were supposed to clamp their carts onto a special escalator-railway system that would allow their carts to accompany them down. Technically, there *was* an elevator large enough to accommodate shoppers and carts, but I wanted so desperately to look "normal" that I was determined to use the escalator just to prove that I could.

Escalators were complicated enough just for me; perfectly aligning my cart's wheels to the railway clasp was another matter altogether. I pushed my cart forward, missed the rails, and pulled it back again.

"Ahh!"

When I finally got the cart into the cart-escalator, I had a new problem. My left hand refused to release the cart's push-bar!

"Whoa, whoa, whoa!" I was being dragged down along with the cart, the tape holding my shoulder in its socket stretching and tearing beneath my shirt.

I managed to extricate myself from the cart-rail before the accident got really serious, and stumbled back clutching my left shoulder.

"Are you okay?" A concerned lady behind me asked.

"Yeah," I lied. "Okay."

My cheeks burned with embarrassment at how badly this simple task had gone.

I went home that day with so much on my mind.

First things first. I needed to make myself a list of topics or icebreakers that I could memorize or keep on-hand to start conversations with strangers. I opened the journal tab on my phone and started brainstorming. The following is a real transcript of what I wrote:

1. "Hello how;s your shopping day going?"
2. "Hi you know what time close here?"
1. "Isnt this weather today great?"
2. "Hi I Adam what's your name?"
3. "Like your.. (any clothing piece)"
4. "Can I talk to youui?"

I thought so hard about what I'd do differently next time that I gave myself a headache. Would the women notice that I wasn't normal? Would I come across as crazy?

Then I realized I wasn't looking for a girlfriend. Not really. I was looking for acceptance.

Over the next few days, I began stopping into any grocery store I could after I got out of work. This was a new frontier for me: I'd gotten almost comfortable at the gym, but talking to strangers in public still terrified me. So, I spent as much time as I could practicing, desensitizing myself, and working up the nerve.

I rarely needed food since Ema often brought me supplies, but I would place items in my cart anyway just to look like a normal shopper. Cereal boxes were my favorite: they were light as a feather to lift off the shelf with my good arm, but they took up so much space in my cart that anyone could see at a glance that I really was shopping for food.

My conversational approaches got better.

"Hi, how's your day going? Shopping for anything specific?"

Some women were not happy to be spoken to, and I was convinced it was because of my disability. Looking back, I now realize that it was more likely that they just didn't want to be approached by strangers while shopping..

Either way it was good to talk to people. I needed social interaction so badly.

I began speaking to almost everyone, including little old ladies and grocery store workers. Every time they smiled and replied, I felt validated. The fact that I had not yet succeeded in getting a single woman's phone number didn't matter.

Once, I decided to try chewing gum as I shopped. I got it into my head that this was something a "normal" person would do, that it would make me look more effortless and casual. As I spoke to a beautiful woman that day, the gum fell out of the left side of my mouth!

"Oh, sorry!" the woman smiled and laughed, but I judged myself harshly for that slip.

I was so happy to talk to anyone at all at the grocery store, regardless of age or gender, that I started to develop a reputation for friendliness. The grocery store became my equivalent of going to the bar: it was where I would meet people in a way that was comfortable for me. I began to drive all over the valley to visit grocery stores for a change of scenery and to meet new people. Sometimes, I would take an entire weekend to travel up and down the coast, visiting any store that provided carts to mask my disability.

As I gained confidence, I adopted a new attitude towards approaching women. "What's the worst that can happen?" I would ask myself. I was successfully desensitizing myself to rejection. I no longer had any real fear of people's reactions to me, and that was liberating. In fact, I would later realize that fear of rejection was one of the main things holding people back in life.

I walked the aisles, deciding who I would strike up conversations with. I made notes about what was going on in my life so I could actually talk about my life with strangers. I used the same system to discreetly glance at my phone notes during conversations that I used at G-Defy to discreetly reference the catalog while speaking with a customer. I even developed a playlist to listen to with an earbud tucked in one ear and get me "pumped," the same way I once did at the gym.

In a way, the grocery store was the gym for my social skills.

"Hello, you have beautiful eyes," I was able to say confidently now.

Or a softer approach: "Do you know where the oatmeal is? I'm lost."

It wasn't really about getting dates. It was just about feeling accepted and equal.

Something remarkable began to happen. The less my disability bothered me, the less it bothered my fellow shoppers. When I seemed frightened and ashamed, they thought something was wrong. I must have been out of my depth to be so anxious. But when I smiled at them and made eye contact, my foot dragging on the ground wasn't a big deal. If it wasn't a big deal to me, they figured I had it under control.

I never told anyone about my grocery "thrills" except Rene. Somehow, I knew that if I told my parents or my therapists, they would view it as their "project" too, and my sense of independence would be lost.

I eventually had to explain to Ema what was going on because she always asked where I was when she called me.

"Adahm efo-ata ose *(where are you)*? It's getting dark, when will you be home eem *(with)* Nelly? ...at the grocery store again?! What could you possibly need?"

Ema was still worried I would get into something I couldn't handle if she didn't know where I was and why. I finally confessed: I had been going to grocery stores to meet women.

A few days after I explained this to Ema, Aba joined me on my deck during one of his visits to the Cody Home.

"Adahm..." he started cautiously. "Ema said you want to meet women now." He seemed almost afraid that it wasn't true. When I nodded, he seemed relieved.

"Tase *(use)* Internet for online dating," he suggested. "Women there are looking for partners, and this way, they get to know your personality before you meet them in-person."

Aba helped me download a couple of dating apps. I'd never had to use one before; when I'd been a top bodybuilder, I usually had success approaching women anywhere I went. Now, I felt helpless and bewildered as Aba talked me through setting up my profiles.

"Do I say I had a s-severe brain injury, Aba?" I asked anxiously, wanting to be truthful.

"Perhaps not 'severe,'" Aba recommended. "Adam, move alla-center shelcha *(to your)* photos."

I frowned, staring blankly at the upload button. What recent photos could I possibly use? We settled on a photo Ema had taken of my cousin Nisso and myself as we celebrated both our successful surgeries, standing in his Long Beach apartment with my cane in my hand.

Unbeknownst to him, Aba had just given me a new type of rehab. Text messaging would allow me to plan what I would say in a conversation carefully, giving me an opportunity to rehearse and reason out complex new streams of thought before sending. Trying to impress women who were looking for a date was considerably more motivating than trying to impress therapists at TBS.

I still had trouble in written communication according to Nick, who I asked to look over my early messages.

"What did you mean here, man?" Nick asked, squinting at my message history. "I can't figure out what this word is supposed to be…"

I struggled to text women on dating apps just as I had first struggled to walk and talk to people at the grocery store. I often clicked "unmatch" after finding that I had no idea how to start a conversation. But that was okay. One general principle I was learning: if I was terrible at something, that just meant I had to practice it as much as I possibly could.

For weeks, I scared away almost every girl I spoke to by talking about my injury.

"Oh-ok."

"I'm so sorry that's, beyond drastic."

"a 10-day-coma? Your family must have been depressed!!"

I was so anxious to set their expectations of me realistically so that I wouldn't disappoint them in-person that I terrified them with the reality of my condition. I had trouble keeping the conversation off my injury for too long because my own thoughts were always on it.

Soon, I decided I preferred the grocery store to the dating app. Trying to choose someone to be in my life for the long-term was too intimidating.

Finally, I connected with a girl I could bear the thought of meeting. Emily was from the Midwest, and she offered to meet me before I'd had a chance to scare her off. This was it. A chance to see how someone would react to spending a whole date night with me.

I was excited for that evening. I even stopped at a barber shop for the first time since the accident.

"Hey bud, what are we going for today?" The barber asked, fondling the left side of my head. I hadn't been able to bring myself to go to Manny's: I was still too afraid of how he would react, having known me before my injury.

"Please keep right side of my head with little more hair," I requested.

That night, freshly trimmed and sharply dressed, I made my way to the cafe early. I wanted to arrive before Emily so she wouldn't see me limp into the restaurant. I also wanted time to study the questions and responses I'd prepared ahead of time. I discreetly took my credit card out and placed it under my napkin on the table so that when the time came to pay, she wouldn't see my left arm flail as I dug into my pockets for my wallet.

On my phone, Ema bombarded me with questions. "Where? What time? Do I know her? Is she Jewish?"

Emily arrived around 7:30 PM. She had black hair and pale skin and sported a stylish dark green jacket over a blue shirt. As soon as I saw her, my plans for making conversation fled my mind as anxiety set in. She apparently found this charming and soon commented that I was a "great listener." I smiled and nodded, grateful that she was leading the conversation.

We had a great time talking until about 10 PM. By now, the night had grown cool. I paid for dinner and got out of my chair as gracefully as I could, then offered to walk Emily to her car.

To my horror, the left side of my body began to clench up as we began our walk. The cold air caused my muscles to lock. Emily walked ahead, but as my limp became worse, she turned to see what was taking me so long. My left leg suddenly locked and shot straight out while my left arm curled in toward my chest.

"Ahh, need to stretch…" I tried, bending to touch my toes with my right hand in hopes of shoring up that excuse.

If I'd explained the truth to her about my limbs and cold weather, she may have accepted it after our lovely conversation. But I was panicking. The lie made things worse: it looked like I was hiding something. Which I was.

Emily said nothing but walked slower. I tried to keep up and my body clenched as I painstakingly counted every step to her car.

"Well, have a good night," I said, looking into her right eye as she got into the car.

As I drove home with the heat blasting, I was exhausted with the maintenance that my new life required. I needed to work with TBS while having a social life. I needed to balance time spent sitting in chairs with time spent stretching to prevent my left side from locking up. Even the temperature needed to be just right for my body to function.

When I got home that night, Nelly greeted me eagerly. I squatted to kiss her as she stood up on her rear legs and whimpered, reaching for me. I poured her dinner and sat down.

There was a candle with three wicks sitting on the kitchen counter. It had been a gift from a friend, and I hadn't lit it yet. I decided to burn just one wick every day as a reminder of the responsibilities I had to balance. Each time I lit the candle, I would be reminded of my balanced needs. If I lit one wick more often than the others, the imbalance would soon become obvious as the candle's wax melted unevenly.

I never heard from Emily again.

Although Ema no longer lived with me, we still tested my abilities together. Sometimes, Ema and I would go to the mall, and she would ask me to find a specific item in a specific store. We would see if my memory and attention span were sufficient to take me to the conclusion of the task.

I later challenged myself to choose a random locker at the gym to keep some of my things in, and remember which locker it was after working out. I didn't lock it, fearful of losing the combination, and I would take a picture of the locker number on my phone in case my memory failed me.

On one occasion, I forgot the locker number but refused to consult my phone. This resulted in me opening about 50 empty lockers before I found the one containing my things.

In the mornings, I'd make myself breakfasts of egg whites and cheese using my right arm. I would sit with my left arm on the counter beside me, watching it for signs of slowing blood flow.

Each morning, I lit a different wick on the candle and burned it until I had to leave for work or TBS.

Balance. Find your balance.

I began to believe that more changes were possible for me. The time came to talk to my parents about the outrageously expensive Colorado rehab called Rejuve, which Andrew Sharp's parents took him to.

I first began to research its offerings to make sure they were really worth it.

In a video from their site, a patient stood on a vibrating platform while other patients sat at IV stations nearby. The equipment looked like hospital equipment, but the environment looked like a spa or a gym with a mini rock wall in the background. They advertised the familiar transcranial magnetic stimulation and hyperbaric oxygen, but also exotic words and acronyms I didn't understand. Some of the articles on their website featured diagrams of molecules that looked very scientific.

It was the stem cell component that sold me. This therapy promised that these cells could regrow tissue that had died or been removed. The video showed the procedure involving IV and nasal injections, the latter being performed as the patient hung upside down!

They cost $31,000 per treatment. But the possibilities...my heart beat with excitement.

I thought of the missing parts of my brain, removed because they were contaminated with motor oil. Who wouldn't pay $31,000 to get part of their brain, part of their self back?

In videos on the website, before and after tapes of people with horrific brain injuries were shown. Patients described their bodies as becoming less fragile, and feeling less imprisoned by their bodies after they received the treatments.

I sat at the computer and glanced down at my ankle brace, my left leg feeling like a dead weight.

I had to do this.

A search of the Internet turned up dozens of articles discussing the use of stem cell therapy to treat TBIs, cancers, various injuries, and other diseases. Claims were made about re-growing bones, hair, and ligaments, and videos of celebrities talking about the benefits of stem cell therapy abounded.

I learned that this therapy was almost exclusively reserved for the wealthy, but there had to be a way my family could come up with the money. Aba was such an amazing businessman, and I was defying my own expectations by earning money every day. I began to fantasize about what would be possible for me with stem cells. I daydreamed about leaving my difficulties behind.

I knew firsthand that the brain controlled the body and that nothing worked without it. I had spent my life egotistically training my body, imagining this to be the greatest achievement possible. In reality, the achievement of growing my muscles was proving to be nothing compared to trying to recover my brain function. I had never appreciated the miracles the brain performed when it allowed me to perform an exercise, seamlessly coordinating dozens of muscles to perform precise movements in synchrony.

I didn't appreciate my brain, and now I'm paying the price. Can I get it back?

I continued to exercise at the gym, gradually making my way up to heavier weights. One day, I ran into Kaylee and her parents.

As I headed to my car, I realized that Kaylee was walking just a few steps behind me with her intimidating father and her mother. I was immediately embarrassed: I hadn't been watching myself too closely, and my left leg had been flailing in wide circles while my left arm swung at my side.

"Looking good, Adam," Kaylee's father said warily when he saw me noticing them. "How's everything?"

I couldn't bring myself to meet his eyes. "Good, goes," I said, staring straight ahead and pretending to be in a hurry.

"Don't walk too fast," he cautioned me, seeing my arm and leg flail as I sped up.

Kaylee didn't say a word.

I didn't know it yet, but our relationship was colored by something I couldn't see. As it turned out, Ema had blocked Kaylee's number from my phone while I was in my coma. She didn't want me to worry about answering messages from my new girlfriend, whom I'd only known for a few weeks, while I was fighting for my life.

As far as Kaylee knew, I'd ghosted her. And as far as I knew, she had ghosted *me a*fter my injury. When I finally remembered enough about my life to wonder why I hadn't heard from her, that seemed the only possible conclusion.

I imagined now that she was staring at me, deciding whether I had recovered enough to be worth speaking to.

As September approached, I decided it was time to graduate from TBS. I was doing so much now, and I found its long days of basic exercises incredibly boring. Everyone was sad to see me go, yet happy that I had regained so much ability.

In a way, I was sad to see them go, too. But if I was not sad to be done with the long hours of tedious exercises.

On my last day, Dave, the occupational therapist, handed me a cup of golf balls.

"Use these as often as you like, Adam," he said, a glimmer of pride in his eyes.

***

As the weeks passed, I had to admit that I needed some sort of rehab. I couldn't bear the thought of going back to TBS's all-day program, but my left arm and leg were getting worse without the help of a therapist.

When I voiced this dilemma to Ema, she suggested I hire a personal trainer to come to my home for private sessions a few times a week. That way, I could continue working and going to the gym almost uninterrupted, and I could get the benefits of assisted stretching and exercise in one hour per day instead of seven.

I thought about my options and remembered Delilah. She'd mentioned that she was a physical therapist now, and had offered to help me if I ever needed it. The fact that we had dated briefly before my injury did not make this a less appealing prospect. In fact, I was excited by the thought. Anything but TBS!

I called Delilah, excited to show her how far I'd come since she had seen me in my wheelchair. But when she didn't pick up the first time I called her, I had a crisis of confidence. I imagined that she didn't want to see me anymore.

"Don't need her anyway," I muttered to myself and began working out a way to try to stretch my own left arm.

Of course, Delilah returned my call within a few minutes. I was still judging myself more harshly than anyone else.

Seeing her name on the screen of my ringing phone, panic set in.

"What you going to say, Adam?" I tried to talk myself through planning a conversation as I swiped to answer the call.

"Hey, Delilah," I managed.

"Adam! How are you feeling? I miss you—you disappeared on me!"

I let out a sigh of relief. She sounded genuinely happy to hear from me. Excited, even. I took a deep breath and let her welcoming energy wash over me.

She told me everything was fine with her work and that she was reliably booked on the side as a personal trainer. I smiled at the news.

"Delilah—always handling h-er business."

She laughed, "I missed how you called me your go-getter girl!"

I'd forgotten that I used to call her my adversary because she was just as ambitious as I was. She was always working on something and could perform a one-legged single-arm deadlift while standing on half a yoga ball with ease. That feat is exactly as challenging as it sounds.

Memories of our old camaraderie came flooding back to me, memories of us talking and laughing and teasing each other at the gym.

Eventually, I got the courage to ask her to be my in-home trainer. Talk about a role reversal: once, I had trained her.

"Oh yes!" she replied happily. "I'd love to come and see you. Where do you live now, Adam?"

I told her my address, and she sounded delighted that my new home was just a few miles from her.

The next week, Delilah stopped by after her hospital shift as a rehab therapist. I answered the door, standing up with my head held high. She had changed into black leggings and a tank top that hung loosely off her fit body. The way she looked at me made me feel like a man, not a patient.

"Hey you," she said smiling, with sparkling eyes. "Nice to see you back to your old self."

I smiled tightly but was saved from having to respond by Nelly.

"Oh, who is this!?" Delilah exclaimed as Three Buttons ran up barking and began sniffing her feet frantically. "So cute, cutie butt! Come here!" She bent down and stretched out her arms as Nelly dodged her playfully.

Delilah followed Nelly into the house. "Show me an open space, and let's see what we can work on!"

I began walking her around my Cody Home, my left foot dragging as we went. I was supposed to be thinking about rehab, but I couldn't stop thinking about the time we'd spent dating. Images of her from before flashed through my mind.

"So this um, here," I walked her to Ema's old room, which I'd converted into a tiny, dumbbell-equipped home gym.

"I brought my tools and mat, is in the car." English was her third language, and I suddenly realized that her occasional word-finding difficulties might help me to feel at home with my own newly acquired speech troubles.

I stumbled as I turned to see her out, and my left knee locked.

"Adam, easy, easy," she cautioned me, grabbing my shoulder to steady me. "You already look great. Just breathe, okay?" Delilah bit her full bottom lip as she looked up at me with her brown eyes, our bodies pressed together as she supported me. Then we tore ourselves apart, and she hurried to grab her equipment.

She spent that day's session assessing my capabilities, asking me to lunge and squat with each leg so she could gauge how well they worked. As she assigned me exercises, I found myself performing movements I had never experienced before. At one point, she pulled out a plastic disk and instructed me to sit in a chair, then showed me how to use the disc to mimic hamstring curls.

I spectacularly failed to perform a hamstring curl with my left leg. My inner thighs were too weak to support the exercise.

Delilah designed an exercise to target those muscles. It involved tying an elastic band around my left ankle, tying the other end around a piece of furniture, and urging me to pull my leg inward against the resistance.

"Basketball stance," she reminded me, mimicking a player bouncing from side to side.

It was a strange feeling to have the same woman I had once showered with flowers, affection, and tender sleepovers giving me orders. Part of me almost rebelled against having her now "in charge of me." The rest of me knew that it was stupid: I needed her expertise.

"Okay, before we finish," she said, once I was too exhausted to continue, "I want to show you a new move. I want you to hold this dumbbell," she handed me a 10 lb weight—one of the same weights I'd once used in my very first PX90 workouts. "Now, with a straight back and chest up..." She started bent over with her butt sticking out gracefully and continued lowering her tanned perky chest slowly to her knees.

I stood staring, hunched to my right as my left arm angled uselessly at my side. "O-okay."

Delilah was determined to get my left hamstring to unlock. I was far from certain this was going to work.

"So keep your chin up, and bend your body until you feel your hamstrings stretch." She later described the move as 'concentration deadlifts.'

I tried the one-arm move a bit lazily, already exhausted.

"Arch, Adam."

To my shock, as I followed her instructions, I actually felt a pull in my left hamstring!

"Ahh!"

"Okay," she softened. "That's it for today, Adam." She handed me my water bottle before helping me sit. "This was an introduction. There are many, many moves we can do."

I immediately signed up, impressed that she could make me feel my left leg.

As it turned out, my enthusiasm didn't last forever. I signed up to have her come three times per week, and this soon became a lot. I'd gotten into the habit of exercising at the gym almost daily since leaving TBS, and some part of me still craved that ego boost.

But I had to admit, Delilah's stretching was damn near perfect. She got into parts of my body I hadn't known I could still feel, and I'd lie, completely euphoric, on the floor of my home gym after she finished stretching me.

Delilah was like a surgeon, identifying precisely which muscles were causing problems and prescribing what was necessary to fix them. She'd leave me in an almost meditative state when we were done. I would lie on the floor in a harmony of complete relief, my limbs and fingers spread wide, loosened, and warm. Until Nelly interrupted my blissful state, sniffing my ears and nose with great interest.

"Rest," Delilah would whisper in my ear as we wound our sessions down. "Relax, Adam." She'd let herself out when she was done, allowing me to lie there in another dimension for a good half-hour.

With Delilah, I never needed weights or resistance machinery. My own body did the work, sometimes with the help of resistance bands. I remembered what she had been able to achieve with her yoga ball deadlift, using nothing but her own body weight to train. I had never seen her pick up a dumbbell or barbell.

"You don't need more resistance," she would tell me in our physical therapy sessions. "Learn ta' use what you've already got."

***

22

Delilah

Total memory recall 54%
Mental Capabilities: 49%
Left Leg: 40%
Left Arm: 19%
Skin State: Scratches
Assistive items: Ankle brace
Age: 18
Weight: 165
Sources: Myself and Dad

Delilah and I first connected at the gym because we had so much in common. Both of us were athletically ambitious, aspiring to push both our physical abilities and our aesthetics to new heights. Both of us were children of immigrants, her family being Ukrainian and mine being Israeli. Both of us had family members with strong military involvement, which created a certain family culture. Now, post-accident, Delilah's caregiving background added a new dimension to our relationship.

Delilah's brother, Vlad, had been stabbed over 18 times in the chest on the streets of Russia. He survived but spent five years recovering from his injuries. Delilah helped to care for him during that time, and those same instincts now kicked in when she visited me.

Delilah had mentioned that I reminded her of her brother even before my injury. She'd said that the way I moved reminded her of him. Perhaps because of this resemblance, Delilah brought more than professional care to our appointments. With tremendous patience, she built a balanced movement routine for me, focusing on my core strength.

My time with Delilah accelerated my rehab in more ways than one. Our conversations helped to rehabilitate my mind and spirit as well. She knew precisely what my capabilities were but had full confidence in my independence. She accepted different levels of ability as a normal part of life and neither denied my disabilities nor seemed at all bothered by them.

I was so at ease with Delilah that I didn't stutter or grow confused when I spoke to her, and this showed me just how much of my speech disability was rooted in my own social anxiety and self-doubt. The more I spoke with this beautiful woman successfully, the more I felt my manhood was restored.

Almost immediately after she began working for me, we began socializing outside of our sessions. We went for coffee a few times and soon began taking trips to distant beaches, which marked the furthest I had driven myself from home since my accident. On the beach, she would have me practice balancing and walking over the shifting sands or while waves lapped at my ankles.

She even helped me change into my sandals and swimsuit. I'll never forget her, dressed in a light blue bikini, commanding me, "Lean to your left, Adam! Put weight on that left knee!" As I struggled to get my shoes off.

I stumbled and fell many times as we walked the beach, and I tried to wade into the ocean. I would trip, laughing at myself as she giggled and bit her full bottom lip.

"Careful, Adam," she'd tease, shaking her head in the glaring sun.

Once, an older man watched me fall, and rushed to help. "Whoa! You okay, dude? Need help?"

I laughed and thanked him for his offer as I climbed back onto my feet. "Thank you," I told him, "but that girl over there is my personal trainer." Delilah walked toward us, laughing with a towel wrapped around her waist.

We'd visit beach shops together, sometimes entertaining ourselves by playing the drums they set out for potential buyers to test. On one occasion, my car keys fell out of my pocket in the waves, and we had to phone Ema and Alex Eskanazi to bring me my spare set.

That day, as Delilah and I sat at a taco cafe waiting for Ema to arrive, Delilah told me about the times she'd witnessed people have "setbacks" in their lives. Her brother, like me, had once been told that he could not possibly recover from his injuries.

As I listened to her talk, I thought about how good her friendship had been for me and how I should treasure every moment with her. Surely, such a strong, beautiful, intelligent, caring woman would not be interested in socializing with a disabled man like me for long.

In October 2019, Delilah and I took a trip to the coastal mountains. She posed against the rugged backdrop wearing Aba's G-Defy shoes as I took pictures of her to advertise the new Mighty Walk product line. I gifted her the shoes after the photo shoot, and one of those photographs eventually became one of G-Defy's most successful marketing images.

She continued to challenge me in our sessions. At the start, I could perform lunges only with her help because my ankles weren't strong enough to do them independently. Lunges required me to consciously align my hips, knees, toes, and core and then force both knees to bend—a combination of movements that would have been unthinkable six months ago.

I was terrified the first few times she instructed me to try lunging on my own. But each time I performed lunges with her, the movements became more automatic. In time, I found that I no longer needed her assistance to accomplish this feat. Taking "lunge walks" across my deck amid the chirping birds became a source of great joy. Doing what I was unable to do before.

As soon as I mastered one exercise, Delilah would add more. She began having me hold light weights in my left arm as I performed lunges and eventually had me start doing something called *reverse* lunges, which tested my brain's ability to control my left hamstring to its extreme limits. Each week, I was shocked by what Delilah proposed, and shocked by what I was able to accomplish.

"Okay, stay straight up, Adam," she'd instruct me. "Don't lean to the side!"

We told ourselves that our affection for each other was purely platonic, perhaps because we both knew I was not in a good place for a romance. The thought of being in a real relationship terrified me, but I loved Delilah's attention. And although she treated me like more, I was still her patient.

We told ourselves that for a long time.

One day, after completing my usual training, she was stretching me on the floor of my home gym. This required her to press my hips into the floor with one hand while pulling on my upper legs with the other hand. While she did this, her body made contact with mine.

"Nice," Delilah breathed as my muscle tension relaxed. "Take a big, deep breath."

Suddenly, her hand slipped just a little bit, traveling further down the inside of my thigh than usual. I had a perfect view of all her curves from where I lay on the ground, and I felt a new kind of desire for her.

Her beauty was impossible to miss. She was wearing her usual crop top and skin-tight leggings, and her face looked exquisite as she frowned in concentration over me. My heart raced. I suppressed the urge to reach for her, but when she glanced down to where my legs met, it became obvious to her that I was excited.

She stopped, glancing up into my eyes.

Adam, you need her as your trainer. Don't be stupid! I berated myself.

Then, all at once, we began to kiss, our bodies pressed together.

"...Adam...I missed you," she whispered in my ear. "I'm so happy you're with me." Her arms wrapped around my waist.

Rapture shot through me.

She kissed my lips and cheek lovingly as I wrapped my right arm around her waist. She moved down to kiss my neck, and then her arms were around me, pulling me to my feet. She helped me hobble to my bedroom, where I immediately threw myself on the bed, and she began to help me take my clothes and unfasten the ankle brace.

This is actually happening.

I tried to climb on top of her and take the dominant position, but I failed. There was no way I could hold myself above her body with just my right arm and locked knee.

"Sorry I'm so broken," I grunted, trying to maneuver my elbows under me.

"Stop. Adam, don't ever apologize to me. I care about and I *love you.*"

Alarm bells rang in my head, but I was too far gone with lust and excitement. It was more than lust: it was validation. I was lovable. I could be loved, even like this. Even by a woman as impressive as her.

She flipped me over and straddled me, moaning softly and biting her lips as she slid me inside her. I met her gaze and stared into her eyes. The physical sensations were overwhelming, but my anxiety took over.

Am I enough for her? I look terrible. I can't be enough...

Memories came flooding back to me. I remembered how I always took control when having sex before my injury. I'd hold myself up and position myself carefully, using my strength to provide my partner with pleasure. Now, under Delilah, I tried to move my hips. But I could only move the right one. Delilah didn't seem to care as she set her own rhythm.

Soon, she gasped, arching her back and closing her eyes. "Mmm," she moaned in ecstasy.

Joy exploded within me at the knowledge that I'd brought such an amazing woman so much satisfaction. I grabbed Delilah's waist with my right arm and redoubled my efforts to move my own hips up and down along with hers.

As she moved above me, I closed my eyes. Afraid she might judge my flailing. The more I wanted to please her, the more anxious I got.

"Yes, Adam...this." Delilah grabbed my left hand and squeezed it. "Feel that?" She asked.

I shook my head, ashamed.

"You *will!*"

I gasped as she changed her rhythm.

"You will one day, Adam," she repeated, swaying back and forth on top of me.

Some part of me was still processing her profession of love, wondering what that could possibly mean. Surely she couldn't mean that she loved *me*, this me, me as I was since the accident. Surely, she meant the me she had known before, the strong, dominant, athletic man.

Yet she was making love to the *current* me, the disabled me, the me who she had seen when I could barely speak.

In the end, Delilah orgasmed, but I didn't. My insecurities drowned my pleasure. She murmured something about me having "stamina" as she curled up beside me in my bed, content.

After we finished, I thanked her for the wonderful experience. But deep down, dread churned in my stomach.

If she really meant what she said about loving me, we had a problem. I was grateful for her love—and totally unprepared to return it. Where once I might have felt romantic toward her, I now sensed nothing but anxiety and insecurity in my body.

"I honestly want you to recover, Adam," she said, as though reading my shamefully hidden thoughts. "I am your friend most of all."

I loved her affection. Yet I knew I could never really be *comfortable* with it. I'd spent our entire lovemaking session fighting with my new body. That was no basis for a lifelong relationship. There was no basis for an equal partnership.

But how could I tell her that? How could I tell someone who I needed, in more ways than one, that I didn't reciprocate her romantic love?

I tried my best to explain that I was early in my recovery. That I didn't know what I felt, that I couldn't feel romantic love through all the anxiety in my body. I had love and appreciation for her, but not the kind she wanted.

I could not bear the thought of losing or hurting her, either as a trainer or a friend. This left me between a rock and a hard place: did I let her continue showing me affection, knowing how she felt, or did I stop her?

I needed her as a trainer as much as I needed her friendship. I kept asking her to push me physically, even asking her to take me to the gym and help me to do a "heavy" workout like I'd done before my injury.

"Delilah, I'll go heavy tomorrow on my arms, then later we'll do our rehab workout. Okay?" I was trying to reassert my old dominant self, hoping that taking that role might help kindle some romantic feelings for her. But I was still so unsure of myself in the presence of someone so authoritative.

We continued like this for many months. I would apologize for not returning her feelings and try to return our relationship to a professional one. But we would end up in bed together, only for her heart to be broken again a few weeks later when she really understood that I was not in love with her.

One day, she knocked on my door, skipping our session and instead presenting me detailed instructions for rehab exercises. She told me that she knew I was now capable of following these instructions on my own and that she could no longer be involved in my life and keep getting hurt.

Losing her was painful. But I understood her decision. Part of me was relieved that I didn't have to choose between leading her on and losing her anymore.

I call that book of instructions "The Delilah Handbook," and I still use it today. I keep it attached to my journal.

I needed Delilah. Not as a lover or a girlfriend, but as a personal trainer and a rehab therapist. She knew me before my accident, but the new me needed her guidance in getting through my disability.

I didn't want to *need* anyone. Her acting as my caregiver just made me feel more dependent.

I think that's why I couldn't reciprocate. Not because she wasn't enough, but because I felt "less than" in her presence. Because I felt that I wasn't enough for her, and I could never be comfortable with that.

I will forever love and appreciate Delilah.

***

23

Stem Cells

Total memory recall 58%
Mental Capabilities: 49%
Left Leg: 40%
Left Arm: 19%
Skin State: Scratches
Assistive items: Hyperbaric Oxygen, TMS, Astronaut
Training Equipment, NAD+, Stem Cells
Age: 18
Weight: 165
Sources: Myself and Dad

On one of my last days at TBS, I saw Andrew Sharp walking!

I stopped dead in my tracks. A month ago, he had been confined to a wheelchair, unable to voluntarily move anything but his thumb. I was told he'd been like that for over a year. Now, here he was, walking through the TBS lobby unassisted. His arms still curled in toward his chest, but it was like seeing a miracle.

I stared. His mother looked delighted, watching Andrew's every move as she walked behind him.

How the hell...?

Stem cells.

I looked down at my own left arm where it dangled, useless, at my side.

When I got home that night after a day spent struggling to grasp golf balls in my claw-like left hand, struggling to keep my balance on a treadmill, I prepared to talk to my parents about Rejuve.

Scrolling through Rejuve's website, I was reminded of the price tag.

$32,000. No insurance would cover stem cell treatments since they weren't FDA-approved and were considered "experimental."

How could I ask my parents to spend $32,000 more on my care?

Could I even dare?

A few days later, Aba and Ema paid a visit to the Cody Home. I was ready to pitch my idea to them.

"I saw Andrew Sharp walking."

That was enough to stop Ema in her tracks. She knew the Sharps better than I did; she and Mrs. Sharp had swapped stories while Andrew and I did our rehab.

"No cane, even," I enthused. "He got stem cells."

Ema looked very cautiously at Aba. She was already thinking the same thing I was. If what I was saying was true, stem cells were a miracle. If what I was saying was true, then maybe, for me...

I stood up and began to pace, wanting to look strong when I made my proposal.

"If Andrew can walk, imagine what I can do if I get stem cells." I glanced furtively at Aba as I paced, still not back to my old, commanding self. "I can recover. I can do everything, Aba. I can be better!"

As I spoke, I began to believe this. I had spent the last year considering so many things beyond my grasp. Assuming that having a career—a *real* career, where I earned enough to support myself—was out of the question with my speech and memory problems. Even Ema had begun to caution me to lower my expectations.

Seeing Andrew Sharp walk made me question all of that.

I felt like I was preaching as I paced across my living room. "This is it! We've been looking for what would help me to recover, and this is it! Know Vital won't cover it, but…" I tried not to let the edge of desperation show in my voice.

Aba watched me with a serious, thoughtful stare. It was the same look he'd had the day I asked to drive his car in the desert. He shifted his weight, considering.

"Is that what you want?" he asked.

"Yes." Was it really possible?

"If stem cells may do this for you," Aba conceded finally, "bo nere (*let's see*)."

My eyes welled up with tears.

Aba didn't have the money to fund the stem cell therapy out-of-pocket. He'd already depleted his savings on the down payment for the Cody Home, and I'd depleted mine on the payments for my car. But Aba knew how to get financing with low-interest rates—that had been a key skill in building his businesses. He used his credit history to find a lender who, if we went through with the procedure, would give him a low-interest loan of $30,000.

Ema, Aba, and I completed my application to Rejuve. We sent them all the medical records Ema had from Thailand, Sunset, and TBS. Then we waited.

Finally, I got the phone call. A Rejuve nurse practitioner named Diane told me I might be eligible for their treatments. But to be sure, I would have to come out to the Rejuve clinic to have more tests and exams performed in-person.

The evaluation alone would cost $1,200.

I sucked in a breath. *How can anyone afford this? I wondered. Anyone whose dad doesn't run a big company?*

Even Aba, with all of his achievements, would need to take out a loan against the future to afford this. I couldn't imagine what an average family would do if stem cell therapy looked like their child's last hope.

But we could make it work. Just barely, by leveraging Aba's perfect credit history.

Six days later, we were on a plane to Denver.

***

To my surprise, Ema brought Nelly to Denver with us on the plane. Nelly's service animal status allowed it, and Ema knew I couldn't bear to be apart from her.

Poor little Three Buttons shook in her seat, surrounded by strangers and eerie noises as Ema fed her water from a bottle cap. But she seemed to prefer this to being left behind.

I limped up and down the aisles to keep my leg from seizing up while Aba conducted business on his cell phone. My family must have been quite a sight.

When we unloaded in Denver, I watched Aba and Ema work together to find the right luggage carousel. They walked close together, speaking softly to each other in Hebrew. I suddenly realized that they never spoke English when it was just the two of them.

Of course. They had grown up in Israel and met in the Israeli Defense Force. What must they be remembering when they looked at each other, and when they spoke Hebrew to each other? No strangers would look at this middle-aged couple and peg them as former soldiers. What experiences had they shared that I could not begin to imagine?

Ema and Aba had been divorced for over fifteen years. Yet here they were, working together to help their son recover.

My heart filled with love and gratitude as I watched them. There had never been any doubt that they would work together if I needed them. When Ema got up to use the airport restroom, leaving Aba alone, I leaned over and expressed my gratitude to him.

"Aba, thank you," I said guiltily. "Sorry. Thank you. Promise I will be better soon."

Sorry. Thank you. Promise I will be better. These phrases had become like my mantra since my injury, my constant apology to those around me for destroying my life.

Aba shook his head, staring out across the airport. "Adam, you are my son. My heart. Everything I created. I love you."

He managed to look at me then, perhaps overcoming a little shyness about being so tender. "Ani yodea *(I know)*...you grow and make mistakes. Aval *(But)*, I will give the world to keep my family and ha olam sheli *(my life)* healthy and secure."

He paused. "Ata neshama sheli." '*You are the air I breathe.*'

I took a deep breath, hearing those words. I so often felt inadequate next to my supremely talented Aba, especially since my injury. But hearing that I was loved made all the difference.

Aba rented us a car and drove us out to the small town outside of Denver, where the Rejuve clinic was located. We checked into the nearest hotel and settled in. Ema insisted on sleeping on the hotel room couch, arguing that the couch was only big enough for a 5' person like herself and not for Aba or me.

"We came here for your recovery," Ema argued as I tried to change her mind and take her place on the cramped sofa. "I need you to sleep well."

Nelly was calm and happy again now that it was just us. She didn't normally get to visit with all three of us all day and all night, and she was going to make the most of it. She ran in circles playfully before curling up next to me.

The next morning, I would visit the mythical Rejuve facility in-person and learn if I was eligible for stem cell therapy.

***

As Aba followed the GPS directions to Rejuve the next day, I was expecting to see something like the Avengers compound. With the slick, futuristic feel they'd cultivated in their online advertising, I expected a glistening tower to rise up from the Rocky Mountains as we approached. Instead, we pulled up to a modest-looking cube of a building with an unusual number of handicapped spaces in the parking lot.

The inside of the building was equally modest. The ceilings felt low compared to what I had expected, just 8' or 9' high, and I felt as though my head almost brushed the door frames as I towered 6'2". A staff person named Julie greeted us and immediately passed us off to a nurse named Geneva.

Geneva looked me up and down, assessing my posture. "You must be Adam." She consulted her clipboard.

We followed Geneva down a long white hallway. At one end was a room that looked like you'd use it to train astronauts. It contained some sort of chair encased in a metal frame and layers of clear plastic. The same room held devices that looked like what would happen if a treadmill had a baby with a yoga mat and a chair with something that looked concerningly like an e-stim device on steroids.

This is fine. This is necessary. I told myself.

Nelly stayed close to me, protective as any guard dog, as we explored the facility. She barked fiercely when the staff came too close to me. She'd then turn and sniff and look up at me with concerned little black eyes to see if I was okay.

I think she sensed my fear.

What if they didn't approve me for stem cell therapy? What if they decided I was too injured, or not injured enough?

Worst of all, what if I got the stem cell therapy and it *didn't work?*

Geneva led us into a room where I was hooked up to an IV, which I was told contained saline and vitamins. As the vitamins began to flush through my system I felt hot, and a strange, tarry taste coated my tongue.

"The concentrated vitamins can make you feel strange," Geneva assured me, "But they're good for the dry Rocky Mountain air." She turned to Aba and Ema. "Can you tell me more about Adam's accident?"

I sat by while Aba and Ema reviewed my early post-accident history with her. Geneva quizzed them about my air transport and its complications, what my vital signs had been during the flight, and my capabilities in the first days after I woke up.

Then, it was time to assess my cognitive abilities. Geneva settled me at a computer screen where questions, images, and videos were displayed. Some questions asked about my feelings, while others asked me to recall details from previous pages. Some asked me simple logic and math problems, reminding me of the class I had abandoned at TBS.

Then I was off to meet a balance and movement coordinator named Steve.

"Hello, Adam, I'm Steve!" He strapped me into a protective harness, similar to the bungee vests Becca had used at TBS, and had me step onto a platform.

We were in a corner room with strange-looking machines lined up against a wall. Instead of a treadmill's flat running surface, they had foot pedals that I was supposed to attempt to balance on. Steve wanted to see if I could remain standing while the surface beneath my feet moved in different ways, both with my eyes open and closed.

"Good, good," Steve murmured as I managed to keep my balance with my eyes open. "Now, gather yourself. I want you to do the same thing but without the visual cues to draw on." He stepped up behind me and slipped a blinding cloth over my eyes, then continued the test.

By the time my first day at Rejuve was over, Nelly was exhausted from sniffing every Rejuve staff member who approached me. She was dead asleep in Ema's arms by the time we got back to our hotel room.

For my part, I felt more hopeful than ever that we'd made the right decision by coming here. If Rejuve was so thorough with its testing, how effective would its treatments be?

The day somehow went both very fast and very slowly. I was buzzing with excitement to be here. But I had been disappointed so many times before. Nelly kept me sane, diverting my attention every time I was about to lose my patience with the endless parade of procedures. I began to feel like I was being subjected to new tests to prove my worthiness.

That evening, we had the final meeting. At an office in the back of the facility, a man in his mid-30s with shoulder-length hair greeted us. I recognized his picture from the website: he was Dr. Blossom, CEO of Rejuve. I remember being impressed by how such a young doctor could have all of the degrees, certifications, and awards the website listed for him. Beside him stood a younger doctor who looked like he'd just walked off the medical school graduation stage. He was introduced as Dr. Graham.

"Welcome, Elnekaveh family!" Dr. Blossom greeted us, smiling and trying his best to pronounce our last name.

Once we were all seated, he leaned over his desk toward us. "Although we cannot give the names of our past patients for confidentiality reasons," he explained, "many of them have made extraordinary recoveries. Assessing Adam, we have reason to believe that he could be one of those patients. I have worked with TBI patients for most of my career, and the therapeutic regimen we use here is specifically designed to stimulate injured brain regions to grow and heal.

"The big question," he said, taking a deep breath, "is the stem cells. This is our most unique therapy, and our most controversial. If you decide to go through with the treatment, stem cells which have been derived from umbilical cord blood from a Utah hospital will be shipped here under refrigeration. The stem cell preparation will be injected intravenously and through Adam's nasal cavity, where blood vessels will take the cells to his brain."

Dr. Blossom watched my parents and me carefully, gauging our reactions. "It may be possible to notice clear changes within the first few days of the treatment. However, it can take up to a year for the treatment's full effects to be seen as the stem cells and their growth factors create new neural pathways across Adam's brain."

I only processed the first part of that statement.

Just a few days? Excitement welled within me and I wanted to shout! I imagined coming back to Los Angeles as my old, strong, and clever self.

"I believe that Adam will probably be able to walk without his leg brace after treatment," Dr. Blossom proclaimed. "He should start walking without it immediately after receiving the stem cell treatment to stimulate his brain to focus growth on those neurons. But you should discuss this as a family," Dr. Blossom focused his attention on Aba and Ema.

"As you know, this treatment is still considered experimental. It hasn't been around long enough for its long-term effects to be studied." Dr. Blossom then shifted his gaze to me. "Adam, I've reviewed your X-rays and MRIs from the accident. Whatever your parents decide, I'm just glad you're not in a permanent vegetative state. It's remarkable."

The discussion continued back at our hotel room.

"I don't know," Ema said doubtfully. "Why is this magical treatment not approved by the FDA?"

An Internet search revealed that the FDA had taken action against the company that provided the stem cells to Rejuve in the past. The FDA argued that there was a risk of cancer if stem cells were taken from one person and injected into another; the stem cells could theoretically form tumors, and immune system reactions could occur against the foreign cells inside the body.

"Look at this!" Ema exclaimed, reading the report. "Adam! You could get cancer! You want to take that risk?"

I didn't have to think about it very hard. The possibility of developing cancer *someday* versus struggling to meet my goals for the rest of my life? I thought about Andrew Sharp walking down the hall at TBS.

"I cannot believe they are allowed to sell this!" Ema exclaimed, scrolling down a long list of negative side effects that had been reported.

I was still thinking about Andrew Sharp.

"This is his decision," Aba said finally after listening to Ema's anxieties and my silence. "It is his body and his life. Adam, tell us…do you want to take this risk?"

They both looked at me.

"Yes," I said instantly. "This has to be good for my recovery." Another moment of silence stretched between us. "Please, Aba," I met his eyes desperately.

"Then it's settled," Aba announced, and stood up to begin packing his bags.

He had to fly back to California the next morning to return to G-Defy. But Ema and I would stay for a full two-week course of rehab, culminating in the stem cell treatment.

***

The next morning, Nelly strained wildly against her leash to greet everyone at the Rejuve clinic.

Ema still seemed anxious, but the staff assured her that they would administer the "minimum viable amount" of stem cells to me to reduce the risk of side effects. And I was determined.

The Rejuve staff wanted to start my day with more cognitive tasks and more questions and problems given to me on a computer screen. I expressed my impatience, looking longingly at the physical therapy machines in the other treatment rooms. But Steve said something that made me see things in a new way.

"Adam, I understand how you feel," he said. "But in order to heal your body, we have to heal your brain. You're already a strong guy, but your mind is just as important to your life as your body. What's the point of having a Ferrari if you can't drive it? Remember, it is your brain that drives your body. If you can't have a good mental state and make good decisions, you can't enjoy your body."

That analogy hit home for me in a way none of the other lectures had. Steve was right: I needed to develop my brain just as much as my body, even if that meant sitting through "boring" cognitive tests.

Over the days to come, I was introduced to more treatments than I ever knew existed. Rejuve had the familiar transcranial magnetic stimulation and hyperbaric oxygen therapy (though this was administered in ziplock tents, not tubes), which were administered to me every day. They also had things I'd never seen before, like "electric water therapy," a device I took to calling a "gyro chair" because its full name was too long for me to remember, and something called "NAD+ IV therapy."

The cold laser therapy was fascinating. It worked by shooting beams of light at my head, which were intense enough to penetrate the skull and brain tissue. The wavelengths of the light were supposed to stimulate cellular metabolism and promote healing. The Rejuve staff targeted the areas of my brain that had been injured in my accident.

The gyro chair—the thing that looked like a piece of astronaut training equipment—turned out to actually *be* a piece of astronaut equipment. It turned out that roughly the same technology that could teach a pilot to function while tumbling through the air could also produce intense activation in areas of the brain associated with balance and motor control.

The specific program of spinning and flipping they assigned me to go through in the gyro chair was meant to target my right sensorimotor cortex. It was damage to this brain area, which was supposed to send movement commands to the left side of my body and process sensations from that side, which was causing the problems with my left arm and leg.

My body did not like the gyro chair. My left hand and foot began trembling violently almost as soon as I climbed into it. It was normal for them to tremble for up to a minute when I tried something new or challenging with them, but with this machine, every position I could sit in was new and challenging.

Dr. Graham told me to grip the metal handles of the gyro machine, which I managed to do only after playing the usual game of tetris with the fingers of my left hand. Then a red light began flashing to let us know that the machine was about to move. The next thing I knew, I was being flipped upside down and spun in circles!

Yes, this was certainly going to stimulate *something* new in my brain.

The machine soon became more uncomfortable than exciting. I had no control over its movements, and I had to constantly adjust to new motions and positions. Dr. Young had me spin and flip for six minutes at a time before giving me a much-needed rest. After a few of these six-minute cycles, Dr. Blossom walked in.

"Great job, Adam," he said, nodding in approval. "Your next task will focus on multi-tasking."

Dread formed in the pit of my stomach. Multitasking was my Achilles heel. I could still barely walk and talk at the same time. But that was probably exactly why Dr. Blossom wanted me to do it. He handed me a tiny blue laser pointer.

"Adam, I want you to hold this in your right hand and point it at the targets while you spin." He pointed to a series of stickers with bullseye designs scattered around the walls of the room.

I took a deep breath and nodded, willing my left hand and foot to stop quivering. I struggled to get comfortable with my right hand clutching the pointer instead of stabilizing me.

Then I was spinning again. I fought desperately to point the laser at the targets, imagining myself in a real-life version of one of the video games I'd played as a kid.

I must have hit some of them because Dr. Blossom shouted: "Yes! Keep it going!" and the speed of the flipping and whirling gyro increased.

After the gyro session, it was time for TMS. Thank goodness. Sitting in a comfortable chair doing nothing was just what I needed.

I sat there and dreamed of how I would recover. How I would become a hard worker and a profitable employee for Aba and make him proud.

Then there was the NAD+.

Oh God. The NAD+.

NAD+ is considered a cutting-edge anti-aging and regenerative medicine treatment. If NAD+ sounds familiar to any of you, you probably learned about it in high school biology class. It's supposed to stimulate cellular metabolism and prompt injured cells to grow and heal.

Some studies in lab mice have suggested that increasing NAD+ in the body can drastically increase physical energy and lifespan and even reduce molecular aging. In mice.

Because this has so far only been studied in mice, many scientists are not convinced it works on humans. But many tech millionaires pay hundreds of dollars per IV bag to have NAD+ infused directly into their veins, and many have testified about NAD+'s transformative effects on the Rejuve website.

This being the case, I went in expecting NAD+ injections to feel like a spa treatment. They did not.

As the day of my first NAD+ treatment approached, Rejuve staff would make comments about how I should "get ready for my NAD+" and how "they knew I could make it through."

In hindsight, these comments were definitely red flags.

The NAD+ IV fluid was a yellow-green color. Geneva would hook the IV bag up, and I could watch the yellow-green color creep through the IV tubing toward my vein.

"Okay, Adam," Geneva said, "I need you to walk while this infuses. Walking is the only way we can ensure it circulates through your body and reaches your brain."

Walking? That sounded simple. Though it had once been a huge challenge for me to walk, I was proud to be able to say it didn't intimidate me anymore. Trailing my IV pole behind me, I started to walk. Ema followed, holding a controller with "+" and "-" buttons to turn the flow of NAD+ into my body up or down.

I made it fifteen steps before it hit me.

My entire body knotted up in excruciating pain. I began to shake. Everything hurt. My vision went white. I wanted to vomit, but my body couldn't seem to unclench long enough to do so. I felt like I was having another seizure.

I collapsed to the floor of the clinic, shaking.

"Hnnngh!"

"It's okay, Adam," Geneva soothed, hovering over me. "Your body will get used to it soon."

"Ema! Turn off!"

She did, and the sickness subsided within seconds. I now understood why they had handed the control to her and not to me. I had no motor control in my hands when I shouted my plea.

Steve picked me up off the ground, still shaking. Then it was time for round two. I had to finish the IV bag to be eligible for stem cell treatment.

"You should not have to go through this, Adam," Ema told me, unsettled as she drove us back to the hotel.

"Have no choice," I told her simply.

The second time they gave me NAD+, I had already developed extreme anxiety about having the IV placed in my arm.

As the days passed, I started to need space. From everything. The Rejuve therapies could be overstimulating, and I was no longer used to living with Ema in a small, confined space. Sometimes I would ask Ema for her car keys and just so sit in the car, decompressing in the solitude.

While I sat out there, I remember listening to the U2 song "I Still Haven't Found What I'm Looking For" on repeat. The story of a man desperately searching for something he could not name, sung with unspeakable longing, resonated with me on every level.

One day, Ema and I went into the nearby downtown to eat at a restaurant and see Colorado's culture. I saw a young man and woman walking down the street hand-in-hand, whispering to each other romantically.

Will I ever be able to hold a woman with two arms again? I wondered, watching them. *Will I ever be able to make a woman proud?*

I had to try.

After over a week of various therapies, the Rejuve staff were satisfied that my brain was ready. The day had come for my stem cell treatment.

The big day started normally. I walked to the clinic alone; Ema was now satisfied that I knew my way around the place. Nurse Patricia put in a vitamin IV, took my vitals, and walked me to the leather TMS chair for my first brain stimulation of the day.

I glanced around, wondering if the silver refrigerator in the corner held the sought-after stem cells.

"Your first stem cell injection," Patricia said, turning to take something out of the silver fridge, "will be intravenous. That means we'll put it into your veins. Later today, we'll administer another injection into your nose."

She had a bag of IV fluids in her hand, and I fought to keep from hyperventilating with excitement.

"For your second injection," she continued, "we'll hang you upside down on an inversion table. That will help the stem cells reach your brain."

Patricia turned back to me. "Ready for the first part, love?" She hooked the IV catheter in my hand up to the new IV bag.

She left me alone in the room, praying. I expected to feel something magical as the $30,000 fluid infused into my veins.

But I felt nothing.

When Patricia returned to check my vitals fifteen minutes later, she realized what was going on.

"You won't feel anything just yet," she explained gently. "It will take days, weeks, even up to a year for the stem cells to complete the process of helping your brain."

I nodded, suppressing a groan. I squeezed my fist tight, wondering if that would help pump the stem cells up to my brain faster. Ema came in, carrying Nelly to keep me company. But her attempts at conversation and Nelly's sniffs did little to distract me from my focus on the stem cells.

When the stem cell IV bag was empty, Patricia came back and walked Ema and me across the hall to a room that housed an inversion table. Patricia strapped my feet in. I knew this was to hold them in place when the table flipped me upside down, but it felt like I was being restrained.

The table flipped me up, my feet toward the ceiling and my head dangling helplessly toward the floor. Patricia disappeared from my field of view for a moment. When she re-appeared, she was looming over me, holding a device with a four-inch-long needle protruding from it.

I had a sudden flashback to the Amityville Horror movies of my childhood.

"Okay, let's get started," Patricia said cheerfully. She dipped the impossibly long needle into a tiny glass bottle, drawing some liquid out of it. "You might feel a *little* poke."

She inserted the needle into my nostril.

I started to have a panic attack.

"Deep breaths," Patricia soothed. I could feel the needle poking through my sinuses and into my forehead. I closed my eyes, praying this would all be worth it.

Whatever it takes.

I hung there 20 minutes—so long that my right foot started to go numb. My head pounded as blood rushed to

419

it. I looked around for any sort of timer that would tell me how long I had to stay like that.

After what seemed an eternity, an alarm beeped somewhere.

"Congratulations!" Patricia chirped. "You're ALL done! There's just one more thing."

Patricia flipped me back down into a normal position, and relief coursed through my body. "What's that?" I asked uneasily.

"You just need to spend two hours in the hyperbaric oxygen tent."

I deflated. "Seriously?" How anticlimactic. I'd had what felt like a thousand hyperbaric oxygen treatments, and I'd never felt as though they helped.

"It's the final step!" She smiled so enthusiastically that I almost believed her. "But don't bring your phone with you. Your brain has to rest right now."

In the hall on the way to the oxygen tents, physical therapist Ronnie passed by and gave me a high five. "You're in the home stretch, man!"

Yes, I told myself. *Home stretch.*

*A*fter an excruciatingly boring two hours of oxygen therapy, Ema drove us back to the hotel where I immediately passed out in bed. I slept for twelve hours, and still needed Ema to wake me up in the morning.

The next day was our final day at Rejuve.

Patricia took my vitals when we arrived, and quizzed me about my eating and sleeping. When I recounted my long night's sleep, she smiled. "That's a good sign. Today will be very relaxing—we'll be giving you tests like on your first day here, to track how your performance has changed since you arrived."

On one hand, that did not sound fun or exciting. On the other hand, it wasn't NAD+.

They started me with an hour in the hyperbaric oxygen tent. This time, I was allowed to bring my phone. Then, it was time to test my balance and motor control skills with Steve.

Finally came the computer quizzes—page after page of questions that alternately felt mind-numbingly easy and impossibly difficult. I clicked through questions about which emotions different photographs of faces were showing for what felt like an eternity.

"I'm not stupid," I murmured. "Can tell if someone's face is happy or sad." I didn't yet understand that there were people with brain damage specifically affecting their ability to read facial expressions, the same way I had brain damage that specifically affected my left hand and foot. These tests I was taking were meant to test just about every area of the brain.

Finally, it was time to meet with Dr. Blossom. I felt excited despite myself. He was portrayed as such a glamorous and brilliant man on Rejuve's website. I felt sure that he would have something exciting to tell me about my recovery.

"Hi, Adam. How are you feeling?" He asked, smiling as Ema and I sat down in his office. I smiled and reported that I felt good; in that moment, I did. I felt hope, and that felt good.

"We will be shipping you exosome treatments to take over the next few months," Dr. Blossom explained, showing us a box of tiny glass vials. "These need to be refrigerated at all times to remain viable. They're tiny little packages of chemical messengers that can get inside of cells and help your brain to incorporate the stem cells. We'll also be sending you home with some testosterone and human growth hormone treatments."

I stared in amazement. Throughout my years as a bodybuilder, I'd rejected steroids even when my peers promised me that they would allow me to achieve superior results. Now I was being prescribed them by a medical doctor to treat my injury?

Wow, the irony.

However, The prescription formulation was carefully controlled and safe, unlike the black market steroids some bodybuilders used, which were often laced with undisclosed drugs to give them an extra "kick."

This might actually work!

"Next, Adam," Dr. Blossom continued, "I want you to start walking without your ankle brace."

I stared, astonished. I'd wanted nothing more than to ditch this brace since I first got it. But the few times I walked without it had not gone well.

"Walking without the brace will activate those muscles and nerves, and stimulate your brain to reconnect to them," Dr. Blossom explained. "That is exactly what we want to be doing right now."

Dr. Blossom got up, knelt down, and loosened the brace on my ankle himself. "Let's start by just loosening it and see what happens."

He returned to his seat, sat back, and looked at me. Looked at me like I was a puzzle. "Adam," he said, "the way you injured your brain is very interesting. I know you prefer athletic tasks, but you will have to exercise all parts of your brain to see recovery. You will have to read, write, and socialize to regain your speech, memory, and reasoning faculties. I believe you can do it; but it will require practice.

"With your type of brain injury, I think that doing things backward will be very helpful for you. Walking backwards or running backwards on an elliptical, for example. That will activate new patterns of motion in your brain and help you regain more control of your movements."

As Dr. Blossom said it, I was shocked that no one had ever thought of this before. It made perfect sense.

Dr. Blossom stood up. "Well, thank you for coming out here and trusting us with your care. I truly believe you will continue to make a great recovery. You have already come so far."

Ema and I thanked Dr. Blossom sincerely and walked out of his office excited. I may not yet have felt like an Avenger, but I had new tools to use to recover.

That night, in the shower, I tried to scrub my body with my left arm. I couldn't move it any more than usual, but I wanted to be prepared for the day when it might become mine again.

On the way home, I stared at my feet, placing them carefully as I walked up and down the airplane aisles with no ankle brace, testing my abilities.

***

24

The Promotion

Attainments: Marketing Department Associate
Mental Capabilities: 65%
Left Leg: 47%
Left Arm: 23%
Assistive items: Netsweet Introduction
Age: 20
Weight: 172
Sources: Sam, Robben, Pen, Evan, and Myself

I was so happy to put my bags down in the kitchen of the Cody Home back in Los Angeles. The thought of sleeping in my bed again was amazing. But first, I sank into the beige recliner beside it to think.

We'd been instructed to make many changes to my life to support the stem cells. We'd been told to add more healthy fats to my diet and to substitute all dairy products with plant-based alternatives. I was supposed to buy all organic foods to reduce the possible impact of pesticides and herbicides on the stem cells. In the next few weeks, a refrigerated package of steroids and exosomes would arrive for me to inject myself with regularly.

These changes sounded unimaginable, especially since getting through the basic responsibilities of life was still a struggle for me.

But, there was the reward. According to Dr. Blossom, I no longer needed my ankle brace. If he was right, I could ditch my last assistive device.

I drifted off in bed that night and woke to find Nelly curled up beside me. I stretched my arms to try to pet her, and to see if my left arm was healed yet.

No. Not yet. If anything, I felt unusually exhausted.

Since I would need to be careful about my diet, I started practicing cooking more. Cracking eggs into a frying pan with one hand was challenging, and this morning was no different. I dropped the first egg on the floor, the second splattering on the stovetop beside the pan. On the third attempt I managed to crack the egg into the pan, but most of the eggshell went along with it. I had to take the pan off the heat and clean the shell fragments out of it.

Time for round two. I bent close to the pan in concentration, my weight shifting onto my right leg as my left leg began to tremor from the effort. Out of seven attempts, I finally managed to get two eggs into the pan without much shell. They made a satisfying sizzle.

I stayed home for a few days, recuperating and performing exercises out of the "Delilah Handbook."

On the third day, I slipped on my old, treasured Nike's for the first time since my accident. Once my constant companion at the gym, the shoes had not been compatible with my ankle brace. I hadn't known if I'd ever be able to wear them again.

The fact that I'd bench-pressed 335 pounds the last time I wore them filled me with mixed emotions. I had a vivid flashback to doing "clap-ups" wearing these shoes, flying through the air after hurling myself upward with two strong arms.

I arrived at the gym and walked on a treadmill for six minutes before I remembered: I wasn't allowed to work out with weights for two weeks after my stem cell treatment. Ronnie had explained to me that working my

425

muscles to the point of developing microtears could "confuse" the stem cells into migrating to repair my muscles instead of my brain.

Well, I thought. *If I'm only allowed to do cardio, I'll make it interesting.* I decided to try to walk for 50 minutes straight without my ankle brace.

I stared down at my feet the whole time, carefully placing one in front of the other to ensure they were properly aligned and I wouldn't fall.

I made it! I walked for 52 minutes without my brace.

On my way out of the locker room, a group of athletes caught my eye. One especially fit man was being recorded by three of his buddies as they exclaimed about his strength and aesthetic looks.

"Man, look at this dude!"

Transfixed by the reminder of my past life, I walked closer to them.

"Nice body," I told the man sincerely as I passed. "Be safe, man." He could not have known why I offered this particular warning.

I was so transfixed that I stopped watching my feet and almost immediately tripped on a dumbbell someone had left out on the floor. I fell, landing on my numb left arm.

"Hey!" One of the buff athlete's friends looked up in alarm, then stepped toward me. "You okay guy?"

"Yeah, okay!" I hastily got to my feet, using my TBS training to push off the ground. "Watch your step, guys!" I shot a warning glance at the stray dumbbell and hurried away, half-limping in my haste.

Only my pride was wounded. But my insecurity was running high.

After the gym trip, it was time to try something new: vegan protein powder. The Rejuve dietician insisted on this, saying that dairy proteins could interfere with my stem cell recovery. Ema had lovingly bought me a vanilla vegan powder, which I mixed up in the Cody Home blender with almond milk.

I took a sip—and instantly spit it into the sink. It tasted like blended chalk.

"This is disgusting, Nelly!" I half-shouted, needing someone to witness my horror.

I glanced at the label, hoping it was expired and spoiled. It wasn't. Then I eyed the blender cup like it was my nemesis.

"Sacrifice, pay the price," I muttered, closing my eyes and raising the blender cup in my right hand. I chugged the rest of the shake as quickly as I could, trying not to taste or smell it.

I was determined to get the full benefits of stem cell therapy and rebuild my life.

As the days progressed, my moods began to swing wildly. It's hard to say if this was some side effect of the stem cells, or simply disappointment that I had not returned from the clinic a new man. I had not yet experienced a miraculous recovery like Andrew Sharp. Although I knew intellectually that Andrew had not started walking until months after he began his visits to Rejuve, I was still frustrated.

Around this time, Aba approached me about finishing construction on the Cody Home's downstairs units and getting me some tenants. "We need help with the mortgage payment, Aba," he told me.

I had almost forgotten the existence of the lower floor, avoiding stairs thanks to Aba's warnings about the danger that I could fall. I nodded as he explained that construction workers would be coming in to finish the new rooms.

This conversation reminded me to look for ways I could contribute to the cost of my treatment and the cost of *everything*. I returned to work at G-Defy the next day and began looking for ways I could add more value to the company.

I searched through G-Defy's web presence, knowing that social media marketing was something I'd been decent at before my accident. I found that G-Defy's marketing was not exactly en pointe: the product photos online were not to my liking, and there was almost no way for people to find or engage with the brand on social media. I began asking around and learned that marketing was only receiving a tiny budget compared to G-Defy's operating expenses.

I had some ideas of how to improve the situation. Working on FitFlow, I had perfected product photography, and knew it was important to show the products being used for different activities to show the consumer their benefits. By showing people performing various activities in G-Defy shoes, we could give a much stronger sense of what was possible with these shoes than by just showing the shoes alone against a white background.

I began writing a list of photographs I would like to see on the company website to help promote three of the top shoe lines more effectively. I added more shoe lines and product photo ideas to the lists.

Part of me felt that this was not "real" work because it came easily to me. But, I knew that if I could capture online audiences more effectively, G-Defy could sell more shoes.

After about two weeks, I had compiled a list of proposed product photos for six different G-Defy shoe lines. I took a deep breath and stood up to walk over to the Art Department, where Director Brian handled marketing.

I approached him cautiously, then held out my list and explained my background in putting together the marketing campaign for FitFlow. I explained the likely benefits and asked how much it would cost to hire professional photographers to take these pictures.

"Adam, this is great," Brian said hesitantly. "But unfortunately, executing all of these photographs with the scenery you describe would cost about $15,000."

My eyes bulged. "Wow, that much?" My mind immediately went to the $32,000 my parents had already spent on my stay in Colorado for treatment, and I felt guilty for asking for even more money.

"Yes, Adam," Brian explained. "Remember, we are talking about professional photographers, models, wardrobe, cameras, lights, etc."

I took a deep breath, struggling with this cost estimate.

"I have an idea," Brian said, squinting at me under his gray hair. "Why don't you present this idea to your father? Show him this list along with a list of the demographics you believe these photos will reach and your marketing goals. If your father is convinced, maybe he will authorize a budget for it. I'll email you a list of the expenses I'd anticipate for this project by the end of today."

I nodded and immediately went to my father's office without doing any of Brian's suggested prep work.

Knock knock. "Aba," I said softly, peeking in the half-open door of the office he shared with John.

"Ken, Aba," my father said, looking up from reading something on his computer.

I stepped anxiously into his office and took out my handwritten photography outline. Fidgeting anxiously, I began to explain my proposal.

Aba just watched me. He never glanced at the paper once.

"Rackrega, (one moment)," he murmured thoughtfully after I finished my pitch. To my alarm, he picked up his phone.

"Evan," he said into the speaker, "bring Robben over. I want a marketing sales meeting."

My heart began to pound—this time with excitement instead of fear—as I realized he was taking me seriously. As I waited for the others to arrive, I braced myself.

Moments later Evan strode in, followed by his assistant Robben. I tensed, feeling like I might collapse inward from the pressure of having to pitch my ideas to all three of these intimidating men at once.

"Okay, gentlemen, have a seat," Aba gestured toward the office furniture. Evan and Robben looked around, but there were only two guest chairs in Aba's office—and I was already sitting in one of them. Awkwardly, I stood up and offered one chair to Evan.

Aba nodded in approval, then, to my astonishment, rose from his own maroon office chair and offered it to me.

"Adam bo, teeshev poe, (come, sit here)."

My heart began to pound harder. Whether Aba saw the symbolic significance of it or not, he had just invited me to come sit in *the owner's chair.*

I did as he asked, walking crookedly around his desk, sitting in his chair, and glancing around, trying to pretend I knew what to do next.

"What's going on?" Evan asked finally, glancing up at Aba.

"Talk to your team, Adahm," Aba said, fixing his attention on me.

I stared at Robben and Evan silently, pretending to gather my thoughts.

"So, basically," I took a deep breath, "I want to take new photos for the c-company website," I said, fixing my gaze on Robben, unable to process talking to two people at once. "I think we should show what people can do with the shoes. Pictures like," I glanced down at the paper still clutched in my sweaty hand and read off of it, "a mother at the park with her kids, or a mailman walking carrying—packages."

After speaking for what felt like an eternity, I fell silent. I glanced up at Aba for approval and realized I was slouching to the left and straightened up.

"Okay, yofi," Aba said calmly, glancing at Evan and Robben for their responses. "Good ideas, Aba. Guys, go back to your work, and we will continue this conversation tomorrow."

Evan stood up, his eyebrows raised, and Robben followed suit. As they walked out, I quickly got out of Aba's chair and circled back around to the other side of the desk. I felt the weight of leadership slide off my shoulders as I did so.

Aba sat back down. "Tov meod *(very good)*. I see that your brain is working more and more," then he looked at me seriously. "What do you want to do for the company, Aba? You want to be a marketing photographer? You want to oversee the company catalog, or its social media presence? What do you enjoy?"

I sat there, confused. Was he really asking me what I *enjoyed* instead of what was good for the company? I'd been totally unprepared for this. I was too stressed to feel any sense of delight.

"I don't know, Aba…" I said finally.

"Let's have you oversee our social media," he suggested, probably recalling my FitFlow business proposal. "You'll learn alongside Robben and Evan. I want to also put you with Pen, our head of software so you can continue to learn about the company system. Learn how it works beyond just taking a sales order and emailing."

I sat there nodding, absorbing maybe 30% of Aba's words.

"Sounds good?" he asked.

"Okay, Aba," I hoped that was an appropriate response.

Emotionally depleted, I headed to lunch. After a much-needed break, a man I didn't recognize knocked on my cubicle wall.

"Hey, Adam, I'm Pen," he told me. "How's it going, man?"

Pen. G-Defy's software engineer. I looked up. He stood there in a sharp green jacket with slicked-back hair.

"I'm here to train you," he said, smiling cautiously when I had no intelligent response. "Alex wanted me to teach you more in-depth about the company Netsweet system."

I smiled in relief, remembering my conversation with Aba.

"But," Pen continued, the words gushing out of him, "I told him that right now, I am working with the company website's coding, the shipping reports, and such. Can we possibly meet next week instead?"

My mind was already spinning from him speaking so fast. In time, I would learn that Pen always spoke the way his brain worked: at a million miles a minute. I nodded, pretending I understood. "All good, Pen," I ventured, since he seemed to be looking for my approval.

In the days to come, I tried to live up to Aba's expectations. I began working for G-Defy almost full-time, asking all the questions I could think of about my new trainers, Robben, Evan, and Pen. When I had spare time, I called Ema, wanting a silly conversation to make me smile.

Aba was pleased, and a new idea was taking shape in my mind.

When I was a bodybuilder, a major marketing mechanism had been influencer marketing. Getting people who were already influencers with hundreds of thousands of followers in the fitness space to have me on their shows, or to talk about FitFlow, was the way to get in front of millions of viewers.

To my knowledge, nobody had yet tried this with G-Defy. I began sending message requests to prominent medical and athletic influencers, along with requests for reviews and sometimes modest sponsorship offers.

The effect snowballed quickly. The more influencers I got covering G-Defy's shoes, the more prestigious the brand appeared and the more influencers joined in. Eventually, G-Defy was accepted as a sponsor by one of the most famous orthopedic surgeons on Instagram.

My time spent as a shoe salesperson now paid off, as I knew which G-Defy shoe line was best to offer to each influencer. Medical influencers were a better fit for G-Defy's shoes designed to help with orthopedic issues, while athletic influencers were suitable for sports and running shoes. I sent a European track runner who had 115,000 followers a pair of XLR8s to review for his audience. Several of our surgeon and doctor influencer-partners had 200,000 followers or more.

Pen began to teach me how to read and manage my "KPIs," or "Key Performance Indicators." This included marketing and sales numbers, total orders, and retail location revenue that were tracked in NetSweet. By tracking these numbers, we could see how well a business strategy was working as far as bringing in revenue.

"Let me say," Pen told me one day, clicking us through NetSweet tabs, "your father has great trust in you. Alex never gives anyone this type of total access. Only you, me, John, and Rap can see all of this data." It was then that I learned Aba had essentially given me CEO-level access to the company's computer systems.

I tried my best to follow along as Pen showed me how to compare earnings from various date ranges, stores, and shoe lines. I often sat at the computer with him, frowning in concentration, until my body reached a point of sheer exhaustion, and long after my mind stopped registering his facts.

"Let's take a break, please," I would finally request when I could sit there no longer and my head had begun to hurt. Sometimes, I would pretend I had something else to do, somewhere else to be, when I really just needed to get out of my cramped sitting position. Fortunately, Pen was always willing to stop and pick up later.

Once, I was so overwhelmed after one of our training sessions that I walked out of the G-Defy office building, plopped down on the curb in the parking lot, and called Ema.

"Ema?" I asked weakly when she picked up.

"Ma kore, mami?" *'What's going on, baby?'*

"Dubi, can't do this. This work, memory…will forget," I tried to explain helplessly.

I felt so out of my depth with everyone talking at me as though I were a knowledgeable businessman. For the first time, I missed TBS where everyone had patience with me.

Ema reminded me to take my training step-by-step. "Your father saw you very hurt; he is mostly happy you survived," she told me. "So just keep asking questions and learn. Everyone will have patience with you. You also kebalta *(got something)* in the mail, Adami!"

Ema sounded so excited. I strained to remember what the new delivery could be.

***

25

New Growth

Attainments: Regional Manager
Mental Capabilities: 68%
Left Leg: 50%
Left Arm: 25%
Assistive items: Steroid Injections
Age: 21
Weight: 175
Sources: Rap, Dad, Chris, Marvin, Chad, Rupert, and Myself

The box on my kitchen counter was gray with rounded corners. It looked like something out of a science lab—and in fact, it was. Inside the box sat rows of tiny glass bottles with metal caps, designed to be punctured by syringes so medication could be withdrawn without letting bacteria in.

Testosterone. Human growth hormone. Exosomes.

I eyed the bag containing the syringes warily. I'd never liked needles, and my experience receiving NAD+ at Rejuve had left me sweating at the prospect of an injection.

I had rejected steroids for bodybuilding. Yet I was willing to do anything to get my life back.

"The injections go in your stomach, Adahmi," Ema showed me, picking up a small syringe. She put on a bright and chipper personality as she always did when delivering ominous news, hoping her confidence would prove contagious.

I fidgeted. I wanted the results. Very much.

Can't get one without the other…

That night, as I lay down in bed, Ema entered with the vials and the syringes. She followed the instructions from the box, drawing on her nursing experience, and slid the needles into the muscles of my belly.

I winced. In reality, the needle was too small to hurt much, but just the *thought* of it was uncomfortable. I didn't like the idea of needles piercing my flesh, injecting liquids directly into me. Even if I knew the injections would give life.

After Ema left I lay on my bed, carefully feeling the skin where Ema had injected me. I half-expected to find it bleeding. I half-expected to feel a rush of superhuman growth. Nothing happened.

I had another training session with Pen the next day.

Aba was pleased with my work, he said in our next meeting. "It's good for your brain to do activities," he said approvingly. "You are making new relationships for the business and building good brand awareness."

I sat there nodding my head. Thanks to Pen's lessons about KPIs, I could now view the company's sales records from each department. G-Defy had gained 8,200 social media followers since I took over the accounts a few months earlier.

"Ani olech *(I am going to)* change your official title to 'Social Media Manager,' Aba said with an approving nod."

I took a deep breath, trying to appreciate the moment without anxiety.

Me, manager? Not possible. Some days, I can barely talk!

Aba leaned forward in his seat. "I want you to focus on the company's Facebook, Yelp, Google, LinkedIn, Twitter, and whatever else we need."

"Okay, Aba." I told myself I would be able to do this. I've survived everything so far.

That day, I tried my best not to stare at the floor as I walked, and tried to keep my chest up and my left arm tucked in. I wanted to carry myself like a manager.

I tried to unlock my car door using only my left hand, sliding it into the opening mechanism. It worked! I still couldn't feel anything in those fingers, but I managed to move them in the necessary way. I smiled, vowing to only allow myself to use my left hand for that task from now on.

"Social media manager," I murmured as I drove back to the Cody Home. Something about that didn't feel quite right to me. That night, I Googled alternative job titles until I landed on one that I like: "Marketing Consultant."

Over the next few months, I spoke with the art department about improving the look and feel of G-Defy's online presence. The company had been using CGI images that didn't look very dynamic, and I consulted with Jennifer about having photographs taken that looked more "fun" and "realistic." Those were the best words I could find to describe the sense of dynamic energy and comfort I felt they needed.

My social media work continued to bear fruit, but it soon became clear that that was a limited avenue for G-Defy. Since the company specialized in footwear for painful orthopedic conditions, most of G-Defy's customers were geriatric. As fascinated as they might be by our content, 20-somethings who followed fitness and health influencers were unlikely to actually buy many G-

Defy products. And there weren't many grandparents on Instagram in 2019.

Feeling like I wasn't making enough of a difference, I looked for new ways to contribute. I asked Aba's warehouse manager, Rap, if there was anything else I could do at G-Defy.

Rap rubbed his shaved head and thought about it. "You know," he said finally, "there's no one coordinating communication between our stores. Each retail store has a manager, but there's no regional manager in charge of monitoring each of them and tracking their sales, stocking, maintenance, local marketing, and such."

Rap glanced at me then, frowning. "We've tried to hire a regional manager before, but the position is too stressful and everyone always quits. It requires a lot of dedication and constant weekend availability. I'm not sure you want that job, Adam. If you take it, you won't get a break."

I was determined to do all I could for G-Defy and Aba. If this was what needed to be done, I'd do it. Anything for him.

That night, I went home excited like a kid on summer vacation. The marketing consultant position had been good, but it didn't have all the results I had hoped for. The regional manager position Rap described sounded like it was sorely needed, and would create results for G-Defy. Working with Pen had already taught me how to analyze each store's sales.

When I got home, I sat down in my recliner and began drafting a business proposal for a new Regional Manager position for Aba.

Pitching this position to Aba felt different from pitching my marketing work. This felt like a bigger leap.

Unsure what to do, I wrote up a short business proposal and sent Aba my resume. This felt like a silly thing to do—nobody was more familiar with my work history than Aba, after all. He had been my first employer, had in some ways been FitFlow's first investor, and had been my only employer since my accident.

Still, I felt I had to go through all the steps that a normal employee would when applying for a new position. I didn't want special treatment.

Aba received my proposal with understandable skepticism. Having me optimize the company's web presence was one thing: it was an area I had a specialty in, and which frankly didn't require much attention since it was not essential to the company's everyday operations. Actually managing stores was something else entirely.

"Ata lo kolet, ani ratseety et ze me kodem lecha azizam, *(You don't understand, I wanted this for you from the start)*," Aba murmured in our meeting. "But your brain has to heal for this. You don't want to try managing just one store first?" He had his usual intense look: fiercely evaluating but ready to trust my answer.

"I can do it, Aba," I enthused. "I need to manage *all* stores, can't just one." There was something almost childlike about the way I said it, but I also made a valid point. Each store already had a manager; what was lacking was someone to oversee all of their operations and coordinate with corporate headquarters.

"Okay, then," Aba said seriously. "Let's give this a try."

Aba soon introduced me to the managers of each of the California locations. There was Chad, the short, stocky manager of the Huntington Beach location; Tom, the tall, skinny manager of the Palm Springs location; Chris, the sharp-eyed manager of the North Pacoima outlet; and Tom, the chipper manager of the Encino location.

News of my new promotion was received with mixed feelings. On one hand, I was their boss's injured young son, and I had just been effectively promoted above them. On the other hand, maybe they could use this situation to their advantage.

Chris immediately positioned himself as the most ambitious of the four—maybe excessively so.

I was tasked with communicating with each manager to review their needs, performance, and schedules. Chris went above and beyond in terms of communication: he *gossiped*.

"Did you see how many XLR8s we sold this week?!!" He'd text me eagerly.

"Did you see what Chad did? Man, that was a bad idea, not following protocol."

"Hey, me and the other managers have been talking. We think it's time for a pay raise."

"I'll ask my Dad," became my knee-jerk response to such proposals. Chris and the others seemed to hope I would be more easily swayed than Aba, so I made it clear that I was helpless to make changes without his authorization.

After a few weeks, communicating with each of the four managers separately became overwhelming for me. I lost track of who had asked me what and sometimes forgot our conversations entirely. I needed a change.

"Hey guys, I'll be making a group chat," I informed the managers one day. "Please discuss your questions and concerns there."

What began as a way to make it easier for me to keep track of conversations soon proved to be a stroke of accidental genius. With all four store managers on the same discussion thread, they rapidly got to know each other.

It was a joy to see some of their competitive hostility fall away. They got to see each other's sense of humor and saw opportunities to help each other. All of them shared a somewhat dry sense of humor, and all turned out to be family men with girlfriends and wives whom they spoke about. Jokes and personal stories were traded as often as business banter, and soon, the four were behaving more like friends or teammates than like rivals.

Except Chris. Whenever I asked Chris how he was doing, he boasted about his sales and talked about what he saw as the failings of the other store managers.

With this more efficient communication, productivity was up, and my workload was cut in half. And there was still plenty for me to do.

I addressed inventory and analyzed each store's best and worst-selling shoes. I visited each store to evaluate its cleanliness, lighting, and how inviting the store's layout was to customers walking in off the street.

I began encouraging each manager to increase their local marketing efforts, recommending that they take staff out of the store and charge them with marketing and publicity tasks instead. The only way to increase sales was to actually increase foot traffic, and you couldn't do that by sitting in a store waiting for customers to come in.

I encouraged them to send staff to bring fliers and make presentations at podiatrist's offices, rehab centers, retirement communities, hospitals, and other places where people in need of orthopedic footwear were likely to be found.

When managers resisted my changes, I would call and give them a pep talk. My speech had noticeably improved since getting my stem cell therapy, and being able to talk almost fluently to people again was a joy. I was confident in my decisions.

But when the time came to present my first retail report to Aba, I was terrified. I rationally knew that it was unlikely that this week's report was *worse* than previous weeks, but now I shared some responsibility for the numbers. I had never had this much direct responsibility for results in business before. The accident happened just before I got the chance to take responsibility for FitFlow.

What if Aba saw the numbers and decided to take away my newfound responsibilities? Worse, what if he was unhappy with me?

Aba's face was always unreadable as he evaluated the data before him and made decisions. I watched him anxiously as he looked over the quarterly reports, wondering what his feedback would be. Finally, he murmured:

"Good, okay. We have to get Chad's sales up. What do you think next, Aba?"

Being consulted as a professional expert made me happy in ways that are difficult to describe. The more I worked as a manager, the more I began to feel manly again. I was no longer just scurrying around hoping for the approval of Aba and his senior staff. People were actually looking to me to give orders and make decisions, and I was succeeding sufficiently to be *asked* for advice instead of receiving it.

Of course, this success was a mixed bag. On one hand, people now listened to me, and I felt pride in earning my keep. On the other hand, Aba kept giving me more responsibilities, which was scary. He soon began to ask me for help with company-wide projects like creating reports on our online sales and modifying our Amazon presence to see how various changes to our Amazon listings affected our sales.

At any given moment, I felt like my head was exploding. Even walking still was not routine for me: I had to consciously think about how to hold my chest up, and how to place my feet. But I embraced and juggled every responsibility I was given as best I could, knowing from experience that the only way to grow my capabilities was to push myself past my limits. I used an intricate system of note-taking on my phone and adaptations like my manager group chats to keep track of everything I'd been asked to do and power through them one by one.

I learned to use Aba's name judiciously. I cultivated an air of being everybody's friend who wanted to help them get things done. This meant that the store managers weren't exactly intimidated by me. But if I told them *Aba* wanted them to do something, it would be taken care of immediately.

I didn't enjoy all the changes that came with my new position. The call center employees who had once been my colleagues now seemed almost afraid to talk to me.

Have I changed in a bad way, or is it just my job title that's changed? I wondered one day, watching a call center employee glance at me and then quickly look away. I wondered if I'd been that intimidated by Aba's senior staff at the beginning and realized, reluctantly, that the answer was probably "yes."

Around this time, I also noticed something about Aba that I'd never noticed before. He typed with one hand.

For all of the amazing things Aba had accomplished, he typed with just one hand. I watched in fascination as his fingers flew over the computer keyboard during one of our meetings, his hand jumping nimbly from one side of the keyboard to the other.

Aba had full use of both hands; maybe he'd never learned to type in the normal way, or maybe he was just that much of a multitasker.

But either way, if he could succeed in business while typing with one hand—maybe I could too.

26

Freedom

Attainments: Being Underwater
Mental Capabilities: 70%
Left Leg: 54%
Left Arm: 29%
Assistive items: - - -
Age: 22
Weight: 176
Sources: Tom, Maya, Mom, and Myself

Now that I was regional manager, I had to actually visit all my stores. I needed to visually inspect them and see what kinds of experiences they were offering customers. I needed to meet the managers and cultivate relationships with them face-to-face.

I had been to the Palm Springs location before, with Aba driving. It was on that 3.5-hour journey that I first asked Aba to let me drive. So what better place, I thought, to test my ability to make a long drive on my own?

I set out from the Cody Home one morning with the intention of driving to the Palm Springs storefront. Aba was in China on business, so he wouldn't miss me. I made sure to pack myself plenty of water and snacks, knowing the drive might take longer if I had to stop and stretch my spasming left arm and leg regularly.

Then, I set off down the winding streets that would lead me to the freeway heading east. I felt nervous, almost as though my mind and body were fighting over my decision.

For the first several miles, I was sandwiched between other cars, fellow drivers weaving between lanes chaotically. After forty-five minutes, sweat soaked my clothes and ran down my legs as my muscles clenched painfully with concentration. Keeping my attention on the road required constant effort.

Finally, freedom! As the traffic thinned, the empty pavement stretched out before me like a promise. I relaxed, listening to my tunes, knowing that from here, the directions were pretty much "go straight."

Los Angeles fell away, replaced by flat desert. It was like an old Western movie, heat waves dancing on the dusty pavement. Every now and then, an actual tumbleweed rolled past. Wind power stations turned in the distance.

I breathed a sigh of relief and pulled over on the side of the road to stretch. My left arm and leg were frozen stiff from the stress of getting through the city, but the heat helped. The muscles relaxed as the warmth penetrated them, blood vessels opening to try to dissipate the heat. My circulation was restored.

I chugged a bottle of water and raised my knee back into the driver's seat.

I felt so free. After being in a coma, my parents told I may never walk or talk again, I was driving myself through the California desert. I remembered how powerful Aba looked as he drove his white sports car, one hand draped on the wheel while the other lounged casually at his side.

His *left hand.* Aba drove with his left hand.

I looked at my right hand where it rested on the wheel as my car ate up the pavement. I had almost no motor control in my left hand, but I could now clutch things with the spasming fingers if I used my right hand to wrap them around the object.

I glanced at my water bottle where it sat in the cupholder beside me. If I could drive these empty stretches with just my left hand on the wheel, I wouldn't need to pull over to take a drink.

I glanced at the road ahead, then behind me in my rear-view mirror. There wasn't another car in sight.

I pulled over again, taking deep breaths. Then, I carefully arranged the fingers of my left hand, wrapping them tight around the top of the wheel. I leaned back, pulling on my left arm to ensure there was a firm grip. It felt like balancing a heavy log on top of the steering wheel, but the fingers didn't slip off.

I kept my right hand off the wheel but kept it close, ready to jump in if anything went wrong. Then, I slowly hit the gas again.

The car sped up. The blue sky ahead seemed endless, fading into the horizon where it blended with the beige desert.

The car rolled on. I slowly relaxed, laying my right arm beside me.

I'm doing it! I imagined I looked just like Aba now, mirror shades over my eyes as I leaned back and cruised the desert with ease. I curled my right hand around my water bottle and imagined holding a woman's hand.

Just two more hours. I reached for my bottle of water and took a gulp, determined to at least s*imulate* having the use of both my arms.

The minutes flew by, desert unfurling around me as the sun wheeled overhead.

Until my phone rang.

I glanced at the caller ID. E*ma*. Anxiety rose up as I sent her to the car's speakerphone.

"Hi, Ema," I said with false cheerfulness, afraid I knew why she was calling.

"Adami! Where are you? Robben said you are not at the office. I went to your Cody Home to see Nelly, and you are not here!"

"... I'm going to Palm Springs, Ema," I tried to say it as though it were the most natural thing in the world. "Need to see Tom."

"You're going to Palm Springs? How?"

"Driving."

"B*y yourself?!*"

There it was. At some level, I would always be a small child in Ema's mind, and my severe brain injury hadn't helped.

"It's fine, Dubi," I tried to laugh it off. "Drove with Aba before. No traffic. Just straight line."

"You are in the middle of the desert in a car b*y yourself?!*"

"...ken *(yes)*, Ema."

"What if you have a seizure while you're driving?!"

"None since medicine," I reminded her. "Almost there. Love you, Dubi. Bye."

I hung up, breathing a sigh of relief.

My phone soon rang again.

"Hi, Aba," I said brightly.

"Adahm!? You are driving to Palm Springs by yourself?"

I should have known Ema would bring in the big guns.

"It fine, Aba," I repeated. "Just drive, straight line."

"It's a four-hour drive, Aba!" My father countered. "You can't do that twice in one day. Get a hotel, at least.

449

Spend the night in Palm Springs and drive back when you are rested. I will get you a room at that little hotel we stayed at."

That, at least, was reasonable. "Okay, Aba." I made a point of sounding exasperated by his concern. "But really, fine."

A pause. "I believe you, Aba. But sleep before you drive back. To be on the safe side."

"Okay, Aba."

I had to admit, my muscles *were* already tired from the long drive. Maybe spending the night before heading back wouldn't be the worst idea.

As the Palm Springs Monterey store drew closer, I imagined how I would walk in looking cool, casual, and unbothered. Looking like a leader.

"Hey, Tom," I would say, extending my right hand for a shake. Then I'd patrol the aisles of his store, waiting for Tom to look away so he would not see me limping before hobbling from one spot to the next. I'd look for anything that needed to be improved.

You can do this, Adam.

I was slowly starting to believe it.

***

Until the Palm Springs incident, Ema had been satisfied with my daily routine. I was going to work every day, either going to the gym or doing a 'Delilah' workout at home afterward, paying bills, and taking on more responsibility within Aba's company. What more could a mother want for her *ben (*son)?

But after my first solo trip to Palm Springs, one thing became obvious: I wasn't satisfied. I wanted more. And in Ema's mind, I needed more rehab to safely claim it.

She wasn't wrong. I wasn't satisfied with the strength of my body or with my control over it. I'd spent the last

450

few months focusing on stretching my mind, learning to handle complex job responsibilities despite short-term memory and speech issues. Maybe it was time to focus on my body again.

Ema first proposed that I sign up for swimming rehab. She'd met an Israeli teacher who had a pool in her home and held rehab sessions there.

Maya had brown, frizzy brown hair that she kept tied behind her head. She wore a one-piece salamander-colored swimsuit, smiling at Ema and I as we entered her home pool for the first time.

"Ze *(is this)* Adam?" she asked.

I didn't meet her gaze. I was too busy staring at my feet as I painstakingly moved them, one after the other, over the concrete pool deck. I hadn't walked barefoot since Thailand. I skidded each footstep with excruciating care, petrified of falling on my face in front of Maya.

"Adahmi, say hi," Ema encouraged me.

I waved awkwardly. Simply removing my shoes had returned me from a confident regional manager to an uncertain patient with the capacity of a child trying to take my first steps.

When I got in the water, everything changed.

I remembered the last time I'd been in the water with Aba. I'd helplessly spun in circles with only one arm and one leg to propel myself. That was almost a year ago, before the stem cell treatment.

My left arm and leg still felt dead at my side, but this time, I was strong enough to swing them around. The warm water flowing around me kept knocking me off-balance, but soon, I learned to tread water. I realized it was easier to move in water than it was on land. I was even able to swim partial laps, and it sometimes felt like I was flying.

451

I loved floating in the water, staring up through my goggles as the sun shone on the blue azure pool. My body was lighter there; I felt freer than I ever did on land.

My favorite exercise was being underwater, emptying my lungs, and sinking to the bottom of the pool. There, I felt no gravity, no rules, no expectations, no limitations. It was pure serenity.

When I got out of the pool after each swimming rehab session, it felt like waking up from a dream. My body would become impossibly heavy as my exhausted muscles felt the full force of gravity again.

After my first lesson, I climbed out of the pool and reached for my water. I picked it up, only for it to slip through my fingers and fall into the pool. My hand and arm were trembling, too weak from the laps to hold onto it.

My left arm and leg were so exhausted after lessons that I was almost powerless to move them. When I began driving myself to lessons, my left foot would be so exhausted, often with skin peeling off of it from the water and the concrete pool bottom, that it would be limp beneath the dashboard. I'd have to avoid it with my right foot   while   pumping   the   brakes. Afterward, I'd go somewhere and grab a triple burger and a vanilla shake, chugging high-protein, high-calorie food. Then, I'd return home and pass out in my recliner immediately.

The expense for private lessons piled up, and I was forced to look for a more affordable option. I found a gym with a pool included in my membership, but I couldn't figure out how I could carry a bag with swim gear and change in public in less than 18 minutes.

Although grateful for any progress, the exhaustion from constantly trying to adapt to my new body was taking a toll on me.

Can't anything be easy anymore?

***

27

Needles, Sarah, & Foot Mud

Attainments: Tenants
Mental Capabilities: 73%
Left Leg: 56%
Left Arm: 31%
Age: 25
Weight: 178
Sources: Eun, Mom, Sarah, and Myself

After months of swimming lessons, I still wasn't satisfied with my physical progress. Ema noticed, and she began researching other options.

"Adahmi," she said to me one day as we sat in my kitchen, "we should try everything that Vital will cover. I was reading through their website; they will cover acupuncture."

I looked at Ema warily. I had gotten used to the regular hormone and exosome injections, but I still hated needles. Lying on a table and having many needles stuck into my flesh sounded like the worst thing I could imagine.

"They cover it because it has been shown to work," Ema explained. "They do not know how, but sometimes it works for damaged nerves when other therapies have not helped."

Well, that clinched it. If it might work where other therapies had failed, I had to at least try. No matter how much I hated it.

The nearest Vital-covered acupuncture practitioner worked out of a nearby hospital. This was both reassuring and dreadful. Reassuring because it was a hospital: that suggested some degree of safety. Dreadful because it was a *hospital:* I did not have pleasant associations with hospitals. Walking the dimly lit hospital halls triggered anxiety, even as I managed to distract myself from the prospect of the needles.

The acupuncturist was a tiny lady who introduced herself as Eun. She asked me to tell her about my symptoms and to perform different motions so she could evaluate my movements.

"Can't move left hand," I explained, holding out my left arm. "Can grasp a little."

Eun nodded, her eyes thoughtfully narrowed.

"Left ankle weak," I offered helpfully. "Trouble—walking."

Eun nodded again and asked me to lie down on the table. I did so, sweating with anxiety.

The first thing she did was start taping small, round objects to my thumbs. I glanced over, trying to see what she was doing.

"Vaccaria seeds," she explained. "The pressure on your skin improves nerve connection to the brain. The thumb has a stronger nerve connection to the mind, so we will start there."

I nodded. In truth, I didn't understand how taping a couple of bright green beans to my body was going to help, but I was happy to be doing *something.*

There was one good thing about the acupuncture needles: they didn't hurt. They were hair-thin, so thin they barely seemed real as they moved in and out of my flesh, creating no pain and leaving no mark.

Still, I hated the thought of needles going into my body. Sliding around inside me. I couldn't make myself believe that they were safe, even though this was a hospital-approved procedure. My heart pounded.

But I lay still, praying for a miracle. Praying that the acupuncture would work with the stem cells to restore my body.

After my first session, Eun removed the needles, and I sat up in relief. Disappointment crashed over me. My left leg was still weak, and my left arm still a dead weight. I flopped my left arm experimentally.

"Wait," Eun said. "I have an idea."

She went to the back of her office and fished around in a drawer, retrieving a small, bright pink object with a strap attached to it. She brought it to me.

"Strap this to your left arm," she said. "Let's train your body to carry more weight."

I stared at her like she was crazy. Making my weak limbs heavier was the *last* thing I needed.

"Only half a pound," she said, hefting the weight in her hand. "Your body will adapt to the heavier weight. Then, when you take it off, the arm will feel lighter and move easier."

My eyes lit up. Why hadn't anyone thought of that before? I grabbed the weight from her and strapped it on struggling to fasten the Velcro straps with just one hand.

"Don't let your arm just hang there while the weight is on," Eun instructed me. "You have to use it to strengthen the nerves and the muscles. Find things to do with it. Any excuse to raise the arm up, grab something with it. The more you use the arm, the faster the results will be.

456

I nodded enthusiastically. This sounded suspiciously like weight training, and that was something I could get behind.

I'd struggled through obstacles that I was told were impossible, learning to lug my arm around. I could learn to carry another half-pound. And if my limbs really did feel lighter when I took the weights off, it would all be worth it.

***

For three days, I wore the half-pound weight on my left arm. At first, I used my arm as much as I could to open cabinets and doors, to barely steer my car, and perched it on top of things at work as an excuse to hold it up.

By the end of the first day, I could barely lift my left arm. By the end of the second day, I felt like I was going to pass out from the effort of hauling around that extra half-pound. I knew "the burn" from strength training, but this was worse. It felt like I had fifty pounds of weight on me instead of 0.5.

On the third day, I relented and took the weight off of my arm, planning to transfer it to my ankle so it would be strengthening *something*.

When I unstrapped the little pink weight, a miracle! My left arm felt light and free! I waved it around in astonishment, staring at the range of motion. For the first time since the accident, I felt like I could run, jump, play basketball — anything!

I couldn't, of course, because of my left leg. But I felt confident that my arm could even throw a basketball, something I never dreamed of a week ago.

Grinning, I strapped the weight to my left ankle.

Putting the weight on felt like my foot was sunk in mud. I had to pull and strain to take a step. But I knew every step I took this way would strengthen my leg, and that when the weight came off, I would feel light and powerful.

I strategized about how I could fit more steps in, pacing around the massive warehouses, staircases, and inventory halls of G-Defy as much as possible.

That little pink weight was my constant companion for weeks. I would eventually purchase a black weight that weighed a full pound in pursuit of even more strength. The effectiveness of these weights was the only thing that persuaded me to stick with acupuncture.

Meanwhile, I had other problems to solve. Aba asked for help making my house payments, and the downstairs of the Cody Home was finally ready. There were three bedrooms, a bathroom, a mini-kitchenette, and a door to the outside down there waiting for tenants.

Now, it was time to actually find tenants. Aba recommended that I contact someone who had helped him in his previous searches: a real estate agent named Melody Welch.

Immediately, inquiries began pouring in. The first inquiry from Melody came from two young women who professed that living so close to the freeway to Los Angeles would help them with their entertainment careers. Madison and Kirra each volunteered to take both rooms in the Cody Home's lower level.

I tried to contain my excitement as I scheduled a date to give them a tour of the place. I would have given the rooms to anyone who seemed unlikely to be a serial killer, but I did not mind the thought of having pretty girls around at all.

I still wasn't thinking about intimacy—in fact, the thought terrified me because having sex could reveal my disability and make me feel inadequate. But I knew that I still found the presence of pretty girls pleasant.

They signed their lease immediately after touring the place.

I barely noticed Madison and Kirra living below me. They came and went through their entrance, rarely speaking to their landlord—a title that still felt strange to me—except for the occasional friendly "hello" when we passed each other in the garage.

As the first rent check came in, I thought about renting out the guest room where Ema had once stayed. The room was on the lower floor but sat right at the foot of the staircase, making it essentially part of my unit. Anyone who stayed there would share my bathroom, kitchen, and front door instead of the tenants-only kitchenette and side entrance.

My parents recommended against renting that room because it would give the tenant access to my own bedroom and bathroom. But I wanted to cover as many costs as I could, so I insisted.

The truth was, having Madson and Kirra so close and yet so far made me realize that I was lonely. I had never lived alone before. Kaitlyn had become like a sister to me when we roomed together, and I missed having supportive company.

I posted the room ad on Facebook and waited. Apparently, Los Angeles was a magnet for beautiful women. The first application I received for my guest room was from another woman who was a fashion model.

Sarah was a stunningly beautiful woman from Pebble Beach who said the location would be perfect to help her pursue her modeling career. When we met for the tour, her warm aura filled the Cody Home and attracted me to her like a moth to a flame. By the time the interview was over, I learned that her dear mother had passed away when she was 20, and now her father had decided to support his 22-year-old daughter in becoming a model.

Sarah rented the room and immediately made my life better. She was open, warm, and kind, so I had no hesitation about asking her to help me zip up my "blouse," as I would jokingly call my hoodie, when we crossed paths in the kitchen. She was gone until 11 PM most nights, so I still had the house to myself most of the time. On Saturdays, she went to the nearby farmer's market and brought back fresh produce and flowers for the house.

She just radiated beauty and had a sweet, sing-songy way of making me forget about my disability. There was no room left in my brain to worry about looking "normal" when Sarah was flitting around like the physical embodiment of sunshine.

If we are being honest, I developed a slight crush on her. In my mind at the time, it was a profound grace of hers that she never seemed to notice my disability, even though I would sometimes bump into things or slap my left arm into them.

Late one evening, Sarah stood in the doorway of her bedroom and asked me to tell her my story. She knew I'd been injured, but didn't know the details. I felt overwhelmed, yet I told her everything as she sat on her bed and watched me.

"...Yea, accident was *very* bad," I confessed. Pulling out my phone, I showed her photos and videos from the accident. Me in a hospital bed, flailing like a toddler fresh out of my coma. My dented and stitched-up skull after the first surgeries.

"Whoa," Sarah breathed, "Wow. I'm so glad you're okay."

Speaking to Sarah that night was so healing. Women have been such a huge part of my recovery: every time a

460

beautiful woman accepted me as I was, I gained more confidence. That was all I needed: just acceptance.

It was the acceptance of beautiful women, who intimidated me and who I always tried to impress, that taught me that perhaps I could begin to accept my new self.

Sarah and I kept things friendly but professional. After all, I was her landlord, and neither of us wanted to invite problems by trying a romantic entanglement.

But I would be lying if I said I didn't have a crush on her. Sarah could have stayed in my home as long as she liked. Forever.

***

28

Reunited with a Racket

Attainments: Tennis
Mental Capabilities: 73%
Left Leg: 56%
Left Arm: 31%
Age: 25
Weight: 180
Sources: Harvey, Anastasia, Mom, and Myself

I continued to refine the skills that offered the most promise of independence. I practiced driving with my left arm straight on low-traffic streets. The road leading up to the Cody Home required the control of my right arm to avoid the cars parked along the narrow, winding lane, but I could still let my left arm hang out the car window as I made my way up with careful slowness.

Driving with my left arm hanging out the window felt amazing. I imagined I looked so free and natural with my left arm dangling, like any chill guy might do when enjoying the summer air. Driving with one arm with my windows down was the closest I felt to my high school days spent pimping my ride and cruising around, blasting the music Nick introduced me to.

At the top of the mountain, I'd have to get out of the car. This still involved using my right arm to lift my left knee out from under the dashboard, then concentrating with all my might to stand up without pitching forward onto the concrete. I still had to concentrate to keep my chest and shoulders up and my left leg under me.

I'd limp up the driveway and into the Cody Home, where Nelly would be jumping up and down in eagerness to see me.

Nelly was a source of confidence and wonder during this time. Every time I came home and found her running to look up at me with excitement, her "three button" eyes beaming out of her tiny white face, I'd feel amazed that she trusted and depended on me.

Not long ago, I had been totally dependent on others to feed and take care of me. Unlike Nelly, I couldn't even walk on my own. Now, I had a little life who trusted me to feed and protect her, whether in the Cody Home or on a walk down the street.

My confidence was growing, but I was still struggling to move. The acupuncture didn't deliver the miracle I'd hoped for, and my weak left leg still put me at high risk for a fall.

"Adahmi," Ema said one day as she visited to help me clean, "you should try tennis."

I laughed. "Ema, tennis? Me? Can barely walk."

"I know a man," Ema insisted. "He was a big tennis photographer. Now, he works with rehab clients at a tennis court off Wilshire Boulevard. I know tennis will be good for you!"

I stared at her. I struggled to imagine myself limping around a tennis court with one leg, swinging a racket with my right arm while my left arm flopped around.

But I *could* imagine it. I could imagine myself jumping from side-to-side like in my past varsity tennis matches. I could imagine hitting a topspin ball *hard* with my right arm, even slicing underhand with my left after I'd taken the acupuncture weight off of it.

Slowly, my skepticism turned into excitement. I could feel a grin creeping across my face.

"Yes, Ema. Want talk to him."

Ema's smile stretched wider.

I began to fantasize more and more about tennis. I had always enjoyed the feeling of jumping athletically around the court and getting the best tan as I yelled jokes to my friends and opponents. It combined everything I loved about dance and basketball, moving my body expressively while smashing the competition.

When I played tennis in high school, I felt *alive*. I would do anything to feel that way again.

Ema arranged a phone meeting. Tennis instructor Harvey turned out to be even more skeptical than I was. Ema had told him about my injury, and what she'd told him must have been *bad*.

"So are you in a wheelchair? You use a cane?" Harvey asked me, audibly hesitant.

"I'm fine!" I enthused. "Really. Little limp, is all. Left hand don't work so good. But I walk, drive myself to work, exercise at gym. It be fine. Just need little patience and work for weak leg, that's all."

Harvey sounded doubtful. That might have had something to do with the fact that I still wasn't forming sentences right.

"Well, let's meet up Sunday," he finally proposed. "I'll take a look. See what you can do on the court."

I kept carefully silent, but I was ready to rage with excitement.

The day of my first tennis lesson, Ema presented me with a gift: my old high school tennis racket! It was red-and-black and scuffed where my young-self had been rough with it. I laid it in my lap and turned it over and over with my right hand, feeling like I'd been transported back in time.

I could smell the asphalt. Hear the *thunk, pop, thunk* of balls being passed back and forth around me. Feel the sunlight on my skin. I had been a normal kid back then, too naive to appreciate the gift of physical ability.

I picked the racket up and, without thinking, took a swat. Imagined smacking an invisible ball, though I didn't swing it full-strength for fear of smashing the racket against the kitchen counter.

"You remember, Dan-Dan?" Ema stood expectantly by the door.

I looked up at her with awe in my eyes. "Love it, Ema."

Let's see what I can do.

Holding my childhood racket made me feel something. Something only those who suffered profound loss could understand.

On Sunday, Ema and I drove to meet Harvey at a tennis court at Westwood Park. The courts were one block from Wilshire Boulevard, a famous Los Angeles street Ema always cherished. They overlooked the buildings fronting the UCLA Westwood campus.

Harvey was a friendly middle-aged man with a deep Los Angeles tan. He was from Brooklyn, and he had a frankness about him that I liked. When he sized me up, he looked me up and down instead of treating me like a child who needed coddling. I held my left arm and leg straight and strong as I could and firmly shook his right hand with mine. I concentrated on looking into his (right) eye, wanting to address him man to man.

Ema stayed excitedly behind me, looking not-very-secretly delighted at how recovered I now appeared.

"You played tennis before, Adam?" Harvey asked, looking me in the eye.

I nodded. "In high school. Before accident."

"You liked it?"

"Love tennis," I confirmed.

"Then let's see what you can do."

Harvey directed me to walk toward a nearby bench. I walked tall and strong, puffing my chest out, gripping my racket, trying to walk as normally as I could.

"Okay, Adam, look sharp!" Harvey served me a ball, a delicate little punt with his racket just to see how I'd react.

I immediately shattered my carefully cultivated image by whirling to try to catch it so fast that I lost my balance. I windmilled my arms, nearly flopping back onto the court behind me.

Harvey squinted.

"Okay," he said. "We've got some work to do."

***

Harvey wasn't wrong. For all the progress I'd made since my accident, tennis meant moving in an entirely new way. There were no day-to-day chores that mimicked the movements required of tennis. It was just a different kind of footwork.

At first, this was impossible for me. There was just no way I could move fast enough to get to the ball while still controlling my weak left leg. I'd often smack my limp left arm with my racket when I swung it in my right hand. It didn't hurt because of the numbness, but it wasn't good for my arm or my tennis swing.

Psyching myself up, I would visualize hitting the ball with a powerful swing as I once did in school. I'd deliver a powerful hit, but lacking fine muscle control, I sometimes sent the ball flying over the perimeter fence!

466

Harvey gave me exercises and served me easy shots at first. I learned to make sure to follow through with my swing across my body. It was impossible to hit the ball properly with my shoulders and chest slumping inward, so keeping my shoulders back and my chest puffed out became a practiced reflex when I picked up the racket. I learned to take my full weight on my left leg and ankle when I needed to move left to intercept a ball.

After a few weeks of lessons, I felt more comfortable moving around on the court. I was even strong enough to try bouncing on the soles of my feet, just like I remembered doing in high school. My left leg could take it for short periods.

I also discovered another unexpected benefit of my disability.

Harvey's students were mostly injured and disabled, and many were more disabled or earlier in their recovery than I was. Stepping onto the tennis court was intimidating for them. When I sat cooling down after my lessons, I saw many shy, disabled kids looking at the ground and many injured patients looking around doubtfully. Ever my socially irrepressible self, I made a point of striking up conversations.

I'd wave enthusiastically with my right hand. "Hey, I'm Adam!"

My being so obviously happy and so friendly drew people out of their shells. Sometimes, they'd approach me cautiously. I'd see them discreetly studying me to see if I was disabled or injured, too.

"Paralyzed left arm and leg," I'd say, flopping my mostly-useless limbs cheerfully. "But doesn't matter. Love tennis. Don't let anything stop me playing."

On occasion, I would even exaggerate my limp as I walked to my car, if a disabled kid was watching. I wanted them to see that they could do anything they wanted without embarrassment, even if they weren't quite "normal."

Seeing those kids helped me see myself in a new light, the way others must have seen me. I couldn't imagine being ashamed of those kids. I wanted the world to accept them as they were without judgment.

The more secure I got in my ability to live independently and contribute to Aba's company, the more comfortable I became talking about my disability. I'd once felt a deep sense of shame at being "broken," partially fueled by guilt at my choice not to wear a helmet, but being around other disabled people made me reevaluate my attitude. Would I ever be as hard on another person as I was on myself?

Even at work, my disabilities had advantages. In my efforts to simplify processes for myself, I simplified the processes for my coworkers. Our communication was more efficient than ever with me in charge, and team morale was stronger as a result. If I hadn't had trouble juggling communication threads and remembering details, I'd never have put the store managers all on a group thread together. Now, our managers had a sense of camaraderie they'd never had when they were strangers who only met up for rare all-staff meetings.

Anything that made me different, I was learning, might be turned into an advantage.

As my tennis game improved, I began to offer Harvey a real challenge. He was still the better player, but after a few months, I could gallop around and swing fast enough to make it through 10 or 15 exchanges before one of us missed the ball.

Harvey and I also became real friends. He was older than me, but he was young at heart. As he told me tales of his exploits as a movie cameraman and his past girlfriends, it became obvious that we had more in common than either of us had expected.

I even got comfortable enough with Harvey, and with my tennis-playing ability, to joke with him about my disability.

"Hey, go easy on the handicapped guy!" I'd sometimes call in indignation when Harvey sent a particularly challenging shot at me. Then, I'd grin at anyone nearby to show that I was joking.

With sales continuing to improve under my oversight and my tennis game making me feel physically powerful, I often cruised home from Wilshire Boulevard feeling amazing. One day, I stopped at Trader Joe's on my way home. I was picking up oatmeal when I stopped in my tracks.

There, walking past the florist section, was a beautiful woman. Her silky blonde hair fell over her shoulders, and her delicate features were creased in concentration as she scrutinized the yogurt options. Her ice-blue eyes scanned the shelves intensely, and she must have been going somewhere interesting because she was wearing eyeliner and a tight black dress that showed off her long, slender legs.

I realized I couldn't simply ignore her. I'd regret it forever if I did. I had to talk to her. But if I was going to do that, I needed to find a grocery cart I could lean on to hide my disabilities. And I needed to find one before she walked out of the store.

I limped hurriedly through the aisles until I found an empty, abandoned cart. I took a moment to steel myself and wrap my left hand around the cart's handle before turning to approach her.

I puffed up my chest, making sure my left leg was planted under me. Then I started rolling my cart toward her with what I hoped was the appropriate mix of confidence and humility. I didn't have the journal with my pick-up lines and conversation starters on me, so I racked my brain for how to begin.

She straightened up as I stopped beside her. I took a deep breath and took the opportunity.

"Hey, I'm Adam."

I offered my right hand to shake. Watched her look over at me. Watched a look of surprise come over her face. I hoped it was *good* surprise.

"Oh. Hi. Anastasia." She placed her pale, delicate hand in mine and shook timidly.

"Sorry if this is weird," I smiled, telling her, "but I would love to get to know you better."

"Uh. Okay..." Her pale cheeks turned pink beneath her piercing eyes.

She seemed flustered to be talking to m*e*. This was going great! I took out my phone, and she reached for it. "Let me give you my Instagram," she told me.

"Cool!" I'd been hoping for a phone number, but I'd take her Instagram any day.

We parted ways a little clumsily, me hoping her awkwardness was *shyness,* indicating she felt as nervous around me as I did around her.

I hadn't dated much since Delilah. Going to the gym and my rehab activities on top of work barely left me time to think about having a social life. But if I could win over such a beautiful woman, it would be one more step towards a normal life.

I got in my car and sent Anastasia a message on Instagram. To my delight, she almost immediately messaged me back. For the rest of the day, Anastasia and

470

I exchanged messages, testing each other's responses and slowly opening up.

I learned she was an immigrant, like my parents and so many people in LA. She was also an entrepreneur, her Instagram filled with stunningly beautiful photographs of herself traveling across Europe, interspersed with pictures of flowers and sunrises with inspirational quotes. She was all the beauty and positivity I could possibly have asked for in my life, and astonishingly, she seemed to genuinely like me.

When I woke up the next morning to find another message from Anastasia, my heart soared. Our ambitions and priorities seemed so similar. She had yet to cling to me, throw herself at me, or treat me like a patient in need of care. I was sure I had successfully hidden my disability from her. As far as Anastasia knew, I was a normal guy who understood her background and admired her ambitions.

For the first time since my injury, I felt like maybe I could be a boyfriend again.

***

29

Healing Hands

Attainments: Pull-ups
Mental Capabilities: 75%
Left Leg: 58%
Left Arm: 35%
Assistive toxin(s): Botox
Age: 27
Weight: 183
Sources: Dr. Arshad, Stacy, Sarah, Anastasia, and Myself

For three blissful days, Anastasia was waiting for me in my inbox when I woke up. We flirted throughout the day as Letty and I once had. I began to feel that some of my old charm was returning, along with my confidence. Maybe I really was ready to start thinking about finding a life partner who could see me as an equal.

But on the third day, Anastasia stopped answering my messages.

At first, I figured she was busy. That was fine. We all had those days. When two days passed with no response, I sent Anastasia another query.

hello. you ok?

By the end of the third day, I was worried. No one knew better than me how life could change in a split second so I was concerned. I decided to search

Anastasia's Instagram to see if she'd posted any pictures recently, just so I could know she was safe.

This was when I discovered that I couldn't *see* Anastasia's Instagram. She'd blocked me.

W*hat the hell?*

I thought frantically back on our recent conversations, trying to figure out what I could have done wrong. I was sure she didn't know about my disability: I'd hidden it carefully, so that couldn't be the reason. I had been nothing but positive and complimentary toward her.

Anastasia?

Five days after her last message, I was distraught. I had thought I was close to having a real relationship, and somehow I had blown it. I was depressed enough that Sarah asked me what was going on as I sat at my kitchen table that evening.

"...remember that girl I met?" I asked Sarah, staring down into my protein shake. I'd told her excitedly about Anastasia as soon as I got home from the grocery store.

"Yeah?" Sarah's brows drew together, her hazel eyes glittering with sympathetic concern.

"She blocked me."

"Oh, Adam. I'm so sorry."

Unburdening myself to Sarah's sympathetic ear, my frustrations poured out. "It was going so well! She didn't even say anything. She just *blocked* me!"

Sarah paused. Shifted her feet awkwardly and leaned on one of the kitchen chairs. "...Adam," she asked. "Did you tell her about me?"

"Of *course,* I told her about you. I told her about the kiwi flowers you found at the farmer's market!"

Sarah sighed deeply, pulled out the chair, and plopped into it. She avoided my eyes. "Adam...that might be the problem."

I stared at her. "Why? It's not like we're together."

"No, Adam, we're not." Sarah managed to meet my eyes this time. "But people might not believe that. Think about it, Adam. A fashion model and a bodybuilder living in the same house. And you speak so affectionately of me. I've heard you talk about me to your mom on the phone."

I felt my cheeks burning. I'd had no problem with Sarah overhearing those conversations because I was just talking about how great she was. But now that she used that word, "affectionate..."

Of course. Anastasia had wanted me too, but then I started talking about another woman. Who lived in my house. And brought me flowers.

I wanted to bang my head on the table. How could this have not occurred to me? And yet, how *could* it have occurred to me? My roommate, Kaitlyn, had been like a sister to me. She'd been a beautiful girl who was attracted to other girls, not to me. How could it have occurred to me that people would assume that just because I lived with a beautiful girl, we were romantically together?

"Adam," Sarah said gently, reaching across the table for my hand. "I think it might be best for both of us if I move out. I've really enjoyed living with you, but...I'm having the same problem. I want to date. I want to find a life partner. But when guys find out I am living with you, they assume I'm not being honest with them about our relationship. And let's be honest: we do have *some* feelings for each other."

I looked down at the table, unsure what to say.

"It's okay. I'll find another place to stay. You've been nothing but professional toward me, Adam, but it seems that other people just won't believe that. We're on the highway to Hollywood, after all. A lot of people here can't imagine a man and a woman living together and not sharing the same bed. It's just the culture out here."

I realized she was waiting for me to say something. "Okay, Sarah…I understand." My eyes burned a little.

She was right. I did have feelings for her. But I also couldn't imagine us as a couple. She was so *much* in the best possible ways: so energetic, so warm, so kind, so profound. The problem wasn't that she was too much for me; it was that I was certain I wouldn't be able to keep up with her.

She didn't have to say it for me to know that she probably felt the same way. And that was why she needed to move out.

It was still strange to me that anyone would have a problem with me rooming with a woman. All my life, I'd seen people of all genders share housing around Los Angeles out of sheer necessity. But then, this was practically Hollywood, with its culture of decadence. And Sarah wasn't just any woman.

Now, there was just one question. Had I lost Anastasia forever?

Over the next few hours, I sent one last series of messages into the void:

hi
how r u?
miss ya.
Anastasia?

***

In the days to come, I tried to pick myself back up. Intellectually, I knew that Anastasia had probably blocked me over Sarah, not my disability. But it was harder to get

475

my heart to believe that. And I had a new symptom that was starting to become a real distraction.

My tennis games had an unintended side effect. Since I was a right-handed tennis player and couldn't perform certain gym exercises on the left side at all, my left arm was being neglected. It would become painfully tight from lack of use, and it got worse as the weeks passed.

I am so tired of having a body that doesn't work. I am so tired of trying to be normal.

When the tightness got bad, my left hand would curl up into a frozen claw. It looked worse than it felt since I still had almost no feeling on that side. But the spasms became more frequent and more severe until Ema became worried. She took to the Internet again, looking for anything that might help.

She found a potential answer in Healing Hands, a rehab center focused exclusively on the arms and hands. I could go there for an hour once or twice a week to exercise my left arm without having to commit to a full day at TBS.

The exercises by this time were familiar. I was assigned to spend an hour at a time picking up golf balls with my left hand, exerting careful control to touch my nose, straining my left arm in an effort to touch my left hand to my right shoulder.

Healing Hands also had a set of dumbbells, and as often as they let me, I would curl the fingers of my left hand around a 5-pound weight and walk the halls with the weight clenched in my hand.

Keeping my hand clenched required constant, excruciating effort and concentration. To strangers, it may have looked like a casual stroll or an awkward one on a bad day. But what was actually happening was that I was pushing my mind and body to their limit with each step.

Clench fist. Right foot. Raise left knee. Lean on left leg. Clench fist! Shoulders up. Pull hips in. Clench fist!

By the end of one of my strolls, I'd be sweating and feeling overwhelmed. But I knew that was the only way I was going to get better.

My efforts didn't go unnoticed by the staff at Healing Hands. Stacy, the head therapist and facility owner, could see that the exercises were not helping much with my arm spasms. They were helping with my arm *strength* but not with the muscle spasms that now ran from my left shoulder through the tips of my fingers.

"Adam, you know anything about Botox?" Stacy asked me one day.

"Botox? That thing ladies inject to stop wrinkles in their face?"

Stacy smiled, amusement glinting in her blue eyes. "Well, yes. It paralyzes muscles. That's how it prevents wrinkles, you know. It paralyzes the muscles of the face so they can't tighten to create smile or frown lines. And it can paralyze *any* muscle. Some people use it to reduce spasticity so they can start using their weak muscles."

My eyes grew wide. Of course! That made perfect sense. If Botox worked by paralyzing muscles, it could offer me blessed relief from the post-exercise cramps.

Probably. But I had concerns.

"Will it weaken my left arm?" I asked anxiously, envisioning a return to the days when it had been totally paralyzed.

Stacy shook her head. "You'll have to ask the Botox doctor that. I'm not an expert on the treatment."

So, I went looking for a Botox doctor.

Ema helped me root through Vital's website again. We discovered that Vital offered Botox for muscle spasticity at a neurologist's office in the same hospital I'd been taken to after my seizure.

Once again, I was not excited to go back to the hospital. But it was necessary.

I walked with Ema through the dimly lit halls of the neuro outpatient offices until we found Dr. Arshad. I was immediately turned off by his attitude. He wasn't unfriendly, exactly, but he seemed preoccupied. I'm not sure he even looked at my face before impatiently waving us into his office and telling me to sit down on the exam table.

"Adam Elnekevah? You are here for left arm spasticity, yes?"

"Yes," Ema replied, seeming flustered by his manner. He bent and typed something into a computer by the exam table. Then he came over and began examining my arm, still without looking me in the eye.

I let him move my arm as he pleased, pulling it through a range of motions. I could see from the expression of concentration on his face that he was feeling for any tightening or resistance in the muscles, and maybe listening for yelps of pain. He could have just *asked* me to tell him if it hurt, but it was a little late for that.

He did eventually ask some questions, after which a nurse walked in, pushing a silver cart. She parked it by the sink, and Dr. Arshad opened a drawer and grabbed a couple of preloaded needles. I instinctively tensed and began sweating.

These needles were bigger than the acupuncture needles. Much bigger. They were bigger than the needles Ema and I used to inject my exosomes into my stomach.

I braced myself as he stuck a series of electromyography sensors on my skin. Then I realized I hadn't gotten to ask any questions of my own yet.

"Will this affect my gym performance?" I enunciated the words carefully, wanting to sound as lucid as I could.

The doctor glanced up in surprise. "Eh?"

"I drive myself to work. Lift weights. I play tennis and swim. Will Botox stop me from doing any of that?"

The doctor blinked, as though seeing me for the first time. "I don't think so. But there's only one way to be sure how the medication will affect you. It will take several days to take full effect—maybe up to two weeks. After that, you will know exactly how it affects your muscles. The targeted paralysis will last for 3-4 months, during which time your spasticity should be greatly reduced."

There was a mixed bag of news if I'd ever heard one. I hated the word "paralysis," but the phrase "reduced spasticity" was tantalizing. I imagined living free from the tightness that interfered with my movement.

"Let's do it," I volunteered.

Then, I braced myself for the needles. The doctor put one injection in my wrist and one in my shoulder. I don't know how much of the unpleasantness I remember was pain from the needles and how much was the pain of anticipation.

Intellectually, I knew I wouldn't feel the effects of the Botox for over a week. Every time I got an ounce of hope, I was restless for results. So naturally, I headed straight to the 24 Galleria gym.

"Limited by Botox, they say... won't stop me..." I murmured hungrily to myself as I parked in the underground lot, bursting through the doors with a confident, if slightly lopsided, stride.

I first went to the treadmill and jogged for 20 minutes straight—a *huge* achievement with no ankle brace or supports of any kind. I remembered the day when I could not even fathom ever jogging again when Becca had to assure me that it was safe for me to 'run' with a bungee harness on because it would catch me if—when—I fell from being unable to support my own weight.

I was so pumped after those 20 minutes that I hopped off the treadmill—yes, actually hopped—and started down the stairs.

I stopped in my tracks when I saw the downstairs pull-up bar. I had forced myself to start ignoring pull-up bars when I passed them, knowing there was no way my left arm could lift even the tiniest fraction of my weight. I'd almost given up on ever doing a pull-up again.

Almost.

When I first started avoiding pull-up bars, I couldn't even hold a 1.5-pound baton in my left hand. Now, I could carry a 5-pound weight in it while *walking*. Now, I could use it to grip a steering wheel or open a car door.

Now, I could grasp a pull-up bar, in theory.

Before the adrenaline of completing my 20-minute jog could wear off, I stepped up to the pull-up station and reached for the bar. I first tried to reach for it with both hands out of habit, but I couldn't get the fingers of my left hand to open. So I pried them open with my right hand, and tetris'd them around the bar, squeezing my left hand firmly with my right to ensure that my grip was secure.

Then I grabbed the pull-up bar with my right hand and pulled with almost hysterical strength.

I felt my chest, then my hips lift as my arms—almost entirely my right arm—pulled them up. I held my breath, waiting for my arms to give out and send me plunging back down.

My feet both left the ground, and my left toes began to tremble in the air!

I was so astonished to feel my shoes leave the floor that my eyes grew wide, and I threw all the adrenaline that flooded my system into keeping the pull-up going. The time I spent soaring through the air, supported by only my arms, felt like an eternity. Will Smith's voice echoed in my mind.

"...for me... It has been about being that guy who does what people say can't be done. The road to success is through commitment and strength to drive through that commitment."

In reality, it was probably only a second or two before my feet touched the ground again.

But a second can change everything.

***

30

An Interesting Change

Attainments: Elena
Mental Capabilities: 86%
Left Leg: 60%
Left Arm: 40%
Age: 28
Weight: 185
Sources: Chris, Elena, & Myself

L eaving the gym after the pull-up, I felt amazing. Anastasia's rejection still stung, but I told myself that her presumption was her loss. I felt so strong, so like my old self again. I felt almost ready to pick up where I'd left off.

With excitement pulsing through my veins, I reached for my phone as I limped towards my car in the gym parking lot. I pulled out my phone and searched for a very special contact: Kaylee.

My last message to Kaylee stared at me from my screen: taunting me:

Kaylee: I'll miss you, baby.

Adam: Yeah, babe. I'll be back soon.

Even that bitter reminder of the life I had planned for myself before was not enough to bring me down. But as I limped towards my car, I frowned, noticing a small message at the top of my phone screen:

You have blocked this number. Unblock?

I stared, puzzled. I didn't remember *ever* blocking Kaylee's number. In fact, I couldn't imagine doing so. I hit "unblock" quickly with my thumb and typed a message.

Hey, Kaylee. Sorry, I haven't been around. Feeling much better now. Would you like to catch up?

I realized it was a long shot, but my last conversation with her parents in the gym parking lot had been friendly enough. And right now, I was bursting with confidence.

As I slid into the driver's seat, I glanced back at my phone. I didn't like wondering why Kaylee's number had been blocked. There were two possibilities: either I had blocked Kaylee myself for unfathomable reasons and then forgotten, or someone *else* had gone into my phone and blocked Kaylee without telling me. I didn't like either option.

Biting my lip, I considered who to call. There was only one person who I knew had access to my phone and who I could see doing something like this.

Ema.

With trembling fingers, I pushed "call" to speak to her.

"Adahmi?" Ema sounded nervously attentive as always when she answered my call. She always worried that if I called h*er,* it meant something was wrong.

"Ema," I considered how to word this diplomatically. "Have question."

"Yes, Dan-Dan?" Relief crept into her voice as she heard that I was alright.

"Just found Kaylee's number blocked in my phone. Don't remember doing it. ...you know why?"

The long pause on the other end of the line told me she was guilty. If she hadn't done it she'd have laughed and fussed at my silliness.

"I blocked her, Dan-Dan," she admitted. "I was worried when you were in the hospital. You'd only been seeing that Kaylee girl for a few weeks, and then you were…" *Dead,* my mind supplied the word she couldn't say. "I didn't want you to be worrying about texting her while you were recovering. I'm sorry," she sounded repentant. "I should have told you. To be honest, I forgot about it. Everything was so intense for so long…"

Now, it was my turn to be relieved. I'd been afraid that I'd blocked the number myself and forgotten about it. I hated the thought that I could do something and, days or weeks later, have no memory of the action or why I took it. Usually, when I learned about something I'd forgotten doing, I could at least see the logic behind it.

"It's okay, Ema," I reassured her. "Just found out. Was confused. Thank you."

"You're welcome, Dan-Dan." She sounded relieved. "Are you thinking about calling Kaylee?"

"Yeah. Just did a pull-up at gym! Feeling much better. Best since the accident."

"Oh, I'm so glad to hear that Dan-Dan." I could *hear* Ema smiling through the phone. "Be safe, lo arbe *(not too much).*" It was her eternal refrain. But today, she added something more. "Have a good day."

I was. I would.

***

I waited for long hours for Kaylee to text me back. In my mind, nightmare scenarios played out. What if she had been texting me for months or years, hurt and confused by my silence? Would she be angry to hear from me suddenly, casually, after so long? How could I explain to her what had happened? I checked my texts for her response when I got home from the gym, as I made dinner before I went to bed.

Fortunately, I had work to keep me busy. Rap wasn't kidding when he said that managing the shoe stores was more than a full-time job. Even with the more efficient communication between the store managers and me, communications between the stores and the warehouse, art, and marketing departments were not going as smoothly.

Most recently, I was dealing with inventory issues. Everybody seemed to be selling out of G-Defy's popular XLR8 sports shoes, and for some reason, wholesale was having trouble delivering enough of them to keep all the franchises happy.

I was on the phone with Chris, the North Pacoima manager, my text to Kaylee temporarily forgotten, as I left for work the next morning. I was on the phone with Chad, the Huntington Beach manager, as I left work in the evening. Both wanted the same XLR8s, but the warehouse was telling me they didn't have enough for both of them. I was trying to keep them both happy as they both argued that being out-of-stock on their most popular models would hurt their sales numbers and that whoever got the shoes and sold them would end up looking better in Aba's eyes.

"It's okay, I promise you," I told Chad on speakerphone as I drove to get sushi after work. "Dad is aware of this situation. He won't blame you for n-not selling inventory you don't have."

"But Pacoima is always selling more than us! It's because inventory always goes to them first! I feel like your father doesn't understand how much demand we have…"

"Got to go, Chad," I said, fighting rising irritation. "Dinner with my mom."

"Of course!" If there was one thing Chad didn't want to do, it was piss off me *and* Aba's former wife at the same time. "Have a good dinner, man. We'll sort this out tomorrow."

Sure, we'll try. I hung up my phone, fighting irritation, and checked my text messages.

My heart jumped. Kaylee had texted me back. I opened her message, wondering if I could resume this chapter of my old life.

Hey Adam, sorry, but it's a little weird that you're always calling and messaging me all the time. I think we should go our separate ways. Please don't contact me again. No hard feelings, but I've moved on.

Kaylee's rejection stung—the second beautiful girl to reject me in a week. But that wasn't what bothered me most.

Always calling and messaging her? Now, that *couldn't* be right. Not given that I'd just unblocked her number yesterday.

Perplexed, I checked my message history. The last message I sent her was from the airport. My phone record showed no calls to her, either.

I racked my brain, trying to figure out if there was another way I could have contacted her and then forgotten about it. Since my injury, I had been known to forget about conversations I had with people. But electronic records didn't lie: I couldn't find any evidence that I had, in fact, called or texted her since I got on the plane to Thailand two years ago.

What is going on?

I read over her message again, analyzing it.

I've moved on.

That was perfectly reasonable: I would have accepted that as an explanation on its own. It had been two years.

Why would she claim I was repeatedly calling and texting her? Did she feel that "I've moved on" was not enough? Was she hoping that I wouldn't remember my own actions, that she could convince me that I'd driven her away so she wouldn't have to take responsibility for turning me down?

I shook my head as I looked at our text message history, scrolling in vain in search of messages I'd sent her. I would actually have felt better if I'd been able to find some. Having clear evidence that I *had* forgotten a conversation (or ten) with her would be better than wondering what I was missing.

In the end, I put the phone down and took a deep breath. *It's okay, Kaylee. I will let go...* She wouldn't have needed any excuse if she didn't want to talk to me.

But still, it hurt. I was constantly reminded that I couldn't pick up where I'd left off in life. And I couldn't meet new girls, either.

I thought back to Anastasia with bitterness on my tongue. I didn't want to resent her, but the possibility that she had assumed I was lying to her still stung. As with Kaylee, a simple "I'm not interested" would have sufficed. I wasn't raised to believe I was entitled to anyone's affection. As far as I was concerned, "no" was a complete sentence.

The idea that Anastasia believed I had been trying to cheat on Sarah with her ate at me. Even worse was the prospect that we could have had something amazing. Maybe she had blocked me because she'd been so hurt by my imagined betrayal.

That bothered me.

I shook my head and glanced out of my car window to where the sushi restaurant Katsuya stood with its blue-and-yellow neon sign blazing in the gathering evening darkness. Just above it loomed the dark, familiar hulk of TBS.

Seeing TBS, I felt a sudden wave of gratitude. *I got out.*

I wondered how Andrew Sharp was doing. Said a silent prayer of thanks to him and his mother for telling me about Rejuve. They'd said it would be difficult to know what was the stem cells and what was my natural recovery, but I'd felt better over the last few months than I'd imagined possible. Despite the spasticity. Despite the discomfort. I was all-but running shoe stores, exercising, playing tennis, swimming, dating. I'd even just done a pull-up!

Having re-centered myself in gratitude, I pushed the sting of two romantic rejections in one week into the back of my mind. Pushed away the insecurities that crept up, the fear that my accident had changed the part of me that appealed to women forever. Delilah had wanted me, but I was convinced that that was only because she'd known me before. I wanted someone who loved me for who I was *now,* and so far, such a woman had been hard to come by.

Well. There was always Ema. I dialed her number and raised my phone to my ear again.

"Yes, Dan-Dan?" The anxiety in her voice was back.

"At sushi restaurant, Ema. You and Oritoosh still here?"

A long pause. This time, it couldn't be an admission of guilt. My mind raced for a few seconds, trying to tell what I was missing.

"I called you two and a half hours ago, Dan-Dan. Orit and I went home. It's late. Are you driving?" I could hear the edge of fear in her voice.

Of course. I glanced at the time readout on my dashboard. *Of course,* it had been two hours since Ema called to invite me to dinner. My sense of time was one thing still affected by my injury, and I hadn't realized it had taken me over two hours to wrap up business at the office.

Now, it was my turn to sound guilty. "Sorry, I missed you, Ema. Busy day at work."

"I know, Dan-Dan. It's okay. You're busy these days."

"Should have told you," I insisted.

"I knew." To my surprise, she sounded amused. "You're not so different kmo Aba shelcha *(from your father that way)."*

That made me puff up my chest a little more. I assumed that every mistake I made was because of my injury, but if Aba, in his focus on his work, was the same way...

"Thanks, Ema. I'll get dinner here, then go home."

"Drive safe, Dan-Dan. It's getting dark out."

"Okay, Dubi. I'll be fine."

I knew she wasn't satisfied as I hung up the phone, but I was glad she didn't push it. After two years of recovery, one of them spent working for Aba; she was beginning to accept that I knew what I could and couldn't do.

My brain was a vortex of pride and insecurities after the day I'd had. I lifted my left leg out of the car and limped toward the entrance of Katsuya.

489

The restaurant was bustling. There was a line of people waiting to pick up to-go orders. As I took my place in line, I saw the woman in front of me and froze.

I stared at her. I couldn't even see her face as she stood with her back to me, but I *could* see that she had the most beautiful, perfectly coiffed golden hair I had ever seen. I felt like I was standing in line behind a Disney princess.

My mouth went dry as she moved up in line, stepping toward the host's desk. In the process,\ she half-turned, her profile facing me, and I beheld one of the most beautiful faces I had ever seen.

Her mouth curved into a warm smile under a tiny nose, and her brown eyes sparkled kindly at the host with a gentle grace. Her voice reached my ears, graced by a Russian accent as she thanked the host and took an enormous bag of take-out sushi into her arms.

I was so smitten that I was staring, literally open-mouthed, when she turned to go. And saw me.

I didn't have time to panic because her face lit up as soon as she saw me. "Oh, hey!" she said.

"H-hi," I stuttered. "I'm Adam."

Uncertainty flitted over her face. Later, I'd learn that she'd greeted me because she'd mistaken me for someone else. But at that moment, I just knew I had to say something.

"That's a lot of sushi. Hold the door for you?" I pushed the nearly-weightless door open with my right arm.

She smiled. And blushed. The sort of smile and blush that suggested she didn't get this kind of attention from men too often. In hindsight, that should have raised questions in my mind. That surprise and delight at being approached by a stranger coming from such a beautiful woman.

But I didn't think of that then. I couldn't.

It took me a minute to realize what I'd done. I'd volunteered to walk her out the door. That meant I'd have to *walk*. It meant that she would probably watch me walk. It meant that she might see I was disabled, and then, I was sure, never talk to me again.

Don't let her see you move.

I did my best to stay a step behind her as she walked through the restaurant doors. I tried to make it look like a "ladies first" situation. I strained with everything I had left in me to keep my hips tucked in, my chest out, my shoulders back. My left leg dragged under me, my left arm braced firmly at my side.

It was a *lot* to keep track of. Especially while listening to her speak.

I don't remember what she said to me in the parking lot. I was too busy focusing on hiding my disability as I walked and too distracted by her beauty. When she stopped at her car, I was able to focus on words again, as she wrangled her giant bag of sushi and searched for her keys.

"Can I ask your name?" I asked her.

She smiled at me, that delighted, flattered smile again. "Elena," she said.

Elena. It was *such* a beautiful name. "Can I...give you my phone number to stay in touch?" I asked hesitantly.

Her face changed. But not in disapproval. In something more like disappointment. "Trust me," there was an edge of bitterness to her voice. "I am more than you want to handle. I have a son, you know." Her expression told me she was used to men running the other way when they heard that.

But nothing she said at that point could have made a difference to me. All I could think was that I wanted to bring a smile to that face.

"That's great!" I enthused. "Have a little brother. His name's Jacob."

Elena paused, her eyebrows lifting in surprise. She turned slowly back to me, regarding me as though seeing me for the first time.

She stood for a moment, watching my face with those warm brown eyes and tiny nose. Shifted her weight from one leg to the other as I desperately tried to stand straight and tall, unable to look away from her.

"Well," she said finally. "I guess you can give me your number."

I tried not to look too much like a kid in a candy store as I gave it to her, typing it into her phone. But I think I must have looked delighted because the smile slowly returned to her face. She waved at me a little flirtatiously as she got into her car. I stood there feeling like a million bucks as she disappeared into the night.

I was too infatuated with the woman I had just met, too overwhelmed by her, to have any insecurities as I swaggered back to my car. I actually whistled to myself as I drove back to the Cody Home.

Petting Nelly in the kitchen, I realized something and began laughing at myself.

I had entirely forgotten to get my sushi.

**

31

Lost & Explosive

Attainments: Speech to John
Mental Capabilities: 87%
Left Leg: 65%
Left Arm: 43%
Age: 28
Weight: 187
Sources: Dad, John, Elena, & Myself

In the days to come, I tried not to think about Elena. I was certain she wouldn't be interested in me if she knew the whole truth. How could she be? So I played it cool, trying not to obsess in hope. She deserved more than I could give her, surely, just as Sarah did.

I threw myself into my work.

At the office, CEO John announced his resignation from G-Defy. It wasn't hard to see why: Aba had mostly withdrawn from the company before my accident, effectively retiring to spend time with his new wife and young son. But having me involved in G-Defy again renewed Aba's passion for running the business with his own hands. Now we were solving problems together, and Aba began imagining G-Defy again as my future and his legacy.

Before my brain injury, I had made it clear to Aba that I did not plan to work for him for the rest of my life. I didn't want to just inherit a legacy from him; I wanted to create my own.

Now, we weren't sure I had that choice. Building my own business from the ground up no longer seemed realistic, and this meant I was fulfilling the dream Aba had always had of me becoming his successor.

All of which effectively meant that John had been out of a job for some time. He was still on the payroll, but Aba now got the final say in all G-Defy decisions. When my very assertive father went toe to toe with his young Canadian-Californian hired help, it was clear who had the upper hand.

The day John prepared for his departure, I was *angry*.

I had been intimidated by him ever since I was a college kid who he assigned to work with spreadsheets to prove my worth to the company. John had been the one I had to impress if I wanted to impress Aba, but he was not especially understanding of my strengths and weaknesses. For a decade of my life, John had been a symbol of the business-educated strength standing between me and Aba's approval.

At the same time, I wanted what John had. I wanted my father's respect and trust. I wanted the title of authority, CEO, which I assumed John had *earned.* That title was a prize I'd thought was out of my league because of my restless physical energy, and later, my injury.

John had that prize, and now he was just *giving it up?* Because he was unhappy with how Aba was running his own company?

I wasn't the only one who felt this way. I'd heard other senior-level staff complain about what they felt was John's obsession with numbers on spreadsheets and his lack of understanding of the actual boots-on-the-ground (pun intended) realities of running the company. I wasn't the only one who was glad to see him go or annoyed by his behavior.

In hindsight, I can see how John departing from the company was best for everyone. His management style was not Aba's management style, nor my own approach. He prioritized different values and expected different things from me. His decision to stay would have only caused conflict.

But two years ago, the situation was far less clear to me. I was *offended* that he was leaving, even as I was happy to see him go.

The senior staff gathered one lunch hour to honor John. Aba sat beside John on the bottom step of the headquarters' tall spiral staircase. Evan, Rap, and I, as well as all the senior managers gathered around to hear John make a speech.

I remember little of the speech. He wished us well and said that it was time to move on. Everyone sat around awkwardly. John had that effect on people: his half-hearted attempts at both camaraderie and judgment left everyone unsure how to relate to him.

John's reserved manner was a major reason we'd never gotten along. I did everything all in and for better or worse.

As everybody tittered awkwardly, suddenly, I could restrain myself no longer. I rose from the couch I'd been sitting on and took a small step forward.

"J-John," I said with nervous conviction, "let me ask you something." My left leg began to tremble as I realized everyone was staring at me. But I'd started this: I had to push through. "...Do you believe in my dad's shoe technology?"

Everybody looked a little bit surprised. None more so than John.

"Well...yes, Adam," he said hesitantly, stroking his beard. "I think it's an amazing technology that helps many people."

Maybe that was true; I think now that everything John said was true. But because he always spoke with such caution, everything he said sounded scripted to me.

"Well," I proclaimed, turning to the others who were gathered, "I believe in this company. And I'm not leaving."

I don't know what I was expecting. Applause, maybe. What I got was an awkward silence, and I immediately realized why. John was my dad's golden arm, and even those who agreed with me were afraid to express disapproval of Aba's choice of CEO in front of Aba.

I was shaking, but I was satisfied that I had spoken my piece. I glanced at Aba to gauge his reaction: he was sitting at John's side, staring at me with the same unreadable fierceness he'd had when I'd first asked to drive his car after my injury.

Later, when we were driving together, Aba suddenly began to laugh. It was a deep, hearty laugh, the kind that was not easy to get out of him. I watched him questioningly as he cracked up behind the steering wheel. Finally, he shook his head, wiping his eyes. "Adham," he wheezed, "I can't believe you actually said that to him. It was a bit too much, but it's okay."

That was all the applause I needed.

***

One day, a week after meeting the beautiful woman at the sushi restaurant, I checked my text messages before pulling out of my parking spot at the gym. I saw something that made me forget what I was doing.

"Hey. Is this Adam? This is Elena!"

I typed back as fast as I could with my right hand:

"Hey Elena how r u?"

In just a few moments, the reply came.

"Fine... How are you doing?"

My heart jumped into my throat. Yes, yes, *yes*, I was doing well! If Elena was the one who was asking, my entire month was going amazing. My whole life could be amazing if I could have her in it.

I began asking about her day, eager to keep her talking. I learned that she lived in the Encino hills, not far from Ema. I told her about my home on the very next mountain and welcomed her anytime for a coffee meeting:

"I cannot meet...I won't have much time."

My excitement fell.

"Alright, whenever you can."

I sent her the address of my Cody Home, trying to act casual about it while trying not to dwell on what might have been.

"No way!" Her response surprised me. *"You're, like, right down the street from me."*

There was no way this was really happening. Did she sound...enthusiastic?

"Oh yeah? why don't you come over for some coffee?"

"Hmm ok, maybe I will stop by. Hows around 8?"

"Ok, sounds good."

Now, I just had to make the place look presentable.

My brain ran a million miles a minute as I prepared the Cody Home for Elena. This time, I thought as I frantically scrubbed the kitchen counters, I had no fashion model roommate to concern her.

497

I stopped dead in my tracks. Now, there was only my disability, which I had tried so hard to conceal when I walked her out of the restaurant. I wouldn't be able to do that here—at least, not nearly as effectively. How could I move like a normal person for Elena's visit?

The prospect of spending *hours* in her presence flustered me enough that I started cleaning again, trying not to wonder if Elena would accept me for who I was...or if she wouldn't.

I made extra sure to walk straight, to keep my hips tucked in, to bend my left leg and step forward with it instead of swinging it out to the side when she rang the doorbell. I held my shoulders high and puffed my chest up as I opened the door and greeted her.

Elena still had the most beautiful face I had ever seen, with serene, delicate features and an alluring, intimate stare.

She smiled and went in for a hug. I just about died wrapping my single arm around when her body pressed against mine softly, my left hand lightly tangled with her hanging purse. I tried to read the intention in the hug, but I couldn't. I was too overwhelmed by my own feelings, by the fire ignited in my veins, to trust any judgment I might make about her greeting.

I took my ground coffee beans out with my back to Elena so she wouldn't notice that I only had one arm to use. Elena's eyes lit up as she watched me pour the grounds.

"Oh, is that brand good?" She melted onto my kitchen counter, leaning forward on her elbows to examine the bag. "I love coffee more than anything."

I tried not to stare at the dress she was wearing. A simple sundress, but it hung on her radiantly, accentuating her perfect form and cute nose. Her eyes were as warm and curious, and her hair as perfect and golden as it had been the night we met.

Does she look like this all the time? I imagined what it would be like to wake up next to her in bed and lightly stroke her beautiful lips and cheeks.

I made us both coffee, careful to do everything with my right hand and try to make it look natural. Careful to keep my left hand hidden. Careful not to move too much, not to walk too quickly lest my left leg betrayed me. Mercifully, when her own mug was done, she picked it up immediately, sparing me the necessity of showing that I couldn't carry a coffee mug in each hand.

"Let's go out on the porch," I proposed, nodding toward the deck, which at that moment was bathed in the light of the setting sun. Elena smiled a delighted smile as she glimpsed the view and started out onto the deck without waiting for me to lead the way.

Thank God.

I followed her, trying not to limp noticeably.

Once we were settled on the deck couches, I discreetly fixed my hips. All I had to do was sit in a way that looked reasonably natural, and she wouldn't realize my left arm and leg didn't work properly.

Once we sat down, I could focus on her words again.

She was telling me how she loved to go to the gym. She'd glimpsed my home gym as we passed through the living room and she appreciated that I valued fitness, too. For Elena, maintaining her body to look good *and* feel good was one of the most important things. We had that in common.

I tried not to let my eyes wander too much as she spoke. Her sparkling brown eyes and sweet nose were enough to transfix me, but when she spoke of her body, my eyes couldn't *not* travel down her throat to her collarbones, to her well-toned chest—

I'd snap back to attention and ask her more questions. I asked her every question I could think of: about her fitness routine, about her family, about her likes and dislikes.

In part, I loved the sound of her voice. In part, I was desperately hoping not to have to talk about myself. I was already getting tongue-tied by her beauty while just trying to formulate coherent questions to ask her. And what, what could I talk about? What was there in my life other than my job, which I didn't want to bore her with, and my injury, which was a subject I wanted to avoid at all costs?

Fortunately, Elena seemed happy to have someone to open up to. She looked delighted, as though it had been a long time since she had a listening ear.

And when she was done talking, it became clear that our chemistry was too intense to ignore.

My blood raced as those brown eyes pierced my soul. It was official: I was speechless. There was too much blood pooling somewhere else for the speech center of my brain to work.

And then, all at once, we were kissing.

And I was lost, lost, lost.

***

32

Intimacy with Elena

Attainments: Her Pleasure
Mental Capabilities: 90%
Left Leg: 68%
Left Arm: 46%
Age: 29
Weight: 189
Sources: Elena & Myself

Elena's hands were all over me. And then my hands were all over her, taking in the slender curve of her waist and her round butt. She crawled on top of me, her warm tongue teasing my lips. Afraid the neighbors would not appreciate our affection, I managed to tear my mouth away from hers long enough to propose that we move inside.

I led her back toward my bedroom with desire, forgetting my limp as Elena watched me with anticipation. Once there, she was on me again, every inch of her curves pressed against my skin and her hands fumbling with my clothes.

We moved closer, closer, separating only to tear each others' clothes off. I was in heaven, and she was too, judging by the noises she was making. She seemed almost high, as though she hadn't been touched in ages. I hoped she was distracted enough not to notice I was using only my right arm.

Finally, her dress was unfastened and unzipped. I inhaled and exhaled through Elena's enticing lips. She felt warm, smooth, and slick against me. Suddenly, she enveloped me, and her blonde hair brushed across my shoulders as I shuddered with ecstasy.

But I couldn't let my guard down. Not entirely. Elena needed me to please her. She was not as dominant as Delilah, who had pushed me down and ridden me while I marveled helplessly.

There was a vulnerability about Elena. When I walked my fingers under her skirt and slipped them inside of her, she went almost limp. Moaning as though she desperately needed to be the cared-for instead of the caregiver, the recipient instead of the doer.

I gently shifted us so that she was partially under me as my left leg remained sharply extended. She cupped my hand around her perfect thigh and moved herself against me. The sensation of Elena squeezing me was an indescribable pleasure, but I tried to think about what would be pleasurable for *her*. Surely, gyrating in this way would be. Surely, thrusting in that way would be.

My left hand dangled weak and powerless, and my left arm threatened to give out. I shifted my weight, ensuring that most of Elena's body rested under my right side.

Struggling to support myself while gazing at the breathless expression on her face, I buried my head in the curve of her neck. I alternated my focus between our intertwined bodies and her flushed cheek, monitoring her reactions to ensure I was doing everything right.

Her muffled moans told me, "yes," as they slowly escalated into squeals.

The feeling of Elena cumming against me was intense. I didn't orgasm myself—but, the validation. As

502

her back arched violently and she threw her head back in ecstasy, her perfect golden hair flew everywhere. I remember her lifting the dress from her body, revealing her flawless breasts and her enticing stomach, as I gazed at them with infatuation.

I can't believe she's giving herself to me. I thought as she settled against me. *Does she have any idea how injured I am?*

I knew that Delilah had had orgasms with me, but she had been so dominant that it always seemed more like her doing than mine.

This—this had been my doing. I softly kissed Elena's cheek as she nestled against me, a pool of relaxed bliss. But after less than a minute, reality struck Elena, and she quickly rose from my bed.

"I don't have much time," she said quickly, walking naked to my bathroom for a shower. I sat half-naked on my bed, heart still pounding, my jeans half-off my ankles, and my shoes lying where I'd tossed them. I heard my electronic toilet opening as it sensed Elena's brisk footsteps passing toward the shower.

I made my way to the shower, limping on my bare feet as if casually strolling in. I nearly stumbled but managed to stop myself from asking her, with her beautifully perfect body, if I could join her.

Elena gently cracked the door as steam filled the marbled bathroom, giving me a view of her in the shower.

Such exquisite beauty, I thought, as water droplets trickled down her tiny nose.

***

My days settled into a new pattern. In the mornings and afternoons, I was always on the clock for work. The evenings were for my gym workouts and for Elena's sporadic text messages.

"I have 5 minutes," she would say.

I was constantly strategizing with the store managers, brainstorming ways to boost foot traffic. Our focus extended beyond merely stocking our G-Defy stores with inventory; we also aimed to increase our brand's visibility on the streets and in neighboring retail outlets.

Elena learned my work schedule, and it was not uncommon for me to have a text message from her by the end of the work day.

"hey, can I come over?"

"Come over," at this point, had become code for either "a quick hug and kiss" or "have wild sex on every available surface in my house."

It was still all about pleasing her for me. I had yet to have an orgasm with a woman since my injury. I had enjoyed and lusted after my encounters with Delilah, and now with Elena. But I had never been able to let my guard down enough to orgasm.

Instead, I was totally preoccupied with my performance. Maintaining an erection was never difficult with such beautiful women seducing me, but I was worried about my technique now that I was partially paralyzed.

Once I realized Elena wanted me, porn and sex advice articles became my study materials. I would study the videos and even take notes, noting what muscles were being used to thrust and what muscles were necessary to maintain certain positions. I delved into understanding a woman's anatomy, her sensitivities, and the art of teasing, pleasuring, and giving extensive foreplay.

Many positions required me to hold myself or Elena up with my arms, which meant that I was obsessively working on my left-sided body strength to ensure I could perform these. I constantly looked for new ways in which

I could please her, and even sometimes read women's magazines to see what women were looking for.

A significant focus of my gym time revolved around the question of "what muscles do I need to strengthen to have better sex?" I couldn't even use the euphemism "in bed," because, as often as not, we were on my kitchen counter, or I was bending Elena over my white kitchen island.

Since many sex positions required upper body strength, I began to focus more on bench presses. I would bench press with one side at a time to enable me to strengthen both arms optimally: if I'd done both sides at once, my right arm's growth would have been limited by the capabilities of my left, and my left arm would have had help from my right arm and not been pushed to its limit.

The bench presses worked approximately the same muscles that were involved in holding my body up off of Elena in some positions, which was currently my biggest challenge.

I knew the optimal length of time between repetitions of an exercise set was 30-120 seconds. That was best for muscle growth, allowing the muscle to recover enough to take more work but not enough to lessen the metabolic stress that would cause the bulging of muscle fibers. I sometimes worried that I was resting each side too long between sets by working only one arm at a time. But when I tried bench pressing with both arms at once, I was quickly reminded that this resulted in one or the other not being pushed to its full potential.

I worked my way up to bench press 30 pounds with each arm—a frankly astonishing amount, given that I had not been able to lift a 2-pound weight just a year or two earlier. With each pump of the iron, I smiled, envisioning Elena in various positions. In front of me. Underneath me. Moaning.

That was some motivation.

I struggled to understand how such an obviously gorgeous woman could act as though she'd been sexually starved, but I figured she did have an infant child. That probably didn't leave much time for sleeping, let alone dates. And in the sushi restaurant parking lot, she had acted as though she expected me to run away after finding out she was a mom. Maybe most men did.

I think there was an adventurous streak in her, too. I think it was more than just being in a hurry that prompted her to sprawl herself across my kitchen counter and shed her leggings, visually begging me to take her there and then. She'd already be wet when I got inside her, and I think she took some special pleasure being in the kitchen, the living room, the shower, as close as we dared to get to the enormous glass doors overlooking the valley.

I deduced that doggy style was her favorite position. I loved it too, but probably for very different reasons than she did. I loved it because it meant I didn't have to use my arms to hold myself up and that she couldn't see my left arm flapping wildly around as I thrust into her vigorously.

I still had high standards for myself in terms of the force I could apply, probably left over from my bodybuilder days. For that reason, I always worried that I wasn't thrusting hard enough or wasn't holding her tight enough with just my one arm. But judging by Elena's reactions, I must have been doing a pretty good job. I suppose most men had never been able to bench press 145 pounds, so my gauge of my own relative strength may have been a bit off.

Yes, that really was my headspace. I loved every minute of sex with Elena. Watching her thrash at the height of an orgasm felt like making a work of art, the most fulfilling thing I'd felt since my accident. I felt incredibly lucky to be able to create that kind of beauty on a near-daily basis.

But you can see why I never relaxed enough to orgasm. For me, the sex was about her beautiful body sliding all over mine, but it was just as much about winning the approval of a woman who I was still, at some level, convinced was out of my league.

Deep down, I still doubted that I would ever be able to please a woman as a partner again. Elena's complete ignorance of or indifference to my disability was slowly beginning to restore my faith that it really didn't matter.

There came a point where I knew that she *must* have noticed my limp or the way I never used my left arm or hand to do anything. But she never said anything about it. I still wasn't sure if she actually understood that I was disabled.

Even having seen my own feelings toward Harvey's child students, I didn't really believe yet that other people didn't judge me nearly as harshly as I judged myself. It would be a long time before I got the message that Delilah and Elena had tried to give me: that women didn't care about my disability so long as I treated them right.

But I didn't need to understand that to be *very* determined to treat Elena right.

For the time being, pleasing her felt like the reason for my existence.

***

507

33

At My Door

Attainments: Heart Racing
Mental Capabilities: 90.5%
Left Leg: 69%
Left Arm: 47%
Age: 30
Weight: 189
Sources: Myself

Elena and I decided to spend Halloween night together. Neither of us were much for parties or trick-or-treating, so she asked me to meet her in a pharmacy parking lot.

That was, in hindsight, a strange thing. The number of early dates we had in parking lots, where she'd jump in my car, and we'd make out. Maybe that should have tipped me off that something was wrong. But it was also sort of a rush, like being a teenager again.

It was dark out by the time I pulled up to the store, with fluorescent lights shining coldly on the black asphalt of the lot under the glowing green sign. I waited with anticipation for Elena's car to pull in.

She circled the lot until she recognized my car. Then she pulled in next to me, opened her driver's side door, and glanced around furtively. Almost as though she were afraid of being seen with me. She hurried up to my car, yanked the passenger door open, and slid into the seat, then glanced behind us, out through the back window. As though to check for someone.

This was enough for me to notice, even through my love-misted eyes. Elena was acting more nervous than usual tonight. And it wasn't a shy sort of nervousness. It wasn't me she seemed afraid of.

She was acting scared of something else. Someone else.

"Elena," I asked, "you okay?"

She smiled at me, but there was something wrong with the smile. Something tight and fragile. Then she squeezed her eyes shut and raised her hand to her face, partially covering it. Her hand was shaking.

"Elena…?"

"Adam," she confessed, putting her hand down and looking away from me, eyes. "I'm still married."

Time stopped.

I didn't know how to process this. Had I been sleeping with another man's wife for what felt like an eternity? That didn't seem like something I would do. And cheating didn't seem like something Elena would do.

I looked closer, scrutinizing her face as though it might hold some clues. Compulsively, my eyes went to her fingers. No wedding ring.

She looked back at me, watching me nervously as though waiting for anger. What I gave her instead was concern. Trust. Maybe it was infatuation talking, but I could not see her as a lying cheater. Something else had to be going on.

"The situation is…not good." She confessed when I did not scream at her. She looked away from me again as though she couldn't bear to meet my eyes as she talked about it. And now there was something in her expression that I'd never seen there before. Something haunted.

And suddenly, it all made sense. Her apparent surprise at my attention in the parking lot. The bitterness in her voice when she tried to convince me I wouldn't want someone like her. Her childlike delight when I asked her questions about herself, listened to what she had to say. Her intense sexual appetite and her need to be taken care of.

Despite her staggering beauty and the kindness that radiated from her every pore, she was not *used* to being treated well by men. By the only man in her life. By the only man she'd been allowed for God-only-knew-how-long. From the way she looked around the parking lot before she got into my car, from the way she glanced out the back window, I wondered if she feared violence from him.

This broke my heart.

"He...stopped paying attention to me, when I was pregnant," she continued, her voice thick as she stared out the window. "I think he no longer found me attractive, or enjoyed me being home all the time. And when I was staying home with Jack, in the first weeks, I found out about...other women. He was using websites to meet them. He was always gone, *always,* and...he never cleared his browser history. He was even late to the hospital when I went into labor. I had to call a taxi."

I did feel anger rising in my veins now, but not at Elena.

I imagined being pregnant. Nine months pregnant with your partner's child and having them lose all interest in you. I imagined calling a Lyft to take myself to the hospital during labor because my partner was nowhere to be found. I imagined getting home from the hospital, logging onto the computer, and...

It got worse. Elena poured out her heart to me and finally told me what she'd been afraid to tell me. Afraid that I would leave her, that I would stop being her partner. Afraid that I'd be angry with her, as her husband often was.

Her husband had been married before. He had two daughters with another woman. This in itself was not a problem: Elena had tried, when she married into the family, to make friends with them. She tried to create a relationship where they could raise their kids together. For a while, it seemed to work.

Then came the restraining order. Elena either didn't know the details, or she didn't tell me. But the first wife, Karen, called her one day and told her grimly never to visit them again. The husband, Frank, had done *something,* and Karen had gotten a restraining order, and she didn't want Elena coming around for fear that this would attract Frank's attention back to her and her children.

"We can't be friends," she told Elena over the phone, her voice flat. "It wouldn't work. Not with Frank involved. Sorry." And she hung up.

But the worst thing, Elena said, was the way Frank had hurt the person she held in the highest regard. Her father, she said, was an honest, pure, hard-working man who would do anything for his family. He had come to visit Elena in California to meet her husband. Once.

Elena had been over the moon, more excited than she had been in years, as she embraced her parents at the airport. But Frank seemed determined to ruin it. To assert his dominance, as though he were threatened by anyone else who loved Elena. By anyone she could go to for support.

She did not give me details, but his behavior toward Elena and her parents during that visit was so hostile that her father could see the situation was unsalvagable. He gave her an ultimatum. He would not visit Elena in the United States again until she divorced Frank and moved out of his home.

He had not been back since. Not even to see his grandson. And Elena was left asking herself if she had been a fool to ever love this man who had at first showered her with gifts and admiration, who had at first been so charming and promised her the life she deserved.

Elena was now crying in her seat, shaking with great sobs as years' worth of pent-up pain spilled out.

Of course. Of course. Her husband was a predator. He'd caught one of the most beautiful women in the world. Caught her in a way where she would be reliant on him, an immigrant with little formal education, no money, no family here in the United States. And then he revealed his true colors.

That was what I imagined, anyway. I didn't know Frank, and Elena said little about him. Except to tell me they were married. Except to tell me about the restraining order.

It wasn't just the words she spoke that broke my heart. It was the *way* she said them. For that moment, I saw an expression of hollow doubt in the most beautiful face I had ever seen. A sense of worthlessness. Of guilt—not, at her own illicit conversation with me, but a guilt that suggested, at some level, she thought some deficiency on her part had *caused* Frank to treat her the way he did.

Even learning about the restraining order had not fully convinced her, deep down in her soul, that *she* was not the problem. That she had not somehow caused her situation. Like me, she felt inadequate at a level that words could not reach. But maybe actions could. Maybe I could help her feel worthy again.

I may have been projecting some of this, imagining how she might feel. But what I *did* read in her face, unmistakably, was devastation. And a kind of terror. A terror that her being here with me was wrong, that anything she might do that made her happy was wrong. She had loved this man once, and he had become a terror to her.

"Elena," I blurted out, "that's ridiculous."

She looked at me sharply, frowning.

"I mean, it's ridiculous that anyone would treat you this way. Let alone when you were pregnant with his baby? That's just...insane." I was staring in genuine disbelief.

Slowly, slowly, she relaxed. Her guard melted. And suddenly, she was looking at me with grateful eyes.

"Oh, Adam," her voice cracked. "I...I know I shouldn't be here. But it has been so long since a man looked at me the way you did in that parking lot. My marriage to my husband is over. Not legally...he has all the money, the house, and he is my only family here in America..."

Her eyes filled with tears, and I had to do something to stop her from collapsing into sobs again.

I reached across the center console and pulled her into my arms. Both of them. The left arm was strong enough, now, to manage a gentle embrace.

"Elena," I said, "it's not your fault."

She smiled fragilely up at me. "Thank you, Mister," she whispered.

"For what?" I asked her. "I love being with you."

She melted into my kiss, and I went to work trying to help her forget everything else.

***

After that night, Elena and I developed real intimacy. What we'd had before was *fun,* but at some level, I'd been hoping for her to let me in. She had always seemed to be in a hurry. Always seemed too rushed, almost frantically energetic.

Knowing her story now, I saw that for what it was. A diversion. It was exactly the same as when I tried to energetically direct a conversation to distract the other person from my arm and leg. Leaving space for silence meant leaving space to be seen. So when I was afraid someone wouldn't like what they saw in me, I had to keep up distractions like a shield.

After telling me the whole story, Elena slowed down. She would stay for longer dates. Long hours spent lying in my bed, afternoons on the boardwalk. She fell in love with my mother, missing her own mother back home. She even began to visit Ema to style her hair while I was at work, and the two became fast friends.

Winter passed. She didn't say anything more about her husband. I didn't ask. I wondered, sometimes, and even worried about how she was explaining the long hours we spent together. But Elena was a smart, brave woman. She knew how to protect herself.

Right?

The first hints of spring were in the air when my cousin Josh invited me to his birthday party.

Josh was close to me in age, and we'd been close as children. In recent years, we'd drifted apart, as childhood friends are prone to doing. I'd started texting him in a fit of enthusiasm inspired partially by my recovery.

And partially by Elena. Taking care of her made me feel like a whole man again. Like the kind of man who might have something in common with his uninjured cousin, who was a successful entrepreneur. And so I took a risk: I invited Elena for an evening out, knowing we might not be back from the party until late.

Up to this point, our dates had been stolen: meeting in parking lots or in my home, sometimes for as little as half an hour. I now understood why that was: Frank could not notice she was missing.

But tonight, she agreed.

Here's the thing to understand about Josh's party: it was *fancy*. Josh and his parents had both worked very hard and acted very strategically to become wealthy, as so many immigrants do. Josh had decided he wanted his 32nd birthday to be held at his parent's mansion in Calabasas, a wealthy city in the west of the San Fernando Valley.

To help you envision it, the Calabasas is the sort of neighborhood where people who go on expensive winery tours every summer live full-time. His parents' home was all white wooden trim and mission-style architecture, with arched doorways, unnecessarily elaborate windowsills, and banister railings to make sure you knew that a lot of skilled labor and loving attention to detail went into crafting this place.

The mansion came complete with a wide staircase that swept down into the front atrium of the house in a way clearly intended for making grand entrances. My uncle was walking down that staircase, all puffed up and ready to party, when Elena and I walked in.

The party was already hopping. The buzz of happy people chatting almost drowned out the throbbing base that leaked in from the kitchen. Everyone was dressed up in that classically Los Angeleno way, where you can't look too formal, but you've got to look *sharp,* perfectly coiffed, and made up while wearing leggings, boots and a jacket.

Which is more or less what Elena was wearing when my uncle caught sight of her and lost control of his body. His mouth fell open and he stumbled, then slipped and nearly smacked down the stairs before managing to pull himself upright using the rail.

He didn't even look upset about it. His eyes were still on Elena, his hand on his heart.

I've got to admit I grinned a huge, goofy grin, watching my uncle's reaction to Elena. I knew she was the most beautiful woman in the world, and it seemed I wasn't the only one who felt that way. Elena raised a hand to her mouth to hide her own giggle of delight.

We turned and wove away into the crowd before things got awkward, seeking a gaggle of fellow young folks to dance the night away with.

We found Josh, but the birthday boy was in high demand, so we ended up mingling with his friends, younger brothers, and acquaintances. His college friends were there, and work colleagues, and even children of his parents' friends who had been invited out for the big celebration. With Elena at my side and the bass pounding, I completely forgot about my limp and my useless left hand.

I felt normal. One of the crowd. Even a particularly *lucky* one of the crowd, from the way passing men and women alike, kept looking at my date.

Elena was at my side, and that alone was enough to make me feel amazing. Seeing her lose herself in the party, in the music, in the sensation of being young again and admired by everyone was an absolute joy.

I was too absorbed in her to notice really anything about myself, but in hindsight, being so absorbed in anything that I *forgot about my disability* was an absolute delight, too. It was just eclipsed by the sweetness of being lost in Elena's bliss.

Elena and I had driven in separate cars for obvious reasons. We embraced for a blissful goodbye, and I got into my car and began the drive home.

When I arrived home, my body was still warm with the buzz of the wonderful evening.

Elena dancing. Looking so happy. Looking like she was remembering what it was to be a free woman. My friends and family admiring her, a little bit in awe of me who had brought her to the party. My body felt warm and easy, not because my disability had vanished, but because the people and the music filled me up. Everything felt warm and easy.

I dragged myself into my bedroom and managed to tear most of my clothes off before collapsing onto the sheets.

***

I jolted awake on Sunday morning to the sound of pounding on my door.

Bang bang bang. Bang bang bang.

I rolled out of bed as Nelly slept, my eyes bleary and my brain foggy. Carefully testing my weight on both feet before standing was now an automatic habit. When I was satisfied that I wouldn't fall over, I stood up.

Bang bang bang.

Who is that? I wondered as I staggered through my home gym, past my living room, and to the front door.

It didn't occur to me to be afraid: in my foggy state, it was the duty of a polite homeowner to answer the door.

Bang bang bang!

Then he shouted:

"Adam, it's Frank!" There was a mocking, hostile edge to the man's voice. "You know that name? Or did Elena not bother to tell you she was married?"

I froze, my hand inches from the doorknob.

"Come out here now!"

**

REBUILDING

ADAM

STAY TUNED

BOOK 2
COMING SOON

Loved this book? Every review you write
helps Adam reach more readers.

Check out Adam Elnekaveh's work, including
his coaching services, at:

strivetodefy.com

Mom and Dad, I apologize for everything we've been through, both you and I. I love you very much and I thank you from the bottom of my heart for giving and restoring my life, not only once when I was born, but also a second time at the age of 27. I pledge that every success I achieve will be dedicated to your honor.

אמא ואבא, אני מתנצל על כל מה שעברנו, גם אתם וגם אני. אני אוהב אתכם מאוד ואני מודה לכם מעומק הלב שנתתם ושיקמתם את חיי, לא רק פעם אחת כאשר נולדתי, אלא גם פעם שנייה בגיל 27. אני מתחייב שכל הצלחה שאני אשיג תוקדש לכבודכם.